A CULTURAL HISTORY OF THE BRITISH EMPIRE

A CULTURAL HISTORY OF THE BRITISH EMPIRE

JOHN M. MACKENZIE

YALE UNIVERSITY PRESS
NEW HAVEN AND LONDON

Published with assistance from the Frank M. Turner Publication Fund.

For information about this and other Yale University Press publications, please contact:
U.S. Office: sales.press@yale.edu   yalebooks.com
Europe Office: sales@yaleup.co.uk   yalebooks.co.uk

Set in Adobe Caslon Pro by IDSUK (DataConnection) Ltd
Printed in Great Britain by TJ Books, Padstow, Cornwall

Library of Congress Control Number: 2022942462

ISBN 978-0-300-26078-6

A catalogue record for this book is available from the British Library.

10 9 8 7 6 5 4 3 2 1

CONTENTS

ILLUSTRATIONS

5. The Coronation Durbar 1911. King George and Queen Mary showing themselves to the multitude, postcard. Photo by Ernest Brooke, Rotary Photo EC, 9493D. Author's collection.

6. Justinian Gantz, *The Ootacamund Hunt Meeting at Mr. Chalmers' House at Gindy, Madras, 1845. The Jackal Pack*, graphite pen and black ink, and watercolour on medium, slightly textured cream wove paper, 1845. Yale Center for British Art, Paul Mellon Collection, B2006.14.21. https://collections.britishart.yale.edu/catalog/tms:54365. CC0 1.0.

7. Adelaide Hunt Club meeting at 'The Brocas', Woodville, Adelaide, 15 August 1870. State Library of South Australia, B2003 (Woodville Collection). Creative Commons Attribution-ShareAlike 4.0 International license (CC-BY-4.0).

8. Thomas Daniell R.A., 'The Assembly Rooms on the Race Ground, Near Madras', from *Oriental Scenery: Twenty Four Views in Hindoostan . . .*, Part 2, London, 1797, aquatint on paper. Cooper Hewitt, Smithsonian Design Museum, Creative Commons Zero (CC0) license.

9. The 12th Bengal Cavalry polo team, winners of the Peshawar Tournament 1898. © British Library Board. All Rights Reserved / Bridgeman Images.

10. Song sheet 'Ranji', dedicated by special permission to H.H. Prince Ranjitsinhji (H.H. Jam Saheb Shri Sir Ranjitsinhji Vibhaji of Nawanagar), words and music by C.T. West. Published Brighton and Hove: Lyon and Hall, 1896. © British Library Board. All Rights Reserved / Bridgeman Images.

11. West Indies cricket team, Australian tour 1930–31 (photographed 1930). State Library of South Australia, Don Bradman Photograph Collection, PRG 682/16/109.

12. 'Melbourne Cricket Ground, 1st January 1864', Melbourne: Charles Troedel & Co., coloured lithograph. State Library Victoria, Australia.

13. Hockey team of the 4th Battalion, 1st Punjab Regiment, 1923. Image courtesy of the National Army Museum, London.

14. Football team of conscripted African drivers serving with the King's African Rifles, Kenya, 1939. Image courtesy of the National Army Museum, London.

15. Edward Lear, *Kangchenjunga from Darjeeling, 1879*, oil on canvas. Yale Center for British Art, Gift of Donald C. Gallup, Yale BA 1934, PhD 1939, B1997.7.3. https://collections.britishart.yale. edu/catalog/tms:5067. CC0 1.0.

16. Cornelius Krieghoff, *Settler's Log House*, oil on canvas, 1856. The Picture Art Collection / Alamy.

17. Paul Kane, *Indian Encampment on Lake Huron*, 1848–50, oil on canvas. The Picture Art Collection / Alamy.

18. Samuel Thomas Gill, *A Bendigo Mill 1852*, watercolour over pencil. National Gallery of Victoria, Melbourne, Australia, The Joseph Brown Collection. Presented through the NGV Foundation by Dr Joseph Brown AO OBE, Honorary Life Benefactor, 2004.

19. Augustus Earle, 'War Speech'. In *Sketches illustrative of the Native Inhabitants and Islands of New Zealand from original drawings by Augustus Earle Esq, Draughtsman of HMS Beagle*. Lithographed and published 'under the auspices of the New Zealand Association' by Robert Martin & Co., London 1838. Ref: PUBL-0015-09, Alexander Turnbull Library, Wellington, New Zealand. /records/22338186.

20. Thomas Baines, *Wagon Crossing a Drift, Natal*, oil on canvas, 1874. The Picture Art Collection / Alamy.

21. Lt Humphrey John Julian, *The Admiral's House, Simon's Town, Cape of Good Hope, 1844*, watercolour, gouache and graphite, with scraping on medium, smooth, cream wove paper. Yale Center for British Art, Paul Mellon Collection, B1975.4.1304. https://collections.britishart.yale.edu/catalog/tms:10760.

22. Memorial to Capt. George Nicholas Hardinge R.N. by John Bacon the younger, St Thomas's Cathedral, Mumbai (Bombay). Photographed 23 July 2012. travelib india / Alamy.

23. National Women's Memorial (Nasionale Vrouemonument), Bloemfontein, South Africa. Photographed 20 October 2010. Ariadne Van Zandbergen / Alamy.

24. Statue of King Emperor George V and obelisk marking the focus of the 1911 Coronation Durbar, Coronation Park, Delhi. Author's collection. Photographed 6 February 2020.

25. Bourne and Shepherd photographers at the Delhi Durbar, 1902–3. © British Library Board. All Rights Reserved / Bridgeman Images.

26. Boer War, South Africa. A large crowd outside the *Cape Times* newspaper office, Cape Town, on hearing news of the relief of Kimberley (11–15 February 1900). Halftone, after J.E. Bruton. Wellcome Collection. Creative Commons Attribution 1.0.

27. 'Egypt in 1882 . . . introducing the Bombardment of Alexandria . . .', Canterbury Theatre of Varieties, Westminster Bridge Road, London. Poster, originally published/produced in Birmingham, 1883. British Library EVAN.1888. © British Library Board. All Rights Reserved / Bridgeman Images.

28. Robert Melville Grindlay, 'Scene in Bombay', coloured aquatint from Grindlay's *Scenery, Costumes and Architecture chiefly on the Western Side of India*, 1826. British Library / Alamy.

29. Capt. George Francklin Atkinson, 'Amateur theatricals on a British station – preparing for a performance by lacing up corsets, applying make-up etc.', from *Curry and Rice (on Forty Plates); or, the ingredients of social life at 'our station' in India*, Day & Son, London, 1860. Lithographer R.M. Bryson. Chronicle / Alamy.

30. A publicity poster for the Argyle Theatre of Varieties, Birkenhead, week commencing 29 January 1912, and Kinemacolor pictures. Courtesy of The Bill Douglas Cinema Museum, University of Exeter, item no. EXEBD 56694.

In text

PREFACE AND ACKNOWLEDGEMENTS

This book constitutes part of the project to rescue, present and analyse the notion of a British imperial culture, both in the metropole and in its global dispersal. It represents decades of collaborative research by many scholars eager to demonstrate that the political, administrative, military and economic histories of empire cannot be fully understood outside their cultural contexts. Such cultural phenomena inevitably embrace many diverse forms while also requiring some understanding of transnational histories and, above all, the racial relationships at the core of the imperial experience. During the past half-century, the practice of history has been revolutionised by a range of strikingly innovative concerns. New fields opened for cultivation have included those relating to the environment, gender, science, and the full range of visual, performance and sporting forms. Diverse areas of popular culture have been accepted as legitimate, indeed central, to the imperial experience. But this developing revolution also featured significant reorientations, among other things shifting the emphasis from above to below and the abandonment of masculinist and racially exclusive approaches.

Hence white male elite history has had to be replaced by histories of peoples across class, gender, race and continental divides. The notion of transnational histories also began to take hold, even before being graced with the name. Sometimes there were signs of a counter-reformation, a renewed insistence upon top-down approaches, as in the dissemination of European institutions, administrative practices, religious forms and educational ideas. This was focused upon a racially defined elite in colonial administration or upon settlers establishing territories expanding the 'western' world. Indigenous peoples seemed to be mainly worth studying when they indulged in violent resistance movements. In any case, some suggested that they were the appropriate subject of anthropology, a discipline founded in the imperial period and which, in its early days, pursued what was in effect an imperial agenda. By the 1960s the developing trends required new theorisation, fresh thinking on the nature of societies and their interaction, and an extension of the range of material appropriate as historical evidence. Later, postcolonial interpretations and notions of globalisation rapidly became significant new approaches.

Among aspects of such globalisation it has become apparent that innovations like sports, theatre and cinema histories, and the placing of art in cultural, social, intellectual and racial contexts, are vital to a full understanding of imperial and postcolonial processes. They are also key to a full understanding of the decline and break-up of empire, the development of new nationalist forces and the emergence of the international nation-state order. Cultural history emerged as one of the new fields, starting perhaps with popular culture and later spreading out into globalised processes in the wider world. Moreover, the field of imperial history was breaking up like empires themselves. Historians were concentrating on opposition, the rise of nationalism and the resulting new nation states. This historiography became firmly established, but transnational history associated with imperialism still had its place, not least in the cultural field. Many cultural forms had been carried on the backs of imperial rule and aspects of the resulting global culture need to be understood. This book is therefore intended as a contribution to this recovery of the transnational. It is also based on the conviction that it is time to bring many specialist studies together into a synoptic work casting light on the wider field of imperial history, while always maintaining a focus on the diversity of the human factor in this phenomenon of cultural dispersal. Although this book may be accused of excessive ambition, such bold aspirations are necessary in charting synoptic new approaches. Nevertheless, it remains impossible to encompass the immensely protean subject of global cultural dissemination in one work, and some selection has been necessary. Yet even the highest academic mountains should be attempted, not just because they are there, but also because they open up many vistas leading to fresh explorations.

At any rate, the work has been based not only on many years of study, but also on contacts, conferences and conversations with stimulating scholars and friends. Rich resources now exist and many friends and colleagues have worked in fruitful transnational and comparative cultural contexts. These include Robert Aldrich, Stephanie Barczewski, Jeremy Black, Liz Buettner, John Darwin, Tom Devine, Martin Farr, Giuseppe Finaldi, Bernhard Gissibl, John Griffiths, Vincent Kuitenbrouwer, Cherry Leonardi, Ulrike Lindner, Justin Livingstone, Sarah Longair, Andrew Mackillop, John McAleer, Berny Sèbe, Matthew Stanard and Stuart Ward, as well as former colleagues such as Stephen Constantine and Jeffrey Richards. I am indebted to Professor Gilles Teulié of the University of Aix-Marseille, Simon Deschamps of the University of Toulouse II–Jean Jaurès, and Professor Vilasnee Tampoe-Hautin of the University of La Réunion for sharing relevant research. David McNab has offered advice in the field of Canadian First Nations people while Michael Belfield was helpful in respect of the Maori of New Zealand. McNab has also kept me up to date on statue, museum and other controversies in Canada. James Burns and Tom Rice provided help with the film chapter. Terry Barringer has been a valuable bibliographer for almost forty years. Undergraduate and postgraduate students at Lancaster, Rolf Johnson and Dominic Omissi continue to produce useful insights. I am grateful to the staffs of the libraries and archives in Nova Scotia, Ontario, British Columbia, Western Australia, Victoria, Tasmania and Singapore, as well as in Auckland, Christchurch and Dunedin. On an extended tour of India in January–February 2020, skilled local guides including Chitra Singh in Delhi, Pandu Rangan in Chennai and points south, and Shatrughan Sharma in Shimla were extremely helpful. Dileep Kumar was both expert driver and valuable guide. The National Library of Scotland in Edinburgh is an invaluable institution, and Roger Jeffery, Jay Brown and the Rev. Neil Gardner are stimulating contacts in that city. As always, Nigel Dalziel has been a vital research associate and helper in manifold ways, including heroic efforts in picture research. Without him this work would have been unlikely to see the light of day. Several chapters were written during the 2020–21 coronavirus 'lockdowns'.

INTRODUCTION

Meeting of settlers and Maoris at Pah Wakairo, near Napier, Hawke's Bay, New Zealand in 1862.

The British Empire was a major globalising cultural phenomenon. Much attention has been paid to the dispersal of political, administrative, legal and religious forms, together with their adaptation in the diaspora, but so far there has been no synoptic survey of the dissemination of cultural characteristics, such as the fascination with ceremonial, the spread of sports, arts, various institutions, the press, as well as manifestations of the theatre and cinema. In some respects these remain the major legacies of empire in North America, the Caribbean, Africa, Asia and Australasia. They were also characteristic of those areas of 'informal empire' which reflected the powerful British economic presence (usually without direct political authority) in South America, the Middle or Near East and the Asian Far East. These dispersals were perhaps seen as the main social and civilising glue that would hold the empire together, the conventional catalysts of conformity that would serve to provide the strengthening of culture to underpin and consolidate political and economic formations. It may be said that these manifestations of an essentially British culture were originally seen as the perquisites and distinguishing characteristics of race. They were designed to express the exclusive aspects of assumed cultural and racial superiority. Missionaries and educators may have desired to spread both religious and related 'civilising' forms to indigenous peoples (and were at times consequently suspected by settlers and colonial administrators), but initially white migrants and expatriates certainly intended to hug these cultural characteristics to themselves. They constituted the badges of racial distinctiveness. But the cultural inheritance of empire around the world has never survived in its pure form. As the following chapters will demonstrate, cultural exports were seized upon by both indigenous peoples and settlers, adapted and converted to their own ends. Indeed, the cultural legacies of empire may seem so strikingly apparent that they appear to represent the more enduring sediments of imperial presence even when the political forms have drained away. Perhaps sports, for example, have remained more powerful and significant expressions of a former global empire than the elements of authority that the British imagined would endure. Moreover, in many societies it was the adoption, adaptation and conversion of cultural forms to the ends of new national identities and the forces of nationalism that served to break up that empire. Imperial cultural phenomena, often hybridised with indigenous equivalents, became vital emblems of a new nation-state international order.

This brief prospectus requires some fleshing out. Empires are, after all, the product of ambitious commercial, territorial and demographic exploitation, imposed by military means and facilitated by technological gaps or superior manpower. To secure their dominance they also have to be culturally expansive. Hence imperial elites insist upon what they consider to be the superior qualities of their culture, conceived as the central aspect of their dominant identity. In modern empires, this was always known as the 'civilising mission', a mission often transferred from the peripheral regions of the metropole to the outer world.[1] In the British and Hibernian Isles, Ireland provides the classic case, with the cultural influence of England on Ireland from the sixteenth century proving to be among the most durable, despite nationalist resistance. To this we can add other Celtic areas beyond the English heartland. Such cultural imperialism offered both the means and the alleged justification for the apparent English ascendancy. As the majority English incorporated the other ethnicities in their 'Atlantic archipelago', the British emerged as a globally significant imperial people, competing with other European empires. Such modern empires, like earlier ones, have made cultural assertions central to their acquisitive designs, both announcing and defending their presence, for example through the built environment. Imposing structures such as fortresses, walled settlements, later commercial, administrative and religious buildings, as well as domestic residences, mark their conquest. New cities and towns rise as both powerful expressions of imperial rule and as alleged evidence of cultural superiority.[2] In addition to this physical presence, a dominant empire seeks to expand the usage of its language, of aspects of its political and legal system, though within the context of autocratic rule, and of its religious observance and associated institutions. It also disperses the character of its social hierarchy, adding further rungs of ethnicity and race. Further, it invariably disseminates methods of socialising the young (in different ways throughout the social and racial structure) through education, youth organisations, religion and juvenile literature. These objectives are achieved through the activities of various imperial agencies and a range of media, all illustrating and utilising the technologies that facilitate the successful expansion of power. These phenomena, both the means and ends of cultural dispersal, are viewed as part of the process of 'modernisation'.

However, the ambition to overlay the cultures of conquered peoples with the supposed cultural and intellectual superiority of the dominant 'race' is seldom completely achieved.[3] Some members of the conquered population may accept the characteristics of the imperial rulers that suit them while seeking to protect the key cultural traits that are central to their identity. But empires are also adaptable in the pursuit of survival and, whether consciously or unconsciously, invariably assimilate characteristics of subordinate peoples. A good example is the creation of a Romano-British culture during the period of Roman domination of parts of Britain in the early centuries of the Christian era. Such elements of hybridity may in certain circumstances make the dominant empire more palatable to some sectors of the population and may also fruitfully extend the cultural base of the empire itself. But, equally importantly, empires also need the acquiescence of their home populations in their expansive activities. Both the strengths and weaknesses of empires may be illustrated by such resilience and imperial decline is invariably accompanied by the reassertion of other cultures, both at home and in colonies, even if such resurgence is characterised by the survival of key aspects of cultural hybridity. These developments are often promoted by the migration of peoples and the creation of multi-ethnic societies, with the consequent intermingling of cultural characteristics. Hence empires are doomed never to be wholly successful in the processes of cultural conversion and always fail in pursuing an ideal of cultural 'purity'.

This is unquestionably true of the British Empire. The formation of the British state and the attempted diffusion of English culture

(English in a linguistic, political, legal and intellectual sense) were fundamental to the emergence of that empire. There can be little doubt that the period between the sixteenth and twentieth centuries saw an English attempt to spread elements of its culture into Wales, Ireland and Scotland (efforts with precedents in the Norman period and in the thirteenth- and fourteenth-century reigns of Edward I and Edward II). The nineteenth-century historian, Cambridge professor, theorist and propagandist for empire, J.R. Seeley, wrote that 'Greater Britain is a real enlargement of the English state'.[4] A common language was key, such that other languages, Welsh, Irish, Scots and Scottish forms of Gaelic, as well as Cornish and Manx, were not only devalued and downgraded, but were subject to efforts at suppression. One of the myths perpetrated by Seeley in his *Expansion of England* was that the British (as well as overseas settlers in 'Greater Britain') were essentially a homogeneous people because the English had culturally overwhelmed the others. Common political systems, social structures, economic institutions, land-holding forms, religious and environmental practices were all more or less seen as central to this, even if ambition was seldom matched by reality, not least when limited by treaty as in the Anglo-Scottish Union of 1707.[5] The nineteenth-century tendency to use the word 'England' as a synecdoche for Britain was symptomatic, although the vigorous opposition to this practice heralded resistance.[6] This pressure for central uniformity secured only limited success insofar as a variety of civil societies, religious forms and cultural identities survived to emerge with fresh vigour in the late nineteenth and twentieth centuries.[7] Moreover, in recent times it has become apparent that, at least to a certain extent, it may have been only the common experience of empire which served to provide the veneer of such a mythic common culture.[8] In any case, supposedly uniform and shared characteristics were themselves hybrid and multifarious, incorporating characteristics of other ethnicities and also increasingly receiving influences from beyond Britain's borders, some of them from empire itself.

The imperial system which emerged from these efforts at the creation of a stiffening and central common culture involved the expansion of forms of settlement and trading activity into an Atlantic (including the Caribbean) and then a wider world. From the late eighteenth century, and more particularly in the nineteenth, major colonies of settlement developed in Canada, Australasia, South Africa and a number of other locations with smaller settler populations, for example in East and Central Africa. This necessarily involved a cultural diffusion which served to bind such populations into what historians have called 'the British World', even although this dispersal reflected at least some of the diversity of cultural forms within the British Isles.[9] If the reproduction of English or British culture overseas was one of the original objectives of settler societies, it was inevitably going to be diluted by the presence of French cultural characteristics in Quebec and Dutch in South Africa, each reflected in distinctive religious forms, Catholic and Calvinist. Moreover, the variations in the 'British World' are typified by the complexity of South African society.[10] Such dilution was to be accelerated by the arrival of many non-British immigrants into all these territories, a phenomenon which speeded up in the inter-war years. The 'British World' idea can also be applied to the 'empire of rule' (colonies in South and South-East Asia, Africa, the Caribbean, the Mediterranean and the Pacific), where British cultural forms were dispersed in notable ways. But the term cannot be taken to imply homogeneity. The 'four nations' of the metropole, Ireland, Scotland, England and Wales, all made significant and distinctive inputs into the British World.[11] Empire may even have permitted these separate ethnicities to flourish, encouraging the survival of their own cultural and religious forms.

The other ideal was the incorporation of indigenous peoples into some elements of this British World. White settlements encountered other peoples, or alternatively transported countless Africans as slaves, and set about controlling them in cultural as well as adminis-

trative and military ways. However, whether slaves should be culturally influenced or absorbed was a subject for considerable debate (for
example in respect of Christian proselytisation). Beyond the territories of settlement, the British Empire became increasingly a phenomenon in which administration was established over other peoples in
order to achieve commercial ends, not least in the extraction of
increasingly varied resources. Starting in India in the late eighteenth
century and expanding in the nineteenth, such rule and its accompanying economic exploitation were facilitated by the diffusion of a
whole range of cultural elements from the centre.

The British Empire thus set out to become a cultural and intellectual phenomenon of global significance. It was one which exhibited the fantasies that have energised empires in human history,
including the fantasy of universal rule, mainly with a monarchical
centre. Others include the fantasy of a supposedly peaceful system,
created by the imperial processes of 'pacification', which for indigenous peoples generally involves violence, warfare, deep personal
suffering (both physical and psychological) and the destruction of
living space and lifestyles, as well as the creation of forms of bondage
and slavery. The imperial power called this the Pax Britannica,
following the Roman precedent of the Pax Romana. The achieve-
ment of these imperial ambitions involves the creation of myths of
martyrdom and sacrifice on the part of constructed imperial heroes,
who become the personifications of processes in the establishment of
imperial power. Imperial authorities celebrate such individuals as
sacrificing their lives for the sake of civilisation, that is for the fantasy
of the creative cargo, the good things empires allegedly carry with
them, forms of religious, economic, legal and governmental 'salvation'. This celebration of imperial heroes and martyrs inevitably fore-
grounds the actions of white people over those of indigenous
peoples.[12] For the dominant citizens of empire, yet another is the
fantasy of free movement, the capacity to use the legal and military
protection of the imperial system to move around the globe. They

can do so as settlers (those generally intending to move permanently to an imperial territory) and as sojourners (those supposedly travelling on a temporary basis as traders, planters, administrators, missionaries and members of other professions). The common tongue that had bound together Britain was seen as superior, sanctified, as they saw it, as the language of Shakespeare and the King James Bible. Through speech, the major fantasy holding the others together is consequently the dream of a global culture, a world-wide set of intellectual, artistic, scientific and technological achievements which, at one and the same time, facilitate the creation of empire, justify its continuing existence, and supposedly act as its binding element. The rise and fall of a global culture is the prime focus of this book.

The visual and material realities of empire result from the fact that these fantastical complexes require to be exhibited. Imperialism, by its very nature, cannot be modest or self-effacing for empires have to be proclaimed and constantly performed. The 'performativity' of empire is a constant imperative for at least four reasons. Rulers and the elite need to convince themselves of the rightness and nobility of the enterprise. The monarchy (republican empires have been in the minority) needs to be exploited to create a common focus of loyalty, displayed on coins and stamps, as well as in portraits, illustrations and statuary. This is designed to underpin conviction in the rectitude of the national and imperial enterprise for both metropolitan citizens and imperial subjects. The co-optation of and authorisation by the domestic population are essential to ensure that the empire is not undermined from within, an imperative more urgent with the spread of democratic politics from the later nineteenth century. Other peoples need to be turned into allies and coadjutors, the mercenaries and collaborators (military, police, minor administrators and some professionals) of empire.[13] Conquered peoples need to be overawed, to be convinced of the grandeur and hopefully the invincibility of imperial power, and, by extension, the hopelessness of resistance. All of this represents the ideal, a set of hoped-for consummations seldom achieved. Empires are in reality complex, messy and variable experiences that intermittently and regularly fall short of theoretical perfection, more frequently as they totter to their fall. Nevertheless, some proponents of the British Empire imagined it as a new type of empire, characterised by the spread of political freedoms, such that it would be insulated from the factors of decline that had infected all previous empires.[14] This was another of the many fantasies of empire, unrealistic because freedoms are, by their nature, self-generating and expansive, inspiring independence of action and national autonomy, encouraging migration of immigrants other than those from the imperial centre to the territories of settlement, and permitting extra-imperial influences to become significant.[15] While some imperialists at least would have liked to see the package of fantasies (for them representing unanswerable truths) operating in their purest form, the fact is that they never did or could. Like all fantasies, they were will-o'-the-wisps, repeatedly fading and strengthening, constantly filled with hopes and disappointments and ultimately vanishing. Yet, when that has been said, many of the physical manifestations of empire invoked by these fantastical dreams do survive and continue to be apparent all around us in the modern world, even if their meanings have often dramatically changed.

The embryonic formation of the fantasies of modern empires can be seen in the eighteenth century. In his book *After Tamerlane: The Global History of Empire*, John Darwin has written of the manner in which Europe came to centre stage in global history late in that century. For him:

> this intoxicating sense of being at the centre of things – the principal source of cultural energy, the headquarters of knowledge, the entrepôt of world trade, and (for the evangelicals) the great depot of truth – had become almost a given in European thought by the end of the century. Not even China could retain its mystique.[16]

9

To gloss this assertion, such 'cultural energy' was generated by aspects of the European Enlightenment, by new economic theory and by the evangelical revival. The Enlightenment promoted the ambitions of Europeans to create a complete taxonomy of the globe, categorising all its natural and human phenomena ('others' in nature and human societies closely bound up with each other), and also developed the theorising of commercial relations and free trade emerging particularly from Scottish thinkers like Adam Smith. While the Enlightenment has been seen as both critical of empire and also promoting it, the fact is that some publications – notably those of the Scottish historian William Robertson – developed significant theorisation that was to be influential in imperial thinking.[17] Evangelicalism was in some respects antithetical to the Enlightenment (though in others helped to spread its ideas) and conceived a passionate desire to spread the Christian religion and vigorous forms of spiritual enthusiasm not only into the supposedly darker places of the new European commercial and later industrial cities, but also around the world. This great explosion (not too strong a word) of evangelical activity brought together working-class Europeans and the diverse ethnicities of the globe as peoples in need of salvation, eventually co-opting the first as agents in the conversion of the second. To this we can add the rapid growth of the printed word, in tracts, pamphlets, journals, newspapers and books. All of these phenomena were to expand mightily in the nineteenth century, closely bound up with the development of the bourgeoisie as the controlling class of empire, with all their cultural and intellectual interests, busily promoting the dissemination of their ideals through the emergence of popular recreations and pastimes, including street ceremonial and performances, topical and spectacular theatre and later the music hall, exhibitions, together with spectator sports, various forms of holidays and participatory pastimes. Not all were pulling in the same direction, of course, nor was this a planned or controlled set of enterprises. They developed an extraordinarily expansive dynamic of their own, furthered by the demands of the consumers, many of them working-class participants enjoying a little more disposable income and leisure time. Moreover, Enlightenment and religion, theatre and church were sometimes in conflict. Press and publishing became major arenas for the great debates of the age, debates including the character of imperialism and its cultural expressions. But such tensions, as well as the inherent complexity of these mental, spiritual and recreational activities, contributed to a cultural energy which was to take European forms across the globe.

If much of this is familiar, all this intellectual, environmental and artistic vigour was to have global manifestations which have seldom been adequately studied. Mental worlds have often received more attention than the material forms through which they were expressed and disseminated. Thus the ways in which the sources of civilisational drive, the articulation and application of new modes of knowledge, and the manner in which world trade connected with the dispersal of a whole range of ethnocentric forms and ideas, as well as evangelical self-confidence and activity, have never been synthesised into a fully fledged cultural history of empire. This book will at least make a preliminary stab at such a synthesis, though any presumption of comprehensiveness is impossible given the range and diversity of the field. We also need to pause to notice that at least some of these phenomena had deeper roots. Interests in the natural and ethnic diversity of the world began in the seventeenth century or earlier. It has been demonstrated that the street, print and theatrical performance of empire was certainly well under way in the early to mid-eighteenth century.[18] Some religious stirrings can also be identified at an earlier period.[19] Above all, it is readily apparent that in the Caribbean and in the thirteen colonies of North America, towns on a European model, with derivative architecture, churches, schools, colleges, intellectual associations and other dispersed cultural manifestations, existed well before the later eighteenth century. Nevertheless, this book will generally concentrate on the era after the end of the American Revolutionary War in 1783. Its centre of gravity will be the second half of the nineteenth century, with significant roots in the previous hundred and fifty years, and continuing developments and a fresh dynamic in the early decades of the twentieth century.

Modernity

The point about all these physical and mental expressions of European culture, particularly as charted from the later eighteenth century, is that they all invariably asserted aspects of modernity. This concept is associated with the growing sense of the 'modern', as defined by Europeans, which grew out of the developing Industrial Revolution with all its urban, technical, transport and intellectual associations. This culturally specific sense of modernity was promoted by the notion that Europeans, uniquely in human history, could embrace the world, develop a universal commerce partly based on luxury goods, partly associated with new forms of global resource extraction and exchange. These ideas received a considerable fillip from the three celebrated voyages of Captain Cook between 1768 and his death in 1779, as well as by his many successors. They were already in place in the age of sail and relatively primitive, though nonetheless effective, firearms – although initially the technological gap with equivalents produced by some other societies was not all that great. Nor were shipbuilding and navigational techniques until significant advances were made in Europe during the following century. An emerging European self-regard was tremendously accelerated in the age of steam and by the many technological developments of that era, including the shift from wood to iron, then steel, in shipbuilding, the invention of the telegraph, undersea cables and much more advanced firepower (some innovations crossing the Atlantic from America to Europe).[20] All of these contributed to a burgeoning sense of difference and of condescension, superior attitudes that became closely bound up, particularly in the popular realm, with ideas of race which had independent origins and were also related to a variety of scientific, medical and intellectual paradigms of the time.[21] Increasingly, Europeans – and their outriders in the Americas – saw themselves as having unique capacities to encircle, embrace, energise and enlighten the world. In doing so they imagined that they could develop and process its resources, which they alone fully understood. They also became engulfed in the processes of demographic 'replenishing of the earth', the scattering of populations, notably in the Americas, in Australasia and in southern Africa.[22] The irony is that much of this dispersal took place because of poverty, famine, violence and marginalisation within Europe. In some ways it was emblematic of the oppression of old social and political systems, of a clash between what were seen as inadequate forms of land use and the dramatic changes associated with technical advances empowering agricultural and industrial revolutions. These set up processes of displacement in Europe which were to translate into dispossession in the wider world.

Among European countries, Britain developed perhaps the greatest conceit. In a supposedly 'advanced' continent, the British saw themselves as the most progressive of all, at least until that 'first prize' in self-regard was taken over by the United States in the twentieth century. In the great economic and cultural race of the nineteenth century, the British saw the older and supposedly decadent empires as declining to a fall, incapable of making the adaptations necessary for the inauguration of modernity. In the wider world, such empires included the Chinese, Mughal, Persian and Ottoman. Within Europe itself, there were decadent empires and states, such as Spain and Portugal, in decline from earlier prominence, as well as backward autocratic systems like the Habsburgs of Austria-Hungary and the Romanovs in Russia. The British, on the other hand, had come through the fires of the French Revolutionary wars, renewing to some extent the supremacy secured in 1763 at the end of the Seven Years' War and overcoming the American setback of 1783. They had the command of the seas, clearly (as they thought) the natural element through which all progressive developments would take place in the future. Their industrial development was the most advanced, as were their degree of urbanisation; the scale of their commerce; the accumulation of capital available for overseas investment; the sophistication of banking, credit and insurance institutions; the alleged liberalism of their politico-legal structures; as well as their ability to produce the population overflow capable of taking over large tracts of the earth. They also had the most highly developed bourgeoisie, both commercial and professional, which provided the necessary energies for imperial expansion. In all these ways, the British saw themselves as constituting the epitome of modernity. Yet their aristocracy had also survived, lending a certain cachet to the politics of the era, to the boards of industrial and commercial firms, and were available for the 'ornamental' aspects of empire such as vice-royalties and governorships. In addition, the export of people lower down the social scale, often subject to elite resistance in the eighteenth century to maintain manpower, now became the mark of their almost overweening dynamism, even if some of that emigration was based on tragedies such as Irish famine or Scottish Clearances.[23] British conceit was so great that they began to compare themselves with great empires of the past, the Greeks for aspects of democracy and intellect, the Romans for power, vigour, maritime expertise and dominance of parts of three continents, Europe, Africa and Asia.[24]

Here, indeed, was a great paradox. Modernity expressed a unique contemporary power, yet it seemed that it was legitimated by appeals to pre-modern worlds. Thus, classical education became the mark of the British elite, celebrated as a preparation, though not necessarily a training, for anything. This ruling, administrative and military elite gave the impression that while their authority was based on modern technologies, still they wished to distance themselves from the modern by such atavistic forms. If the dynamism of the British economy largely came from practical individuals whose self-training led to their personal economic and social advancement, the ruling classes and professions were classically educated, exhibiting educational accomplishments later seen as valuable for the running of an empire. Industry and trade were looked down on, even though they created the world upon which the imperial elite depended.[25] Social hierarchies and snobberies in India and elsewhere were based on these dichotomies and had distinct cultural manifestations. This was particularly true of England and it helps to explain why so many of the exponents of the practical professions – medicine, engineering, surveying, architecture and the rest – came from Scotland and Ireland or, for that matter, from the military. It also helps in understanding the fascination of the elite with traditional rulers in Asia and Africa (particularly in the second half of the nineteenth century) while still banishing some of them.[26] It additionally has connections with the great debate about the relationship between industrial and craft production which emerged in the same period, a debate that eventually produced a reaction in favour of crafts.[27] This was connected with another paradox, the vision of a nostalgic rural Arcadia contrasted with the thrusting world of cities and ports. Such a vision was transferred to the empire in the creation of botanic gardens (though they also had a severely practical purpose), in the public parks and green spaces of colonial cities, and in the visual representations of colonial environments. Thus 'Arcadian' and 'imperial' should not be juxtaposed.[28] They were part of the same complex of thinking which the British carried everywhere. Industry and crafts, Arcadia and the industrial/commercial complex, were central to a mutually reinforcing debate which nineteenth-century Britons transferred overseas. It may be that we can add to this the dichotomy between the 'savage' and the 'civilised', such that the epithet 'savage' could transcend, in some contexts, all the negative, backward connotations of the word to symbolise something more appealing, more basic, closer to nature, the antidote to an over-developed, over-sophisticated world.

Hence for much of the imperial period, these appeals to a pre-modern past ensured that the cultural dispersals to empire were invariably rooted in the worlds of Greece and Rome. Classical education gave the British the self-confidence to imagine that they could connect themselves with the great cultures of the past, while creating the additional tier of the economic and technical prowess of the present. While this imagined emulation of the achievements of Greece and Rome contributed to their sense of self-worth, it also provided them with deep misgivings. For all their greatness, Ancient Greece and Rome had passed into history. Edward Gibbon's multi-volume *History of the Decline and Fall of the Roman Empire* was published between 1776 and 1778, at the very time of the loss of the American colonies, yet on the cusp of British global power. From then until the twentieth century, it was favourite reading matter, a signifi-cant tool of education, and also a dire warning.[29] As the eighteenth-century Grand Tour, with its emphasis on the remains of the classical world, gave way to a bourgeois tourism (and associated guide books) in the nineteenth, there was a shift in perspective from classical to global.[30] Yet the first influenced, informed and energised the second. Global visions could be founded on the ways in which Ancient Greeks and Romans had successfully, at least for a period, dominated their respective worlds.

This obsession with the Ancient world seemed to offer a template for modern political, legal, philosophical and literary sets of ideas while offering the British valuable imperial lessons. One was the concept of 'barbarism', so central to the self-image of Greeks and Romans in their conceptualisation of their relationships with neigh-bours and 'others'.[31] Gibbon popularised the notion of barbarians in his apocalyptic vision of Goths, Huns and Vandals, creating evoca-tive terminology for the future, in bringing down the greatness of Rome. The highest civilisation was capable of being brought to its knees by supposedly inferior peoples. The British both adopted and greatly developed such a set of binaries. This thinking became prevalent in British imperial education and categorisation of the rest of the world in the alleged progression from savagery to barbarism to civilisation, stages of development (linking economic modes with their social and political equivalents) much refined in Scottish 'stadial' theory. Connections might well be made through the word 'dark', the manner in which, to many Victorians, Roman civilisation gave way to the so-called 'dark ages'. The British in the nineteenth century also sent explorers to the 'dark' regions of the world, for example to Africa, specifically designated as the 'dark continent', at least anywhere south of the Sahara.[32] North Africa, after all, had been a key part of the Roman Empire well before the Arab conquests. But just as the word 'savage' could acquire positive resonances, so could 'barbaric' when those pursuing alternative cultural modes saw the opportunities provided by the 'barbaric' for new freedoms in physical movement, dance, elements of performance and in art.

Conventional and cultural histories of empire

Historians of the British Empire have shown relatively little interest in these cultural dimensions. In the plethora of books published on the history of British imperialism, hardly any have escaped from the political and administrative, economic and military complexes that seem to have remained historians' stock-in-trade. There are a number of reasons for this. The first is the fact that training in imperial history has always primarily concentrated on politics and economics, starting with a historiographical tramp through the work of earlier masters (until modern times, scarcely any of them women) and then fitting new ideas into that tradition. The second is that historians have invariably regarded work in archival documents as the essential component of *pukka* historical research.[33] And such official documents – at least in the great state archives – seldom have much to say about cultural contexts. Breaking free of that obsession has not been easy. The main thrust of such a break-out came as late as the 1980s, with attempts at new approaches utilising different kinds of sources, alarming a historical Establishment wary of dangerous originality. The third reason has been the reluctance of that historical tradition to embrace aspects of multi-disciplinary research. Architectural, art, theatre, sports and intellectual historians have beavered away exposing significant landscapes of imperial cultural history, but these have seldom been incorporated into the mainstream. Cross-disciplinary studies, for example those embracing anthropology, historical geography and literature, have rarely been recognised by conventional historians of empire, although they have indeed been significant in what are sometimes called area studies, concentrating on specific regions or peoples. Moreover, despite the influential development of the postcolonial studies school, the great majority of recent books surveying imperial history have continued to ignore such developments. The distinguished environmental historian and authority on cricket Ramachandra Guha has written that emerging fields such as environmental and women's history have tended to remain in ghettoes.[34] This is also true of aspects of cultural history.

Two explanations for this silence commend themselves. The first is that British imperial history has so often been written in isolation, remote from comparative approaches to other empires.[35] In considerations of Ancient or medieval empires, say Roman or Norman, the cultural dimensions are invariably obvious, given their striking material remains. It is now perfectly normal, for example, to consider aspects of the social history of the Romans from their gravestones and funerary monuments.[36] While the British Empire's material remains are obviously extensive and impressive, they have received little notice in the canon of conventional imperial history. This is perhaps even more true of cultural phenomena. A fully rounded estimation of imperialism requires analysis of the cultural dispersal that took place both within cities and towns as well as in rural areas where most indigenous people were settled. Christian missions were particularly significant here. Thus cultural dispersal and change have to be considered in terms of audience: peasants and traditional rulers, urban workers and emerging bourgeoisie.

Moreover, the division between integrated imperial history and more focused and localised area studies has served, perhaps, to obscure cultural phenomena. This division has led to a distinction between the view from above and the perspective from below. General imperial history often pays too little attention to indigenous peoples or to what is happening on the ground. This distinction has perhaps led to a contrast between the characterisation of the British Empire as 'ramshackle', its power spread so widely and thinly that its effects were both diluted and ephemeral, and as 'rampaging', that its influence on the ground in environmental, ethnic and economic ways was actually considerable and often transforming.[37] Cultural history offers an oblique but enlightening angle for considering this contrast. These ideas have been taken up by Antoinette Burton in introducing the six volumes of the *Cultural History of Western Empires*, which examines empires in a comparative way from the Ancient world to modern times.[38] Burton has rightly suggested that 'culture is arguably the carrier of a number of historical forces that attention to politics or economics alone cannot capture', that cultural phenomena are to be identified in a 'diverse array of formations and spaces illuminating dimensions of hegemony and power' with a capacity to shed new light on old paradigms. In the case of the British Empire, there are diverse and particular cultural forces that have never received sufficient attention. Such dimensions have constituted a minority interest, despite their apparent and growing importance in infusing and modulating politics, administration and economics. One reason for this bias is that cultural history has seldom been prominent in British historical training. It has been left to the French, with their adherence to social and cultural theory, perhaps more recently to Americans. Yet, as Peter Burke has pointed out, cultural history offers an opportunity to surmount fragmentation, to create a holistic approach to a frequently splintered phenomenon.[39] Part of the strength of cultural history is that it can operate at both the micro- and macro-level, from anthropological 'thick description' to a much more highly integrated approach. It can also deal with both the elite and the popular, together with combinations of, or negotiations between, the two.

Various phases of cultural history have included concerns with the symbolic, with historical anthropology, situational and ceremonial drama, scenarios, mentalities, representations (including questions of misrepresentation), misunderstanding, and incorporation. To all of these we can add the supposed certainties and ideologies of empire, not least ideas about race and allegedly martial peoples, approaches to the body and clothing, perhaps including sports, spirituality, traditions and their invention, as well as the transfer of ideas and language. In addition, there are interactions and negotiations between concepts of the environment, botany and animals, science and medicine. There is also the question of the handling of space, the cultural dimensions of the ecology of empire, in its racial and economic disposing of landscape in both rural and urban forms. These embrace matters that can be subject to data and description, or they can be amenable to the qualitative and imaginative element central to cultural history, which according to taste can be appealing or disabling. In considering the British Empire, they also introduce notable networks and webs of interaction, between centre and periphery, metropole and colonies, among colonies and different imperial powers, between evaluations of historical phenomena and the present, among different classes and ethnic groups. In all cases, cultural history is necessarily inter- and multi-disciplinary.

In short, the range of cultural history can seem limitless, as much a source of bewilderment as of enlightenment. The historian, additionally, has to be concerned with dynamics, with the extent to which all of these are subject to change, gradual or dramatic, in the phases of establishment, development and collapse of imperial rule. Cultural situations can never be frozen in a moment of time. They change in complex ways, varying according to climate, peoples and social settings. Such transformations, as with biological evolutionary phenomena, can take place in highly competitive or reasonably cooperative circumstances. They can be peaceful or violent, encounter major resistance or even a degree of receptive equanimity. Moreover, the cultural cannot float in a vacuum. It must be firmly rooted in economic and social contexts, since all cultural phenomena are both dependent upon and in turn influence such conditions. As in all historical questions, origins, causes and effects are central to all explanations and require some disentanglement.

Defining 'culture' and 'cultural'

It is perhaps necessary to explain the meanings of 'culture' and 'cultural' here, not least because this will help to define the boundaries of the book's material. The word 'culture' has many different meanings. It can denote, as in anthropology, the complete socio-economic, religio-mental worldviews of specific peoples across the globe. These can be constituted through elements of performance and of exchange, incorporation and adaptation. In archaeology, 'culture' can refer to the totality of past 'civilisations', as expressed and interpreted through surviving material remains, artefacts, inscriptions and other evidential fragments. The word can additionally have horticultural and agricultural connotations, as well as meaning anything from a crop of micro-organisms grown in a laboratory to refinement in thought, manners and tastes. All of these definitions imply a dynamic phenomenon, constantly undergoing change, growth, decline, and never in equilibrium. The word 'culture' can also be used loosely to refer to the arts in general, which can be defined as the performing, visual and material aspects of culture, and the modes through which these are generated and communicated to wider publics. It is the latter meaning, placed within social, intellectual, economic and political contexts, that underpins the material of this book. But this approach to the so-called arts has environmental, intellectual and ethnic contexts. It

21

therefore embraces some, at least, of the anthropological notions of culture, particularly because imperial culture operates in the context of dominant and subordinate societies. Most importantly, it is always about exchanges, acceptance and rejection, attempts to create common fields of cultural endeavour, all invariably in the service of promoting and developing imperial power, but also at times encouraging its disruption. Such exchanges have come to be known as cultural traffic, traffic which, while starting (briefly) as apparently unidirectional from the metropole, soon became multi-directional and international. Cultural traffic is an aspect of the cultural economy, which, like all economies, represents the combination of goods and services, employment arrangements, as well as exchange within and beyond territories. The imperial cultural economy involved entertainment forms requiring a large spectator base, underpinned by the emotional economy, a concept particularly applicable to the Victorian era and subsequent years.[40] The following chapters will provide descriptions and analyses of the dimensions and significance of cultural economies and the traffic engendered.

To add a further complication, we need to consider whether we are dealing with 'cultural imperialism', with 'imperial culture' or with 'the culture of empire'. Definitions of these may vary, but they can be distinguished as follows. 'Cultural imperialism' involves the conscious efforts at conversion to an imperial culture, the proselytising urge, for the home population, the settler diaspora and indigenous peoples. It constitutes the ambitious attempt to create a genuine imperial community united by political, legal, religious and social ideas, lubricated by forms of language, sports, entertainment, ceremonial and art. All these inclined towards offering a specific allegiance to a symbolic centre, notably the monarchy and the metropolitan state. Cultural imperialism is the business of Christian missionaries, not just in religious proselytisation, but also in education, clothing, economic practices, gendering and many other elements, although this has been the subject of controversy.[41] The objectives of cultural imperialism can also be pursued by secular educationalists, administrators, some aspects of the press and the community of authors, and even some fragments of a newly emergent and culturally assimilated indigenous elite.

An 'imperial culture' may be the desired result emerging from the processes of cultural imperialism. It is the wished-for product, which energises the economic aims of the imperial state and creates the cohesive community through which imperial objectives can be attained. Finally, the 'culture of empire' can be interpreted as the various vehicles through which an imperial culture is disseminated. These can be the instrumental forces already mentioned – missions, schools, press, higher education, the propaganda of writers and official publications – but can also be associated with town planning, architecture, infrastructures, musical, dramatic and, later, cinematic performances. Importantly, they embrace ceremony, ritual and all the other ways in which empires display themselves. These all represent an ideal and it is the gap between that ideal and reality which is the space through which imperial ambitions fall. All discussions of forms of imperial culture must highlight the responses, exchanges and independent appropriations by indigenous peoples. Terms such as 'cultural bonds' and cultural 'agents', 'impositions' and 'legacies' have been used, but are probably too simplistic. They imply passivity on the part of the recipients whereas all these processes are part of a dynamic of active adaptation. After all, what is intended as a bond can often become a source of competition and division.

The cultural history of the British Empire

Pioneering work on imperial cultural history has generally concentrated on the third of these formulations. A brief essay on some aspects of the culture of empire, with a metropolitan focus, was incorporated into an otherwise conventional book by Ronald Hyam in the 1970s.[42] He later wrote works on sexuality and empire but has largely concentrated on familiar political fields.[43] It was, however, a journalist and popular author who truly pioneered the cultural history of empire. Jan Morris published her engaging trilogy on imperial culture between 1968 and 1978, and followed this with illustrated books on architecture and the spectacular characteristics of empire.[44] Though infused with a rather romantic tone and limited by a failure to make connections with wider imperial historiography, these books were path-breaking and subsequent cultural historians owe them a debt. They are stimulating despite their eccentricities and often misplaced interpretations. On the other hand, the academic approach to cultural history has invariably come through cross-disciplinary influences, notably from the 1990s. Anthropologists like Geertz, Thomas, Dirks and Cohn have all been important, producing works that have influenced some areas of history but have never fully entered the historical mainstream.[45] Coming from a literary tradition, the highly influential Edward Said linked the words 'Culture' and 'Imperialism' in his book of 1993, which followed his seminal *Orientalism* (1978). His approach adopted the post-structuralist theories of discourse that became central to the postcolonial school and largely differs from that adopted here.[46] Said's take on imperial culture was to scan the nineteenth-century literary canon, which acted as a 'polyphonic accompaniment' to the expansion of Europe, interpreting works in the light of contemporary imperial contexts. He convincingly argued that:

> so vast and yet so detailed is imperialism as an experience with crucial cultural dimensions, that we must speak of overlapping territories, intertwined histories common to men and women, whites and non-whites, dwellers in the metropolis and on the peripheries, past as well as present and future; these territories and histories can only be seen from the perspective of the whole of secular human history.[47]

By this time, the field was opening out in various ways. Several anthropologists, notably Nicholas B. Dirks and Nicholas Thomas, produced works relevant to the cultures of empire.[48] Historians were also producing comparative work relating to several empires.[49] One related work examined a range of cultural phenomena, including film, photography, food, music and dance, education, propaganda and exhibitions in the French Empire.[50] The editor suggested that many historians of the French Empire had missed these phenomena, and argued that the multiplicity of imperial images, triumphalist and oppositional, consensual and radical, spanning the full political spectrum, required much greater study and analysis. From a somewhat different standpoint, Kathleen Wilson was instrumental in carrying some of these cultural and imperial themes into an earlier period, while other works examined issues connected with concepts of the nation, with the important question of gender, and with aspects of identity – although some of these took a predominantly metropolitan focus.[51] The significance of the cultural dimension was then acknowledged in a number of works.[52]

Other key works on the culture of imperialism included those by Maya Jasanoff and Holger Hoock. These examined collecting cultures, including cultural crossovers among European empires.[53] Jasanoff and Hoock concentrated mainly on the metropolis and were less concerned with the wider dispersal of British cultural characteristics to the empire. There have also been rather more popular approaches, in some respects following the interests of Jan Morris.[54] However, it remains true that there has been more interest in the influence of empire on British culture than on the dispersals that concern this book. The question of the reciprocal effects of empire and the extent to which the British constituted an imperial society has indeed produced a lively debate, recently reignited by a bestseller by Sathnam Sanghera.[55] There have also been comparative studies and a series of works on education, emigration, medicine, the environment, policing, fiction, language, travel writing, masculinity and gender, juvenile literature, sport, cities, science, museums, sites of memory, female gentility, clubs, music, royal tours and advertising, as well as aspects of the varied ethnicities of the United Kingdom.[56] While all these touch on cultural topics, others focus more closely on relevant themes.[57] Various innovative studies include one on the manner in which British country houses reflect both imperial cultural connections and investment, while others survey the reception of royal tours in the colonies.[58]

The cultural history of individual Anglophone settler colonies, Canada, Australia, New Zealand and South Africa, has been subjected to a good deal of study.[59] These have confronted the problem of the extent to which imperial sentiment survived in the late nineteenth and twentieth centuries, and how far the development of a more national focus could coexist with loyalty to the British World, and if so in what proportion. The second issue is whether the involvement of colonial troops in the Anglo-Boer War 1899–1902 and the First World War constituted evidence of imperial or national affiliations expressed within a necessary class analysis. It has been suggested that the common culture created in the later nineteenth century, made up of racial dimensions, concepts of masculinity, youth organisations, public displays and imperial adventure literature all served to ensure the 'Call of the Blood' at the time of the First World War.[60] This proposition has to be tested in the light of the development of national cultures of various sorts in those territories. The two were not, however, incompatible. In a landmark book, Carl Berger argued that a certain degree of adherence to the imperial British World constituted a form of Canadian nationalism.[61] Certainly the Canadian situation was complicated by the awareness of the cultural, political and, in the past, military threat of the United States. Moreover, Canada has continued to adhere to the British monarchy as a means of keeping the confederation together. A valuable work by John Griffiths examines imperial culture in antipodean cities and reveals the care that must be taken to avoid easy conclusions based on the British case, not least in the light of the need to recognise the development of local cultural nationalisms in tandem with the apparent survival of imperial sentiment.[62] His book uses a definition of culture that includes architecture and city layout as well as popular music, dance, new twentieth-century entertainment buildings, the press and much else. These themes were all treated with a focus on the white immigrant populations and it might be expected that attitudes of indigenous peoples would take more ambivalent forms. However, the cultural phenomena examined in the following chapters, taking a broader sample than that of Griffiths, might offer richer perspectives.

South Africa has always constituted a different case, and it is only there that indigenous people have retaken the levers of power. This has ensured the development of an exceptionally vibrant rewriting of cultural history on a national basis, recovering the Black dimension and reinserting it into a national past formerly dominated by white perspectives.[63] Similar recoveries of indigenous histories have occurred elsewhere, though in different political contexts, overturning the European imperial notion that people without writing, and consequently lacking documents, have no historiography. This idea was prevalent in the 1960s, though it coincided with countervailing projects for recovering oral histories. Cultural research of various sorts has also proceeded apace in the non-settler imperial territories, notably in India and other Asian territories, not least because it has been recognised that such histories are important in the formation of modern identities.[64] In the case of Sri Lanka, Sujit Sivasundaram has revealed important aspects of the cultural forms that interweave with social and economic history.[65]

The rationale and structure of the book

Despite the existence of published work on modern nation states, there has been little attempt to create an overall cultural history of empire. Though such a project is a daunting task, it is potentially a valuable one, involving the creation of a multi-disciplinary synthesis of work produced by many scholars working in other fields.[66] The

British Empire not only dispersed peoples and a whole range of political and economic behavioural characteristics across the globe, it also spread elements of leisure and recreation, entertainment forms like the theatre and the cinema, as well as significant cultural vehicles like sculpture, ceremonial and, very importantly, extensive press and publishing. To these we can add the dressing of the human body, dance, music and visual arts such as painting and photography. Few if any of these were unique to Britain. They had multiple European origins, some embedded in past 'cultures' while others were heavily influenced by the burgeoning United States. Another major dispersal was the English language and its literary forms. These were also influenced by variants originating in the USA, increasingly influential in the twentieth century. English also developed colonial variations and even hybrid forms such as 'pidgin'. Indeed, no cultural forms disseminated from Europe ever retained their supposed 'purity', but were subjected to processes of interpenetration, interaction and hybridisation in different geographical contexts, climates and environments. Additionally, a full understanding of the globalisation of aspects of British culture (including different elements of the 'four nations') leads us beyond formal empire into its informal manifestations, notably in South America and the Far East. In such informal imperial enclaves similar cultural developments took place and interacted with adjacent societies.[67] All this will be related to such activities as horse racing, equestrian and other sports, as well as leisure pursuits (at least for the elite or for bourgeois groups) in hill stations or seaside resorts.

It is apparent that the field of cultural history is immense and that there are many different ways of analysing its imperial dimensions. What follows is necessarily a selection, as is the case with all works of history, and not all the areas mentioned in the previous paragraph can be covered. While it seeks, unusually, to cover the entire empire in all its forms, it represents a personal choice which highlights themes (some of which have been considered in different ways by other scholars) that have not been brought together into this particular conjunction before. It sets out to move the focus from the consideration of the influence of empire on British domestic society, as in the case of my early work on the propagation of imperial ideas through ephemera and the manner in which empire was repeatedly illustrated in artefacts, advertisements and various cultural forms.[68] This has been much developed by other scholars while the consequences of the possession of empire upon European societies has become a significant area of study in the case of French, Dutch, Portuguese, Italian, Belgian and German imperialism.[69] In more recent times, reflections on reciprocal effects of colonial rule on metropolitan culture have been expanded into an important comparative study of the cultural effects of decolonisation.[70]

The chapters that follow, however, shift the focus from Europe to the so-called periphery with the intention of examining various cultural modes given global expression through empire. The opening chapter examines the manner in which imperial acquisitions often started with ceremonies and certainly ended with them. There were overt expressions of imperial ideology, performances of hegemony and power relations, as well as efforts to impress, entertain and overawe the populace. Several succeeding chapters consider dispersals intended to be vehicles for cultural dominance but which stimulated striking reactions of adoption and adaptation. A prime example is sports, a central characteristic of British cultural imperialism that produced counter-imperial responses. Sports and pastimes were adjusted to local predilections and sometimes came to perform important political and economic functions in creating key social networks, but later contributed to forces of political nationalism and a sense of newly formed identities. Sports could energise the military and civilians, as well as indigenous peoples, in both rural and urban settings, ultimately breaking down racial separation. Two chapters seek to cover some aspects of this important field of sport. Empire was also the location for the creation of new kinds of art, mainly invoking forms of exoticism in landscape, light values, architecture, some aspects of portraiture and of the depiction of colonial peoples, artistic endeavours that created dynamic principles developing throughout the imperial period. In the twentieth century, western artists began to respond to indigenous forms, recognising in them ways of extending the language, mood and subject matter of art. This development became a means of establishing a distinctive national character no longer associated with the European origins of settlers or with imperial hegemony. In India and the so-called dependent territories, it became a route to the reassertion of vital indigenous cultural forms. It was in this area that interchanges between European and local ethnicities became most profound. Visual representations were also subject to new technologies, initially through photography and then through moving film. In these the original intention was often to 'speak' to an audience in the imperial metropole, but they became increasingly significant in addressing colonial populations, initially settlers and sojourners, but also indigenous people. Once again, the expansion in the ethnicity of practitioners ensured that these artistic forms were converted from imperial into nationalist and culturally revivalist forms, reflecting again the themes of dispersal, adoption, reaction and response.[71] Such artistic display connects with statuary and sculpture, which represented symbolic adherence to forms of martyrology and hagiography celebrating those considered heroes and notable figures, mainly military and administrative and almost entirely male. Associated events such as unveilings or annual celebrations were the highly visible public performance of empire, with the military and officialdom as key actors in ceremony. Such practices were later taken up by postcolonial states to emphasise wholly new affiliations.

Ceremony involving statuary was highly theatrical, and theatre history is another form which binds cultural phenomena together. Yet again, theatrical events were significant throughout the colonies, including the intriguing phenomenon of travelling acting troupes, undoubtedly spreading a sense of 'Britishness' wherever they went. But they were to be overtaken by new forms of national drama in the twentieth century. Press and printing advertised theatrical events, and both newspaper founders and journalists were initially highly mobile. Such professions were closely involved with the creation of a global English-language culture, as well as with the processes of intellectual reproduction and cultural dissemination. All cultural activities, sporting and otherwise, revealed the capacity of empire to marshal large labour forces and consequently transform environments.[72]

In each chapter, key examples serve to illuminate the topic and hopefully suggest parallel examples. Nevertheless, there are notable omissions. Language and literature are such major areas of study that it is impossible to incorporate them into this already over-ambitious work of synthesis. They require a specialist scholarship and have been extensively covered by experts in the fields. Consequently, despite their centrality in the imperial experience, they will only be touched on where relevant to other forms. Education and mission stations were obviously significant conduits of cultural dispersal, but they too constitute large and separate studies. Architecture and buildings have been examined elsewhere.

The importance of covering imperial culture on an empire-wide basis lies in exposing the cultural dimensions of globalisation.[73] This can be readily confirmed by looking around us. In many postcolonial countries it is hard to escape the fact that the visitor is looking at essentially British forms, even when through a lens revealing hybrid-isation with elements of local culture or modified by climate and location. Similarly, the French, Dutch or American character of other places can be equally apparent. But empire left more than footprints. Visual and mental worlds associated with metropolitan culture, in all its varieties, remain apparent. Strikingly, such cultural dispersals must be linked to other more familiar aspects of imperialism, not least the manner in which visual, religious, artistic, intellectual, even environ-mental inheritances are closely bound up with the expansion of the nineteenth-century bourgeois public sphere and related economic activities.

This was also true of the clothing of the human body. Here there was often a tension between maintaining European 'standards' and adapting to whatever was more appropriate for the tropics or for cold weather as in Canada.[74] In their early encounters with Asia, Europeans often adopted local dress, but abandoned this with the hardening of racial distinctions.[75] But later western dress was seen as a vital signifier when some emergent indigenous bourgeois figures adopted it, perhaps as a means to social advancement or to international connections, whether through the church, migration in search of further education, or in modern politics and diplomacy. Later, the nationalist urge and the resurgence of indigenous cultures led to the conscious rejection of such clothing. Women seem to have been more likely to stick to traditional forms.

This adjustment and the reaction also occurred in respect of several scholarly disciplines as well as sporting and other activities. Thus many cultural and intellectual associations found themselves, almost without intending it, in a dynamic process of adjustment. Sports adaptations often responded to climatic and social conditions, as in Australian-rules football. Christian forms sometimes adapted to the religions and related mores of peoples they were attempting to convert. This sometimes served to encourage new conversions or as a means of heading off schismatic independence. Cultures are never static but repeatedly demonstrate their porous character, constantly and selectively soaking up the conditions around them. The dynamics of such adaptations constitute an important theme of the book.

Disclaimer

An important disclaimer is called for. It is not intended for a moment that this concentration on sporting, artistic, printing, theatrical and ceremonial forms should obscure the brutalities and violence of empire.[76] The inequalities of power crucial to the whole imperial system were invariably reflected in such cultural forms. Peoples were dispossessed, often in violent ways, in order to create new urban centres, as well as access fresh areas and forms of resource extraction, agricultural or geological. They were forced or persuaded into unfamiliar and debilitating forms of labour in urban settings or mines, foreign ways of living (including land-holding or domestic buildings), into unfamiliar social customs (monogamy for example) and alien mind-sets, encouraged to worship or be educated in new ways (sometimes fiercely resisted, often embraced enthusiastically). New cultural activities were incorporated into traditional societies. A classic case is the adaptation of dance and musical forms by indigenous peoples, usually in intriguing variants and often connected with efforts to grapple with modernisation and generational tensions associated with economic and social change.[77] Indigenous peoples also learned to drink western forms of alcohol, sometimes adopting them all too eagerly as a means of assuaging the deep anxieties of the dislocation of traditional lifestyles. Europeans veered between encouraging this for profit (and perhaps social control) and attempting to prevent it, sometimes at the behest of missionaries. Indigenous people were subject to wholly alien laws (for example in the control of hunting and other environmental matters) and were tried in unfamiliar courtrooms amidst, for them, arcane legal mumbo-jumbo.[78] They were incarcerated in prisons or labour camps that were the brutal sharp end of the western system.

They were also subject to propaganda about the 'good things' brought by the West masking what they knew to be reality. For example, Europeans viewed their alleged command of the environment as a notable attribute, a capacity for control of natural phenomena exhibited in drainage of marshes, digging canals, canalising rivers, clearing agricultural land and generally 'disciplining' the environment to their own ends. This vision infused both settler societies and colonial authorities in Africa and Asia. The environment could be anthropomorphised, sent to school, emerging with a new personality. Indigenous peoples, according to imperial propaganda, were incapable of this. They were at the mercy of their environments, blown hither and thither by its whims and caprices. The reality could be very different. Peoples living in their environments for many centuries knew how to handle them, subtly and effectively, in a manner which it took Europeans many decades fully to understand. In any case, such peoples were by then often divorced from their environments and subjected to the unpredictable fancies of Europeans whose understanding was a good deal slighter than their self-confidence. This conflict between imported ideas and local practice constitutes a backdrop to many of the cultural forms surveyed here. They are also a vital component of the creation and extension of towns, military encampments, European settlements and sporting and ceremonial spaces.[79] Europeans were particularly confident about the practice of western medicine. The spatial dimensions of settlement were often dictated by what Europeans considered to be essential for the main-tenance both of their defensive security and of their health, including 'cordons sanitaires' between themselves and indigenous populations. For similar reasons, hill stations (in the Caribbean, Africa, Australia, India and South-East Asia) became places of European resort.[80] All these conditioned the locating of transposed cultural forms and sometimes inhibited indigenous participation.

Yet, when all these points about violence and displacement have been repeated, it also has to be noted that while Europeans in the settler 'neo-Europes' or in the territories of the 'empire of rule' were busily adapting to their new environments, some indigenous people, even if a minority, scrambled over the 'white cargoes' that were depos-ited in their midst.[81] Some seized new forms of education, hoping that they offered a route into grappling with the invasive forces around them and, in the process, maybe (for a few) delivering a newly affluent lifestyle. For a large number, this led to disappointment and some-times failure, but western education could be turned against their oppressors. Many people migrated to the newly dynamic western-style cities, seeking opportunities and frequently failing to find them.

If any were overawed by the great buildings of such cities, the reality of their lives was more often centred upon traditional structures on the periphery, shanty towns and wholly inadequate sanitary, medical and social arrangements, not least in the twentieth century.

Europeans in settler territories also passed through phases of cultural dispersal, adaptation and renewal. Initially, migrants were keen to see themselves as fragments of the parent society, eager to proclaim their 'Britishness' or its sub-sets of 'Irishness', 'Scottishness', 'Welshness' or 'Englishness' as promoted in churches, clubs and associational culture.[82] They were, however, soon sucked into the necessary adaptations to their new environment and began to take on fresh identities, even if such identities failed to be mutually exclusive in respect of ethnic origins. As well as adjusting to climate, environment and indigenous neighbours, migrants soon had to adapt to the arrival of fresh waves of immigrants from other parts of Europe, and later from other continents, notably Asia.[83] But still the built environments of their towns and cities, the character of their domestic settings, dress, and their cultural and educational institutions continued to bear at least some of the marks of European origins. Cultural influences flowed in from the United States, Asia and indigenous hinterlands, but aspects of 'British' cultural forms survived. Generally they still spoke the English language, albeit with different accents and with elements of a new vocabulary, persuading others to 'perform' aspects of heavily adapted British culture.[84] Imperial territories contributed to the considerable distinction in numbers between those speaking English as a first language and those for whom it is a second one.[85]

Finally, it may be said that most historians now accept the notion that there are essential similarities among all imperial territories, no longer making a clear distinction between those of settlement and rule.[86] These include the dispossession of indigenous peoples, the structural violence of conquest and settlement, commercial exploitation, the capacity to promote environmental change, and the nature of political authority. This book will adopt much of this unifying approach since the processes of propagation of imperial culture were often similar, regardless of constitutional difference. The cultural history of empire smooths out at least some of the political and administrative differences. Much of the 'imperial imaginary' was similar wherever located. It was rooted in material and physical things, including significant cultural forms, connected as they were with political and economic relationships. All were coupled with the imperial mind-set central to the business of empire, the inherent sense of superiority of the ruling people, the striving for security and successful growth and 'development', even the re-creation, at least in modified form, of the class structures of the metropole. The dispersal of cultural forms can be framed as a hegemonic process, implicated in the creation of the racial hierarchies of empire. That was the intention of the original propagators of elements of cultural imperialism in their efforts to create a supposedly uniform imperial culture. But such cultural diffusion had the capacity to be disruptive, producing counter-hegemonic results. Cultural forms were challenged, changed and converted in complex ways (and by both settlers and indigenous others) across the empire. Hence the cultures of colonies turned out to be both parallel and varied. Processes of intellectual reproduction and cultural dissemination became arenas for the development of hybrid affinities and cultural resistance. These cultural interplays are central to the arguments of this book. This will mark some revision (but not necessarily displacement) of the notion that empire is centrally characterised by dissent and disruption, resistance, anxiety and fear.[87]

In assessments of decolonisation the cultural dimensions are the most difficult to pin down. Political change, however problematic and sometimes illusory, can be linked to specific dates. Economic decolonisation has always seemed problematic since there can be little doubt that decolonising empires always attempted to maintain economic continuity in relationships with former colonies. Social change is also difficult to evaluate since, in many former colonies, an extensive impoverished underclass tends to be a continuing feature of the post-colonial era. The relocation by migration of large numbers of colonial peoples, fleeing warfare and poverty, has been a striking characteristic of modern times. In the British case, this has involved the settlement of West Indian, South Asian, West African, Cypriot and Far Eastern peoples, as well as refugees from conflicts involving militant Islam. On the other hand, the familiar concept, 'the decolonisation of the mind' is easier to proclaim as an ambition than to identify as a reality. It can perhaps be linked to the notion of the decolonisation of culture, again difficult to delineate in its state of flux. Cultural continuity is more insidious and harder to disentangle, particularly when entwined with various forms of indigenous culture. Ireland offers a good example (in general terms omitted from this book) since so many cultural aspects of Irish life remain essentially English. Parliament, educational systems and common law are survivals, however much modified. The greatest of Irish writers, like Yeats and Joyce, wrote in English. The landscape of fields and hedges, division into counties, as well as much of the architecture of the British period all survive. Post empire, many colonial traces remain, even in arenas of cultural inter-leaving and interpenetration. The cultural accretions of empire can be resistant to change. They are not mere illusions, stage sets easily collapsed when no longer required. Unlike statues, cultural forms, while dynamic and changeable, do not always fall.

Finally, a work like this leaves hostages to fortune. It runs the risk of being approached by scholars who are authorities on one chapter or even one section of a chapter. It is to be hoped that readers in that category will be indulgent and recognise the significance of its overall design, the ambition of its conception, and the need for exceptionally concise analysis. They may also be forgiving if they recognise that works like this can act as portals for non-specialists to encounter expert work in fields they might otherwise have missed. Given the fact that a vast number of books and articles has been consulted, perhaps tolerance may be extended when authors discover that their important work has been unaccountably missed. Perhaps readers will note the desire to remove so many of these cultural studies from their former ghettoes and bring them into the mainstream of imperial history. It may well be that the complex history of empire should receive some considerable illumination as a result.

1
IMPERIAL CEREMONIAL

King Emperor George V and Mary, Queen Empress, at the Coronation Durbar, Delhi, 1911.

Ostentatious spectacles and pageantry were central to imperialism. Imperial elites throughout history have always felt the need to display themselves and were prepared to spend large sums of money doing so. Since empires cannot be self-effacing, repeated processions and ritualised events were partly designed as acts of self-regard, to fortify and offer reassurance for the participants. They can be viewed as highly ephemeral and insubstantial, passing processions that disappear over the horizon. But they can also be analysed as instrumental in, or at least revelatory of, significant aspects of the imperial condition. Imperial rule has been characterised as involving coercion and collaboration, confidence and competence.[1] The rituals of empire were intended to convey all of these. The involvement of the military and the police represented the forces of coercion; the inclusion of indigenous rulers often signified collaboration; the highly public character of the stylised pomp of such occasions was intended to inspire confidence; while the successful choreography of the pageantry and performance of the stereotypical and solemn conventions of the protocol were designed to demonstrate competence in marshalling and organising people. Ceremony was thus intended to be emblematic of the forms and processes of imperial rule, representing its hierarchies leading to the ultimate authority of the Crown. Such ceremonial was also highly masculinist, with almost all participants (apart from in smaller-scale events) being male. In a manner symptomatic of the age, women were expected to play their role either as consorts or as spectators. Yet for much of the nineteenth century imperial ceremony ultimately glorified a female monarch whose gender was, perhaps, equivalent to the feminine personifications of idealised characterisations of Victory, Peace, Justice, Mercy and Wisdom. Shakespeare perfectly summed up the paradoxes of ceremony, a word he used in its widest meaning. On the one hand, it was hollow, but on the other it was symbolic of rule. Henry V lamented that kings have little that ordinary people 'have not too, Save ceremony, save general ceremony'. For Shakespeare the worth of such ceremony represented 'place, degree, and form/ Creating awe and fear in other men'.[2]

Ceremony performed many functions in the British Empire. The acquisition of territory was invariably declared through formal ceremonial, the announcement of possession, the raising of the flag and so on. This often created a foundation myth, as in Algernon Talmage's 1937 painting *The Founding of Australia*, depicting Captain Phillip laying claim to the land in 1788, 150 years earlier (see Plate 1).[3] Later, it was used to symbolise the relationship between imperial rulers and indigenous peoples, quasi-diplomatic performances that in fact symbolised the power relations of the new order while often sanctifying the continuing power, on sufferance, of collaborating chieftaincies and other rulers (see Plate 2). Such ceremonial was thus mutually beneficial to ruling elites. But it was also significant in symbolising the effects of conquest, the termination of wars or revolts, and sometimes the dispossession of those who had resisted. Ceremonies also accompanied the arrival and departure of viceroys, governors general, governors and other imperial officials.[4] Some ceremonies were intended to impress indigenous people; others to embrace mainly settlers and expatriates. In the urban setting, processions were vital in announcing the presence of the various levels of authority in the laying of foundation stones, the opening of buildings, dedications of various sorts, the erection of statues, the ubiquitous celebration of royal events (like jubilees, coronations and birthdays), key dates in the calendar such as the birthday of Queen Victoria and later Empire Day, eventually the inauguration of councils and other political developments. The most elaborate of all ceremonial came to surround the royal visits to colonies that began in the 1860s. While enforcement authorities were always present, ceremonies were also sanctified by the presence of church clergy. Masonic orders were regularly central to such events because their rituals and formal protocols were key aspects of the fraternal bonding of the brotherhood as well as their mythic association with construction, supposedly emblematic of imperial relationships and the growth of empire.[5] Significantly, the senior elite of empire, including members of the royal family, were themselves invariably freemasons. Such staging of key moments in the life of colonies and of empire could occur on a grand scale in capital cities, but also in more modest form in many smaller settlements. In all cases, it constituted theatre, the performance of loyalties to monarchy, its local representatives, sets of imperial ideas and the institutions that sanctified them.

Aside from the differences in scale and grandeur of such events, there were common elements: the presence of uniforms, robes (for civic leaders, judges, Christian clergy, and lawyers), horses as mounts for senior officers and officials, music (with regimental, local, youth organisation and school bands), elephants in India, all exhibited through processing.[6] Very often in press reports and memoirs it was said that part of the solemnity of occasions like Empire Day or the proclamation of a new monarch was derived from the fact that the participants knew that similar events were taking place at the same time (subject to different time zones) in the metropole and across the empire. Such ceremonies were thus designed to promote a sense of imperial unity. They offered participants, particularly those of the dominant imperial people, a sense of being part of universal phenomena much larger than themselves and their immediate circumstances, something so grandiloquent as to be global and perhaps grander than any rivals. They were designed to unite both participants and specta- tors in symbolic adherence to the imperial ideal, acceptance of its fundamental ideologies and pride in its achievements. In the villages, towns, ports and cities, as well as in rural areas, these were mounted in a classic imperial hierarchy through different levels of pomp and numbers of participants from the truly spectacular to the vaguely ridiculous. Such displays were meaningless without audiences. People turned out into streets, squares and villages to be entertained and awed, or perhaps alienated, even simply rendered indifferent. They were encouraged to do so through the declaration of holidays, through the participation of schoolchildren and the members of youth organisa- tions, through the appeal of music, uniforms (particularly colourful dress uniforms with medals), animals (elephants, horses, camels, mili- tary mascots) and processional displays. Sometimes, the appeal was enhanced through quasi-architectural decoration in the form of banners, arches and other fleeting structures. Moreover, many of the grander ceremonies were consciously rendered more appealing to the viewing public through a carnival atmosphere with entertainments, sports and market sales. They occurred everywhere from the Caribbean islands to remoter corners of Africa, from congregations of white settlers to the more significant Asian locations. How far or how rapidly such ideals began to fade is a matter of debate for individual colonies. Yet it is apparent that the tradition of ceremonial was taken over by the settler colonies in symbolising new national loyalties and, later, even by independent Asian and African states in proclaiming their independence, search for national unity and often maintenance in power of specific elites. It may be that this continuity resulted from the capacity of colonial authorities to appropriate and perhaps pervert indigenous ceremonial.

Appropriation of indigenous ceremonial

Where indigenous people were expected to be spectators, albeit sometimes at the fringes, ceremonies attempted to project a ritualised demonstration of dominance and authority, as well as a sense of cultural difference. Yet ritual ceremonial was equally central to indigenous societies, events promoting social binding and cultural uplift throughout their histories. In Canada, spirituality was central to such ceremonies among First Nations, Métis and Inuit peoples.[7] In a variety of ways, this was also true of many peoples in Africa, the Aboriginals of Australia and the Maori in New Zealand. Among the Maori, ceremonial protocols were of great significance. Their notion of ceremony and appropriate diplomatic behaviour was often conditioned not so much by the event as by the status of the people involved, the *rangatiri* or chiefs often lending their significant presence to such occasions. The Maori word for protocol is *hui*, with rules at a lesser level covered by the word *kawa*.[8] For the Maori, greetings are of particular importance, covered by the word *powhiri*. In Australia, the Aboriginal corroboree, with its spiritual and theatrical elements, the interface between the here and now and 'dreamtime' was never fully penetrated by Europeans. Sadly, relations between Europeans and

Aborigines were invariably more violent than diplomatic, right down to the twentieth century. The corroboree did, however, feature in the work of the Tasmanian artist John Glover as early as 1832, and in the 1890s in that of two Aboriginal artists, Tommy McRae and William Barak, who worked in a medium influenced by western techniques.[9] Buddhist societies of Asia were also exponents of processions and ceremonies, for example in relation to the initiation of a new monk. There were many royal and funeral events in such societies, sometimes involving elaborate wheeled structures. Among Indian princes and rulers, processing and ceremonial with ritual exchanges of gifts were crucial.

The traditional spiritual and diplomatic content of indigenous rituals was seldom fully understood by invading Europeans who often sought to intrude themselves in attempts at appropriation and incorporation. Some traditional rituals were viewed as the survival of backward indigenous forms, others were seen as open to subversion for Europeans' ends. Some ceremonial meetings included discussions at the end of conflicts and attempts to frame treaties, often involving the extension of territorial power.[10] Other ceremonies might be more workaday, as in the arrival of a collector or district officer (in India) or a district commissioner (in Africa), or various local authority figures in the settler territories. Indigenous people were often expected to turn out to demonstrate their respect for these local rituals of power and dominance mediated through their own traditional hierarchy of chiefs and headmen.[11] By the twentieth century, encounters between Europeans and Canadian First Nations had come to be popularly and inaccurately known as 'pow wows'. Under the consolidatory Indian Act of 1876 and subsequent amendments, much indigenous ceremonial was banned as part of the alleged process of 'civilising' First Nations people and incorporating them into European Christian civilisation. The potlatch ceremony among West Coast peoples was banned in 1885 and the Plains Sun Dance ceremony in 1895. A key aspect of these acts was the banning of the regalia central to their performance. Just as bodies were clothed in imperial insignia in British ceremonial, so were magnificent forms of clothing central to indigenous performances.[12] Such cultural suppression (generally driving indigenous rituals and regalia into secret performances) was gradually ameliorated from the 1950s. In some parts of Africa, there were 'palavers' which is a word derived from the Portuguese and largely lacks African authenticity. For example, the Prince of Wales on his African tour of 1925 had a 'palaver' with chiefs in the western province of the Gold Coast (Ghana). The book of illustrations of the tour described the event as being 'a riot of brilliant colours', with an excited crowd of onlookers watching the great chiefs under their big umbrellas moving past the prince's pavilion in slow procession, paying homage, offering gifts.[13] It was apparently the last of a whole series of 'palavers' in the Gold Coast. When the prince moved on to Nigeria, such events were called durbars, perhaps in deference to Islamic rulers in Northern Nigeria. But the favourite word in Africa for meetings between Europeans and African *indunas* (chiefs) was '*indaba*', a Nguni word, made famous by the Zulu, with similar usage by the Xhosa and Sotho-Tswana peoples. Europeans came to spread it throughout southern Africa (partly helped by the dispersal of the Nguni people in the movement known as the *Mfecane* into the Transvaal and north into Zimbabwe, Mozambique, Zambia and Malawi). The Zulu repeatedly performed indabas for royal visitors. In June 1925, the Prince of Wales was in Eshowe where, it was claimed, 50,000 Zulus were encamped. Their war dance was so convincing that onlookers thought the Prince was at risk when regiments stopped their charge a yard in front of him.[14] He also attended indabas in Northern Rhodesia. In 1934 Prince George, Duke of Kent, attended a 'great indaba' of Zulus in Pietermaritzburg on his southern African tour since he did not have the time to visit Zululand. Thousands of Zulus, in full war accoutrements, danced and waved their assegais (short stabbing spears), theatrically performing past conflict in the supposedly peaceful ceremonial present.[15] In Basutoland (Lesotho), the Prince attended a *pitso* (the local ceremonial equivalent) of the Sotho people, allegedly involving 50,000 horsemen and 40,000 spectators. The 90-year-old king, Jonathan Moshesh, grandson of the great Moshesh of the nineteenth century, welcomed the Prince and spoke at some length, demanding that the independence of his kingdom should be maintained.[16] Thus an event designed to create acquiescence in imperial rule was manipulated to the king's own ends.[17]

Some have predicted that the protocols of traditional societies might decline in modern times, through the influence of Christian conversion and of a younger generation responding to the modern world. But traditional forms have survived as part of cultural revivalism, particularly in settler territories where indigenous histories and behavioural forms have been rediscovered and re-emphasised. In Africa some have become associated with nationalist cultural assertion, even if under the political control of modern politicians, thus symbolising to a certain extent the subservience of traditional rulers to the new nation state. Others have been suppressed. Hence, while imperialists clothed themselves in ceremonial at every level of their exercise of power, invariably attempting to overlay the protocols of indigenous societies, they often merely added an additional level to long-standing traditional practice. Imperial ceremonial was more than just the 'flummery' of power: it was in the business of appropriating or suppressing indigenous forms in order to replace them with allegedly more 'civilised' or Christian substitutes. The spread of youth movements (see later in this chapter) became another aspect of the incorporation of indigenous peoples into imperial rituals.

Various questions arise about this engrossing of imperial subalterns into empire ceremonial and the apparent interest of some in its forms. Indians, particularly in the princely states, seemed to see the British rituals as, in some ways, a modified continuation of their own. It is clear, however, that attitudes and reactions would differ according to the status of the participant or the observer, although the British often made the glib assumption that Asian people tended to be impressed by such spectacles, and that their provision was good for the maintenance of the myths of political authority and social control. In some places in Africa, Africans seem to have been enthusiastic participants. Chiefs often appeared to amalgamate European forms into the rituals of their courts, attempting to reassert their authority among their own people and their prestige in respect of neighbours. Some Africans seemed to imitate, in indigenised adaptations, certain European performances, including dress and even music. This was true, for example, in the case of the dance societies in East Africa, Malawi and South Africa which developed in the late nineteenth century. It may be that such appropriations acted as routes to accommodating Europeans through the assumption of aspects of modernity or as a means of connecting with (and controlling) the new order. But such apparent imitations of European activities could also be satirical in intent, offering opportunities to blunt the cultural impact of dominant peoples. The complexity of the purposes of dancing is further illustrated by the notion that it could represent the resistance of the youth to control by a tribal gerontocracy.[18] It may even be that the adoption of such parroted, sometimes distantly echoing, reproductions of alien ritual constituted bridges to fresh nationalist activity in the twentieth century.

Some diplomatic encounters occurred in Britain itself when there were several visits by traditional rulers in the later nineteenth century. Such ritualistic encounters are classically symbolised in Thomas Jones Barker's celebrated painting *The Secret of England's Greatness* of 1863, in which Queen Victoria presents a Bible at an audience in Windsor Castle to an unidentified African, sometimes described as an 'ambassador from East Africa'.[19] This image can be interpreted as an icon of British power, expressing the unambiguous confidence of imperial rule, although modern interpretations see it as concealing mysterious doubts and uncertainties.[20] Barghash, Sultan of Zanzibar, visited Britain in 1875, partly as a reward for signing his anti-slavery treaty of 1870, partly to impress him with the industrial and military power of the imperial metropole (his successor returned in 1929). With different intentions, three Tswana chiefs from what is now Botswana, Bathoen, Sebele and Khama, arrived in 1895 to request British protection to ward off the depredations of competing local South African powers, including the Afrikaner-ruled Transvaal and Cecil Rhodes's British South Africa Company.[21] Dressed in European suits, they overcame opposition to their visit and were more or less feted while being introduced to imperial power and sophistication. Khama was generally referred to as 'king' and became a considerable favourite, not least among missionaries since he converted to Christianity and prohibited alcohol in his kingdom. The real prize for indigenous visitors was to be able to attend royal jubilees or coronations. King Lewanika of the Barotse (Lozi) of western Northern Rhodesia attended the coronation of Edward VII in 1902 and the Lozi were allegedly 'delirious with excitement' on his return. The missionary Coillard reported Lewanika's famous remark about his prospective encounter with Edward VII that 'when we kings get together we always have plenty to talk about'.[22] His successor Yeta III succeeded against official resistance in attending the coronation of George VI in 1937.[23] The kingdom of Buganda in East Africa sent its *katikiro* (loosely equivalent to 'chief minister') to London for Edward VII's coronation, a visit recorded by the katikiro's secretary Ham Mukasa.[24] In colonies, coronation fetes were held for the edification of indigenous people and for the encouragement of white officials and others. While Indian princes were generally secure in their status, despite the great disparity between the grander and lesser ones, as symbolised by the number of gun salutes they were allowed, African chiefs and kings were in a more ambiguous position. Often colonial authorities were opposed to the use of the word 'king' for paramount chiefs holding authority over other chiefs. Despite the fear that they might develop ideas above their station, 'king' was still used for some of the grander rulers of East and southern Africa. Muslim titles like *emir* were more common in West Africa, while the larger states of

Uganda also had convenient indigenous titles like *kabaka* in Buganda, *omugabe* in Ankole. In Barotseland the administration refused to permit the paramount chief to be called king and the traditional royal salute was to be delivered only to the administrator of the territory and the High Commissioner.[25] This changed, however, with the full implementation of Lugard's policy of indirect rule in the inter-war years. While some chiefs succeeded in keeping the honorific of 'king', others attempted to take on the full panoply of imported notions of kingship before losing power to nationalists.[26] However, such policies of operating through indigenous rulers had a tendency to freeze the fluidity of indigenous population groupings, even creating 'tribes' which had scarcely existed in the same form before.

The military

The military involvement in ceremony was of long standing. In 1819, the young Colin Campbell (later Lord Clyde) sailed to Barbados with his regiment. He found that it was the duty of all captains there to parade their companies before the governor every evening between 6 and 7 o'clock. Such a display was designed to bolster the governor's authority, give confidence to white society and demonstrate the fire-power available in the event of slave unrest.[27] While slave societies were an extreme case, all military involvement in ceremonial carried similar significance. For example, on the Queen's birthday in 1878, the Governor General of Canada, Lord Dufferin, took the salute at a large military review of 3,000 troops outside Montreal. Considerable crowds looked on, some climbing trees to get a better view while 'the surrounding hillsides were packed'. 'Bands played, cannon fired in salute, and the event culminated in mock re-enactments of famous British triumphs.' The carnival mood was described as 'Derby-like' by the governor general's wife, while the 'triumphs' clearly bolstered pride and confidence. The review was taking place in Lower Canada or Quebec, the location of the British conquest of New France in

1759.[28] Such public enactment was powerfully symbolic of imperial authority.

New technology also played an essential role in diplomacy and ceremony. Steam vessels, for example, represented a means of over-awing traditional societies through exhibiting a potent instrument of coercion. An excellent example of such an effect, involving regular ceremonies of arrival and departure with accompanying military contingents, occurred in Burma (Myanmar). The initial conquest in 1824–25 featured an early steam vessel, the *Diana*, while the repeated diplomatic missions to the northern Burmese kingdom at Ava and Mandalay were rendered easier by the opportunity to travel more than 400 miles up the Irrawaddy (Ayeyarwady) in steam vessels. Several envoys did the journey by steamer between the 1850s and the conquest of the kingdom in 1885–56, indicating that British steam technology and military power were to be reckoned with. The vice-roys Dufferin and Linlithgow followed, respectively, in 1886 to cele-brate the conquest of the north and in 1937 to mark the transition of Burma from Indian province to separate colony, while the Prince and Princess of Wales (later George V and Queen Mary) appeared on the river in 1906.[29]

India

In India, the British merely added an extra layer of ceremonial to a long-standing tradition of display. It is intriguing that one of the last of the 'old school' of British artists, Frederick Christian Lewis, landed there in 1834 and made his reputation by painting large pictures of ceremonies in Indian states.[30] That raises interesting questions. Were his patrons demonstrating their emulation of the British in deploying ceremony or were they asserting their longer and more distinguished ceremonial tradition, and that the British were mere imitators? Working in a western artistic tradition, Lewis was producing cross-cultural images. Yet, while imperial ceremonial attained its notably overblown manifestations in the later nineteenth and early twentieth centuries, such elaborate ceremonial was already important in the East India Company period from the later seventeenth century. Company officials imagined that commercial activities required the keeping of equivalent forms to those of Indian rulers. The President of the Surat factory apparently 'lived in almost as great state as the Mogul Governor'. Servants with silver staves apparently followed him from room to room, and liveried guardsmen and Moors under two standards marched before him. He had well-filled stables, his own chaplain, physician, surgeon, linguist and mintmaster. Trumpets blew to herald him while at church festivals, 'the President and his lady' were carried in palanquins in solemn procession, the 'Council in ox-drawn coaches of special splendour' with seats inlaid with ivory.[31] The Company may in practice have been an imperial state and arrogated to themselves the appropriate dignity,[32] but technically, unlike governors and viceroys, Company officials were not representatives of the imperial monarchy

Yet it is intriguing that in early Company days it was the Indian princely states that were more eager to impress the British with ceremonial than the other way round. Thus the princes sought to overawe them to turn aside their apparent threat to the existing order. But the British developed their own responses later in the century, seeking to make themselves appear 'more Indian' by adopting what they conceived to be powerful resonances of Indian splendour. During the era of violent advance in the late eighteenth and early nineteenth centuries, ceremonial and rituals were central to the rise of the Company power.[33] Between June 1814 and October 1815, the Company's governor general, the Marquess of Hastings, journeyed from Calcutta across Central India in a vast flotilla of over 200 boats on the Ganges, his entire party numbering some 10,000. He repeatedly held durbars with Indian rulers and exchanged '*nuzzurs* ' or ritual gifts, which he ceremonially touched.[34] In the 1820s, Captain Mundy considered that the pomp, ceremony and entertainment at princely courts visited by Lord Combermere, commander-in-chief of Company forces, reminded him of the visit of a feudal superior in medieval England. The kingdom of Oudh provided an example when the young prince met them on the road at the head of an amazing cavalcade and spectacle, including courtiers, cavalry, infantry and hangers-on. 'Our party was led by the band and the 11th Dragoons and Native Cavalry squadrons, followed by our elephants 15-abreast to which we transferred from our horses.'[35] For an Indian potentate elephants were much more appropriate to such ceremonial than horses, providing the dignity and grandeur required and suggesting the assimilation of the British into Indian norms. The two processions duly combined in a cloud of dust, and the prince joined the commander-in-chief in the howdah of his elephant (a regular ritual of companionable processional travel), part of a group now 40 elephants strong. The British party had two escorts accompanied by princely heralds 'calling the high-sounding titles of the boy-prince'. These 'Cavaliers' showed off their horsemanship and military prowess around the procession. The British and 'native' bands played music, vying with each other for discordant mastery. After breakfast, with 'nautching and singing', presents were swapped, a tradition which Mundy hoped would be abolished.[36] What may be described as intercultural ceremonial took place on the approaches to the great city of Lucknow and its many magnificent buildings, later to be so comprehensively damaged.

The incorporation of the British into Indian processional display is perfectly illustrated by a painting from the studio of Ghulam Ali Khan, c.1840–44, with the British Agent to the Delhi Court, Thomas Metcalfe, riding an elephant followed by a profusion of elephants, horses, soldiers, banners, drummers and lances.[37] Metcalfe is presumably attending a durbar with Bahadur Shah, the Mughal Emperor or King of Delhi. While ceremonial events occurred in all colonial settlements, great and small, it was inevitable that encounters between the imperial authorities and indigenous rulers would be particularly grandiose in India, with its own history of ostentatious rituals. The incidence of these undoubtedly grew in the later nineteenth century, not least with the great durbar pageants. A particular Anglo-Indian word described this characteristic ceremonial: *tamasha*, which was described as a spectacle that provided a popular excitement, thus suggesting an element of entertainment.[38] Fireworks were common, indicating technical accomplishment. Propaganda and entertainment often go together in imperial ritual – the sugaring of the pill of power. The ideology of imperialism was repeatedly asserted through highlighting its leading characters, and there were many different registers of production and reception, as intended by organisers and received by onlookers.

Such ceremonial became more grandiloquent as the century wore on. A typical reception for a new viceroy was described by Mary Lutyens, granddaughter of Lord Lytton. In 1876, the Lyttons landed at Bombay and were received with 'royal salutes from the Arsenal and a guard of honour'. They 'landed through an arch of palms, beyond which was a large red-carpeted area where "all the rank and fashion of Bombay were assembled"'. Cheers accompanied their 'slow passage in a procession of carriages to Government House at Parell'.[39] They later set off by special train to Calcutta. But realities intruded when they were told that there were coffins on board for disposing of those who died of heat apoplexy. At Calcutta, there were neither crowds nor cheers and Lytton delivered a speech 'to an appallingly frigid audience'.[40] Viceroys and governors were not always received with acclamation. Henry Beveridge (invariably a critical observer) distinctly sent up his participation in the durbar with the Maharajah of Bhopal in 1899. On arrival in the princely state, 'a carriage and pair drove me to the camp, while an enormous *shigram* drawn by two camels on which rode two helmeted syces conveyed my poor little baggage. There is a street of tents and on one was my name.'[41] Curzon and Lady Curzon were expected to arrive from different directions the following day (see Plate 3). He concluded that 'viceregal visits cause immense trouble and expense without effecting commensurate good'.[42] They also created exhaustion. Violet Jacob, aristocratic wife of an army officer, spent time with fellow Scot, the Vicereine Lady Elgin in 1896, finding her 'worn and delicate', 'terribly homesick'.[43] On another continent, Governor General Dufferin found his progresses across Canada 'extremely hard work'. At every station and town, 'long eighteen-hour days would be filled with openings, receptions, visits, dances, concerts, addresses – each requiring costume changes and polished little speeches in response'. They attracted large crowds and he had to smile through 'the periods of boredom, illness and exhaustion'. The darker underside is that he considered First Nation Canadians to be 'feckless' and saw them as being akin to his Irish tenants, a typical conflation of Irish and colonial indigenous.[44] Such gubernatorial progresses could be replicated across almost all colonies, but particularly in Australia, New Zealand, the Cape and Natal, later South Africa. If they symbolised the long reach of monarchical symbolism, they could also be manipulated by politicians and local officials.

While ceremonial accompanied the grand events of empire, ritual occurred at every level of the imperial condition. All ritual has clear intentions, but the effects of its manipulation can be highly complex. As well as the laying of foundation stones, there were ceremonial openings of buildings, the inauguration of railway lines, the unveiling of statuary, the completion of public parks, sports facilities, annual horse-racing meetings, the switching on of fountains, together with the arrival and departure of regiments, all prompting public ceremony. Apart from the more overblown events, there were many local manifestations of imperial-wide rituals. One example was the proclamation of the new monarch, which occurred throughout Britain and in every colony. Though an older tradition, this public performance became global with the proclamation of Edward VII and his successors. Most cities and important settlements had sheriffs, titular appointments connected with the High Court, as in England. In

Calcutta in the 1930s the sheriff was a businessman, Colonel Sir Charles Gordon Arthur, who had commanded the Calcutta Light Horse in the 1920s.[45] Although the sheriff's office rotated on virtually an annual basis, he found himself proclaiming the accession of two monarchs, Edward VIII and, after the abdication, George VI. The position of sheriff has continued in the modern Indian republic.[46] Elsewhere, mayors and lord mayors issued the proclamation. These ceremonials were accompanied by marching troops, patriotic band music, trumpet fanfares, hopefully cheering crowds, with leading figures often arriving in horse-drawn carriages. Newsreels exist from the proclamation of Edward VIII, illustrating the extent and grandeur of the ritual, the universality of such colonial ceremonial clearly designed to bind the empire together in loyalty to the monarch.[47] The ritual of Empire Day constitutes an interesting case. First mooted in the 1890s, this formal celebration of monarchy and empire developed in Edwardian times after the second Anglo-Boer War, when imperial patriotism was particularly potent.[48] The day chosen was the birthday of Queen Victoria, 24 May, which became a public holiday in many territories. This celebration also occurred at every level from great capital to small town as well as in widely dispersed mission stations. Schools, missions, youth organisations and many other associations were swept up into these ceremonies, giving them an extensive incidence in both urban and rural areas.

Missionaries were party to imperial ritual, for example in Bombay in 1889, when the opening of a Methodist Soldiers' and Sailors' Home was accompanied by considerable pomp. The Methodists had recently re-established themselves in Bombay and the minister the Rev. George Clutterbuck was attempting to create a chapel, a school, and a home in the Colaba area on a site provided by the government.[49] The home was intended to provide social and religious support, with an emphasis on temperance, for soldiers and sailors visiting the city. The existing Royal Alfred Sailors' Home, wrote Clutterbuck, 'is a very fine establishment, but its drinking bar is a snare to many'. These Methodist plans were fiercely opposed by the Anglican Establishment (who declined to attend monthly inter-denominational meetings to discuss matters of mutual interest),[50] but the ceremonial opening of the home went ahead on 1 July 1889. Decorations and flags had been arranged by soldiers of the garrison while: 'Native police, under the superintendence of European officers, kept splendid order; and soldiers of the garrison, men from HMS *Kingfisher*, and civilians were present in large numbers. The band of the 2nd Gloucestershire Regiment performed suitable selections of music, and the whole affair went off with great éclat.' The musical stimulation of enthusiasm included the singing of 'Home, sweet home', with the general commanding acting as master of ceremonies.[51] The home subsequently received high-profile visits from the Duchess and Duke of Connaught and the Governor Lord Reay with Lady Reay, and Rear Admiral Fremantle, commanding the East Indies naval squadron.[52] While these ceremonies were primarily for 'expatriate' consumption, the Methodists clearly hoped to carry their message to an Indian congregation, helped by 'native' pastors and lay preachers, and there were presumably Indian onlookers to the events. Later the foundation-stone for the chapel was laid by Lady Reay with Governor Lord Reay in attendance.[53]

If Clutterbuck had succeeded in spiking the opposition of the Anglicans, there were inevitably some ceremonies that were failures. Ceremonial could reflect tensions among the ruling elite or could be destroyed by bad weather. When the new viceroy and vicereine, Lord and Lady Minto arrived in Bombay in November 1905, their landing was without pomp. Curzon, most autocratic and arrogant of viceroys, was so outraged that his resignation had been accepted that he resolved to cold-shoulder his successor. The arrival was so ignored that the new viceroy's staff had to hurriedly pick out of the crowd 'Sir Denzil Ibbetson, the Maharajah of Kashmir and two or three other leading men who had come over from the Yacht Club as mere spectators. These were presented to their Excellencies and thus some kind of formal reception was arranged.'[54] Dunlop Smith, the secretary of the new viceroy, was brave enough to tell Curzon how disagreeable this had been. In 1907, the unveiling of a statue in Dalhousie Square, Calcutta backfired spectacularly because of heavy monsoon rain. The speeches of the participants turned to pulp.[55]

Durbars

Indian durbars represented the high point of the symbolic relationship between imperial monarchy and empire. The word 'durbar' has Persian origins and was widely used for encounters between the British and Indian rulers (see Plate 4). In East India Company times, in October 1841, Governor General Lord William Bentinck met the Sikh ruler, Ranjit Singh, on what was described as the 'Field of the Cloth of Cashmere', a durbar characterised by vast numbers of retainers and troops, with elephants, camels and horses, and hugely opulent tents.[56] The modern usage, however, is often traced to the efforts of Viceroy Canning to secure the fealty of princes in the aftermath of the 1857 Indian Revolt. In 1859, Canning held a sequence of durbars in Lucknow, Kanpur, Fatehgarh and Agra, living in a vast tented camp and receiving the chiefs and princes in spectacular ceremonies.[57] As the idea developed from Lytton's 1877 extravagant assemblage it became increasingly connected with the rituals and performances of the imperial relationship, not least the creation of ever more complex hierarchies of honours, titles and gun salutes.[58] But dramatic changes took place between Lytton's Imperial Assemblage, the notorious great durbar of 1903, and the 1911 event. Lytton had shied away from using the word because he considered his event would be much grander than the prototype regular durbars.[59] He set out an impressively visual and mobile discourse of dominance in its most grandiloquent form.[60] These ritualised ceremonies reaffirmed and sacralised hierarchies of power; they were propaganda, spanning imperial territory and metropole. Inevitably during the period 1877–1911, both the tone of the events and metropolitan reactions changed dramatically. To a certain extent, Lytton's emphasised medievalism, Curzon's modernity, while that of 1911 was more directly about displaying the monarchy to India and the world, utilising modern technologies. Their projection in imperial popular culture was transformed in the twentieth century, mainly because fresh technology enhanced the popular penetration of news and images. There was a considerable irony about the medievalism of such ritual, since the supposedly chivalric orders and medals associated with them represented a striking atavism for a supposedly modernising imperial regime.[61] Moreover, considerable tension accompanied the processes of incorporation of Indians: how far was this to go and where were the lines to be drawn? Initially, the emerging bourgeoisie, with its dangerously radical nationalism, was to be excluded. By the inter-war years of the twentieth century, limited incorporation was to be extended to try to blunt resistance.

The Imperial Assemblage of 1877 was designed to announce the elevation of Queen Victoria as Empress of India, the culmination of the processes initiated by the Queen's Proclamation of 1858, the creation of the hierarchies of princes in the 1860s, the visits of the Duke of Edinburgh in 1869 and the more celebrated one of the Prince of Wales in 1875–76.[62] It was the apparent success of the latter that encouraged Disraeli to create an imperial throne. In his speech on the Royal Titles Bill, he laid out a succession of myths of British rule that were to remain standard.[63] India, he said, consisted of a whole range of princedoms requiring to be united in allegiance to a common emperor, as supposedly under the Mughals; the vast regions ruled directly by the British were inhabited by nations (significantly plural) of Indians who were highly heterogeneous in ethnicities, cultures and religions. Indians were consequently incorrigibly disunited and only achieved unity through British rule. The Assemblage and later durbars were required to emphasise that synthetic unity by performing in overblown pageantry a materialisation of the administrative and monarchical pyramid that was the Indian Empire. The assemblage/durbar therefore incorporated Indians into the hierarchy of rulers and representatives of the empress.[64] Lytton also hoped that his Assemblage would influence public opinion in Britain, by which he presumably meant middle-class opinion, since the electorate had not yet been transformed by the extension of the franchise in the acts of 1884, 1918 and 1928.

The Assemblage met with a good deal more opposition than the later durbars with frequently hostile comment in the British press. It took place on New Year's Day 1877 at a camp covering 20 square miles on the Ridge above Delhi (symbolically the military encampment from which the 1857 assault on the rebel city was mounted) and was accompanied by grand banquets and military reviews. It was described as a 'modern field of the Cloth of Gold', a scene of 'gorgeous brilliancy', with no fewer than 100 elaborate standards prepared for presentation to the chief princes, the banners designed by Dr Birdwood of the India Office. All the supposedly well-orchestrated solemnity was followed by the 'comic business' of 'races, balls, amusements'. There was also some unintended and potentially dangerous comic business when a British officer, demonstrating his inadequate Urdu in the presentation of medallions, used the word 'suwars' (pigs) instead of 'sowar' (trooper) and 'billi' (cats) instead of 'billa' (medallions).[65] No fewer than 16,000 prisoners were emancipated from the jails, a conscious following of a supposedly 'Oriental way of celebrating'. But descriptions were quickly racialised. 'Orientals' would be awed 'just as children at home are dazzled by the mock splendours of panto'. While it was certainly of 'historical importance', press and politicians attacked the whole affair. The words 'gewgaws', 'tomfoolery', 'farce' and indeed pantomime frequently appeared in articles and speeches, as did phrases like 'tinsel pageantry'.[66] The 'natives' it was said were not greatly impressed and the attempt to overawe the Russians, threatening the North-West Frontier, was a failure. Sir David Wedderburn, proponent of Indian nationalism, viewed it as an 'expensive fiasco'.[67] Seen as a brainchild of the Tory party, it was opposed by senior administrators including the governors of Bombay and Madras who resented its pretentiousness and cost, time and effort, at a time of famine. Some saw it as essentially un-British, like the title of Empress itself, carrying the taint of autocracy, unsuited to British democratic pretensions. Even its official artist, Val Prinsep, found it horribly vulgar and lacking in taste.[68] Organisational problems included the disruption of the ceremony by a stampede of elephants and horses panicked by the shots of the *feu de joie*, causing deaths and injuries. Thus, although huge numbers of people were involved, 84,000 by one count, the feudal and elitist character of the Assemblage seemed to ensure that its impact upon popular culture in Britain was slight, and the books published afterwards had turgid titles and enjoyed limited circulation.[69]

The two twentieth-century durbars had different thrusts. Theoretically, they proclaimed Victoria's successors as king-emperors, with George V uniquely present in 1911. But other forces were at work. They were supposedly designed to resolve the paradox of the binary nature of British rule, through the princely states on one hand and by direct administration in the presidencies and provinces on the other. But as in 1877, it was the pageantry of the princes and their retainers, with their supposedly traditional and hugely opulent garments, jewels and military accoutrements, which stole the show. Governors, lieutenant governors, commissioners and vast numbers of British and Indian troops from directly ruled India found it hard to counter this luxuriant princely display. This was despite the fact that, according to the Census of 1911, the so-called princely states contained just under 71 million of the population, while British India accounted for over 244 million.[70] Such figures have to be treated with caution since enumeration was obviously difficult, but the relative proportions are clear. Moreover, if the durbars were supposed to demonstrate the symbolic order imposed by the British, by extension suggesting that bourgeois nationalists had little chance of creating such unity, then this was clearly a failure. Similarly, the two great 'boons' announced by George V in 1911 were intended to draw some of the sting of the nationalist movement, but in reality only fomented it. These were the revocation of the partition of Bengal and the move of the capital from Calcutta to the more traditional site of Delhi itself. The partition, brainchild of Curzon, had stimulated the nationalist movement while Calcutta lay in what the British regarded as the most disaffected region of Bengal. But the two ultimately cancelled each other out. Curzon fiercely opposed these policies and cannot have been pleased when *The Times* described 1911 as an 'incomparably bigger and more majestic spectacle' than 1903.[71] Moreover, the mounting of these durbars – and the subsequent building of New Delhi – involved the requisition of large areas of land and the clearance and destruction of as many as a hundred indigenous villages and their traditional ways of life. The events caused both dissension and destruction.[72]

While the imperial objectives of the durbars changed, the location on the Ridge and the basic format did not: 'To the Eastern mind,' a Press Association report averred, 'Delhi is the only natural place to proclaim the Emperor.'[73] Yet the intended audience for the durbars significantly shifted. They were designed to impress several different audiences: in India the princely aristocrats, their retainers and subjects; elsewhere the professional elite; and perhaps even the general populace. In Britain, politicians considered that the public at large would be swept up in imperial fervour. Then there was a global audience consisting of the rest of the British Empire and international observers. Unlike 1877, the involvement of press and media had become a key factor in enhancing British prestige and justifying imperial rule.[74]

Press reports indicate that the two durbars were subject to far fewer criticisms than in 1877. *The Scotsman* even proclaimed that the cost of the earlier Assemblage (£100,000) was 'small in comparison with the political advantages it won for Britain'.[75] The 1903 durbar would cost a lot more, but would bring real economic benefits.[76] The descriptions of the actual events (supplied by the Press Association, Reuters, and the special correspondents of various newspapers) were uniformly ecstatic.[77] 'All spectacles of our time fade into dullness by comparison', while the durbar encouraged modern infrastructural development such as railway extensions (with ten stations for the durbar camps), the spread of electric light, and telegraphic communications with Lahore, Bombay and Karachi.[78] British power was projected as 'justice and beneficent rule'.[79] Moreover, modern media created a new relationship with popular imperialism.[80] The durbars were notable publishing events. Press coverage was considerable, with many photographs and early moving film. A number of books appeared after 1903, including one lavishly illustrated by the artist Mortimer Menpes.[81] Early moving film was shown extensively and there was major press coverage throughout the empire.[82] The spectacle may have impressed Indians rather less than white colonists, though what was described as the surprising stillness and silence from the Indian onlookers were explained away as being means by which Indians showed respect.[83] But it may well be that Indians were not seduced by the effort to 'disguise politics as aesthetic entertainment'.[84]

Architecturally the durbars constituted a mix of vast tented encampments and temporary buildings (such as the Orientalist pavilion housing the major display of Indian arts and crafts in 1903), and structures such as amphitheatres and surrounding arcades. As well as large numbers of troops and princely retainers, the durbars featured no end of receptions, presentations and processions.[85] In 1911, 50,000 troops and military personnel were reviewed with the centrepiece the proclamation of the actual monarchs present and the offering of fealty by the assembled princes. The new emperor and empress displayed themselves on thrones on the roof of the Red Fort, a striking appropriation of the great Mughal imperial building (see Plate 5). Once again, the Indian crowds (but not the British) were strangely silent and it was considered 'a great mistake' that the king/

emperor had ridden into Delhi on a horse rather than an elephant.[86] In 1911, the attention of the British press was even more expansive, at a time when other significant events, such as labour strikes, were taking place. Newsreel had now reached higher levels of length and quality and special durbar film showings filled cinemas and theatres all over Britain and the major cities of the Dominions.[87] There can be little doubt that the last durbar was more significant in impressing the white rather than Indian public. The announcement of the new capital in New Delhi would lead to a building project that proved to be a striking architectural swansong.

The durbars were also gigantic elite social events. A newly launched P&O liner was chartered to bring out guests.[88] As well as titled aristocrats, these included five Maharajahs, various provincial governors returning from home leave and a bishop. Few events seem to symbolise so profoundly both the enormous privilege of such a class and the manner in which the overblown Edwardian age was coming to its climax. The *Official Directory* of the rituals ran to 388 pages, listing all those present and all who received honours and awards or participated in sporting events.[89] With the exception of the proclamation of New Delhi as the capital, irrelevance seems to speak from every page. Modern India has not, however, sought to obliterate all memories of the Durbar.[90] The site on the Ridge is now known as Coronation Park, with an obelisk to mark the location of the actual crowning.[91]

Youth movements

A prime means of pulling 'native' peoples into imperial occasions was through the dispersal of the concept of the youth organisation. The rapid spread of these bodies throughout the empire was a remarkable phenomenon, sweeping up both white and 'native' social groups into ceremonial. Members of youth movements enhanced the numbers participating in religious and secular rituals everywhere.

The Boys' Brigade (BB) was founded in Glasgow in 1883 as a specifically Christian organisation, closely involved with mainly Protestant and dissenting churches. Within a few years there were BB companies in New Zealand, Canada, Australia and South Africa. Initially such companies had purely white membership, but in the early twentieth century largely Black companies were founded in Nigeria (1909) and Nyasaland (1910) among others in the Caribbean and elsewhere. The significant characteristics of the BB were its quasi-military uniform and rankings, the importance it placed on drilling, church parades and major processions. Many BB companies developed brass bands which became a vital aspect of their public performance, as well as emphasising gymnastics and the comradeship of camps. The BB thus socialised the youth of empire into a combination of Christian, military, and imperial performance.[92] A quarter of a century after the founding of the BB, Robert Baden-Powell created the Boy Scouts.[93] The Scouts owed their origins to the Anglo-Boer War, symbolised by the colonial and frontier uniform of shorts, shirt and broad-brimmed hat. If the BB was originally urban, the Scouts emphasised the outdoors, wildlife, tracking and camping. Scouting quickly spread to the colonies (and beyond, notably the USA) and soon became a world-wide movement. Both the BB and the Scouts developed branches for girls and committed themselves to ceremonial in rituals of membership and awarding of badges. However, imperial rulers were not always happy about the spread of such organisations to indigenous people. Since the BB was essentially Christian it became popular in the missions, but Baden-Powell himself was far from being racially liberal. The Scouts became essential components of the ceremonies of 'Empire Day' in the settlement territories, but the rapidly expanding Indian scouting movement passed through a cycle of encouragement and discouragement. In 1921 the All-India Scout Council was formed with the Viceroy as the Chief Scout, such that Indian scouts entered the ceremonial sphere. However, with developing nationalism, the necessity of the oath of loyalty to the king-emperor became problematic and Indian scouting severed its ties with London in 1938.[94] In Northern Rhodesia, Governor Sir Herbert Stanley was keen on the Scouts as a means of African social control.[95] Encouraging the founding of troops, he even suggested the creation of a school on scout lines. But in southern Africa the colour bar was a major problem and Africans were directed into an organisation called the Pathfinder Scouts, distinguished from white scouts. Nevertheless, the African Scout movement prospered and the discriminatory Pathfinder branch ultimately disappeared.

All the youth organisations, but particularly the Scouts and Guides, pulled members of the British royal family into attendance at their major displays, camps and in the Scouts' case 'jamborees'. Their central purpose of training and socialising the young inevitably took imperial forms as useful adjuncts to aspects of civic, colonial or national ritual. On his extensive tours, the Prince of Wales regularly reviewed Boy Scouts and Girl Guides. For example, in Baroda in 1921, scouts and guides attended the large garden party in the grounds of the palace of the Gaekwar, the ruler of the state, such that the chronicler of the tour suggested that 'all castes and creeds were merged' in their comradeship.[96] Later, he attended a large rally of entirely white Scouts and Guides in Durban in 1925.[97] By the 1930s and the tour of Prince George, future Duke of Kent, the emphasis was on 'native' youth. He encountered a 'native kiltie band at the great indaba in Bloemfontein', inspected 'native boy scouts' at Kimberley and watched 'native girl guides' dancing at Gaberones, Bechuanaland (Botswana).[98] Among local events, scouts were involved in the celebrations of George V's Jubilee in 1935 in Kakamega, a remote corner of Kenya.[99] Missionaries sometimes liked to take ceremony into their own hands. A visiting bishop at an Anglican mission in western Kenya in 1916 found that one Sunday hundreds of adherents were uniformed and drilling, with every supposed military rank represented.[100] In more modern times, notably since decolonisation, youth movements in the 'third world' have become more concerned with multiculturalism, social cohesion and, to a certain extent, the renewal of traditional forms.

Royal tours

Of all ceremonial events, it was perhaps royal tours which had the greatest public and press prominence in colonial territories. These promoted rituals of visibility supposedly reflecting the mystique, global diplomatic leverage, theatrical effects and imperial marketing power of the British royal family. They embraced an endless round of ceremony, featured in the illustrations of the many commemorative books published in their wake. Throughout these tours, ceremonies symbolised monarchical mystique and authority in relation to indigenous rulers.[101] The British monarch stood at the head of a hierarchy of lesser rulers and opportunities were provided for royal birthdays, deaths, coronations and other rites of passage to be celebrated in various invented ways. For settlers, such events fashioned 'communal mythologies and identities in the languages of Britishness and imperial citizenship'.[102]

Royal tours can be seen to have started with the Royal Navy and the British army. An eighteenth-century Prince of Wales, the future William IV, and his younger brother the Duke of Kent were stationed in Halifax, Nova Scotia, the former in the navy between 1786 and 1789, the latter in the army 1794–1800. Their service was inevitably punctuated with ceremonial events which rendered them the precursors of royal tourists. The service by these royal princes is still celebrated in the Citadel, the significant 'heritage' building of the city. The more modern concept of the royal tour was created in 1860, with the visit of the teenage Prince of Wales, later Edward VII, to Canada and his younger brother Alfred to South Africa. These princely journeys were capped by the central significance of the Prince of Wales's tour of India in 1875–76, with its powerful political and social resonances, expressed in widespread ceremonial, not least in respect of the Indian princes and the later proclamation of Queen Victoria as Empress.[103] Mortimer Durand noted in his diary a detailed account of the ceremonial connected with the Prince's arrival in Calcutta, with many Indian princes, in elaborate regalia, lined up to meet him. The celebratory illuminations in the city included the Fort, Government House, the High Court and 'the new museum', while the investiture of the Order of the Star of India provided an excuse for another grand ceremony and procession. The Prince had 'a large gold umbrella over his head, and four more borne on all sides of him. His pages, two middies from the Fleet, were dressed in the style of Charles II, wigs and loose trousers and plumed hats, and very high-heeled shoes. The Viceroy's pages were much the same, barring the wig.'[104] Here was an extraordinary combination of supposedly Asian custom, the gold umbrella for the high and mighty, and a curiously atavistic western dressing up, perhaps a reference to the British earliest days in India? The point about ceremony was that it combined multiple elements, geographically and chronologically, in the search for a culturally polyglot form. Here was an alleged transculturalism with emphasis on the historical depth of the British relationship.

The major climax of these tours comes with the extensive empire tour of the Duke and Duchess of York (future George V and Queen Mary) on HMS *Ophir* in 1901, when they visited Gibraltar, Malta, Ceylon, the Straits Settlements, New Zealand, Australia, South Africa and Canada.[105] Between mid-March and early November they covered 50,000 miles, 38,000 of them by sea. As usual, the emphasis was on the unity and loyalty of the empire, with the additional intention of expressing gratitude to the populations of key territories for support in the Anglo-Boer War, although it was not yet over. Another purpose of the tour was the distribution of war medals (well over 4,000) and of various honours to colonial politicians and prominent citizens. It also incorporated the central occasion of opening the first parliament of the new Commonwealth of

Australia in Melbourne, which was to produce one of the most important paintings of imperial ceremonial.

In many respects, however, it was a tour of the architecture of empire. The experienced journalist, travel writer and chronicler of the tour, Sir Donald Mackenzie Wallace, tended to judge all cities and towns according to the quality of their built environments. Buildings were explicitly seen as symbolising the extent and civilising effects of the empire. In Melbourne he observed that grand buildings were interspersed with smaller houses not yet redeveloped, while the grandstand of the racecourse at Flemington seemed to be colossal. In north-east Victoria he thought that the towns had a rough and unfinished look with small box-like structures. Christchurch seemed to him to be something of a disappointment after Auckland and Wellington. In Dunedin, there was no hotel large enough to accommodate the royals and their suite and consequently they had to stay at the Club and in private houses. He expected Perth to be 'Wild West', but instead encountered a fine city. The architecture of Montreal was 'solid and graceful'.[106] This obsession fitted a prime objective, the ceremonial laying of foundation stones, including the new town hall and railway buildings in Wellington, various hospitals, the cathedral in Brisbane, a wing of the Museum and Art Gallery in Perth, law courts in St John's Newfoundland and various statues and memorials to Queen Victoria.[107] In Cape Town there was a 'day of foundation stones', including a new hospital and the cathedral.[108] In Pietermaritzburg, the town hall was inaugurated. The institutions of the bourgeois public sphere were regularly visited, including museums, botanic and zoological gardens, as well as university convocations where the Duke usually received an honorary degree and watched students graduating. Extensive ceremonies took place everywhere, generally attended by vast crowds, particularly drawn by the fact that the tour occurred just months after the death of Victoria and the succession of Edward VII. There were inevitably levées, state dinners and massive reviews of troops. Temporary structures such as triumphal arches often reflected the economy of the territory. Perth had arches in timber, gold and coal, while apples were celebrated in Melbourne. Processions and decorations there were particularly grand, reminiscent, Wallace thought, of a full state entry. Ceremonial matched that of London while he considered that the Exhibition Building, where the opening of parliament took place, was probably finer than the Crystal Palace, so vast that it could accommodate 15,000 spectators.[109] Discordant notes were sometimes sounded. In Ceylon, the royal party heard from the planters of 'the unsatisfactory state of the tea industry caused by low market prices'; several times the success of German trade was mentioned; and in Melbourne the Governor General had to read out the prayers because the Christian denominations could not agree on which clergyman should officiate in the Exhibition Building.[110] George and Mary subsequently toured India in 1905–6 and returned as emperor and empress in 1911. Despite the crescendo of press and visual coverage this was a major turning point in the development of Indian nationalism, but this in no way inhibited royal touring. The royal tours of the inter-war years continued to highlight monarchical relationships with indigenous rulers, a counterpoise to developing nationalism. While dominion politicians were always key players in settler territories, it was only after the Second World War that royal tourists began to meet African and Asian nationalist leaders.

Apart from all the usual arrivals and departures, processions through the streets, civic events, investitures and receptions, there were carefully choreographed encounters with indigenous rulers. Even the railway journeys between centres became part of the spectacle. Periods of relaxation usually took the form of hunting trips, offering further opportunities for encounters with Indian princes in a shared pastime. The visits of Prince Alfred, Duke of Edinburgh, to the Cape were accompanied by hunting safaris resulting in hecatombs of slaughter of African wildlife. Gendered distinctions ensured that accompanying female royals visited hospitals and women's associations, and undertook cultural tours. Later in the twentieth century, the whole family started, occasionally, to travel together. Nevertheless, declining efficacy was perfectly illustrated when the royal family's highly visible 1947 tour of South Africa (king, queen and two daughters) signally failed to hold back Afrikaner nationalism and save the political fortunes of the Anglophile Jan Smuts. After that, the relentless and impeccable touring of Elizabeth II was much more 'ornamental', designed to cement the creation of the Commonwealth. Although not unique to Britain, the ceremonial and pageantry of the British events were perhaps the most widespread and carefully organised.[111] The colonial press always covered these events at some length, even if sometimes critically. The tours were accompanied by multiple publications of special supplements, magazines and books, supposedly to enhance popular knowledge of and interest in their alleged significance.[112] Such journalistic comment, replicated across the empire, was invariably accompanied by engravings, later photographs. From the early twentieth century newsreels and films covered the outdoor ceremonial, often creating a sensation when shown in theatres and early cinemas. These highly visible events were designed as expressions of imperial identity, as well as of modernity in technological and economic change. Royal and other tours adopted strikingly atavistic forms while innovative transport in the vessels they arrived in (and escorting naval ships) and trains represented modernity. Yet we know from private diaries and letters that the royal participants were often bored and impatient, less than totally absorbed and excited by the rituals to which they were subjected. Some of the visits of the Prince of Wales in the 1920s were met with sullen resentment, particularly in urban settings in India. Occasionally interest perked up. When the Prince was present at the Poona races in November, the 'Royal Race Meeting' featuring the Prince of Wales Cup was hailed by *The Times of India* (British owned and edited) as 'a brilliant success' in which the course had 'rarely presented so gay a scene'.[113] There was allegedly 'tremendous enthusiasm' for the appearance of the visitor, who met winners, trainers and jockeys in the paddock. Horse racing had become a prime showcase for visiting royalty, as in the United Kingdom.

Yet those who planned royal visits in London invariably failed to foresee the ways in which public ceremonies could be manipulated by officials and politicians 'on the spot' or the manner in which they were variously interpreted by colonial peoples, settlers, expatriates and, above all, indigenous people and their rulers. Some governors seized the opportunity to use royal visits as a means to forward their own agendas. Indigenous rulers might aim to turn encounters to their own advantage, seeking to bypass the local authorities by requesting concessions of various sorts. Moreover, both in vernacular papers in India and in some settler journals in the colonies of settlement, comment often moved from celebration to criticism or reinterpretations of the purposes of the visit. In Africa and India, the members of the emerging educated elite were kept in the background. The tours indeed had multiple meanings and messages, such that visits that were designed to be principally ornamental could became instrumental and a source of contestation in the eyes of indigenous rulers and colonial politicians.[114] Rather than encouraging settlers to become 'real Britons' overcoming any sense of inferiority, the tours may have either emphasised the 'cultural cringe' or encouraged the emergence of separate cultural and political nationalisms. All this perhaps illustrates the limits of ritual as a technology of rule.[115] It is ironic that as the practice was in apparent decline, publications and other depictions of the tours became more prolific.[116] Perhaps all such performances become more assertive and noisy in retreat. This mirrors the long-standing fact that as the political power of the monarchy declined, the ceremonial and symbolic ritual around it greatly increased. The efficacy of the clear diplomatic intentions of the travels of George VI and Queen Elizabeth in the 1930s was indeed limited.

The Special Service Squadron tour of the empire

Ceremonial and pageantry were also important functions of the Royal Navy. In 1923–24, the 'senior service' indulged in the most dramatic piece of imperial 'naval theatre' in its history. A 'Special Service Squadron' comprising two battle cruisers, *Hood* and *Repulse*, and four light cruisers (augmented to five) spent nine months sailing around the empire. The ships called at Sierra Leone, major ports in South Africa, Zanzibar, Kenya, Ceylon, Malaya, Singapore, Western Australia, South Australia, Victoria, Tasmania, New South Wales, Queensland, several ports in New Zealand, Fiji, Western Samoa, British Columbia, Jamaica, Nova Scotia and Quebec, with additional calls at places outside the British Empire, including Honolulu and in South America.[117]

The object of this extraordinary global display of naval might was described as being to meet 'our kinsmen overseas', emphasise the ties that bound them to Britain, as well as express renewed hope after the First World War and the depression that had followed it.[118] The 'kinsmen overseas' seemed overjoyed to be visited, judging by the vast crowds that turned out everywhere to greet the ships, the festivities in every port, the frequent ceremonies, including processions of sailors and marines (often more than a thousand men) hailed in the streets, together with lavish hospitality and seemingly endless sporting events. The speeches of governors, colonial prime ministers and the vice-admiral in command were redolent of imperial patriotism and efforts to reconcile it with a new sense of Dominions' nationalism. Astonishingly, no fewer than 1,936,717 people were alleged to have visited the ships in ports of call, often including indigenous chiefs and sultans. Of the total, 1,423,157 were Australians and New Zealanders. For their part, crew members showed their imperial allegiance by deserting in considerable numbers: 151 in the first six months, of whom 141 chose illegal immigration to Australia and New Zealand![119] For them, the cruise was a means of free migration.

In British Columbia, the newspaper the *Vancouver Sun* astutely put a number of questions to the commanding vice-admiral, including enquiring about British expenditure on the navy, its continuing cost and commitment, the extent to which the empire should help, and the guarantees that might be given that colonies and Dominions could expect the Royal Navy to protect them in future conflicts.[120] Western Canada, like territories elsewhere, must have been well aware that this 'Empire Cruise' followed the Washington Naval Agreement which had destroyed both the British navy's 'two-power standard' and the Anglo-Japanese Alliance of 1902. The admiral's answers were reassuring enough, but politicians and public must have realised that this display actually masked considerable weaknesses, likely to be exacerbated in the future. In any case, these big ships obscured the fact that empire had generally been about the smaller gunboats, which had established British authority in African rivers, in the Persian Gulf, on the coasts of South-East Asia and the Far East. They had been important in port protection, minesweeping and in many other offensive and defensive precautions. Naval campaigns against Germany on the East African lakes had been instrumental in securing German colonies subsequently transformed into League of Nations mandated territories.[121] The 'Empire Cruise' had, however, revealed the importance attached to propaganda and the 'social and cultural outreach' that the navy could achieve in the maintenance of imperial sentiment. Politicians imagined that such a flotilla could overawe indigenous peoples in West and East Africa, as well as in Asia and the Pacific, where 'native' rulers and members of the elite were welcomed on board.[122]

Ceremonies of retreat

The British indulged their passion for ceremonial to the very end. When Mountbatten arrived in India as the last Viceroy, he did so by air. His daughter recounted the horrors of being expected to participate in an arrival ceremony after a long, bumpy and literally nauseating flight. After a reception in Karachi, that in Delhi on 22 March 1947 was considerably grander, complete with a Sikh Bodyguard and the Royal Scots Guards with their pipe band. At the viceroy's palace, they discovered that the staff numbered 555 'or so', with several thousand dependants requiring a separate school and clinic. On the following day they paraded to the airport to see the departure of the Mountbattens' predecessors, the Wavells. On 24 March the Mountbattens processed with great ceremony to the Durbar Hall and occupied the thrones for the swearing-in ceremony. Such ceremony was now recorded on newsreel cameras as well as by large numbers of press photographers. Within months they would be immersed in independence and then departure ceremonial.[123] As is well known, the British were to indulge in many more such ceremonies throughout the former empire, ceremonies which have been described by Martin Shipway as:

> quirky, self-deluding, but ultimately rather comforting rituals which marked British transfers of power that they loom so large in British accounts of the end of empire; indeed, the 'transfer of power' can seem almost synonymous with decolonisation itself, thus implying decolonisation as pre-planned endpoint, rather than as an often messy political process.[124]

The British adherence to such 'Ornamentalism' apparently contrasted with the French republican avoidance of such delusions.[125] The decolonisation events culminated with the departure from Hong Kong in 1997, which, with Chinese complicity, was one of the grandest of them all, featuring Charles, Prince of Wales and the last Governor, Christopher Patten. The Chinese, no less an empire, put on a remarkable display to match that of the British. The tradition of imperial ceremonial thus continued to the end in its essentially royal formats, demonstrating again the British 'obsession with social rank and status'.[126] Philip Murphy saw such ceremonies as having 'Gilbertian overtones' and constituting a 'rearguard action' in the upholding of the notion of hierarchy. For him the subsequent breaking down of such hierarchies of class constituted the true end of empire, though many would doubt whether such a breakdown has actually occurred.[127] Moreover, it is apparent that the global invention of traditions coincided with and mutually influenced similar inventions within Britain. Thus, as with so many aspects of imperialism, there was a peripheral–metropolitan reciprocity at work. The jubilees of Queen Victoria in 1887 and 1897 were notably imperial events, greatly influenced by the equivalent ceremonies in the empire. The continuing imperial echoes resounded down to the reign of Elizabeth, with ceremonial continuing to uphold the hierarchies and conservatism of the status quo. That perhaps was the prime purpose of imperial ceremonial, however hollow it seemed to many.

2
EQUESTRIAN SPORTS

THE GAME OF POLO.
MATCH PLAYED IN ALBERT PARK.

Polo match played in Albert Park, Melbourne, 1875, revealing the rapid spread of the game throughout the empire.

Background

The British Empire was an empire of sports.[1] Sports seem to have been central to the lifestyles of the British in every colony, but such activity has to be seen as much more than aspects of leisure, a means of relaxing from the more demanding duties of imperial rule or from the challenges faced by settlers. Sports became firmly embedded in imperial ideologies, elevated to the status of a moral system that not only underpinned empire, but also, in some senses, justified its existence. One of the many fantasies of empire was the notion that the dominant people were uniquely qualified to play such sports, that they reflected their physical and mental superiority, mirroring their allegedly virtuous and principled status.[2] For this reason, the British sometimes sought (usually unsuccessfully) to maintain the exclusivity of their sports. At other times they were actively in the business of disseminating them as part of their civilising mission. Training indigenous peoples, particularly in Asia and Africa, in the sports of the imperial rulers (a process that was occasionally reversed even if in recycled forms, as in polo) became a notable imperial objective, part of the desire to spread European culture, although indigenous players often took matters into their own hands. For many people, sport produces quasi-religious reactions and Christian missionaries certainly incorporated sports into their efforts at proselytisation. They considered that sports were a means of inculcating, as they saw it, the moral force of individual endeavour and group solidarity, the 'one for all, all for one' mentality. Thus sports, with their alleged moral superstructure, could constitute a significant accompaniment to Christian conversion, seeming to blend well with missionary objectives. But if sports had the capacity to be a setting for inter-racial activity they were also a location for the perpetuation of racial and communal divisions. Many aspects of sporting encounters, certainly those involving physical contact, were resisted and sports were carefully demarcated into those that were suitable for transmission and those that were not. But however much imperial rulers attempted to hedge their sports around with various criteria of suitability, indigenous people became more adept at adopting and adapting what appealed to them, taking what seemed to fit their own social, cultural and indeed political requirements. Sports increasingly became a major field of intercultural behaviour, with complex patterns of intended and unintended exchange, with boundaries and rules that were erected and broken down. By the inter-war years the British were keen to consolidate imperial sentiment, and take a leaf from the Olympics' book, by founding the Empire Games, to be held every four years two years distant from the Olympics. The first took place in Hamilton, Ontario in 1930. The games were renamed the British Empire and Commonwealth Games between 1954 and 1966, when Empire (and later British) was dropped. They thus shadowed constitutional changes and still enhance the ties of the Commonwealth on a basis of national and cultural equality.

For the European imperialist, sports were perhaps a consolation for exile, a reassuring reminder of home in the midst of unfamiliar and exotic surroundings. Sports could be recreated in alien places, which also offered the opportunity to learn new ones. Some sports were specific to the geographies and climates in which settlers and imperial rulers found themselves, whether in India or in the ice and snows of Canada. Moreover, in the 'empire of rule', sports may well have been an antidote to the boredom of the imperial condition, not least for the military between campaigns.[3] The passion for sports can be interpreted as part of the anti-intellectualism of the British, derived partly from the traditions of the English 'public' (actually private, fee-paying) schools. For many colonial administrators and other products of such schools, the cult of 'athleticism' (regarded as morally more significant than intellectualism) engendered in them was carried to the empire.[4] For settlers of other social classes, it may be that sports represented new freedoms not available in the metropole, for example in hunting and shooting or freshwater fishing, a release from tight poaching laws.[5] For those concerned about the licentious behaviour of the soldiery, particularly in the stricter moral climate of the late nineteenth century, sport (particularly football) might be seen as a means of sublimating sexual desire through the injunction to 'sweat the sex out of you'.[6] In such a context, sports were also a means of creating physical fitness and the inculcation of personal and group discipline. They additionally emphasised the class distinctions in the military and acted as a preparation for some of the techniques of combat. The officer class demarcated a number of sports as emblematic of their status and symbolic of their role in command both in peace and in conflict. Sir Evelyn Baring, Lord Cromer, wrote illuminatingly of the clear class distinctions of the military:

> From the political point of view, the main characteristic of the British officer is his exclusiveness. In whatever clime he may serve, he carries his insular habits and national pastimes with him. In Egypt he rarely mixes with any society which is not English, and he abstains from doing so, partly because of his ignorance of any language but his own, and partly because his social habits differ from those of the cosmopolitan society of the Egyptian towns. What does the Frenchman or Italian care for horse races, polo, cricket, golf, and all the other quasi-national institutions, which the British officer establishes wherever he goes, whether his residence be in the frigid or the torrid zones?[7]

Indeed, as well as not fraternising with foreigners, the officers seldom indulged in team sports with the other ranks, partly because anxieties about bodily contact operated at class as well as racial levels. Athletic and sporting ability were also seen as vital attributes for colonial administrators, very much part of their fitness to rule.[8] This led to the celebrated quip that it was invariably blues (the status given for sporting excellence at Oxbridge) who ruled Blacks. If the army was the prime agent for the conquest and expansion of empire, it was also the main medium for the dispersal of sports. This was true over a longer period, but it became particularly the case in the later nineteenth century, when sports linked with the Haldane army reforms designed to create a more professional and efficient force. It is alleged that sports were also the means of bringing the army into a closer connection with the society that spawned it – and perhaps by extension in the imperial context, even with the societies which it came to dominate.[9] For settlers and others, sport also had the alleged purpose of guarding against the diseases potentially rife in their new environments. Thus sports could fulfil a wide variety of functions, though many were clearly pursued by members of all classes for the sheer pleasure of pitting themselves against animals, the environment and other people. It is perhaps indicative that, on the long sea voyages on the way to colonies and places of settlement, sports were eagerly pursued on ships. One of the first concerns among the passengers on such vessels was to elect a sports committee to organise the tournaments in deck tennis, deck quoits, shuffleboard and other activities. Such tournaments became a principal means of both killing time and maintaining fitness on such voyages.[10] The committee chairman was usually an elite figure.

The study of sports thus offers clear routes into the character of social and racial relationships in the empire, into the multiple hierarchies of class and race (including those based on occupations) of the imperial condition. They reflect attitudes towards gender and provide indications of a sense of national identity and of the role of popular imperialism. Sports offer insights into the imperialists' connection with and aspiration to dominate the environment, for example in the distinction between the urban and the rural, and also through relationships with the natural world in hunting, shooting, angling, pig-sticking (in India), and the acclimatisation of animals both as prey and as auxiliaries. They were thus emblematic of rule as well as of local and wider hegemonies. There were also significant economic dimensions, stimulating business and trade in the supply of equipment, firearms and the breeding for export of horses and dogs.[11] They additionally reflect the manner in which land was demarcated into areas suitably reserved for field leisure pursuits. Sports required not only the creation of courses and playing fields (for horse racing, athletics, cricket and so on), but also the construction of grandstands, club houses, stables and other structures. For example, horse racing became universal and involved the laying aside of relatively large areas of land in urban planning as did (to an even greater extent) the more individualist environmental game of golf. But more than this, all sports, including athletics and team competitions, offer routes into understanding the key articulations of class, status and race in both military and civilian life, as well as of the creation of a competitive culture which was central to imperial ideologies. Sports were a notable generator of clubs and associations, often emphasising the homosocial character of empire. As such, they also operated to facilitate various levels of social solidarity and networking, offering opportunities for bonding and the maintenance of class and racial demarcations. Similarly, sports might offer a means of surveillance of the working classes, encouraging them to participate in rational and health-giving recreation rather than (analogous to the military) pastimes like drinking, gambling or the temptations of vices available in empire (all thought to be particularly debilitating, morally and physically, in a colonial setting). They were closely associated with ceremonial (for example the major Indian durbars were accompanied by sporting events), with royal tours, and with relationships between governors and indigenous rulers, particularly in India. It is perhaps significant that many sports, both in Britain and in the empire, were only fully organised in the period of what historians have called the 'new imperialism' of the late nineteenth century. Sports pursued in haphazard and informal ways in the past were subjected to the framing of all sorts of rules, regulations and even legislation, not to mention the recording of scores, the keeping of records and the creation of historic lore of various sorts. The collection of data was a crucial urge in imperial rule and this came to imbue sports as well as other aspects of life. They further became a means for inter-colonial (and later international) competition which developed considerable racial overtones, only broken down well into the twentieth century. Sports which had relatively deep histories in Britain, such as football and cricket, only came fully into their own in the nineteenth century and were properly codified in the second half of that century. If it took some time for sports to develop along inter-class lines in Britain, so too did competition between the dominant and subordinate peoples in the empire. This, however, started in the later nineteenth century and became a more common feature of imperial rivalry during the twentieth.

It is true, however, that sports of one sort or another are universal in almost all societies.[12] The urge to pit humans against the environment, with or without the help of animals, and against each other is of long standing. India had many traditional sports, such as *kabbadi*, *gilly danda* and *kho-kho*, often specific to different regions of the country, though gilly danda has a wider distribution in Asia.[13] In Burma, the favourite sport of a riverine people was the racing of large canoes, often with as many as a dozen paddlers. For a variety of reasons many of these have been predominantly male pursuits, the perquisite of masculine status, partly because they were often designed as a preparation for warfare. Women, generally of high status, did however assert themselves in respect of horse-riding, hunting from horses, and in shooting and angling, although this was sometimes restricted by religious taboos. In modern times, throughout the empire female school pupils and girls associated with youth movements such as the Guides, began to create sporting spaces, for example in netball and in hockey. Such sports had become significant in female private schools in England and, by imitative extension, in the grammar schools. Gymnastics and callisthenic exercises also became female pursuits in the later nineteenth century, sometimes viewed in Britain as capable of producing a healthy ideal of womanhood, creating biological fitness for the reproduction of the imperial race. But regardless of objective, all these soon spread far beyond the social confines of the dominant people of empire.

Important conditioning factors for the development of sports in a variety of locations were climate, environment and cultural considerations, such as the problems of using leather balls among the Hindu population in India. It was apparent that ice hockey was likely to become characteristic in Canada. Subject to such conditions, sports were propagated not only by educational institutions and missionaries, but also by companies with large numbers of employees, no doubt creating a sense of group solidarity and loyalty to the brand. They were also significantly promoted by ethnic associations. One such, which took surprising hold in many parts of the empire, was Highland or Caledonian games, in which athletic sports together with activities particularly characteristic of the form, such as the 'heavy events' like 'tossing the caber' and 'putting the shot' were combined with often competitive dancing and band playing.[14] Such Highland games generally took place once a year in different locations and were thus much more intermittently pursued than other sports. However, on the days when they occurred, they put entire communities 'en fête' and dates were scattered across the calendar to permit competitors, dancers and musicians, particularly important once professionalisation had arrived, to move from one to the other. Indeed, many sports provided opportunities for bringing large numbers of people together, such that the carnival nature of surrounding events was very much part of the attraction. Such social contexts of sports offered employment opportunities as well as the chance for small traders to secure income.

There can be no doubt that, as military memoirs reveal, sports were a major passion in India by the late nineteenth century. For example, Lieutenant Colonel Henry Tyndall wrote that sport was central to the lives of the British in India, 'an obsession which stemmed from the fear that unless one kept fit one would catch "some dreadful disease or other"'.[15] Indeed, Tyndall's diary reveals just how regularly an officer in peace-time Lahore was playing sports. There are repeated references to polo, rackets, cricket, tennis, not to mention related horse and dog shows. Sometimes he played more than one sport in one day and kept himself fit by cycling from one location to another. Despite such passions, the sporting history of empire was hardly a recognised subject for study until the recent phenomenal growth in interest. To attempt to summarise this material in a pair of chapters is indeed a bold operation. Even a single book would require a considerable feat of compression. These chapters are therefore selective, both in terms of the sports and the colonies covered. This one deals with equestrian sports and hunting, while the next covers team sports, all presenting valuable insights into the imperial condition.

Horses and other animals

It is well known that western Europeans setting out to explore and potentially conquer the post-Columbian so-called New World in the Americas from the sixteenth century were concerned to take horses with them. Horses were the principal means of locomotion in Europe, for individuals (usually high status), for the transport of goods and above all for the military. Where horses were unknown, as in Central and South America, they became a key element in conquests by the Spanish and the Portuguese. Down to the twentieth century, horses (and in some locations other animals like camels, mules and donkeys) were a vital component of warfare.[16] The horse was equally a key auxiliary in the British Empire, its practical and militaristic purposes ensuring there were large numbers in use throughout the colonies. Yet it would be a mistake to see such horses as being sourced in Europe. On the contrary, they came from a variety of different places. They existed throughout Asia, and it was Arabian and Mongol horses that greatly influenced the equine diaspora. Horses had been introduced into the East Indies by Muslim traders and a small 14-hand pony became a well-known feature of transport in Java. It was these Javanese horses that were introduced into other parts of Asia and also into the Cape in southern Africa.

Elsewhere, horses appeared in North and West Africa from c. AD 600, but they could not be used in many sub-Saharan zones where the presence of the tsetse fly, and therefore of the disease trypanoso-miasis, limited their survival. The Cape was a healthier region for horses, although some horse sickness did occur there. This colony thus provides an interesting test case.[17] The Dutch arrived at the Cape in 1652, but the Dutch East India Company resisted the first settlers' demand for horses since the Cape was only intended to be a 'refreshment station' on the route to the East. When horses did start arriving, they were generally sourced from Java rather than Europe. As in other colonies, notably the Iberian ones in South America, the Cape colony soon selectively bred a horse which was most useful for local requirements, for transportation, the control and protection of stock, and human defence. The small horses introduced from the east generally thrived and bred successfully in the Cape's environmental conditions. They not only facilitated expansion into parts of the interior, but were also valuable on shooting expeditions, for the pot, for animal products like skins and horns, and inevitably also for sport. It was only in the later eighteenth century that thoroughbreds from Europe began to arrive in the Cape. They had appeared in Britain from the seventeenth century and were bred from Arabian, Turkish and Barbary horses. Once introduced into the Cape, they began to play a major role in sport. By this time, there had developed, here and elsewhere, a split between 'utilitarian' horses (though these were also sometimes used in informal sports) and the thoroughbreds specifi-cally bred and introduced for racing.

Although horses had been well known in India before the arrival of European imperialism, nevertheless military requirements ensured that large numbers were introduced during the British period. They became a key component of trans-Indian Ocean trade between Australia and India since extensive horse breeding in New South Wales was stimulated to supply the demands of the Indian market. The trade in these horses, often known as 'Walers', developed from the 1830s, and for almost a hundred years from the 1840s there was a constant export to British India for the voracious demands of the cavalry. The steady development of the ubiquity of horses throughout the colonies, combined with the need to train the soldiery, ensured that they became a vital component of sport. They had played a part in sports (and of course warfare) in the early empires of the Mediterranean and Asian worlds. In medieval Europe, they were vital for the elite sport of jousting. In many colonies, equine sports included riding to hounds, some forms of shooting, gymkhanas, racing, pig-sticking and polo, all pursued as both military and civilian pastimes. Even the more niche 'dressage' (the elegant means of testing riders and horses in skilful movements) was transferred to some colonies.[18] But all equine sports became passions of the British and spread throughout the empire. Riding to hounds had become a significant pastime in Britain by the eighteenth century and duly spread to many colonial territories. Nothing would seem to be more English (or class-specific) than this particular sport and colonial settlers and sojourners seemed determined to reproduce it in the empire.

Another hunt with dogs, coursing (the pursuit of animals by sighting them, followed sometimes on horseback), seems to have been in existence in India at an early date, already reported as taking place on Bombay's Malabar Hill. Moreover, it was said that the East India Company had started a pack of twenty hounds at Karwar (in Karnataka, South India) as early as 1692.[19] It is possible that in the colonies the social reach of such a sport – with its associations with a landowning elite and their tenancy – might have been wider than in the metropole. Sports involving dogs were often pursued by the use of what were known as 'bobbery' packs, informal combinations of assorted mongrels.[20] In early nineteenth-century Bombay, a 'bobbery hunt' met in front of the church each Sunday morning.[21] Nevertheless, there are many references to a trade in hounds from the last decades of the eighteenth century. Robert Lindsay, who boarded the *Prince of*

Wales Indiaman in the spring of 1772 to take up a writership in Bengal, wrote that the commander, Captain Jonathan Court had a pack of foxhounds on board. Being valuable animals they were provided with their usual allowance of water while the passengers were put on short commons.[22] Apparently, food provision on the voyage was poor, while the captain ignored the complaints about the lack of water. We also learn that Charles Chisholme sailed to Calcutta in the autumn of 1778 in command of the *Gatton* and brought as his 'investment' a large pack of hounds, 'then in great demand by the Bengal sportsmen' as well as 150 pipes of Madeira wine.[23] But the supply of Madeira was so plentiful that its price had collapsed. He got around this by instructing his purser to indicate that anyone taking four pipes at 300 rupees would be entitled to receive two pairs of hounds at the market price. He promptly disposed of both wine and hounds at a profit of over 100 per cent.[24] John Jones was the captain of *Boddam*, an East Indiaman which made three voyages to China between 1791 and 1801. His private ledger survives for his first voyage and reveals that he invested the enormous sum of £11,000 in goods to be sold in Madras and Canton, including a pack of foxhounds, making a personal profit of nearly £4,000. The continuing trade in dogs into the nineteenth century is evidenced by a pack of hounds being transported to Burma on the Paddy Henderson vessel *Martaban* in 1885. She encountered a violent cyclone near Aden and once again the valuable dogs appear to have received privileged treatment. They were stowed by the lamp-trimmer in second-class cabins and survived sixteen hours of terrible tossing, for which service he received a handsome gift from the Rangoon Hunt Club.[25] Perhaps the most celebrated hunt with hounds was located at the hill station of Ootacamund (Udagamandalam) in the Nilgiri hills of South India.[26] Here jackals were hunted as a substitute for foxes (see Plate 6).[27] The landscape around the town was known as the Wenlock Downs (after Lord Wenlock, governor of Madras from 1891 to 1896), adding another familiar reminder of the English equivalent. *Murray's Guide to India* announced that:

The Ooty Hunt has a history dating from 1847, unbroken except during the Mutiny, and boasts of a pack of from 50 to 60 couple of foxhounds, partly imported year by year from England, and partly bred and reared on the hills, together with excellent kennels and a large staff.[28]

References to hunting with hounds can be found relating to various colonies. For example at the Cape Lord Charles Somerset, Governor 1814–26, was actively involved in the Cape Hunt Club which gathered at Alphen in pursuit of the jackal.[29] In 1828, Captain (later General) Mundy discovered that there was good sport to be had in the countryside near Delhi, where he 'had some excellent coursing with English greyhounds for hares and foxes'. On one of his visits to Cape Town, he was impressed with the Cape horses, well bred with 'English blood'. He found two packs of foxhounds near Cape Town with foxes plentiful.[30] Foxhounds were even taken on campaign.[31] Emily Eden recorded in one of her letters that at 'Umballa' (Ambala) she encountered several officers of the 16th who had returned from Kabul, presumably just prior to the disastrous retreat of 1841, and 'are bringing back in safety their pack of foxhounds'.

In Western Australia, hunting the kangaroo as a source of meat was a common activity among rural white people by 1831. Such kangaroo hunting was pursued informally with 'Kangaroo dogs', which were cross-breeds between mastiff and greyhound or foxhound and Scottish deerhound. By 1890, more formal hunting with packs of hounds had been instituted (see Plate 7). As well as drag hunts and paper chases, the western grey kangaroo, the brush-tailed wallaby and the red fox (introduced from Britain) were enthusiastically hunted. Such hunts were a feature of winter weather and the horses were often used for polo during the summer. However, maintaining packs of dogs was expensive and some of the hunts developed financial problems. The discovery of gold in the colony from the 1880s promoted immigration and more hunt clubs were founded. Some expertise was even imported from the celebrated Leicestershire Quorn Hunt through the immigration of a son of the 7th Duke of Newcastle. Such hunts were patronised by the governors from Sir Arthur Lawley (governor 1901–2) onwards. Restrictions on the hunting of indigenous animals were introduced from 1945, but the imported fox remained fair game.[32]

There is a photograph of the Western Australian Hunt Club meeting, possibly in the 1920s, in which a large crowd of members are shown on horseback wearing formal hunting clothing and hats, with a pack of hounds in the foreground. This indicates the extent to which the appearance of such sporting activities created business opportunities. The hunt club commissioned a particular tailor (Simmonds of Maylands) to supply their coats, while suppliers were required for other aspects of the livery, for horse tack, not to mention the food and drink for the many accompanying social events. Other opportunities for suppliers are revealed through discussions about the appropriate dress for both men and women for evening events, while the importation of horses and dogs constituted another lucrative business.

Horse racing

The racing of horses has been a commonplace in many equestrian societies and the British were obsessed with it.[33] In the early days of a colony, it must often have been a relatively informal activity. Owners rode their own horses. Members of the cavalry raced for fun, to train themselves and their horses. Such racing with amateur military or civilian riders became a popular colonial spectator sport and offered early opportunities for gambling. But wherever the British went, the laying out of a racecourse was an immediate ambition and racing became an increasingly formalised activity. Thoroughbred horses were imported or were locally bred as specialist racers, either on the flat or (more rarely) over jumps. Deeply embedded in metropolitan British culture in the course of the late seventeenth and eighteenth centuries (the English Jockey Club was founded in 1750) its ubiquitous spread in imperial territories was a uniquely British phenomenon.[34] The number of racing clubs was rationalised and turf clubs were established as the overall authority to oversee and regulate the sport. There were efforts to control dubious areas prone to abuse, such as betting arrangements and the access of shady characters to courses. Professionalised jockeys, some developing international careers, became the norm. A characteristic of all colonial racing was the strict social hierarchy which was reflected within its organisation and arrangements for spectators. Turf and jockey clubs tended to be highly exclusive bodies, run by the colonial elite, placing the supervision of racing in the hands of the well-to-do, sometimes associated with the indigenous traditional elite. When grandstands and social spaces were created, they were always divided into zones reflecting social and racial divisions, although inter-community involvement was always possible at the social top end.

Inevitably, India offers the most striking example of the shift from the informal to the highly regulated. Informal racing, particularly among the military, was already common in the East India Company period. It was certainly an established part of the social scene in Calcutta and Madras from the late 1760s and 1770s. Later, once hill stations were established, racing became part of their leisured culture. Ponies and horses were raced at Annandale, the sports annex to Simla, and there were gymkhanas there and at Ooty.[35] Emily Eden described an impromptu racing meeting in Simla in October 1839. Some gentlemen got up some races which, she writes, the Sikhs attended. Apparently the Sikh horses were not quite up to it and their efforts became a source of amusement. In camp at Kurnaul the following month, she described more racing, in which apparently Captain 'Z' was a very effective jockey because so lightweight and won two races. Even more bizarrely, the final race was apparently run by fifteen of the grass-cutters' ponies.[36] But the dispersal of the formalities of racing was already under way at the end of the eighteenth century. The Royal Western India Turf Club dates its origins to 1798 and still sports the 'Royal' designation acquired in 1935. Racing took place for a long time in Byculla, then the centre of many of the cultural and social activities of Bombay, before moving to the racecourse in Mahalaxmi in 1883, where it remains.[37] It has been suggested that the inauguration of the races was partly designed to encourage the breeding of horses in the Bombay area.[38] The progression from the participation of army remounts to the 'Walers' imported from New South Wales to the involvement of the British Bloodstock Agency was to take place through the nineteenth century.[39] The Western Turf Club also administered racing in Poona (Pune) and later in Delhi. The Royal Calcutta Turf Club (again retaining the 'Royal') managed the premier races of India, at least until the twentieth century, with the named races here and elsewhere following the British precedents, such as Derby, St Leger, Oaks and 1,000 Guineas.[40] Racing in Calcutta was established on the maidan, where it remains.[41] It should be remembered, however, that the dedication of areas of land to these imported sports some-times involved the dispossession of indigenous people. In Madras racing began at Guindy in 1777, which the Madras Race Club proclaims as the oldest racecourse in India (see Plate 8).[42] It was created on land granted by the government and removed from two Adyar villages, Vankapaturam and Velacheri, a classic case of sporting demands leading to losses of indigenous settlements. After the start of racing there in 1777 it almost came to a premature halt because of the war with Hyder Ali. The Madras Race Club was constituted in 1837 and maintains that name in Chennai. In 1798 Thomas Daniell painted *The Assembly Rooms on the Race Course near Madras*, indicative of racecourses becoming key centres of sociability for the British.[43]

Various other racing traditions were established by the ruling princes of India, such as in Hyderabad, active at least from the 1860s, and Mysore from 1891.[44] Racing was mainly on the flat, although some steeplechasing took place, for example at Tollygunge in Calcutta and in Poona. But maharajahs and maharanis were also active in the race meetings in British India. For example, the race card of the Poona races in 1921, the year in which the Prince of Wales was present, reveals several of them listed as owners.[45] British precedents were followed, such as the viceroy being conveyed in state round the Calcutta course in the finest carriage available, like the monarch in England, as well as the many associated social events displaying the particular status of the imperial elite. Evidence of an interaction between Australian and Indian racing comes in 1878, when the winning horse of the Melbourne Cup also raced in Hyderabad. Racing became a key setting for British interaction with Indian princely families, as well as encouraging the cooperation of trainers and the internationalisation of the jockeys' profession. The spread of racing and the prominence of racecourses are well illustrated by the manner in which Kipling in *Kim* makes several references to the race-course in Umballa (Ambala).[46] Racecourses could be useful in other respects: in the twentieth century a cavalry regiment was billeted at the Peshawar course, with the officers' mess in the grandstand.[47]

The Cape again offers a striking example of the social and cultural significance of colonial horse racing. Two years after the British conquered the colony, taking it from the Dutch, the first Cape Town races took place at Green Point in 1797 with an African Turf Club founded for the purpose.[48] From the start, the spectators at the races revealed their extraordinarily diverse composition in terms of class, gender, race and ethnicity. Thus, the popularity of the races consti-tuted a means of bringing communities together in one place, while still emphasising difference. As might be expected, such races were 'supported enthusiastically by the British military contingent'.[49] But the early races were highly informal. Lady Duff Gordon reported that she had seen a 'queer-looking' Cape farmer's horse ridden by a 'Hottentot' beat a thoroughbred ridden by 'a first-rate English jockey'.[50] Informality could produce upsets. After the Treaty of

Amiens and the return of the Cape to the Batavian Republic between 1803 and 1806 no races took place. But they reappeared after the British reconquest. An African Turf Club made a hesitant return in 1810, more formalised as the South African Turf Club in 1814. From an early period, the races were particularly popular among the Cape 'Malay' population (many of them former slaves). But not everyone approved. The early governor Lord Macartney (1796–98) despised racing and some thought it not quite socially acceptable. However, such inhibitions vanished once racing was promoted by the aristocratic Governor Lord Charles Somerset between 1814 and 1826. His passion for horses and horse breeding may have arisen from the fact that he was brought up near the centre of the British equine cult at Badminton and was familiar with horse sales at Newmarket. He contributed to improving the quality of horses in the colony (known as Capers), and even the development of exports to other areas of the empire. He was engaged in all related sports, and encouraged the regularisation of racing at Green Point racecourse, which soon became one of the principal social gatherings of Cape society, with the white elite marked out within the hierarchy by the quality and style of the conveyances in which they travelled to the meets. The sport soon spread to other settlements: Paarl in 1815, Uitenhage and Stellenbosch (1816), Graaff-Reinet (1821), Grahamstown (1823), Somerset East and Swellendam (1825). The British command of the Cape was thus marked by the racing cult expanding in tandem with imperial authority. Horse racing was to remain a central recreation of the white population, apparently evidence of the refinement of their society, yet also shared by spectators from so many other (segregated) communities. Within eleven years of the arrival of Somerset no fewer than ten venues were active.[51] Thoroughbreds became increasingly common after 1860, and in the twentieth century the top racing fixtures were concentrated in eight notable courses, two in the Western Cape, two in the Eastern Cape, and two each in Kwa-Zulu Natal and Gauteng.[52] Kenilworth, the oldest, was opened in 1881, stimulating nearby horse breeding.[53] Its extensive land also incorporates a biodiversity conservation area. In the Transvaal, the discovery of gold ensured the development of horse racing in 1886–87. The immigrant gold diggers (*uitlanders*) and above all the emerging class of wealthy Randlords constituted respectively punters and owners, the latter prepared to put a lot of money into the sport. When General Sir William Butler visited Johannesburg shortly before the Anglo-Boer War of 1899 he was 'taken to see one of the largest of the racing stables belonging to one of the many cosmopolitan millionaires on the Rand'.[54] He was shown very valuable animals intended for the major races in South Africa.

A survey of the development of horse racing in the various territories of empire reveals the emergence of significant transcolonial themes. Strict segregation was obviously a characteristic of racing on Caribbean islands, where the first importation of bloodstock to Jamaica from England took place as early as 1775 and plantation owners often took to horse breeding. In the early days, it seems that jockeys were sometimes slaves. Racing spread to other West Indian islands, such as Barbados and Trinidad, promoted by army officers, plantation owners and wealthy merchants. Turf clubs were founded by the early twentieth century. It was perhaps inevitable that there would be some connections between the islands and horse racing in the United States. The patronage of colonial governors, invariably from the class of horse-racing enthusiasts in Britain, was often significant throughout the empire. On the Indian Ocean island of Mauritius, where the British inaugurated racing soon after they conquered the island in 1810, the sport was promoted by Governor Sir Robert Farquhar, an East India Company merchant who had also served as governor of Penang and of Réunion. He suggested that it would constitute a means of reconciling French settlers on the island to the new British administration. Farquhar, who had a wife of French extraction, duly authorised the use of the Champs de Mars, where the French had trained their troops, as the racecourse, and it retains this function today. It was used for the proclamation of the independent territory in 1968. Horse racing was introduced into the Falkland Islands soon after their seizure by Britain in 1833. By 1847, a Governor's Cup was a spur to competition and racing became part of the sporting and social traditions of a remote pastoral society.[55] Racing and other sports were also reflective of a protective national identity and popular imperialism in the islands.

In Singapore, formal horse racing was delayed until the formation of the Singapore Sporting Club in 1842.[56] Informal races almost certainly happened at an earlier date, including the racing of *gharry* (horse-drawn cab) ponies on the Esplanade. But well-to-do figures in the island colony planned something more formal in establishing the Sporting Club. Once a large piece of land, covering 50 acres, had been identified, a racecourse was laid out and grandstands were built with seating areas for the 'second class' and for 'natives'. The role of racing in reconciling various elements of a polyglot population seemed to be reflected in the fact that various communities, such as the Chinese and Arabs, donated winners' plates. But the hierarchy remained clear: for much of the colonial period, the governor and the Sultan of Johor were invariably the patrons of the races. In the early days, the horses were generally imported from Sumatra, revealing again the power of local trades. Further turf clubs were founded in Penang in 1864 and in Selangor in 1896.[57] Another characteristic of colonial racing was that it was facilitated by cheap labour. The syces or grooms in South-East Asia were invariably Boyanese (or Baweanese), a people from East Java who started migrating to Singapore from the early years of the nineteenth century. They were experienced in working with horses and became celebrated in Singapore for helping to construct the racecourse, or acting as grooms, sometimes jockeys and even trainers, also as gharry drivers.[58] We know too that racing was developed in Rangoon, Burma, soon after the British conquest of the 1850s. There is some indication that it was associated with the active red-light district that developed in this port city.[59] Nevertheless, reminiscences of the early days of racing in Rangoon appeared in the *Rangoon Times* in 1912, describing the atmosphere of those times, indicating the prominence of an Indian called Mr Burjorjee and the significance of the Stewards Cup and the Burma Plate.[60] The indigenous horse of Burma, the Shan pony, was initially used by the British for polo and for racing, though it was not particularly suitable for either. There is a photograph by Felice Beato of racing in Mandalay in the early 1890s, just a few years after the British conquered Upper Burma.[61] The traditional white railings are lined with spectators who appear to be mainly of European and Indian origin, while there is a small grandstand with a roof with distinctly Burmese elements. The racecourse was near Mandalay Hill where its remains can still be seen from the summit, but the generals who ruled Burma after the Second World War closed down racing because they disapproved of gambling. Further east there were racecourses in both Chinese (and also Japanese) treaty ports, for example in Shanghai and Tianjin, after 1842.[62]

In Canada horse racing had a hesitant start and experienced only intermittent success. Clearly the Canadian climate militates against the year-round breeding and training of horses. Moreover, the social origins and tone of the settlers were also less amenable to the sport than, for example, in Australia. The religious character of the settlements additionally ensured that the sport was often seen as a rather shady activity. Nevertheless, it was French settlers in Quebec who inaugurated early racing. It is said that the first official horse race took place on the appropriately flat lands of the Plains of Abraham in Quebec City in 1767 and the first turf club was founded there in 1789.[63] There must have been some informal racing taking place in Nova Scotia because in 1771 the Halifax authorities banned the sport, suggesting that it rendered the citizenry idle and turned them into immoral gamblers.[64] Horse racing only really developed in Ontario in the last decades of the nineteenth century, with racing in Toronto from 1860 and a jockey club founded there in 1881. While the gubernatorial patronage of the Marquess of Lorne in 1883 encouraged developments, still betting and bookmakers were seen as sufficiently disreputable to be banned by the Canadian parliament in 1910. The sport survived this legislative action and the problems of the great depression of the 1930s to become more significant in modern times, although the scale of interest and number of race-courses and meetings never came anywhere near matching the remarkable growth in Australia.

Horse racing was indeed developed to a greater extent in the Australian colonies than anywhere else, such that it has been said that horse racing 'might almost be called the Australian national sport'.[65] There are a number of reasons for this. From the early days in New South Wales and Victoria, the Australian colonies were essentially pastoral economies (primarily sheep running) extending over vast areas, rendering the possession and use of horses essential. The environment was also convenient for the health of the animals and for breeding. Moreover, the free settlers who arrived in Australia seemed to have had a particular penchant for racing and colonists soon became obsessed with it. Each of the colonies had informal racing from their earliest days, and the typical creation of turf and jockey clubs followed soon afterwards. Formal racecourses were established from an early date. In Parramatta, New South Wales, racing commenced in 1810 and the town opened its racecourse in 1825.[66] Similarly, racing seems to have begun in Sydney at least from 1810, with many of the mares coming from the Cape or from Timor, with some early stallion imports from India. Initially racing was often closely connected with the military and the departure of a regi-ment could cause a hiatus, but soon such dependence ceased. Courses quickly appeared in other towns such as Newcastle and rural racing was also keenly followed. In Tasmania, Victoria, South Australia and Western Australia, racing followed close on the heels of settle-ment, often stimulated by the interest of the governor. In Western Australia, an early governor, James Stirling, was himself a breeder of thoroughbreds.[67] Economic developments, notably the discovery of gold in Victoria in the 1850s and in Western Australia in the 1880s and '90s, greatly stimulated interest in and spending on racing. It has been claimed that Western Australia ended up with more racecourses in relation to the population than anywhere else in the world. In Victoria, the Flemington racecourse inaugurated the Melbourne Gold Cup in 1861. It became the most celebrated race in Australia, known as 'the race that stops a nation', indicating the manner in which racing became one of the components of Australian identity even before federation in 1901.[68] The sport seems to have been fully professionalised by the 1870s and 1880s, and many of the courses ran races with celebrated names in the Anglophone world, such as Derby, St Leger and Queen's Plate. By that time, there were many successful stud farms. The sheer scale of these developments becomes obvious from the statistics in 1955, when there were 3,500 race and hunting meetings per annum, with some 25,000 people dependent on the sport for their livelihoods. By this time women had also come to be significant as breeders, trainers and jockeys.

The first horses may have been introduced to New Zealand by the Rev. Samuel Marsden in 1814, supposedly a gift from Governor Macquarie of New South Wales. Their importation to Wellington began in 1840 and, as elsewhere, military garrisons started racing and developed the sport. In 1841, soon after the founding of the colony, citizens of Auckland and Manukau resolved to hold a race meeting at Epsom, a name with obvious resonances, and competed for the Auckland Town Plate. Epsom racecourse was duly laid out and in those early days it was traditional for the owners of horses to do the riding. The first racecourse boasting a grandstand was organised at Burnham Water and races spread throughout New Zealand. Interestingly, they always became a feature of commemorations. For example, there were races at Dunedin in 1849 celebrating the first anniversary of the Otago settlement, and similarly in Christchurch in 1851, the year after the founding of Canterbury. The Canterbury

Jockey Club was founded in 1854 and a racecourse at Riccarton was leased the following year.[69] Soon there were races at all the major settlements and also some smaller ones. The Otago Jockey Club appeared in 1861 and it was said that 'racing mania' took over in that province in the 1860s, despite its Presbyterian origins.[70] There were various conflicts in the founding of an integrated Racing Conference and Jockey Club, with difficulties over gambling, the totalisator and other significant features of racing. At last an overall New Zealand Jockey Club was recognised and received the imprimatur of the Jockey Club in England. This sport, as with others, thus saw itself as tied to the prototype in the metropolitan country. Its popularity was such that, at the end of the First World War, a Christchurch professor claimed (and due allowance must be made for academic cynicism) that New Zealanders in Canterbury were more intent on heading for the races than welcoming troops returning from the war. When they seemed to study the newsagents' placards it was the race results rather than war news which interested them more.[71] By the post-Second World War period there were 71 racing clubs and 17 hunt clubs in the country.[72]

Polo

Polo was a sport which the British famously picked up from India. There is substantial evidence that it is an ancient game, played in Persia from an early period, then spreading across much of Asia eastwards through Central Asia and Mongolia to China. Allegedly the main square of Isfahan was used as a polo pitch. There are depictions of polo being played in China as early as the eighth century and in Persian miniatures from at least the sixteenth century, though the game is much older there. Its utility was obvious in training in horsemanship, particularly for cavalry and for the elite. The Viceroy Curzon devoted an entire essay to polo, later posthumously published, describing what he had seen of the sport during his travels in both the north-west and north-east of India in the 1890s.[73] While it has often been regarded as inseparably associated with the British army, in fact its origins were as much civilian as military. At any rate, it seems that after a period when the sport lapsed into obscurity, it may have been rediscovered in the frontier regions where Curzon later saw it. There is some dispute as to whether it was resurrected by tea planters in Assam or by British officers in the nearby state of Manipur in the 1850s, reflecting civilian and military streams. As a sport which was undoubtedly learned from colonial subjects, it constituted 'a shared cultural space', though generally (but not exclusively) associated with high status.[74] It is claimed that the first polo club was established by planters in Silchar, the headquarters of the Assamese Cachar district, in 1859. But it was certainly Captain Robert Stewart, the Superintendent of Cachar, and his assistant Lieutenant John Sherer who took it to Calcutta, where the polo club was founded in 1862. Its world-wide dispersal was then under way. It reached Britain in 1869, brought by Lord De L'Isle and the later Lord Manson. The 9th Lancers and 10th Hussars played a match in Hounslow in 1871. The Hurlingham Club was established in 1874 and became the sport's centre in the British Empire, establishing the rules and regulations (again symbolising the metropolitan validation of such sports). It was this careful regulation, so central to sports in the period, that separated the British version from the general mêlées and informality described by Curzon. Hurlingham became so important that its lands were considerably extended (at some cost) in 1879 and 1912.[75] By 1878 inter-regional tournaments were taking place in England and an Oxford and Cambridge fixture had also been created.

If horse racing was the classic and most common equine sport throughout the British Empire, one in which almost everybody could participate as spectators and betting punters, polo was a much more exclusive affair. It involved the ownership of polo ponies, smaller horses that came to be bred for their bursts of speed, stamina and agility. Each player had to own at least two such ponies since they had to be rested and substituted during the chukkas or sections of the game. As well as the ponies, various other items of equipment were required, and in addition polo grounds had to be set aside, much larger than other sports fields (five to six times the size of an Association Football pitch, for example), usually with a club house for sociability and changing, while stabling was also sometimes required. These might well require the employment of extra labour, another cost upon players, members and spectators. In the colonies, however, the cost of grooms, recruited from the indigenous population, was considerably cheaper. Thus, it generally remained a high-status sport throughout, often considered a prime interest of princes and kings. It might, however, embrace a wider social group in places where large numbers of horses were central to the economy, for example in cattle ranching or plantations.

A vital characteristic of polo was that since it lacked immediate physical contact it could be jointly played by British and Indians, which of course meant elite Indians, invariably associated with the princely states.[76] For this reason, it was a characteristic sport played at the durbars. It could, however, be dangerous. At the Assemblage of 1877, at one of the first major tournaments in India, the unfortunate Captain Clayton, extra ADC to the viceroy, was killed on Christmas Day as a result of a polo accident and was buried with full military honours.[77] At the subsequent durbars, there are regular references to polo in the official programmes and in the home press. In 1902, it was reported that excellent polo grounds and club houses were erected for £2,000.[78] A 'grand polo tournament' was duly inaugurated and continued through the early days of January 1903.[79] At the 1911 Durbar, a polo match between Bhopal and the Imperial Cadet Corps aroused great interest and was watched by 15,000 spectators. Bhopal won 7–3 and one Bhopal player, Imtiaz Ali, was highlighted as having played brilliantly.[80] The Imperial Cadet Corps was a unit made up of Indian cadets and British officers, so the polo team was inevitably similarly mixed. Captain Skinner and the Rajah of Ratlam were much praised.[81] Polo was also played in Rangoon, where there was an Indian team (of immigrants) in addition to the European ones.[82]

It has been suggested that in India, polo took over from pig-sticking as the characteristic imperial sport, though pig-sticking certainly continued into the twentieth century.[83] Winston Churchill was a passionate enthusiast for polo, emphasising its alleged wider significance in politics and moral uplift:

> I could not help thinking that polo has had a good deal to do with strengthening the good relations of the Indian princes and the British officers. It may seem strange to speak of polo as an Imperial factor, but it would not be the first time in history that national games have played a part in high politics. Polo has been the common ground on which English and Indian gentlemen have met on equal terms, and it is to that meeting that much mutual esteem and respect is due. Besides this, polo has been the salvation of the subaltern in India, and the young officer no longer, as heretofore, has a 'centre piece' of brandy on his table night and day. The pony and his polo stick have drawn him from his bungalow and mess-room to play a game that must improve his nerve, his judgment and his temper.[84]

Churchill certainly put this prescription into effect (though he continued to like his brandy). When he sailed to India as a subaltern in the 4th Hussars in 1896, he and his colleagues devoted themselves to 'the serious purpose of life' which was polo. All officers donated to the funds of the regimental polo club and, having landed in Bombay (where all Arab ponies and horses were imported by the Byculla stables), they proceeded to Poona and purchased the entire polo stud of twenty-five ponies from the Poona Light Horse, their ambition being to win the Inter-Regimental Tournament. They spent every day, he wrote, living for the hour of polo. Stationed in Bangalore they became involved in the Golconda Cup of Hyderabad. This was watched by 'enormous masses of Indian spectators of all classes'. Ultimately, his team did indeed win the Inter-Regimental Tournament Cup at Meerut.[85] Many officers showed a keen interest in the acquisition of polo ponies: Henry Tyndall recorded in his diary that he bought 'an Arab pony from Dunlop for 200 rupees' (about £13–£14) in October of 1899. In 1900 Tyndall reported on a polo tournament in which the state of Patiala played the Guides.[86] In Kipling's *Kim*, the horse trader (and spy) Mahbub Ali was involved in trading polo ponies (and picking up information) for British officers. Polo became so endemic in India that well into the twentieth century it was easy for a British army officer to get leave to participate in a polo tournament.[87] When the Prince of Wales visited India in 1921, he regularly played polo, usually in Indian states, and also in Mandalay in Burma and Colombo in Ceylon. On a later tour, he played polo in Kano, northern Nigeria, and in Maseru in Basutoland (Lesotho).[88] In 1934, there was a polo championship in Calcutta. There is a Pathé news film of the event, in which the Viceroy Willingdon rides in to review parades of troops and then watches Jaipur, 'captained by its young Rajah, defeating Kashmir'.[89] The last Viceroy, Mountbatten, was an enthusiastic polo player, describing it as 'the best game in the world'.[90] He was still playing in 1949 when he was a member of a Maltese team which took on Italian military players, demonstrating the spread of the sport into Europe.[91]

But not everyone in the military shared the polo enthusiasms of Churchill or Mountbatten. As Mason and Riedi have recorded, a major controversy broke out about the way in which cavalry regiments became obsessive about polo (see Plate 9).[92] Objections included the amount of money spent on ponies and tournaments, such that cavalry officers had to have a considerable private income, limiting the reservoir of talent and also leading to the dangers of considerable indebtedness. This was exacerbated by inflation in the price of polo ponies as a result of pressure on the supply. Another was the fact that many hours spent on polo cut into time available for military training, while regular accidents involving injuries and even deaths on the polo field were noted.[93] Polo, along with the keeping of horses and other equine sports like racing and hunting, was already banned from Sandhurst in 1894. The failings of the army in the Anglo-Boer War brought some of these issues to a head, although the controversy inevitably broke down into arguments between reforming and traditionalist parties, as well as discussion of the contrast between the allegedly 'scientific' German approach and the British notion of being 'ready for anything'. The fundamental issue was therefore whether equine sports like hunting, pig-sticking and polo could legitimately be seen as essential to officer training. All this was overtaken by the transformation in the methods of war in the twentieth century.[94]

From a largely civilian point of view, the spread of polo around the empire was almost an explosive phenomenon. For example, it rapidly became popular once introduced into Australia. The first match in New South Wales was said to have taken place in Moore Park, Sydney in 1874, while the sport was inaugurated in Victoria in Albert Park, Melbourne in the following year.[95] The New South Wales Polo Association was founded in 1892 and, after the creation of the Commonwealth of Australia in 1901, various cups and trophies were donated to encourage tournaments both within and among the states.[96] A programme of the tournament for the Australasian Cup in 1933 indicates that competing teams came from all the states of Australia and from New Zealand.[97] It had reached South Africa in 1874, the first match being between the Gordon Highlanders and the Cape Mounted Rifles on the Kingwilliamstown parade ground in the Eastern Cape. Civilian clubs appeared in 1886 and 1889 and the South African Polo Association was founded in 1906. By 1886 it was in Singapore, introduced by officers of the King's Own Regiment.[98] After the Second World War, the polo ground had become a squatters' camp, but polo enthusiast Mountbatten author-ised its clearance and return to the polo club. The social tone of

Canterbury was indicated by the manner in which the Christchurch Polo Club was founded in 1888, shortly after its introduction to the colony.[99] The Auckland Polo Club was founded in the same year and the New Zealand Polo Association was in existence from 1890. By that time there were a number of polo clubs and Captain Savile, ADC to the governor general, presented a cup for an inter-club tournament.[100] By the late 1880s the West Indies Regiment had taken it to Jamaica, where there was a large stud farm and a polo ground was established on a plantation.[101] It reached Selangor by 1902, the polo club unusually having an urban ground in Kuala Lumpur.[102] Polo was unquestionably dispersed as a result of inter-colonial movement. For example, Nyeri Polo Club in Kenya was founded by soldier-settlers who had served in India and played the sport there. Makuyu Club sprang from the playing of polo by early farmers in the district.[103] Edward Atiyah, a Syrian brought up in the Sudan who became a British administrator, remembered that in Khartoum there was a perpetual procession of 'tall commanding figures, riding out to play polo on their well-trained ponies'.[104] Famously, polo also spread into areas of informal empire that were culturally influenced by Britain, notably Argentina where it became an important activity. It was also introduced into Chile, where horses were said to be ubiquitous.[105] In addition, it became popular in the United States.[106] Women's polo became a feature of the sport in many colonies from the 1930s and arrived in South Africa in the 1940s.[107]

One sport using ponies which was almost exclusively restricted to India was pig-sticking, sometimes known as hog-hunting. This sport, involving the hunting of wild boar to be killed by the use of a long lance or spear, seems to have developed first in Bengal in the late eighteenth century, but it soon spread to the Deccan and from there to other parts of the subcontinent. There may be some connection with the much older cavalry sport of tent-pegging, common in both Asia and Europe, in which the horseman attempts to pierce a small ground object with a sword or a lance. This was certainly practised in

British India, but pig-sticking was more important. The latter was formalised by being organised into hunts or tent-clubs and was regularly justified as a means of keeping down animals which were destructive of the crops of peasants. It was also suggested it gave a 'sporting chance' since the boar had a good possibility of escape. It became competitive and cups were offered for the largest number of kills. The most important cup, the Kadir, was presented at the 'Grand National of the Hog-Hunter's Year', at Meerut.[108] Often pursued in broken country, it could be dangerous for the hunters, both ponies and humans. While partly overtaken by the popularity of polo, it remained a favoured military sport until well into the twentieth century, indulged in by visiting 'royals' like the Prince of Wales in the early 1920s. Baden-Powell was a propagandist for its combination of training in horsemanship and preparation for battle, famously writing a book about it.[109] The military were indeed always highly resourceful in the use of animals in sport. Camel racing was well known in the Arab world, but the British Imperial Camel Corps also took it up when operating on the North-West Frontier of India in the early twentieth century. There were camel races (with betting) and 'there were also a number of more imaginative, if slightly ludicrous, competitions – soldiers wrestling each other while aboard their camels, or participating in camel-mounted egg and spoon races'. Somehow they also managed 'to play a version of musical chairs aboard camels'. It was however observed that the camels, their dignity offended, did not seem to enjoy these experiences.[110]

Horses were sometimes used in imperial big-game shooting, but in the most celebrated cases of such hunting, in India and the interior of Africa, we find the great contrast between the use of elephants and (because of the presence of the tsetse fly) walking. Shooting of this sort has received a lot of attention, but it can be said that from the early nineteenth century it certainly acted as an imperial demonstration of command of the environment, as a source of ivory, horns and skins for trade, and as a major means of creating imperial interior decoration.[111] It was also a key activity in demonstrating the supposed worthiness of the British officer in the marshalling of auxiliary human beings.[112] One of its alleged justifications was that it allowed imperial officials to protect indigenous people from predatory wild animals, such as man-eating tigers. In the inter-war years of the twentieth century, one high-ranking official delivering a recruiting address in Oxford considered that big-game shooting in India constituted a sort-of cure for Liberalism.[113] It can also be said that it would not have been possible without the expertise of both African and Indian trackers and beaters, who, through their superior knowledge, constituted the environmental advisers for European hunters. In both India and Africa it also involved relationships with indigenous rulers, which were either cooperative or sometimes antagonistic.[114] It was a passionate interest of military officers who contributed to the obsession with statistics of the size and number of kills. As well as supposedly protecting agriculturalists, it was a means of entertainment for travelling VIPs and members of the royal family. In these guises it continued into the twentieth century. Such hunting has often been viewed as a major expression of masculinity, not least because of the concentration on male prey carrying the desired trophies, but the reality is that many women were also hunting and shooting in the late nineteenth and twentieth centuries.[115] However, no other sport went through such a rapid transition from an acceptable and central aspect of imperialism into an activity regarded as dubious, with the capacity to damage environments and seriously reduce the numbers of increasingly rare animals. Indeed it became apparent that indigenous hunting had been far more sustainable and by degrees hunting fervour was transformed into disillusionment.[116] The concerns with first preservation and then conservation (through successive game laws) emerged from within the sport, which gave rise to the development of game reserves and national parks for game viewing by tourists, and for shooting with the camera rather than the gun. Baden-Powell formerly fierce in his extolling of pig-sticking and shooting during his career, even incorporating the use of guns into the early editions of his *Scouting for Boys*, changed his mind in the 1920s.[117] It may be that for some like him, the experience of the carnage of the First World War made the substitution of camera for gun an attractive proposition.

The sports covered in this chapter were distinctively pursued by Europeans, but indigenous people became increasingly involved in roles other than as auxiliaries. The ownership and riding of horses in the empire were generally symbolic of wealth and power, although more humble whites used them in pastoral societies as in Australia. Elite Indians enjoyed the same status and, during the informal era of horse racing (for example at the Cape), Hottentots (Khoi) and Africans were sometimes riders. In most places, however, access to a horse was economically restricted to both the ruling 'race' and, in India, the indigenous elite. In the next chapter, the situation is very different. Team sports were taken over by the indigenous peoples of empire in many strikingly important ways.

3
TEAM SPORTS

Football match between 59th Regiment and Garrison teams at Kandahar, Afghanistan, 1878.

During the heyday of empire, the British imagined that team sports could constitute a prime vehicle for disseminating imperial ideologies. But if imperial rulers thought such sports would transform the consciousness of indigenous peoples, transmit forms of discipline and even create a means of surveillance, all on their terms, they actually became more significant in creating national

identities and contributing to the development of cultural and political nationalisms. Moreover, sports played a key role in inter-
colonial relations and in the international connections that served to
erode the notion that the relationships of empire were paramount.
They consequently served to lubricate the transition from the network of empire into that of international diplomacy. But they may
also have helped in the cohesion of the Commonwealth, the empire's
successor of free and equal states. What is intriguing is the manner
in which different team sports have become characteristic in various
territories of the former empire. It is interesting to analyse the environmental, climatic, cultural and physical reasons for these apparent
preferences. If sports had significant effects upon environments they
were also important in inter-racial relationships. As we have seen,
indigenous team sports were already a characteristic of Asian and
African societies. In the case of Africa, one scholar identified ball
games among the San (Bushmen) and in various societies stick
fighting, oxen racing, wrestling, water games and athletics.[1] Even
competitive dancing can be seen as a form of team sport. This was
well established in parts of eastern Africa, later in the central and
southern regions and was additionally used as a means of satirising
colonial attitudes and ethnic differences among the British.[2]

More individual games like golf, boxing, athletics and tennis,
although common throughout the empire, have received only
marginal attention as they offer fewer opportunities for political and
inter-racial comment. Some sports, such as basketball and volleyball,
were important in being taken up by both European women and
indigenous players, but their origins lay outside the British Empire
and cannot be seen as having either promoted or undermined the
imperial spirit, at least in the period covered here.[3] Indoor games
have also been omitted, even when they have significant imperial
connections – as in the case of snooker, famously invented in India,
with its rules created in 1884 by Colonel Sir Neville Chamberlain
in Ootacamund. The rules of badminton were also formulated by

officers in India and exported back to Britain. But in imperial contexts some sports can be viewed both as key cultural transmitters of the values and attitudes of colonists and as vital counter-hegemonic forces for the colonised. They contributed to the dynamic which ensured that so many British cultural exports went through processes of absorption and adaptation. The sports considered here perfectly reflected these processes, as well as indicating the fallacy, so often propagated by right-wing politicians, that they can supposedly float free from political contexts.

Cricket

Of all the many sports globally dispersed in the nineteenth and twentieth centuries, it was perhaps cricket which had the greatest imperial resonance. In the early twentieth century the historian Cecil Headlam suggested that the propagators of imperialism were 'the hunter, the missionary, and the merchant, next the soldier and the politician, then the cricketer'. Of these, he went on to suggest, the cricketer did 'least harm'.[4] For Sir Ralph Furse, the celebrated (or notorious) recruiter to the Colonial Service between 1910 and 1950, the benefits bestowed upon the world by the British Empire included 'the abolition of slavery ... the example of justice and fair play ... the introduction of cricket'.[5] What they both failed to see was that it was cricket which ultimately provided the most powerful counter-hegemonic force. The surprising thing about this notion of the centrality of cricket is that it was regarded as quintessentially English, a leisurely sport strikingly associated with village green or urban field and a temperate climate. Its first-class games were scheduled to take five days until the modern development (in 1974) of one-day cricket. Above all, its practitioners see it as a sport of great subtlety, of refined and elaborate technique, requiring considerable environmental and psychological insights in the setting of fielders, the appropriate style of bowling (fast, slow, spin, etc.) or the order of the batting. In the colonies it was initially regarded as a sport likely to be restricted to the imperial ruling 'race' and to British migrants to settlement territories, thus unlikely to be transmitted to indigenous peoples. Requiring as it did distinctive clothing, relatively expensive equipment, a convenient piece of land and a carefully prepared wicket, not to mention leisure time and related social arrangements (the ritual of tea-breaks, for example), it was also regarded as very much a middle-class sport. It therefore came as a considerable surprise that it was taken up with such enthusiasm by so-called native peoples and former Black slaves in the Caribbean. But adopted it was. For the Trinidadian C.L.R. James, cricket on the recreation ground opposite his home 'was the only game'.[6] It was a sport which was thought to carry with it a complete ideology, the supposedly classic English ethos of the team spirit, of humility in victory and magnanimity towards the defeated, of acceptance of the umpire's decisions, ultimately of the restraint, modesty and lack of pride that were said to typify the English character (largely excluding the more fiery 'Celtic fringe' of Welsh, Scots and Irish). It was a set of qualities embracing the 'public-school code' as inculcated by Thomas Arnold at Rugby between 1828 and 1841, serving to reform institutions that had previously been somewhat anarchic, even organisationally chaotic. James alleged that this complete moral system was largely accepted by its players in the Caribbean and elsewhere, to such an extent that cricket occupied a separate sphere, which the code regulated, rather than the rest of life where very different standards and passions might prevail.

Despite its alleged association with Englishness and the imperial mentality, in the twentieth century cricket became a game inseparably associated with the sporting response to imperial rule, in some respects a key to the development of national identities and to political resistance, particularly in Asia, the Caribbean and some Pacific islands.[7] Thus, if it became a national institution in Britain (perhaps more accurately in England and Wales, though it is enthusiastically played in some places in Scotland),[8] then it was to become a nationalist focus in colonial territories. Association football or soccer, on the other hand, might have been expected to secure a greater global reach. It seemed to have a wider meteorological suitability, playable in any climate except excessive heat, with very few 'start-up' costs or environmental requirements. It was, moreover, a game with a more 'demotic' tone, one which many missionaries seemed to be more intent on propagating, particularly in Africa. In South Africa, both soccer and rugby have been seen as important counters to apartheid, while rugby has been viewed as an exceptionally significant factor in the development of New Zealand national identity.[9] But surprisingly it was cricket that became most associated with nationalist reactions to empire and was used to demonstrate that its colonial practitioners, of all races, were capable of beating the imperialists 'at their own game'. Cricket is also, in some senses, a literary game, inspiring a great deal of prose and journalistic endeavour. It has had a notable effect on the English language, contributing a remarkable collection of cricketing metaphors to ordinary speech, almost a score of them, which also went around the world.[10] It is, moreover, cricket which has tended to produce masterpieces of historical and contemporary analysis, works of the stature of C.L.R. James's *Beyond a Boundary* and Ramachandra Guha's *Corner of a Foreign Field*.[11] Both authors would see cricket as central to the histories of their respective regions; for Guha it was a sport embedded in 'the overarching themes of Indian history, race, caste, religion and nation'.[12] Both deny Trotsky's claim that sports were an imperialist plot to sow 'false consciousness' in subordinate peoples. While Guha surveys the communalism of sport in India, he also sees it as a location for the reformation of Hindu social rigidities while also presenting an opportunity for Indians to adopt a British game and quickly outdo its progenitors in skill. In the Caribbean, C.L.R. James, living through the key years from 1901 to 1989, saw cricket as vital in the development of the self-confidence and national awareness of West Indians, as well as the (albeit all-too-late) overturning of racial discrimination.[13] In each case, the game created a social bond of considerable significance in response to imperial rule. As both writers reveal, among its fanatics it produces a fascination with the statistics of runs scored, batting averages, wickets taken, ideal squads imagined. Such data (and the dream teams) are carefully recorded, constituting the enduring history of the game and encounters at all levels, from the local to international test matches.

The dissemination of cricket to the empire, as with so many other sports, occurred principally from the late eighteenth into the nineteenth centuries. Although the origins of the game were almost certainly rural, created by those who worked in an agricultural economy, it was invariably widely dispersed by the military. The first recorded cricket match in India may have taken place in Cambay, Gujerat, as early as 1721, when sailors (both officers and ratings?) from a naval vessel came ashore for a match. Famously, the first visual evidence of cricket in India comes from an aquatint by Thomas Daniell dating from 1792. This illustrates Fort St George in Madras with a cricket match taking place outside the fort.[14] As this painting demonstrates, defensive precautions against the French, the clearing of land around forts to enhance the field of fire, created open land available for sports, including cricket. The maidans or esplanades in all three of the major East India Company centres of Calcutta, Madras and Bombay became the sites of cricket matches, additionally ensuring that the sport was highly visible to the indigenous community. If the military introduced it, civilians were swiftly involved.[15] The first cricket club in India was founded in Calcutta in 1792 and, by the early nineteenth century, Company officials and Old Etonians were competing in matches. This not only reflects the association of cricket with the English public-school tradition, even before the Arnold reforms, but also illustrates the early translation of such loyalties to imperial territories by official personnel. One recorded match among Europeans in Bombay, among the many that must have taken place, was when a military team took on civilians in

1897.[16] In these English and military incarnations the game was imbued with social snobbery: in both army and navy it was entirely associated with the officer class and its exponents had a tendency to decry any effort by 'other ranks' to take it up.[17] This emphasises the irony of its adoption by Indians and the appearance of inter-racial matches. In August 1897, Violet Jacob recorded a game between the military at Mhow and the 'Indore Mohammedans' at which her husband, Arthur, the brigade major, made a good score.[18]

In Bombay, cricket was quickly copied by the Parsi community. Parsis were immigrants to India from Persia who became heavily involved in commerce, some of them amassing considerable fortunes, not least in the opium trade. As a people they were prepared to absorb aspects of British culture, including language, music, freemasonry, dress and sports, helping them to enter British professions such as the law and administration.[19] They were also keen on the British habit of forming clubs. Indeed, young Parsis were already copying the British fascination with cricket as early as the 1830s and 1840s.[20] In 1848, some of them formed a cricket club and Parsi sporting clubs were soon proliferating. At first their version was relatively primitive, with matting wickets and miscellaneous pieces of wood serving as bats and stumps. But wealthy Parsis soon offered proper equipment to those wishing to play. As imitators, the Parsis were willing to move out of their traditional clothes into cricket 'whites', a process eventually followed by other Indian cricketers. The community's leaders encouraged these developments and, by 1870, inter-club prize competitions had begun to be the norm. This may have reflected the Parsi desire to ingratiate themselves with the British or simply the fact that the attraction of cricket was irresistible. Competitive encounters were essential to improvements in the quality of play and the opportunities for such rivalry were expanding. This was enhanced when bowling changed from underarm to overarm in the 1870s, a new technique disseminated around the world. But cricket in Bombay, often regarded as the game's original Indian home, continued to be played on a communal basis until well into the twentieth century. The Bombay Union Hindu Club was formed in 1866, and Muslims took up cricket in the 1890s, forming their own gymkhana. It is a moot point whether the Parsi adoption of cricket encouraged these communal arrangements or whether the religious basis of teams resulted from the city's natural social organisation. For the Parsis it presented an opportunity for a small community to play on equal terms with much larger ones. Europeans were also keen on these racial and religious divisions. The Parsis sent teams to England as early as 1886 and 1888 (representing the Parsi Gymkhana Club founded in 1884 and financed by a member of the wealthy Tata family) and the English first sent a squad to India in 1889.[21] Between 1895 and 1906 Bombay witnessed annual fixtures between Europeans and Parsis. The Hindus turned this into a triangular arrangement in 1907 and Muslim teams joined in from 1912. These quadrangular tournaments became immensely popular and were inevitably managed by a committee which putatively became the Bombay Presidency Cricket Association in 1928, the year of the founding of the All-India Cricket Board of Control. In the 1930s, the Bombay body became the Maharashtra and Gujerat Cricket Association, indicating the emergence of a considerable administrative superstructure for the sport. In 1937, the Quadrangular became the Pentangular by the admission of a new team, 'The Rest', comprising Sikhs, Buddhists, Jews and Indian Christians. The social basis of cricket, at least in Bombay, thus remained resolutely communal.[22]

Guha has convincingly decried the notion that the British taught Indians cricket and encouraged them to take up the sport. The game seemed to have a natural attraction and imitation was much more influential than instruction. Instead, the British sometimes put obstacles in the way of indigenous cricketers, with a classic case occurring in Bombay where cricket was played by young Indians of the various religious persuasions on the large piece of land known as the Esplanade or parade ground. After the European Bombay Gymkhana was permitted to enclose some of the land for its various sports, a dispute arose between the cricketers, who played on the unenclosed land, and military polo players who required a large space to play twice a week. Polo and cricket were obviously incompatible since the hooves of polo ponies inevitably cut up the ground. From 1879 the cricket players attempted to assert what they regarded as their rights and started sending petitions to the governor. In 1882, the petitions were successful: 'native' cricket would take precedence over European polo, but in 1883 the decision was reversed and the conflict revived. As Guha ironically put it: 'the Asian game played by Europeans became the emblem of patrician power, and the English sport indulged in by natives the mark of plebeian resistance'.[23] The controversy continued into the 1890s governorship of the indolent Lord Harris, whose reputation for favouring cricket has been dented by the undoubted fact that his fundamentally racist views took precedence over his cricketing passion. He thus continued to favour European polo players over Indian cricketers. He would also have concurred with the acts of social discrimination that ran through the relationships between European and Indian cricketers. Playing together was one thing, socialising quite another. Although the Hindu cricketers had first defeated the European Bombay Gymkhana team in 1887, Harris averred that 'the Indian [cricketer] would never be the equal of the Englishman' and doubted that an all-India team could ever be as good as the best of English county sides.[24] It is ironic that India produced its first Test team in the very year Harris died, 1932.

The conservative inclinations of Harris could also be represented in ceremonial, which Indians increasingly regarded as both ridiculous and obfuscating. In the winter of 1892 when Lord Hawke (a cricketing peer who played as an amateur for Yorkshire and England) brought a visiting side from England to tour Ceylon and India, Harris decreed that in Bombay the tourists should receive royal treatment.[25] At the Victoria Terminus railway station the team was welcomed by representatives of the governor and other dignitaries. The visitors were provided with carriages and horses, a particularly magnificent one for Lord Hawke. The newspaper *Native Opinion* commented that apparently 'the reception of cricket teams is as sacred a function of the Government as the reception of a Viceroy or a prince of the royal blood', a notion taken 'beyond certain limits'. Another commented that there would no doubt be an official levée with balls and fetes and that perhaps the cricketers should have been received with a salute of eleven guns, one for each member of the team.[26]

Despite all this, land was reserved for the Hindu and Muslim gymkhanas on an area known as the Kennedy Sea Face and the quadrilateral, then pentangular tournaments took place there. But conservatism in cricket was not just a British preserve. Hindus indulged in caste discrimination, as in the case of the Dalit or Untouchable bowler of considerable distinction, Palwankar Baloo, who took some time to be socially accepted among upper-caste cricketers and never received full recognition through appointment to the captaincy of Indian teams. By the time that Baloo's brilliance gave him social *entrée*, cricket had spread throughout India and there were literally hundreds of clubs, often demarcated by regional rather than communal affiliations. Cricket had also been taken up in Karachi and other areas of what would later become Pakistan, with its own international presence. Cricket in East Bengal, later East Pakistan and Bangladesh, went through a similar trajectory, plotting the various political changes. By this time cricket was commonplace in Indian schools, colleges and universities, and Indian teams began to take their place on the international stage. Things had certainly moved on from the days when the princely Ranjitsinhji regarded himself as an 'English' cricketer (see Plate 10).[27] Through cricket he achieved the remarkable status of an international figure, a person of highly fluid identities, but his elite trajectory occurred somewhat outside the development of Indian cricket and, to a certain extent, he withdraw once he succeeded as ruler of his state. He did, however, give his name (and donate the trophy) to the Indian first-class Ranji

Tournament, inaugurated in 1934. This tournament was hailed as an opportunity to emphasise regional rather than communal loyalties. The other cricketing locus had been the princely states, where rulers enthusiastically took up the game, established cricket grounds and paid for celebrated cricketers to come to provide demonstrations and train their players.[28] This may have been part of the princes' strategy of seeking cultural acceptance – as in their interests in architecture, museums and other institutions – or perhaps out of eagerness to emulate the British and appear 'modern'.

Throughout this, cricket shadowed the fever chart of Indian politics. In the years of maximum resistance to the British in the 1930s and 1940s, tournaments had to be abandoned. Moreover, as the Congress party became increasingly associated with nationalist fervour, its leadership, notably Gandhi, saw the communal basis of cricket as cutting against the united society of their ambitions. On the other hand, the performance and 1930s success of the discrete Muslim team seemed to promote Jinnah's notion of a separate Pakistan, an alarming prospect for Congress. Gandhi himself decried the communal cricket teams and called for their abandonment. Other writers insisted on the complete rejection of cricket as emblematic of British rule, and as a game which aroused major passions and caused days lost at the workplace or in schools and colleges. In 1937, a critic M.N.M. Badruddin saw cricket as a source of British cultural power that should be resisted, suggesting that playing it was essentially an aristocratic pastime enjoyed by 'those who liked to attend ceremonial parades, rich dinners, and to pass away their tiresome hours in their club rooms and cricket fields'.[29] The desire of Congress politicians to kill off communal cricket was, however, achieved by Partition and its tragic aftermath. While there had already been a number of tours of the subcontinent by British and Australian teams, the 1950s saw Indian teams pulled into a Commonwealth cricketing network, including Pakistan, later Bangladesh, the West Indies, Australia and New Zealand. Cricket had been seen as the forger of imperial bonds. It had instead fostered national self-awareness and now became a key aspect of the Anglophone relationships of India. It remains the national sport, fostered by radio and later television, well represented in the continued opening of new stadia, sometimes at considerable cost.[30] By then it seemed to be more an Indian sport than an English one.[31]

As C.L.R. James graphically described, the game also became the national sport of the Anglophone Caribbean. Yet in the West Indies players seldom had the advantage of turf wickets and often played on matting, although in certain circumstances this might have developed their game. It may be that the cricket passion in the islands was particularly helped by the relatively small-scale character of the territories. Cricketers were well known within their communities. Once there were international players, they were sprinkled around and were naturally much involved in local matches, both on individual islands and in inter-island fixtures. Brian Stoddart has pointed out, however, that the difficulties of inter-island travel inhibited such contacts for some time and gave Jamaica an advantage by being a larger territory, more likely to receive touring teams.[32] It may even be argued that the populations of the Caribbean islands, having largely replaced the original inhabitants with coerced plantation slavery, needed to create their own traditions. While they maintained some oral traditions from their African origins, all the same fresh musical, dance and other cultural forms developed in new contexts, formations into which cricket fitted well. Cricket journalism developed very early and was a source of fascination and a promoter of passions. Despite island fragmentation, the West Indian Board of Control was established in the early 1920s and still exists, coordinating the administration of cricket in fifteen former colonies, islands and the mainland territory of Guyana, English-speaking with one exception (St Maarten). Thus, while the West Indies political federation only survived between 1958 and 1962, this supra-national cricketing board has continued (and been enlarged) from colonial to postcolonial periods. But Caribbean cricket was inevitably disfigured by racism, exemplified by the fact that the captaincy of the West Indies continued to be consistently racially exclusive such that a mediocre white player often led a team of players superior in quality to himself. It was only after a lengthy journalistic campaign by James that this situation was overturned and Frank Worral, from Barbados, at last became captain of the West Indian side in its Test tour of Australia in 1960–61.[33] Although Learie Constantine was denied the West Indies captaincy, he toured India and contrasted the relative lack of racism in Australia with its rigidity in India, where white opinion was 'half a century behind the rest of the world'.[34] Plate 11 shows the mixed West Indies cricket team that toured Australia in 1930–31, clearly managed by white people.

One of the great advantages of imperial sporting cultural traffic was the manner in which the seasons dovetailed between the northern and southern hemispheres. This was particularly true in the case of Australia, South Africa and New Zealand. Moreover, in India, cricket is played in the winter season, to avoid excessive heat, so even in the northern hemisphere there was a convenient fit. Hence during the British winter, games could be played in the southern hemisphere summer or in winter India, although the sea voyages to accomplish this remained of very long duration until air travel became more common. In Australia, cricket may well have been played in New South Wales from the early days, though the middle- and upper-class tone of the English game may have inhibited its early development in the convict settlements. Nevertheless, a match was played in Sydney in 1803 and by the time that the first inter-colonial matches were played in 1850–51 cricket was clearly well established. The earliest of these was played between the newly created Victoria (carved out of New South Wales) and Tasmania, then Victoria against New South Wales in 1856. The most extraordinary event in the development of Australian cricket and imperial cultural exchange was the tour of England by an Aboriginal team in 1868, by far the first indigenous sports team to arrive from anywhere in the empire. The explanation for Aboriginal skills was that the players worked as stockmen on cattle stations in western Victoria.[35] There, and notably on the Lake William station of William Hayman, they were taught to play cricket for the obvious reason that there were insufficient Europeans available to make up two teams. Trained by Tom Willis, they played at the Melbourne cricket ground and then in Sydney in 1866 (see Plate 12 for the Melbourne cricket ground in 1864). The 1868 touring team was captained by Charles Lawrence, a professional cricketer and immigrant to Australia, and played no fewer than forty-seven matches against largely amateur opponents, winning fourteen.[36] These were well attended, perhaps because of the additional attraction of seeing the Aborigines demonstrating supposed native sports by throwing spears and the boomerang. Despite some racist comment in the English press, the tour was closely followed, notably in reports in *The Times*, and the players were seen as civilised, displaying a 'manly and dignified bearing'.[37] Generally the tour was viewed as a success. But the early flourishing of indigenous cricket was stifled by colonial racism. Legislation in Victoria in 1869 (with the euphemistic title of the Aboriginal Protection Act) confined Aboriginal people to a reserve such that they required permission to leave.

English cricket teams toured Australian colonies in 1861–62, 1863–64 and more significantly in 1873–74 and 1878–79.[38] The celebrated W.G. Grace was with the tourists in 1873–74 and again in 1891–92, though his transparently imperial and class-conscious attitudes did not go down well. The first Test is regarded as having taken place in 1882 when the Australians won and claimed that English cricket had died, the origins of the notion of the 'ashes'. After that, there were many such reciprocal tours and the Australians also sent tourists to other parts of the British Empire, notably in the inter-war years, laying the foundations of the modern Commonwealth Test series. The multilateral nature of cultural traffic was thus firmly established. Moreover, as in India and the West Indies, the success of Australian cricket, starting in its golden age between the 1890s and

1914, had significant repercussions for Australian national identity and the political responses of the so-called imperial periphery. Before the First World War, cricket received a great deal of press attention and, from the inter-war years, radio became significant in propagating news of and commentaries on games, while after the Second World War, television became increasingly important. Of all sports, cricket in Australia achieved the widest following across both the country and the generations, with a very high proportion of the population expressing an interest in it. Richard White and Hsu-Ming Teo have commented on the dualities forged by cricket, including the inter-state matches that nonetheless pulled the federation together and both the sense of the sympathetic binding of the British Empire together with the development of Australian nationalism. This received a blow in the notorious 'bodyline series' of 1932–33, when the visiting English team bowled 'bouncers', a tactic designed by D.R. Jardine to neutralise the batting of Don Bradman.[39] The Australians felt, according to visiting UK Cabinet Secretary Maurice Hankey, that the British 'had lowered [their] standard of sportsmanship'.[40] This created a fresh imperial iniquity requiring to be expunged by Australian victories, as indeed it was in full measure in repeated Test series.

It has been said that cricket had become the national sport of New Zealand by the 1890s,[41] but it must be apparent that in terms of international visibility, it is perhaps rugby that seems to fulfil this role. There were problems in New Zealand – a wet climate and ground that was often muddy and cut up. As in other places, missionary educators were important in establishing the game and the presence of British regiments also helped. The Wellington Cricket Club was founded in 1842 and by the 1850s cricket was being played in other centres: Auckland, Christchurch, Dunedin and Nelson. Christchurch players had the advantage of a cricket ground in the centrally located Hagley Park, though the class tone of the game was emphasised by a gentlemen versus working men game as early as 1851, a year after the foundation of Canterbury.[42] It is interesting that the Maori never took to the game (unlike rugby) and remain under-represented in New Zealand cricket to this day. Cricket was also played in many other colonies, often again with racial overtones, including South Africa and even on island possessions like St Helena, where the topography was scarcely appropriate to its requirements.

It is, however, instructive to note the places where cricket did not catch on. Ali Mazrui has pointed out that in Africa both cricket and hockey were race specific. Cricket had 'failed to capture the imagination of Black Africans' and was restricted to expatriate whites and to people of Asian ethnicity.[43] This seems curious when we consider its history in the West Indies. But the fact is that different parts of the empire produced varying responses to sports. Horton has demonstrated the manner in which sporting responses in Singapore and Australia turned out to be different.[44] An additional variable is the factor of the differing preferences of the 'four nations' of the United Kingdom. The main sporting influences undoubtedly emanated from England, but wherever Scots were prominent (whether as missionaries, educators or prominent in the settler population), it was invariably football that was more significant than either cricket or rugby. The Irish constituent of the Australian settler cohort has always been seen as culturally influential and this may also have been true of the development of sports.[45]

Hockey was considered a potential rival to cricket, with many in India considering that it would make a more appropriate national sport. While it was also a military game, it started to be organised into clubs in India in the 1880s and an Indian hockey federation was created in 1925, accepted internationally in 1927.[46] An Indian men's team participated in the Olympics in 1928 (when a relatively small group of teams took part) and this mixed team of Europeans and Indians won the gold medal (see Plate 13).[47] India proceeded to win the gold medal at every Olympics from that date until 1960, when, significantly, it was defeated by Pakistan.[48] During these years there were mutual hockey tours (among other sports) between India and

Australia.[49] It may be that hockey was particularly suited to hotter climates because the hard ground made the game faster and more skilled. Some even suggested that it was an ancient sport, played in Asia in various forms before the days of the Raj and therefore not distinctively British. Nevertheless, it was a popular game in the empire, particularly in schools, which helped it to become a sport for both sexes. Hockey spread throughout the empire (and in Canada ice hockey)[50] and also became significant in Malaya/Malaysia. However, it took even longer for women's participation to reach the international level than it did for Black players to captain, for example, cricket teams.[51]

Football and rugby

Association football unquestionably became the national sport in Britain itself. Its origins are murky, but violent and chaotic versions were certainly played in medieval Scotland. In 1424, King James I outlawed the game because it was being played so regularly that it was inhibiting archery and other more useful practices of war.[52] Amateur football clubs appeared in Britain in the late eighteenth century and it soon became the classic game of the soldiery. The modern game emerged as a more controlled and elegant affair once the Football Association was founded and rules formulated in 1863. Cup competitions were inaugurated in the early 1870s with the leagues formed in England (1888) and Scotland (1890). The founding of many teams throughout the country ensured that it became the game most passionately followed by the working classes and in the twentieth century a principal aspect of both local and national identity. Yet its role in the British Empire never matched its significance in the metropole. The military certainly took it everywhere, and both missionaries and educators propagated it among those they attempted to convert, perhaps notably in Africa, but cricket, rugby and even hockey can be viewed as more significant in many colonies. While this may be partly a function of climate, football has also been seen as the product of a particular social environment. In India, rugby was an exclusively white sport such that when the young Mortimer Durand arrived as an Indian Civil Service magistrate in 1873, he began to play rugby with his younger colleagues.[53] In the 1930s, in the hot conditions of Rangoon, Alister McCrae, an employee of the Irrawaddy Flotilla Company, played rugby with younger colleagues (all white) at the Gymkhana Club in the late afternoon.[54]

In India it seems that the arrival of a contingent of the Northumberland Fusiliers in 1886 brought the 'new game of football with them'.[55] Thus the dispersal of the game was stepped up once its rules and organisation had been formalised in Britain. It then became the classic and universal game among the rankers in the army.[56] As such, it also spread to other peoples. The military playing football, as with cricket, was often a very public affair that drew Indian spectators to the touchlines. There is a charming story that football gained popularity because a young Indian boy watching a soldiers' game on the Calcutta maidan in the 1870s became involved by kicking the ball back to the players. Violet Jacob recounted another example of imitation in 1899 when Indian boys at the Kumaon lakes near Naini Tal watched her young son kicking a football with her servants. Soon the spectators were kicking around a ball made up of rags and a local headman sent for a proper football for them, 'so Harry will have introduced the football to the Kumaun district'.[57] At any rate, by the 1890s a string of regimental teams played for a number of cups. There were also Indian teams, notably Mohun Bagan Athletic Club, founded in 1889, and Mohammedan Sporting, perhaps inaugurated in 1891. The latter team indicated the extent to which football, like cricket, had a communal affiliation. Cup competitions were rapidly created, starting with the Durand Cup in Simla in 1889,[58] the Rovers Cup in Bombay in 1891 and the Indian Football Association Shield in 1893. The model of the English Football Association was closely followed and the teams competing for these trophies were largely white in the early days. However, a major turning point was reached when Mohun Bagan won the IFA Shield in 1911 by beating an all-white East Yorkshire Regimental Team, having defeated three other regimental teams on the way. This event was immediately given a nationalist spin.[59] If Bombay has often been seen as the cockpit of cricket, then Calcutta was the main driver of football. Throughout this period, there was a tension between those who wished to maintain football's white exclusivity and those who sought to develop the competitive spirit by training Bengalis and other Indians in the moral and physical force of the game.[60] The Rovers Cup in Bombay had been the preserve of British regimental teams since it was founded in 1892, but the Mohammedan Sporting team was successful in winning it in the 1930s and in 1937 the final was played between two Indian teams for the first time. This was another case of Indians beating the British at their own game and again football prowess seemed to march in step with growing nationalism. Within the army itself, inter-racial team competition was banned, but such a prohibition did not extend to civilians.

The other great disseminators of football in India were undoubtedly the mission stations and schools, where British sporting values were imposed in a more ethnocentric and dominant way. For example, Europeans had to overcome the natural aversion of Hindus to playing with a leather ball, as well as persuading members of the upper castes to participate in an activity which might be viewed as both unclean as well as socially and physically beneath them.[61] These inhibitions were overcome and the products of English public schools and Oxbridge (such as Theodore Pennell and Cecil Tyndale-Biscoe in the north-west of India) were instrumental in spreading the sport.[62] It is intriguing, however, that such figures did not attempt to propagate rugby, which would have been a game with which, given their backgrounds, they would have been more familiar.[63] Was this because it was a contact game with close physical proximity or was it because the educators saw football as the more demotic game more suitable for imperial people? It is, however, apparent from the study of these missionary approaches to sports like football that they could be strikingly overbearing in their desire to impose the game, its mores, rules and dress upon their charges. Nevertheless, once initial opposition had been overcome the players were prepared to devote themselves to it with real enthusiasm. In Burma, football (as well as cricket and rugby) was actively played in Rangoon from soon after the British conquest. There was a police football team and matches were played between an All-Burma eleven and the Ceylon equivalent.[64] After the First World War, the Burma football team took on one in Calcutta.[65] Elsewhere in the colony football was allegedly used as an instrument not only of westernisation, but also of pacification. Sir George Scott (1851–1935) was a Scottish journalist and colonial frontier administrator who worked in Rangoon, Mandalay, and particularly in the Shan states. Football was his passion and he persuaded the Burmese to take it up as a supposedly key part of their Anglicisation both within and outside the new British schools.[66] Once again, football became the vehicle for a major cultural transition, not least in the clothing of the body, such as the wearing of trousers. On the other hand, we learn from Richard Sidney that in the Victoria Institution in Kuala Lumpur (founded in 1887), Malay students hitched up their sarongs to play the game.[67] At this exclusive school, the Tamboosamy Shield was presented to the house (a very English division of the school) which secured the highest aggregate scores in football, badminton, cricket, hockey, rifle shooting, scout craft, boxing and the Futt Yew Athletic Championship (the latter to be decided at the annual school sports).[68] Such a galaxy of sports could no doubt be replicated across many schools in the empire. Here we find evidence of the manner in which donors of Indian and Chinese heritage, no doubt securing wealth in the colony, had contributed to this dissemination of imperial sports. Yet, even at such an English-style school, Asian culture was also present when rooms in the school were hung with Chinese lanterns and other decorations, as well as the playing of music that reasserted the cultural environment, though one more Chinese than Malay.

War was particularly effective in spreading the playing of football. It reached Afrikaner men during the Anglo-Boer War (1899–1902) since they were taught to play by their jailers in prisoner-of-war camps in St Helena, Ceylon and India, a development encouraged by the British authorities, no doubt to avoid dangerously idle leisure time. Thus, Afrikaners, generally resistant to cultural traffic from the British, had little alternative but to accept it and, no doubt, found it an antidote to boredom. They proceeded to disperse the game further on their return.[69] In the Western Cape, mule drivers from the Cape Coloured community (South African ethnic group consisted of persons of mixed European and African or Asian ancestry) took it up during the same war and gave their teams various British names, such as Sussex Rovers and Argyll Rovers, some of which survived until recently.[70] Some British battalion teams included Cape Coloured players in their number and military matches began to attract audiences, particularly in the port cities of the Cape. Sports were also disseminated by the King's African Rifles and the Royal West African Frontier Force. Military service in the Second World War further encouraged African interest and participation in football, and after that war, the sport took off in West Africa and elsewhere. The British continued to recruit to African regiments after the war and sports became very much part of officer training in these years leading to decolonisation, no doubt in the effort to ensure that African countries would remain 'on side' in the postcolonial era. This has been seen as promoting the vigour of sporting life in post-independence African armies.[71]

The foundations for this were certainly laid in earlier years. Some Europeans played football with Africans they were working with in the 1920s.[72] Meanwhile both missionaries and colonial officials had been effective in spreading the game far into the interior of the continent among Africans who had none of the taboos or social inhibitions of Indians. There is abundant evidence that missionaries were already using football in East Africa as a key aspect of educational training and religio/cultural conversion from the 1890s onwards.[73] One educator, Arthur Douglas, proclaimed that at his African school on the shores of Lake Nyasa, the pupils were free to play football each day at 4 p.m. The daily schedule seemed to him an ideal life, keeping African pupils happy and disciplined. In these ways, missionary educators thought that they were establishing a complex network of loyalties, of pupil to pupil, team to team, footballers to teachers and the institution, and, no doubt, ultimately to the Christian God. Gordon Memorial College, built in Khartoum between 1899 and 1902 (now part of the University) was provided with seven houses and football was regarded as central to its training.[74] However, not all disseminators of British sports were men. The Scottish Marion Stephenson was keen to introduce football (and also tennis) at her school in Tumutumu in Kenya. She considered they played an excellent role in both attracting and disciplining the boys at the school, not least because it led them away from 'fighting and bad dances'.[75] So football might even have encouraged attendance at the school. In West Africa, the presence of a white mercantile elite, as opposed to a more upper-class non-mercantile one, has been seen as crucial to the spread of football. The game quickly became popular among Africans, generally playing barefoot. As elsewhere it was propagated by educators and missionaries, though we should never forget the involvement of observant street players. A Nigerian African team first toured Britain in 1949, revealing the considerable talents of the players, and this helped to bring African football to the international stage, while also updating it (for example in the use of boots) as well as ultimately wresting control from white people, who continued to manage the game as in so many other colonies.[76]

In the twentieth century football played a part in resistance to apartheid.[77] Prisoners enduring the brutal regime on Robben Island resolved to play football but had to fight the authorities for their opportunity to do so. They formed the Makana football league, made up of five teams, and games occurred over a period of twenty years, offering psychological support for the inmates as well as permitting them to feel they were opposing apartheid even on this offshore island. Africans indeed were to emerge as exceptionally talented players of international standing. In South Africa, the sport was inhibited by apartheid, though it was played enthusiastically in many African areas of the country. Since the end of white supremacy a complex league structure has been formed in the various provinces and it has developed a truly popular following, helped by the country hosting the World Cup in 2010. Elsewhere in Africa it was encouraged by the fact that the game was extensively played in the French Empire, such that in modern times West African teams emerged as significant on the world stage. In the territories of white settlement, football is significant everywhere, but it has never reached the heights of its popular status in Britain, which helps to explain the reason for celebrated UK teams enjoying supporters around the Anglophone world and beyond.

While cricket can be seen as the main sport influencing the formation of national identities in India, Pakistan, Sri Lanka, Australia and the West Indies, it is unquestionably rugby that has been more important for South Africa, New Zealand and some of the Pacific islands.[78] There is no question that in Fiji rugby is the national sport. The game is said to have begun there when Europeans and Fijian soldiers played in 1884. However, it remained a white-dominated sport for some time. In 1913, white settlers founded the Fijian Rugby Football Union and in 1913 the New Zealand All Blacks visited the island and played a European team, defeating them comprehensively. The relationship with New Zealand naturally developed in the 1920s, by which time indigenous Fijians were taking over from white people, following the founding of a native Rugby Football Union in 1915 and its associated competition. The Fijians honed their skills in inter-island matches with Tonga and Samoa, where rugby had been introduced respectively in the early twentieth century and 1920. The game was brought to Samoa by Catholic missionaries and became popular so quickly that a union was formed in 1924 and the first international, against Fiji, played in that year.[79] Tonga won its first match against Fiji in 1924. The success of rugby in the Pacific islands is a major phenomenon, such that teams compete on the world stage and individual players have joined teams elsewhere, including the UK. Such internationalisation of individual rugby players is an important aspect of labour migration, in some cases providing financial security for players, families and wider communities.[80] The question arises why these Pacific Islanders (with low populations) took to rugby and turned it into their national sport.[81] Fijians, Tongans and Samoans are Polynesians, like the Maori of New Zealand (Aotearoa). It may be that the Maori took to rugby because there was an indigenous game which had affiliations with sports involving some variant of ball-handling. Perhaps this was also true in the islands. The muscular Polynesian physique is also clearly appropriate for rugby.

Among white settler colonies, there can be no doubt that rugby has been most important in New Zealand and South Africa. In modern times, they have vied for first place in the world rankings, having won three World Cup competitions each. The relationship between them has been characterised by partial racial inclusion in New Zealand, in terms of Maori players, exclusion with regard to Black people in South Africa, as well as by international boycotts of apartheid South Africa which the New Zealanders seemed most eager to flaunt. Yet Maori players have been involved in New Zealand rugby from its beginnings in the 1870s and have played in New Zealand international teams since 1884. Maoris have also established their own All Blacks team which has been exceptionally successful in international fixtures. In 1928, 1949 and 1960 Maoris were excluded from All Blacks teams playing in South Africa, a surprisingly craven capitulation to South African segregation policies which has only been expunged in modern times. In 1970 Maori appeared as 'honorary whites'. Touring continued until 1980–81, but after that South Africa was largely excluded from international competition, which (along with other sporting bans) may have helped to heighten the country's sense of isolation.[82] Yet the Maoris' eager adoption of rugby certainly contributed to New Zealand's All Blacks rugby team becoming so successful internationally and the country's undoubted national sport. In the case of South Africa, by contrast, African and Cape Coloured people took up rugby soon after its introduction to the country in the 1880s, but were only able to reach the national team after the dismantling of apartheid in the 1990s, although it took some time for the white control of the game to be overturned. Only in 2019 was it possible for an African to be captain, whereas a player with Maori heritage captained the New Zealand team as early as 1896.

The South African history of rugby reveals the fact that English public schools other than Rugby also created similar sports. The first rugby-type sport to appear at the Cape was Winchester football introduced to the Diocesan College in 1861–62. Winchester football spread, but it was completely overtaken by the Rugby version after its introduction in 1875. The latter experienced a rapid dispersal throughout the Eastern and Western Cape and Natal during the 1880s, and the South African Rugby Board was founded in 1889 (a union had already emerged in Kimberley in 1886). But the most interesting aspect of South African rugby is that it was so rapidly taken up by young Afrikaners. It was already being played by young Boer farmers in Stellenbosch in 1886 and moved from there to the independent states of the Transvaal and Orange Free State. Indeed, in a sense South African rugby was 'federated' before the country became a Union in 1910. In 1891, a British team visited South Africa, financed by Rhodes and President Kruger of the Transvaal, and played a team made up of players from both the British colonies and Boer states. The Currie Cup tournament was created in 1892. While Cape Coloured and African play was entirely segregated from white, Afrikaners curiously identified with this British sport which contributed to their sense of distinctive ethnicity. Black and Nauright have argued that rugby has:

represented at different times and in differing places imperial connections, Afrikaner nationalism, Islamic masculinity and [Cape] Coloured community identity, sporting identity and culture among the educated African elite, racism and ... a new pan-South African national identification.[83]

Until relatively recent times, when women have come to play rugby (in both its Union and League forms), it has also been emblematic of male dominance and 'manly' qualities. If empire can be seen by some as a relentless display of masculinity, then team sports were a major cultural expression of such masculinity. In this guise rugby has unquestionably been a significant sport in Australia, where four different types of football prevail: soccer, Rugby Union, Rugby League and Australian Rules. Soccer emerged in Australia in the later nineteenth century, coterminous with its codification and organisation in Britain. As elsewhere, it was a game of the military and of the police, but it developed in a highly competitive environment and it only aspired to national popularity and international status in relatively recent times.[84] It was taken up by Aboriginal players among whom it has become very popular.[85] They brought skills derived from a hunting culture and from an indigenous game, but they were prevented from entering at a higher level until modern times. Rugby League has a considerable following, as has the other 'handling' (and running) game, Australian Rules football, originally invented (around 1858) to keep cricketers fit during the winter. It was preferred to the growing popularity elsewhere of the rugby of Rugby School, partly because players were anxious about the dangers of tackling and falling on to the hard ground.[86] Although this sport has a major league and a massively enthusiastic following in Australia, it has a lower international profile. It is, however, interesting that it featured in an Australian painting with the title *The National Game* as early as 1889.[87] Rugby Union has been seen as a middle-class sport and its spread tended to follow the development of a bourgeoisie, as for example in Queensland in the 1880s.[88] It thus tracked socio-economic change, a characteristic that must have been replicated in other settler territories. In Western Australia, however, rugby had a chequered existence. It started to be played in 1881, but interest flagged and clubs converted to Australian Rules in 1885. Rugby was revived in 1893 following the arrival of players from New Zealand, Britain and New South Wales during the gold rush. Declining again in the early twentieth century, it was resurrected in 1928, with Rugby League arriving in 1948.[89] Aborigines have never been as active in Australian rugby as Maoris have been in New Zealand. Some eight Aborigines have played in the national team, but they have generally been educated in private rugby-playing schools suggesting they were from the elite or were lucky enough to secure scholarships. It has been said that rugby has an image problem among indigenous Australians, partly because of historic racism, and partly because it seemed to be a game for 'toffs', for upper classes who formerly could afford to be amateurs.[90] Racism has continued to be a feature of Australian sport until relatively recently, as when a player in the Australian Aboriginal Football League responded to racist abuse by raising his shirt and proclaiming his pride in his origins.[91]

Other sports

This chapter has concentrated on team sports because the insights they provide into cultural transmission also reflect the intersection of race, politics and national identities. Naturally, there were other physical activities dispersed by empire, including athletics, tennis, jogging, boxing, fencing, even tugs of war. In the case of boxing, this has invariably been seen as an urban pursuit and has received some scholarly attention, not least in its class and racial dimensions.[92] Tennis became virtually universal, a sport associated with the countless clubs of empire since the amount of land required was slight and it needed relatively low investment. It was a sport that could be played by both men and women, either separately or together. However, until modern times, it was never likely to be a major spectator sport. Among settlers, there was an additional raft of sports: wherever there were rivers, harbours or other areas of sheltered water, the British introduced nautical events, including various forms of rowing, canoeing and yachting. The latter was invariably organised through major and exclusive clubs like the Royal Bombay Yacht Club (RBYC), the Singapore and Hong Kong yacht clubs, and many others in the ports of the settler territories. These were elite social clubs, complementing their sailing activities. The RBYC, founded in 1846, acquired its grand waterfront building in 1881.[93] These clubs have been taken over by postcolonial elites, but it is tempting to imagine that, in addition to so-called martial races, there were maritime equivalents enjoying competitive activities on the water, literally marine races. Such sports were also used in the navy as training for mariners and pastimes in naval bases. In addition, the British were keen on establishing swimming clubs, for example (of many) the Kokine Swimming Club in Rangoon.[94] Again, it must be said that many indigenous peoples have used water to secure food and other resources or as transport systems, sometimes also for recreational activity, though never perhaps to the degree pursued by leisured Europeans.

Two sources reflect the importance of sports for the culture of empire. The astonishing range of sports is illustrated in the listing at the Delhi Durbar of 1911, recorded in the official programme. This announces that the polo, hockey and football tournaments will be 'played off' on the polo ground opposite the Foreign Office camp. The fine gradations of those permitted to take part are obvious in the various instructions and arrangements. Seventy-six teams were entered for the hockey tournament, and this was open to the entire 'native army' with only three officers permitted to participate in each team. Hockey seems to have been a sport which lent itself to inter-racial participation, the sticks helping to maintain social distance. The football tournament, on the other hand, was open to the entire

British army in India, in other words only the Europeans in that army. As late as 1911 the notion of a mixed team of British and Indians seemed unacceptable. In addition, there was a highly competitive military tournament and a boxing tournament, which was open to officers and men separately illustrating class divisions. The military tournament involved the presentation of individuals, again divided into officers and men, each being judged 'at arms' and 'bayonet-to-bayonet', 'sword-to-sword' and in tent-pegging, with many prizes in each category. The point-to-point horse races were conducted over two different courses, one of 4 miles of natural country and another of 3 miles. They were categorised according to different kinds of horses, including 'English' and 'Australasians', 'country bred' and 'Arabs', illustrating the complexity in the breeding and origins of horses in India. 'Native Sports' (that is for Indians) were placed in a separate category, comprising wrestling, quoit-throwing, Sonchi,[95] sword and shield play, and a flat race (presumably athletics).[96] Additionally, the sporting passion among settlers is reflected in an observation by Julian Huxley when visiting Nyeri in Kenya in 1930. This town in the principal area of white settlement in the Highlands north of Nairobi boasted a full-size cricket field, golf course, tennis club and polo ground. Huxley remarked that: 'Truly the British are a remarkable race. No imperialists save perhaps the Romans have ever exported their domestic habits and their recreations so wholeheartedly all over the empire.'[97] Such lavish sporting facilities would have been used by a relatively small settler population at that time. But the white people there would have had substantial leisure time, not least because they were supported by indigenous servants and other workers. Thus indigenous peoples underpinned white leisure, but were also the new seedbed in which such sports could be sown.

In many ways, settlers and expatriates surrounded themselves with sporting opportunities not only as a powerful projection of their dominant masculinity, but also as part of their sense of cultural exclusivity. Richard Sidney, in the 1920s, wrote of the manner in which '[we need not] be deprived of our customary games, for hospitable European Clubs will ask us to play Cricket and Football, Hockey, Tennis and Golf'.[98] As the years went by, all imperial sports became deeply embroiled in the capitalist endeavours of empire, not just, as noted above, through the supply of equipment and the construction of facilities, but also increasingly in the twentieth century through sponsorship. Such interests started to finance sports as a means of establishing corporate identities and loyalties among their workforce. This was true of large employers (like the railways or the banking system in India) and other major corporate interests. Major companies were interested in linking the visibility of their reputations, 'names' or products to sports with popular followings. Whether this helped to transform the character of the sports is a matter of debate. But what can be said is that imperial sports negotiated the dramatic social, racial, gender and political transformations of the various colonies from the high point of empire through to its demise. As empire declined, sports flourished and took on significant new roles both in nationalist and in gender terms. While women had participated in individualist sports like golf and tennis, they increasingly participated in team sports, starting perhaps with hockey. There can be little doubt that sports should enter the mainstream of British imperial history, where they have scarcely featured in the past, since they constituted prime examples of 'cultural traffic' within the wider economy. They also illustrate the complex multi-directional nature of such traffic.

4

ARTS OF EMPIRE AND OF NATIONS

Carting sugar at Rose Hill, the residence of Edward Jackson, Trinidad, British West Indies, c.1836.

There is a remarkable intersection between imperial sports and the art of empire in Thomas Daniell's 1792 depiction of Fort St George in Madras. This unveils both the centre of British power in South India and the key sport taking place on the fort's cleared land,

Europeans playing cricket. This image combines a familiar English pastime with imperial military architecture in an alien environment. But imperial art more generally was concerned with exotica, with the capacity of the imperial thrust to unveil all forms of the unfamiliar, in topographies, peoples, flora, fauna, natural phenomena, human customs and architecture. Such art represents the imaginative grappling with difference. Yet, despite such striking images and in common with many studies of aspects of British culture, the visual arts have been generally disconnected from the experience of empire. This has been described as 'a spectacular act of erasure' in many ways reflecting ideological silences.[1] On the other hand, one area that has received a good deal of attention is the appearance of Black servants in British paintings, a reflection of the social influence of Caribbean slavery in the metropolis.[2] It is also true that scholars in each major territory of the former British Empire have produced studies of art in those countries, often seeking to find the origins and development of national styles, but there has been very little attempt to draw the arts of empire together into an integrated whole.[3] More recently, some studies, together with major relevant exhibitions, have redressed this omission.[4] This chapter will briefly consider the origins of imperial art in the eighteenth century, followed by its full flowering in the nineteenth before national artistic responses disrupted the heroic traditions.

Several key points need to be made at the outset. The first is that the art is as much marked by omissions as inclusions. While the discovery and intercontinental transposition of botanical specimens are featured, the economic processes of extraction and exploitation are often ignored, at least until the coming of advertisements and propaganda in the nineteenth and twentieth centuries. Hence the production of crops and resources for European consumption, for trade goods (e.g. opium), or conversion into crafted and industrial products was central to the imperial economy, but was seldom represented in art. The realities of working conditions of humans central to these processes, whether the baleful trans-Atlantic slave trade to plantations in the Caribbean and the Americas, or indigenous and indentured labour throughout the empire, were usually absent. Third, it should be noted that many of the artists were not white. In India and the Far East Europeans tapped into older artistic traditions, converted them and persuaded indigenous artists to contribute to cross-cultural artistic endeavours. Some of these artists seized the new opportunities afforded by Europeans, adapting styles to new commissions. Such intercultural processes served to modify western art, feeding back influences that have often been missed. Imperial art progressively became an exchange between its original wellsprings and the images and techniques encountered in the 'field'. Yet from the late 1700s, art elevated colonial conquest into the heroic domain, transforming it into an aspect of British national identity. This was heightened in the following century reaching a climax in the high imperial period after 1850. At the same time, it became more visible, more democratically available, part of the popular culture of imperialism. However, this soon heralded the end of a true imperial art.

All art is about forms of discovery, but European voyages into the wider world created a vastly new potential for visual revelations. From the earliest days, artists were key personnel on such expeditions. They were required to produce proof of success, images of strange places and peoples encountered.[5] Such art achieved much greater quality and significance in the three celebrated voyages of Captain James Cook between 1768 and 1780. A number of artists accompanied Cook, producing remarkable depictions of the places, peoples, environments and meteorology of the Pacific and Antarctic regions.[6] However, the emphasis changed, from botany in the first voyage under the influence of Joseph Banks to the illustration of meteorological and topographical effects in the second, while the third focused mainly on peoples, exotic ethnographical images. A remarkable corpus of art was produced, in turn influencing artistic developments elsewhere, such as the East India Company's grappling with

India. Yet, there was a paradox. Artists had to find a visual language which would render images of exotica accessible, to attract rather than repel their audiences. The revelation of the strikingly unfamiliar had to be produced within conventions familiar to the viewer. Emergent European notions of the sublime and the picturesque became vehicles for the revelation of places very different from those in Europe. Moreover, as settlement proceeded in the early nineteenth century, some at least of the early visions of settlement colonies had the look of the English pastoral about them. Each colonial 'school' had its origins in gentler landscapes – the Maritimes or the banks of the St Lawrence in Canada, the coastal regions of south-eastern Australia or Tasmania, the long-settled agricultural lands of the Cape, and scenes in the North Island of New Zealand. Even some West Indian landscapes, particularly after the dramatic ecological changes such as the destruction of native tree cover wrought by the English in the seventeenth century, lent themselves to this bucolic tradition.

However, striking developments in imperial art took place in India. The presence of the East India Company, utterly disruptive as it was, served to attract many artists to the subcontinent. There they set about painting dramatic landscapes, striking architecture and unfamiliar peoples, notably of the princely states and of the Mughal royal court. There were also considerable opportunities for western portraitists. It was well known that British and other European individuals in India were making considerable fortunes and sought to record their presence there, as well as that of their families, invariably of mixed race. Portraitists of some stature, including Tilly Kettle, Johan Zoffany, Thomas Hickey, Ozias Humphrey, Robert Home, George Chinnery and Francesco Renaldi worked in India in the last decades of the eighteenth century and early in the nineteenth.[7] Several, including Kettle, Zoffany, Home and (later) George Duncan Beechey went to Lucknow to work at the court of the Nawab of Oudh. There were also opportunities in the trading posts in the Far East. Artists quickly began to translate the major European movement of Romanticism into the depiction of Indian scenes. They were also, together with Indian artists, active in unveiling scientific developments.[8] Indians were soon working in hybrid styles, creating significant cross-cultural influences, as in the school known as Company paintings.[9] The artist William Hodges constitutes a key link between the Cook voyages (he was artist on the second) and developments in India.[10] After his arrival in 1778, patronised by Warren Hastings, he travelled on a sequence of journeys up the Ganges and into Central India. Using *plein air* technique, he drew and painted dozens of Indian buildings, often set in botanical and topographical settings.[11] Many, including Allahabad, Cawnpore, Murshidabad, Benares, Agra and Akbar's abandoned capital at Fatehpur Sikri were later reissued in a lavish book.[12] There were also neat and restrained images of Indian men and women, while additionally he offered advice to other artists travelling east. Many images of India were revealed to an elite audience, including a depiction of the Taj Mahal. Hodges was swiftly followed by two other remarkably versatile artists, Thomas Daniell (1749–1840) and his nephew William Daniell (1769–1837), who arrived in 1786 and returned to Britain in 1794. They made three memorable journeys from Calcutta, first (1788–91) up the Ganges, across Central India and on to Kashmir; second (1792–23) a tour from Madras around Mysore, already subject to the predatory gaze of the East India Company; the third (1793–94) took them to the sites of the Bombay area, including the caves of Elephanta. Like other artists, they often travelled through areas seriously disturbed by warfare and lawlessness, yet their artistic achievements were considerable. Their depiction of Chowringhee Road in Calcutta revealed the developing elegance and grandeur of the Company's capital. They produced many illustrations of Indian antiquities which, together with landscapes, betray no hint of decline and decay, sometimes seen as inherent in western representations of the Orient. The Daniells' work includes Indian architecture, holy and scientific places, people, landscapes and sports (including tiger hunting on elephant-back), generally rendered in the spirit of a western picturesque. They produced the first impressions of the Himalayas seen in Britain. Back in London, they spent many years working up their drawings into watercolours and oils.[13] They produced aquatints, published in six volumes of 144 prints which, though highly priced, sold well and appeared in libraries.[14] The Indian picturesque style was much developed by the artist Sita Ram, who accompanied the governor general on his tour in 1814–15 and produced remarkably extensive portfolios of more than 200 watercolours.[15] The activities of the many artists in India have been described as 'a phenomenon without parallel in the history of art'.[16]

Many amateur artists were also active. Some were members of professions in which artistic training was useful, including army officers, revenue officials, surveyors and engineers (see Plate 21). Some of their efforts were later worked up by professionals and some, for example by the brothers James and William Fraser, have been published in recent times.[17] Some sought professional training and several amateurs met in Calcutta to discuss and critique each other's work.[18] There were a number of women painters of portraits and miniatures in the late eighteenth and early nineteenth centuries, while some elite women pursued artistic endeavours.[19] The celebrated diaries of Emily Eden, in India with Governor General Auckland 1835–42, are full of references to sketching and painting, with drawings often sent home to illustrate letters, while Charlotte Canning, the wife of the last East India Company governor general, was an artist in the 1850s.[20]

Conquest and heroic deaths

Meanwhile, the main thrust of art in the thirteen pre-revolutionary American colonies was in portraiture as settlers sought to demonstrate their self-confidence and the 'civilised' nature of their lifestyles. This self-congratulatory mode ensured that they seemed more interested in themselves than their surroundings. This increasingly sophisticated colonial society produced two of the most significant artists in the development of the heroic tradition of imperial art. These were the contemporaries John Singleton Copley (1738–1815), born in Boston, and Benjamin West (1738–1820), born in Springfield (now Swarthmore) Pennsylvania. Both moved to Britain and became academicians, and West was later President of the Royal Academy. West developed his expertise by painting portraits in Pennsylvania but left for Italy in 1760 to continue his artistic training and gain experience.[21] He settled in London from 1763, becoming one of the most influential artists of the day. His paintings such as *The Treaty of Penn with the Indians* of 1772 and events of the Seven Years' War, notably *The Death of General Wolfe* of 1770 (commemorating an event of 1759) brought him considerable fame and were regularly reproduced in engravings.[22] These were elevated into mythic moments, imaginative reconstructions with such profound ideological content that image took over from reality. Complex histories were reduced to single images with profoundly instrumental effects. The *Death of Wolfe* was the most influential imperial painting of the age, and death scenes became the staple of such heroic art. The death of Captain Cook on the Sandwich Islands (Hawaii) in 1779 was another iconic moment, depicted by several artists, despite the dubious circumstances in which it occurred.[23] John Webber, artist on the expedition, was the first to portray it, though it became an increasingly heroic and tragic moment, notably in Johan Zoffany's painting of 1794. Engravings, by stripping the image into its essentials, further enhanced the sense of a heroic martyrdom, with Cook converted from an apparently aggressive to a passive figure. Whereas Wolfe died in battle between Europeans, Cook was 'martyrised' by an attack by Hawaiian Polynesians. West took up the heroic death theme again by famously painting *The Death of Nelson* soon after it occurred.[24] This became a classic, the hero dying, like Wolfe, at the moment of victory. Nelson's death, a key turning point in the increasing dominance of imperial Britain in struggles with France, symbolised West's transposition of the grand manner historical style ('epic representations' he called them) into the empire, confirming his fame as a foundational artist of imperial heroic imagery.[25] Crossovers with theatrical representations became common, starting with staged versions of Cook's death in the 1780s, either with dramatic plays or with tableaux reproducing the paintings.

Copley also developed his talents and his income by painting well-to-do contemporary Bostonian colonists, providing them with an appealing aura of civilised elegance. In 1774 he sailed for Europe and after visiting the Continent settled in London in 1775. As well as accomplished portraits of such imperial figures as the Marquess Cornwallis, Copley contributed to the heroic tradition of contemporary history painting, as in his *Death of Major Pierson* in St Helier during the retaking of Jersey from the French in 1781, and canvases devoted to the Siege and Relief of Gibraltar in 1781–82.[26] He contributed to Napoleonic war iconography, for example in his *Surrender of the Dutch Admiral de Winter to Admiral Duncan* of 1797.[27] The heroic grand manner was also transferred to portraits of notable figures of the day.

West and Copley had no direct experience of the settings of their heroic pictures: they were imaginative exercises in both locale and composition. This was also true of depictions of key moments in the British advance in India. The storming of the fort at Seringapatam in 1799, which brought the Mysore wars to an end, produced a flurry of works both inside and outside India. In London, the event was celebrated in one of the spectacular pictorial media of the age, the Panorama.[28] Sir Robert Ker Porter produced imaginary paintings of the battle for a 180-degree panorama shown in 1800 at the Lyceum Theatre to celebrate British military prowess.[29] One of the most heroic of imperial paintings relating to the same event was painted almost 40 years after it had allegedly occurred by another artist who had never been to India. David Wilkie's *General Sir David Baird discovering the body of Sultan Tippoo Sahib after having captured Seringapatam on the 4th May 1799* of 1838 depicts Baird surrounded by Indian onlookers and British soldiers.[30] The body is close to the grille of the prison where Baird had been incarcerated years earlier while the elongated figure of the general, lit by a torch held by a Scottish soldier, dramatically points to a supposedly more civilised future.[31] It is a classic icon of imperial ideology by an artist better known for unheroic genre scenes. Unencumbered by the struggle to render unfamiliar landscapes in the language of the picturesque, artists thus forged a new instrumental art of imperial heroism, imaginary depictions of symbolic events that would be highly influential in the nineteenth century. Thus, while landscape art contributed to the creation of a global British artistic culture, when it came to historical events ideology took over from attempts at faithful representation.[32]

At the same time, art became less the preserve of the elite, new technologies serving to democratise it, spreading imperial ideology to a wider population. Developments in engraving and later, the mechanisation of printing ensured that an explosion of imperial images reached a much larger audience. Visual representations were now popularised, available for the eyes of the British and migrants across the empire. New illustrated journals contributed to this, including the *Illustrated London News* (founded 1842), the *Illustrated Times* (1855–62), the *Penny Illustrated Paper* and *The Graphic* (1869), all containing engravings of principal events. Further advances, such as electrotyping from roughly the middle of the century and the printed reproduction of photography from the 1880s, rendered pictures even more available. Journals and popular books supplied myriad images, many relating to empire. Art's apparent commitment to imperial ideology promoted a profound sense of cultural superiority. At the same time, the new profession of war artist became the major means by which the British public was made aware of India and other colonies. The outbreak of the Indian Revolt in 1857 coincided with this dramatic growth in availability of images and the result was severely ideological portrayals of resistance and its defeat, the struggle between the alleged evil of rebellion and the supposed morality of imperial suppression, however bloody. A cartoon by John

Tenniel, published in *Punch* in September 1857, displayed the female incarnation of Justice with shield and upraised sword surrounded by slain Indians. Graphic and prejudiced images of the revolt in illustrated journals included the Relief of Lucknow, the killing of British women at Cawnpore, the capture of the Emperor Bahadur Shah and his sons, with British officers raised to heroic status. The artist William Simpson arrived in India in 1859 to produce pictures of places associated with the revolt, many published in Britain.[33] While 1857 provided countless opportunities for illustrations, it also served to create some anti-British art, not only by Indians, but also by the Russian artist Vasily Vereshchagin, who painted graphic images of British brutal vengeance such as the blowing of rebels from guns.

Highly partisan images of colonial campaigns became central to imperial art. Heroic iconography incorporated powerful racist ideology, with officers and troops shown valiantly confronting the racial other. Richard Caton Woodville, an 'embedded' artist in the Second Afghan War, produced celebrated images such as *The Saving of the Guns at the Battle of Maiwand* in 1880. In Africa, another icon painted by the French artist Alphonse de Neuville was of Lieutenants Melville and Coghill saving the colours after the Battle of Isandhlwana in 1879 in the Anglo-Zulu War. Perhaps the most regularly reproduced scene of imperial heroism was G.W. Joy's *The Death of General Gordon at Khartoum* in 1885, depicting the supposed self-sacrifice of a Christian martyr, which appeared in many media, including stained glass.[34] Most nineteenth-century ideologically charged heroic images featured high-ranking figures, but one project 'democratised glory'.[35] Louis William Desanges conceived a scheme to paint all recipients of the Victoria Cross, among whom there were many private soldiers and non-commissioned officers. Between 1859 and 1862, he produced over fifty oils of heroic moments during the wars of empire in Asia and Africa. Displayed in London, they secured a wide audience and were published in a book. Desanges also painted senior figures like generals Wolseley and Roberts in the Ashanti and Afghan wars.[36] Such images contributed to the extraordinary rise in the social and cultural reputation of the military of the period.[37] Other imperial events included the artistic recording of the visit of Albert Edward, Prince of Wales in 1875–76 and later the various durbars.[38]

By the late Victorian era, it is possible to see a sense of imperial pageantry and grandeur entering into the depiction of domestic ceremonial in art. An excellent example is Sir John Lavery's painting of Queen Victoria opening the Glasgow Exhibition of 1888. This contains distinctly Orientalist elements, including the robes of civic officials and uniforms of the military, creating a municipal durbar unquestionably influenced by India.[39] Moreover, from Edwardian times commercial companies exploited imperial imagery in advertising. In theatres throughout the country, stage scenery, *tableaux vivants* and panoramas featured imperial scenes.[40] Some elements of the picturesque style of 1770–1830 survived into the art of Edward Lear on his visit to India between 1873 and 1875 (see Plate 15), and resurfaced in advertising and posters in the twentieth century.[41] In all these ways artists struggled to portray the cultural differentials of advanced societies in Asia, with material cultures older and grander than those in Europe, as well as what were seen as 'primitive' indigenous societies in the Americas, Africa and Australasia. But still, artistic output was emblematic of the great burst of energy in the European encounter with the outer world. Images also contributed to the extraordinary growth in knowledge of the products and character of the globe encompassed in imperial ambitions. Artists powerfully reflected and generally supported the political, military and economic phenomena of the age.

Fragmentation of imperial art

The incorporation of wider sectors of the population was promoted by the global development of the colonial bourgeois public sphere. The universal growth of the middle class prompted the creation of fresh cultural institutions, characteristic of growing cities of the settler territories, India and other colonies. From the 1860s, art societies were founded, art schools created, journals instituted and public art galleries opened for the first time. Moreover, almost all the industrial exhibitions of the period had art sections providing an international audience for colonial art. This was true of such exhibitions in colonial cities, for example the Dunedin Industrial Exhibition of 1865, which gave opportunities for the display of works by both local artists and some from Australia. Wealthy patrons sometimes offered prizes for paintings to create competition and attract publicity. Such prizes, however, could become a drag on artistic innovation with patron and judges promoting conservative tastes. The development of such a bourgeois apparatus also brought together artists to encourage and criticise each other's work and promote opportunities for training aspirant painters. This encouraged debate, establishing the lines of conservatism and radicalism, and promoting the search for national schools. Such a development became an ambition in many colonies at a time when the creation of transport infrastructures enabled artists to travel to seek patrons for portraits or find topographical scenes for landscapes. The penetration of railway lines into remote rural areas and the opening up of steamer services along coasts or up rivers (for example in Canada or New Zealand) all helped. Later, roadbuilding and the development of the internal combustion engine became similarly effective. While artists had been notable travellers in the days of sail and the horse, international exchanges became easier with the growth of steamship lines, ensuring easier transport to and from Europe and between the colonies themselves. The original sense of the pastoral and the familiar was dramatically disrupted by revelations of strikingly vast, snow-covered or desert landscapes in the territories of settlement. Increasingly, the art of the Dominions became profoundly about portraying aspects of difference, even if early manifestations were expressed through a powerfully romantic lens. It was only later that the next stage was reached, namely the application of different techniques and method-ologies to the representations of contrasting environments when new artistic styles arrived from Europe. But soon a wholly new art emerged through the fusion of modernist approaches with the traditions of indigenous arts. In India, the final stage took place over a longer period and had a largely different objective, namely the search for hybridity, which would both reinvigorate Indian arts and render them more comprehensible on an international stage. These developments will be considered in the individual territories.

Canada

Settler art in Canada reached back into a French tradition originating in the seventeenth century.[42] Quebecois art, however, only took on a truly local style in the late eighteenth and early nineteenth centuries, when the British conquest and French Revolutionary Wars largely separated it from its parent culture. A fine tradition of both portrai-ture and landscape then emerged. In both Quebec and Anglophone Canada painters inevitably produced portraits of leading officials and citizens (often Catholic ecclesiastics in the case of Quebec), a valu-able means of securing an income. There was also a market for reli-gious and biblical subjects. But there is little that is distinctive about their work, except perhaps when it adopted ethnographic subjects. It is also important to recognise that despite the British conquest a French colonial culture continued, in terms of religion, language, literature, and also art. An example of a portrait of a leading Quebecois citizen is that of the Honourable Antoine Juchereau Duchesnay, Seigneur of Beauport by François Baillergé dating from 1782–84.

However, any survey of paintings in the Ottawa National Gallery of Art reveals the extent to which artists were fascinated by the cultures and appearance of Indian or First Nations people.[43] The economic and cultural interactions of the fur trade had prompted the exchange of regalia and artefacts characteristic of First Nations and European

151

cultures, an inter-ethnic cultural traffic which appeared in paintings. Interestingly, naïve artists were sometimes particularly adept at conveying the detail of First Nations clothing and other cultural details, including the interior and decoration of a 'tepee': an example is the painting of Micmac (or Mi'kmaq) Indians by an unknown artist, possibly dating from 1850 and described by the National Gallery as 'one of the jewels of the collection'.[44] But the key to many such depictions of First Nations people, particularly in the nineteenth century, was the conviction that they were potentially doomed to extinction (culturally if not demographically), so art created a record for subsequent generations who would be deprived of the reality. The Quebec artist Antoine Plamondon produced a classic of this genre in *The Last of the Hurons of Lorette (Zacharie Vincent)* in 1838.[45] The subject, Vincent, was himself an artist and, perhaps activated by the same fear, produced ten self-portraits. Rather more sympathetic portraits of First Nations and mixed-race people were produced on ivory miniatures by Lady Hamilton, Matilda Jones and others.[46] Plamondon also painted still-lifes and portraits, notably of religious figures, a continuing assertion of the Catholic character of Quebec. Théophile Hamel was another Quebecois artist who painted portraits of leading Quebecois, significant Anglophone figures and visiting 'Indian chiefs'. He travelled to Europe and also extended his interests into western Canada.[47]

After the Seven Years' War (1756–63), a British school of army topographers and watercolourists emerged in Canada. Initially their work was imitative rather than distinctive, largely following British conventions and tending to suggest that these lands could be made familiar, that through conquest they could be rendered (both literally and figuratively) more like Europe. By the 1830s, however, artists were beginning to be interested in depicting Canadian scenes in a more typical manner. For example, the maritime trade and commerce of Canada were illustrated in the painting of the port of Halifax of c.1835, possibly by the visiting British artist John Poad Drake. In the same period, Robert C. Todd painted two views of the *Timber and*

Shipbuilding Yards of Allan Gilmour and Company at Wolfe's Cove, Quebec (viewed from the south and west), indicative of economic developments in the territory.[48] There is, however, an interesting connection between army artists and the development of Canadian art in Quebec City. Robert Coulson, a Grenadier Guards officer stationed there from 1839 to 1842, for example, painted watercolours of the city from the Pointe de Lévy, featuring the dramatic citadel overlooking the river. This may have influenced the Canadian landscape artist Joseph Légaré who painted the scene in oils from the same viewpoint.[49] Although artists continued to produce the income-generating portraits of leading citizens into the central years of the nineteenth century, they increasingly recognised that they should depict the distinctive topographical and meteorological characteristics of Canada. These were to be found in frozen rivers, waterfalls and snow, with people surviving arduous journeys or in snow-covered houses. The Amsterdam-born Cornelius Krieghoff, a popular Canadian artist of the period, created many winter landscapes that bring a partly Dutch, partly German sensibility to bear on Canadian subjects.[50] A notable example is his *White Horse Inn* of 1851, with horses and humans coping with wintry conditions, no doubt anticipating a warmer interior.[51] Habitations set in snow became an important trope (see Plate 16), emphasising the courage and grittiness of the pioneer spirit in surviving difficult climatic conditions. Henry Sandham's *Hunters Returning with their Spoil* of 1877 revealed another classic snow-bound activity.[52] Canadian artists also derived influences from Scandinavian counterparts, where terrain, foliage and northern light were not too dissimilar.

Almost contemporary with the work of Krieghoff, several artists were heading westwards to the Pacific. The finest of these, Paul Kane, travelled from Toronto to the great lakes and reached the west coast between 1846 and 1848 (see Plate 17). He produced highly romanticised and idealised paintings of Indians set in the grand scenery of British Columbia. He painted over a hundred canvases of the West and when exhibited in the early 1850s they created a sensation.[53] Later they were regularly exhibited overseas and came to epitomise Canada. Gold discoveries in British Columbia from 1858 drew other artists westwards, including Fred Verner, Kane's pupil. Although gold transformed the economy of the West and helped to develop its cities, Verner concentrated on scenes of travel, camping, canoeing and, above all, the buffalo hunt, which became almost an obsession. The West was consequently unveiled well ahead of the building of the transcontinental railway. Meanwhile, in the East other artists were beginning to depict ordinary Canadians at work in characteristic occupations, such as smiths and lumberjacks. George Reid's *Logging* of 1888 is a good example.[54] Subsequently, Charles F. Comfort explored the aesthetic possibilities of industrial landscapes.[55] Later in the century, artistic production in Canada continued to develop its transcontinental ambitions, matching contemporary economic and infrastructural developments. Although Kane and others had led the way, the development of railway communications rendered Canadians more aware of the geographical extent and topographical range of the territories. Several artists associated with the Canadian Pacific Railway sought to supply images emphasising the scenic magnifi-cence of the territory and reflecting the political development of Confederation from 1867, thus unveiling its wonders to settlers and tourists. Sir William Van Horne, the company's chief executive, was a major patron of Canadian art and recognised the value of paintings in advertising. He and other patrons were looking for powerful and 'typical' landscapes conveying the grandeur of the epic of imperial enterprise and its burgeoning economic success. Such images were supplied by the classic painter of the period, Lucius O'Brien, who became the leader of the Canadian art establishment, as well as by John Hammond who was commissioned to travel on the Canadian Pacific Railway to produce magnificent images of the Canadian West for use in company posters. Thus Canadian art seemed to come of age, matched by the foundation of institutions such as the Royal

Canadian Academy of Arts of 1880 (with Lucius O'Brien its first president) and various art galleries, together with artistic training for students. Opportunities for international exhibiting were also expanding. Such growing confidence helped to sharpen the divide between establishment and radical younger painters. If Canadian art had emerged as a major means of projecting the country's grandeur and settler opportunities, it had largely maintained its adherence to a lush romantic conservatism. By the end of the century, however, it was receiving influences from new movements in Europe. In 1893, no fewer than twenty-five Canadian artists were studying in Paris and many came to be influenced by the Barbizon group, stressing ordinary agricultural activities and everyday rural life, as well as by the techniques of impressionism.[56]

Artists in Canada were increasingly concerned to depict its vast spaces, forests and snow-covered landscapes in a particularly effective lean and understated form. Even though the white populations of these territories rapidly became highly urbanised, the physical image presented to the outside world was of huge unpopulated areas, over-whelmingly grand terrains, striking (and romanticised) indigenous peoples, with farming or ranching on a scale unknown at home. In this they were influenced by self-consciously anti-industrial European artistic trends. In addition to the *plein air* Barbizon school, these included impressionism, post-impressionism and rural revivalism. The stress upon ordinary agricultural activities found its Canadian counterpart in the work of Wyatt Eaton and Homer Watson, while impressionism achieved its most distinguished Canadian followers in James Wilson Morris and Maurice Cullen. But the emergence of a genuinely national Canadian school had to wait until 1913 when the celebrated 'Group of Seven' came together in Ontario. Amid contro-versy and conservative criticism they held their first exhibition in 1920 and were well represented at the Wembley Empire Exhibition of 1924–25. This group, sometimes known as the 'Algonquin School' because of their devotion to the landscapes of the great Canadian

Shield, included Tom Thomson, J.E.H. Macdonald and Frederick Varley. Despite Thomson's early death, they became the establishment artists of the 1920s, particularly once their work was praised abroad.[57] In maintaining the landscape tradition in a heavily urbanised country, they combined influences from impressionism and Japanese art. Trees were rendered in spare and symbolic ways and features of the terrain were reduced to their essence. The range of the colour palette contracted to highlight the symbolic character of natural features. Thomson's notably spare painting *The Jack Pine* became an iconic image of Canadian art, a lone tree in a reduced landscape.

Contemporaneously with these artists, Emily Carr was pursuing her interests in the Canadian West. Born in Victoria, British Columbia, she returned to Canada in 1912 after training in France and England. She then set about exploring the possibilities of First Nations communities on the north-west coast, their habitations and their carvings, as well as creating images of towering landscapes and forests.[58] Carr's paintings have been seen as mercifully lacking the air of melancholy, the sense of doom, of earlier art depicting First Nations peoples. Nevertheless, artists had kept alive images of native Canadians and their arts of carving at a time when Canadian legislation often sought to suppress the cultures of indigenous peoples. Such laws failed, only stimulating the survival of cultural forms in hidden and 'underground' ways. Carr's paintings, coming as they do in the twentieth century, present her subjects with the full dignity of triumphant survival. From the time of Carr and her successors it was apparent that art in Canada had become distinctively Canadian, leaving behind its imperial origins.

Australia

Australian art has demonstrated the same obsession with landscape and, to a certain extent, its indigenous peoples. But there is a major difference from the Canadian experience. Thomas Keneally has written that after the Enlightenment fascination with Antipodean exoticism, there developed a powerful sense of rejection of the interior, even a 'self-loathing' for a landscape regarded as an affront to that of the civilised world of Europe.[59] He sees this inferiority complex as having been overcome by the work of Australian artists. It may be that this is a little overdrawn (and the artists' role somewhat exaggerated), but clearly there is an element of truth here. The interior, so extensively made up of desert, was indeed much feared, sometimes known as the 'dead heart'. Any examination of Australian art inevitably moves from that sense of initial, if wary, allure of the coasts through the conscious perception of anxiety about what lay beyond, to the eventual extolling of the unique beauties of the 'outback', with its vast expanses, remorselessly dry character, striking light values, unique vegetation and biological life. Yet one of the iconic images of Australian history carries none of this sense of the environment but rather celebrates the coming of age of the continental (white) nation.

This is the celebrated monumental painting *Opening of the First Parliament of the Commonwealth of Australia by HRH the Duke of Cornwall and York, May 9th 1901* by Tom Roberts. This event took place in the Melbourne Exhibition Hall built in 1880, and is a highly romanticised depiction of the founding of a modern state, complete with 269 actual portraits of people present.[60] It took the artist two years to complete and may well have had a deleterious effect upon his health. A second image of the same event was produced by Charles Nuttall and is generally regarded as being more representational, but more prosaic. Roberts' painting represents a distinctively late depiction of imperial ceremonial, the creation of a new dominion within the British Empire, but it stands at a central point in the chronology of the development of Australian art. The creation of this classic imperial image, albeit a marker on the route to the modern independent multicultural nation, is in a sense ironic since Roberts was an artist in the forefront of creating a new national style, strongly rooted in the environment. Aboriginal people were excluded, indicating the realities of Australian settler cultural and political policies of the day. It was to be some time before Aborigines would be recognised as the true owners of the land, as the living and vibrant demographic and cultural denial of the *terra nullius* theory, and as the progenitors of the truly natural and spiritual art of Australia.[61]

Setting 1901 aside, the major 2013 exhibition of Australian art at the London Royal Academy and the superb catalogue which accompanied it provide a valuable starting point.[62] In addition, there are extensive collections to be seen in the National Gallery of Australia in Canberra and the National Gallery of Victoria in Melbourne, as well as in many regional centres and the capitals of other states. Australian art constitutes a remarkably rich and varied resource, like Canadian art passing through a sequence of phases, from the early colonial era to the time of settler expansion and the eventual discovery of a distinctive national style. Later, Australian art moved into its post-impressionist and modernist phase, becoming more aware of indigenous art and the need for cross-cultural hybrid approaches in the twentieth century. From this point the great antiquity and continuity of Aboriginal artistic traditions were emphasised, revealing the extent to which immigrant, European-style art constituted a notably late arrival.

In the initial stages of settlement in New South Wales painting usually imitated – and sometimes extended – British models. The exotic was often viewed as repellent, such that colonial scenery was rendered in a more familiar, almost English form. The early paintings of the settlements around Sydney (some of them by transported 'convicts' who had some artistic training) tend to be sylvan, gentle affairs, with familiar-looking buildings set into the landscape. Hence from the 1790s, convict and free artists regularly depicted Australia in terms of the sympathetically familiar. Nevertheless, there was also a desire to reveal some of the colony's exotic natural characteristics in trees and vegetation. The forger Thomas Watling arrived in the colony in 1792 and is generally regarded as its first professional artist. He was pardoned in 1797. Initially, the scientific imperative was paramount and Watling, in association with the colony's surgeon general, produced realistic paintings of animals and plants unusual to European eyes. His landscapes, including *Direct North View of Sydney Cove* of 1794 included some exotic trees.[63] Watling was very much aware of indigenous artists and sometimes worked alongside them. His successors were John Eyre (reached Sydney 1801) and Joseph Lycett (1814). Both drew and painted the settlement at Sydney and the surrounding country, providing a valuable historical record and some striking landscapes. Lycett worked both in New South Wales (in Sydney and further north in Newcastle) and Van Diemen's Land (Tasmania), producing portraits and scenes including miniatures of private properties. In 1820 he painted an Aboriginal kangaroo hunt, a striking depiction of indigenous exploitation of animals. Lachlan Macquarie, the influential governor of New South Wales (1809–22), promoted the Georgian style of architecture and the artists painted the grander houses in their almost English parkland.[64] Here, to a certain extent, was a tamed and elegant terrain on the fringes of a vast, unfamiliar and remote continent. Macquarie encouraged Lycett and his pastoral scenes, no doubt confirming the governor's sense of creating an enclave of civilisation on a distant shore.[65] But there continued to be an awareness of earlier artists. William Westall who accompanied Matthew Flinders on his coastal voyages was conscious of Aboriginal rock art and sought to reproduce it.[66]

However, since artists in Australia had no European parallels to draw on, they had to find their own means of representing the strength of southern hemisphere light and the effects of ultra-violet luminosity, strikingly different geologies, unique flora and fauna, and of course very different indigenous peoples. Augustus Earle, who also painted in New Zealand, depicted the encampments of Aborigines, heightening a sense of their supposedly primitive character. In the 1830s, a romantic approach began to be pursued more widely. Robert Dale painted a remarkable watercolour of a panorama of King George's Sound, in the colony of the Swan River, later Western

Australia. Meanwhile, the artist John Glover, who had established a considerable reputation as a watercolourist in England, arrived in Van Diemen's Land in 1831 at the age of 64 and quickly established himself as one of the founders of Australian landscape painting. Initially living in Hobart, he painted there before moving to a property on the Mills plains where he painted his own residence and garden together with surrounding scenery, exhibiting striking clarity of both light and colour. In 1832 he painted an indigenous corroboree and various other images of indigenous Tasmanians, who were subjected to considerable violence and ethnic genocide. The military amateur artist Godfrey Mundy's *Mounted Police and Blacks* provides an apparently honest depiction of such violence. According to Lydon:

> Mundy's image was a stereotype of frontier conflict widely reproduced across the nineteenth century in imperial print culture, and specifically the visual economy formed by the engravings reproduced within illustrated newspapers, periodicals and books. In the fixity and repetition of such scenes we see a fundamental device in colonial visual culture, seeking to show Aboriginal people as less than human, subordinate to British military prowess.[67]

This would be equally true of many other non-European peoples caught up in the empire.

In contrast with Glover's fascination with the rural, S.T. Gill arrived in Adelaide in 1839 and became the artist of early city life.[68] He painted buildings in Adelaide and Melbourne and by the early 1850s was illustrating social and working life on the Victoria gold diggings. Never seeking to romanticise, he depicted the hopes, drudgery and disillusion of gold seekers (see Plate 18). He was an artist of the people, distinctively basic and raw, presenting a lust for living and a humour typical of the riotous lives of the diggers in a manner later recognised as typically Australian. His lifestyle of heavy drinking and gambling limited his artistic output. Yet, although

Bernard Smith saw Gill as every bit as Australian as the Heidelberg School (see later in this chapter), he was little known when he died in 1880, his qualities only fully recognised in the twentieth century.[69] Interestingly, he introduced photography into his work, owning a daguerreotype camera which he sold to Robert Hall, one of Australia's earliest commercial photographers.[70] By the time he was working, artists from other European traditions were arriving to make their mark upon landscape painting and portrayals of the major home-steads already appearing in the various colonies.

In Australian landscape art representational problems were posed by the vegetation as well as the contrasting colours of downs, desert, rocks and the dry climate. The Aboriginal technique of firing the bush to encourage new growth also became a pictorial fascination. These topographical and meteorological challenges produced strug-gles between realistic representation and efforts to concentrate essences in colour and symbolic form, the latter phase influenced by French and Japanese art. However, while solutions to these environ-mental problems were being sought by artists, the gold strikes of the 1850s and after not only created a new interest in the developmental processes of resource extraction, as with Gill, but also brought in more migrants, many with cosmopolitan origins in Europe and China. These events elicited examples of socially realistic art even as Australian settlers rapidly became urbanised. But the artistic obses-sion with landscape remained more important than the recognition of urban, industrial, economic and social realities. Although there were some examples of artists working in urban contexts, by and large art with grittier content had to wait until the inter-war years and the post-Second World War period. But the search for a rural idyll seldom produced calming relations among artists: they became embroiled in considerable controversies about the appropriate ways of depicting their environments.

Art aspired to be truly Australian only when it was influenced by a group of painters who had been trained abroad. In the late 1880s and

1890s Tom Roberts, Frederick McCubbin, Arthur Streeton and Charles Conder established the Heidelberg School on the outskirts of Melbourne. They introduced *plein air* and impressionist principles and set about emphasising the dignity of the lives of ordinary people while shifting towards the higher, brighter tones of the powerful Antipodean light. The eucalyptus or gum tree, which had posed major problems of design and colouring, was now rendered in more satisfactory ways by the German Hans Heysen and the 'sparkling impressionist landscapes' of Frederick McCubbin.[71] (McCubbin also painted settler life and urban scenes.) With their work an Australian national school with a recognisably appropriate and distinctive landscape style came of age, though, particularly in the hands of Streeton, it ran the danger of becoming over-formulaic, a tired repetition of a successful recipe. Antipodean art found more successful nationalist vehicles when it set out to blend the starkly opalescent hues of its environment with the rediscovery of indigenous art. Women artists had already established themselves, but they became even more significant in the inter-war years. One of the leading post-impressionists was Grace Cossington Smith, while Jessie Traill was a notable printmaker. Soon, a new school, of whom Sir Sidney Nolan is the best known, set about juxtaposing symbols of European material life with local scenes and indigenous motifs, mostly conveyed in the shrill colours of the Australian interior. Painters were now actively resisting colonial conventions. Nolan did this through his sequence of paintings of the Ned Kelly legend. The art of Australia had shaken off its imperial origins and adopted a largely distinctive and unique national style. The days of the patronising view that colonial art had to be stimulated by displays of paintings from the metropole, still current in 1887 for example, were over.[72]

New Zealand

The original depictions of New Zealand botany and terrain date from the Cook voyages, with work by Sydney Parkinson (1769), William

Hodges, and John Webber.[73] As *pakeha* (white) settlers arrived in the 1830s and 1840s, artists remained fascinated by landscape, exotic flora, and above all the Maori. A rapid shift took place from ordered Enlightenment visions towards a more romantic style. In later decades discovery in art marched hand in hand with economic, topographical and ethnographic surveys, images to encourage settlement.

In the imperial hierarchy of indigenous peoples of the period, the Maori occupied a position seen as superior to many African peoples and to Australian Aborigines. This was symbolised by the 1840 Waitangi Treaty, although the Maori were also victims of colonial violence and acts of dispossession of land and culture. Nevertheless, Maori status is well represented in the paintings of Augustus Earle, who travelled extensively throughout the world (see Plate 19). Arriving in New Zealand in 1827, he idealised the Maori physique, drawing inspiration from classical precedents and romantic visions of people in landscape. In 1832, he published a book about his experiences.[74] He thought Maori warriors were 'exceedingly handsome' and athletic, contrasting with the 'savagery' of their society in taking and mistreating slaves.[75] George Angas and William Strutt, who both visited and painted in South Africa and Australia, also romanticised the Maori, documenting their fortifications, carvings, customs and daily life in infinite detail.[76] Their art did little to reveal the social and economic reality of Maori life.[77] Admiration for the Maori was continued by Gottfried Lindauer who arrived in New Zealand in 1874, producing portraits of the Maori of 'stunning realism', respectfully revealing their dignity.[78] His paintings were particularly valued at the peak of late romantic idealism in the early twentieth century.

But art in New Zealand also took more practical forms in the work of surveyors such as Charles Heaphy and Edward Ashworth in the 1840s. Both employed by the New Zealand Company, they painted watercolours as practical aids to surveys of economic resources, propaganda for settlement, all reflecting fascination with landscape. Ashworth had trained as an architect and painted buildings in

Auckland, the capital from 1843 to 1860. As elsewhere, military officers constituted another group interested in art and their numbers were swollen by the wars against the Maori, when topographical understanding helped combat operations. But it was gold that galvanised the economy and the rate of settlement. Gold strikes in 1861 quickly introduced artists to interior landscapes, to fresh social contexts, and to characteristic colonial 'types', diggers and other inhabitants of gold-rush townships. The Otago diggings in the interior of the South Island drew painters towards the spectacular West Coast. The obsession with stunning scenery was exemplified by artists like John Buchanan and William Hodgkins, who joined the circle of artists gathering in Dunedin. Buchanan's painting *Milford Sound, looking north-west from Freshwater Basin* of 1863 is often seen as an early masterpiece. New Zealand's inland agricultural and stock-rearing potential promoted interest in pastoral scenes. But New Zealand landscape, according to Hodgkins in a lecture to the Otago Institute in 1880, presented a problem in that distinguishing the colony's unique character was hindered by notions that it was supposedly reminiscent of Scotland, Switzerland, Norway and California.[79] Such allusions were emphasised by the naming of the Southern Alps and the acclimatisation of so many plants and animals from Europe. Landscape artists had to create something distinctive to escape the tyranny of the comparative.

Landscapes of orange browns, dark foliage and vast bright skies were produced by John Gully, John Hoyte and Hodgkins himself, New Zealand artistic counterparts of the Canadian O'Brien. Hodgkins was familiar with the work of J.M.W. Turner and had read Ruskin's *Modern Painters*. It has been suggested that Gully, despite his technical expertise, worked to an established formula and was not particularly inventive.[80] By the 1880s, the institutional apparatus of New Zealand art was firmly in place. Dunedin was the main driver. After the 1865 exhibition's fine arts section, Hodgkins organised an exhibition to coincide with the visit of the Duke of Edinburgh in

1869, the first royal tour to the country. The Dunedin School of Art, the first in New Zealand, was founded in 1870; the Otago Art Society followed in 1875; and the first Dunedin public gallery opened in 1884. Similar developments occurred in the other three major centres: Auckland, where the Society of Artists was founded in 1869 and Christchurch, with the Canterbury College of Art established in 1881. The New Zealand Academy of Fine Arts appeared in Wellington in 1882 followed by the Wellington Art Club in 1892.[81] The supporting art apparatus was thus firmly in place.[82]

It was perhaps this growing evidence of sophistication which attracted three notable artists: Petrus van der Velden (from the Netherlands in 1890), James Nairn (from Scotland also 1890) and G.P. Nerli (from Italy, who was intermittently in New Zealand from 1889 to 1898). They settled in Christchurch, Wellington and Dunedin respectively and between them taught the next generation of painters.[83] Nairn, who had been associated with the celebrated group the Glasgow boys, worked in oils and was highly influential in introducing aspects of impressionism. European influences were quickly transformed by the local environment. Later in the century Thomas Ryan was beginning to move towards a new vision, still of dramatic natural power, but with more glowing colours, while in the early twentieth century Margaret Stoddart and Alfred Walsh focused on more closely observed, clearer and brighter images that finally broke free of Victorian conventions. New Zealand landscape painting came to reflect not just the brightness of light but its translucence. Frances Hodgkins, pupil of Nerli and daughter of William, is often seen as the first great colonial-born New Zealand artist. She was trained in Europe and lived there for lengthy periods later introducing a succession of modern movements (such as Cubism) to the colony's art. Her sister Isabel may have been equally important. They mark a significant tradition of female painters working in New Zealand landscape art, including Dorothy Richmond, Margaret Stoddart and Rita Angus. The contrast in approaches is beautifully represented by comparing two paintings, first *Dunedin from the Junction* of 1869 by George O'Brien, who was a surveyor and architect. A perfect piece of topographical reproduction, accurate in every detail, this work is now greatly appreciated, though initially rejected. On the other hand, Rita Angus's *Central Otago* (1954–56) uses a Chinese technique of creating a 'composite landscape' by building different elements on top of each other in a non-natural conjunction.[84] Painters have continued to produce poetic interpretations of New Zealand scenery, sometimes (as in work by Robin White and Colin McCahon) in intriguingly spare and angular ways. The twentieth century also saw the major rediscovery of Maori artistic and design traditions, not least in their approach to architecture and crafts. As elsewhere, New Zealand art then moved from the imperial to the national phase. Parallel with Sidney Nolan's reinvocation of the Ned Kelly legend, the New Zealand artist Trevor Moffitt took up the story of James McKenzie, notorious nineteenth-century sheep-stealer, for a series of 'ballad' paintings. Here was a story from New Zealand's past which could be given a fresh legendary twist.[85]

South Africa

The artistic tradition in South Africa was the latest to emerge and remained the most conservative.[86] While the emphasis was again upon landscape, it took some time for major European movements to have any influence. Impressionism, for example, did not arrive until the 1920s and various streams of modernism not until the 1940s. Nevertheless, the prime focus of South African art was to render the essence of its landscape and meteorology, indigenous peoples, botany and zoology, in terms of its unique character and distinctive values of light and colour. Botanical and zoological drawings and paintings were produced by some of the travellers into the interior in the early nineteenth century, of whom the most effective was perhaps Samuel Daniell, another nephew of Thomas and brother of William, who reached the Cape in 1799 and was artist to expeditions to Bechuanaland.[87] He became noted for the publication of aquatints of southern African people and animals, including Khoisan and their villages, as well as Trekboers and their encampments.[88] But the most important explorer/artist was Thomas Baines, active between 1842 and his death in Durban in 1875 (see Plate 20).[89] In 1846 he painted aspects of the Cape frontier campaign known as the 7th Kaffir War, while in 1854 he was appointed artist to Augustus Gregory's expedition to northern Australia and developed further his feel for the colouring of exotic landscapes. Best known for his work on Livingstone's Zambezi expedition from 1858, Baines was also a prospector, geologist, writer and cartographer. He explored the southern African interior, including the region of Zimbabwe, and painted Africans and their material culture (such as musical instruments) as well as plants and animals.[90] Grand landscapes appealed to him and he both wrote lyrically about and painted dramatic perspectives of the Victoria Falls (the first artist to do so). George French Angas, better known for his work in Australia and New Zealand, also visited South Africa. He travelled to Zululand, painting both the Zulu people, so celebrated in Victorian times, and their environment. The artistic connection between Australasia and South Africa reflects inter-colonial influences.

The first South African artist of distinction was Hugo Naudé, who was trained in London and Munich and produced significant portraits and landscapes. Working from his home in Worcester in the Cape, he painted a mountainous terrain alive with bright colours of spring flowers. Later his work became simpler and highly spontaneous, though always infused with sun-drenched colour. While he occasionally painted semi-urban sights, such as his *Malay Quarter* and African portraits such as *The Washerwoman*, his work contains none of the racial or social realities of South Africa of the period. Although Naudé painted at a time when impressionist influences were sweeping art in Canada and Australia, he never fully adopted their techniques. Other artists who adapted aspects of impressionism without fully surrendering to it were the Dutch immigrant Pieter Wenning and Hendrik Pierneef. Wenning's work was small scale, intimate and highly evocative, and was the first to inspire a South African school of painting. His work became extremely popular after his early death in 1921. Pierneef was devoted to discovering the essence of South African topography with its striking trees, notably the baobab. Paradoxically, his reputation was eventually made by the grander murals he created for South Africa House in London and the main Johannesburg railway station.[91]

In the twentieth century, Constance Greaves became celebrated for her countless 'native studies'. Strat Caldecott introduced a full-blown impressionist style in the 1920s while Maggie Laubser and Irma Stern brought German expressionism to South Africa. Erik Laubscher adopted modernist approaches to landscape while suburban subjects were portrayed by Gregoire Boonzaier. But the emergence of modern styles had to weather some local support for Hitler's attack on 'decadence' in art, and South African conservatism is neatly epitomised by the acclaimed paintings of Tinus de Jongh depicting South African landscapes in a sumptuous Amsterdam style continuing well into the twentieth century. But later South African art caught up, if in radically different ways, with developments in other former Dominions.

Dominion art and international perspectives

Colonial artists never worked in a vacuum, securing a wider audience through international exhibitions. As early as 1855, artists who had worked in Australia, George French Angas, Conrad Martens, Frederick Terry and Adelaide Ironside, were featured at the Paris Exposition. Some colonial art appeared at the great exhibition in London in 1862. Other artists were exhibited at the Paris Exposition of 1867 and (in large numbers) at the 1886 Colonial and Indian Exhibition in London. At the latter, Canadian painters, depicting topographical grandeur and romantic indigenous peoples, aroused particular interest.[92] Canadian paintings were featured at American exhibitions including Philadelphia (1876), Chicago (1893) and

Buffalo (1901). Images of New Zealand Maoris also created a considerable sensation. The largest collection of colonial paintings appeared at the Wembley Exhibition of 1924–25 when major disputes between conservatives and radicals, traditionalists and 'modernists' came to a head. In the case of Canada, the split was between the somewhat traditional Royal Canadian Academy and the more adventurous National Gallery (both founded in 1880). The latter was successful in ensuring that the Group of Seven were represented while, for Australia, the Heidelberg School exhibited. New Zealand was seen as not yet possessing a truly national style.[93] Nevertheless, the publicity in 1924 ran along traditional lines, colonial paintings viewed as products of 'Daughter Nations' developing from 'the English school'. Although the text of the catalogue suggested that the paintings proved the triumph of imperial dispersal, the exhibition shows enabled artists of the Dominions to interact with each other in the development of national styles. Moreover, metropolitan critics often expressed more favourable views than counterparts in the colonial press. By 1924 dominions art was beginning to reach maturity. It is perhaps ironic that in the same year a survey of imperial art was published which interpreted the visual arts in purely utilitarian and patriotic ways. A chapter on 'The art of the Empire' reflected on the advertising of shipping and railway companies and concluded that: 'our Colonial artists are doing an immense service to the Empire by slowly developing, on sane and uplifting lines, the art of each part of our Dominions, Colonies and Dependencies. . . . This is their contribution towards the encouragement of colonisation.'[94] This survey saw the prime function of colonial artists as the issuing of propaganda for settlement, thereby extending the sense of imperial community in both demographic and cultural terms. Conservative attitudes were thus part of the publicity of 1924, when the transition from imperial to national art was well advanced with impressionism and post-impressionism finding adherents and adaptations to local conditions in Canada, Australasia and South Africa.

As wider modernist global fashions took hold, as well as remarkable exercises in cultural syncretism, the older traditions of imperial art, and its objectives of power, were clearly dying, though art was still being marshalled for imperial economic propaganda. This representational art, though often with a modern twist, was the product of the Empire Marketing Board created in 1926 to persuade the British public to buy empire products. This was designed to create a mutually beneficial imperial economic community to ward off the cyclical turns of the world economy, particularly after the Wall Street crash of 1929 and ensuing depression. A major poster campaign, directed by Frank Pick, celebrated for his London Underground posters, harnessed a number of artists, including Charles Pears, Frank Newbould, Austin Cooper, MacDonald Gill, Clare Leighton and McKnight Kauffer. They produced strikingly bold images of agricultural, stock-rearing and mining production in many colonies.[95] The campaign fell short of the ambitions of its founders, but a remarkable collection of poster art was created redolent of contemporary attitudes to empire and indigenous workers, who can be seen labouring in a Sudan cotton field, on a Nyasaland tobacco farm, in a manganese ore mine, at a Ceylonese tea garden or on docksides loading ships. White people appear in a supervisory capacity, often smoking pipes. Art thus reflected imperial realities in this depiction of economic endeavour. Additional posters were produced by shipping lines and by the General Post Office. One of the latter series, designed by John Vickery in 1937, displayed the diversity of ethnicity and transport systems of postmen delivering mail in several colonies.

The resurgence of indigenous art

It was always rightly said that the British were never successful in introducing the metropolitan population to the arts and cultures of indigenous peoples of empire, unlike the more sympathetic French.[96] Nevertheless, dominion artists searching for uniquely nationalist forms began to draw upon the motifs, pigments and abstract spiritual concepts of indigenous art. By the middle of the twentieth century, this fusing of local symbols with European techniques had become standard throughout the territories of white settlement. Yet it represented an attempt to create a syncretic art which, in different forms, already had a long tradition within the British Empire, a tradition which had been initiated by the so-called native peoples of empire themselves. In the eighteenth century, Indian artists created works which attempted to adapt western perspective and subject matter to the conventions and colour schemes of Mughal and other local art.[97] Artists working in a number of Indian cities over many years produced paintings for European clients, now recognised as a major school. Parallel movements developed in Burma (Myanmar), Ceylon (Sri Lanka) and the Chinese ports.

In the nineteenth century, Indian artists increasingly tried to emulate European art, though in distinctive ways, particularly after western-style art schools were founded in the principal cities.[98] This culminated in the work of the South Indian 'Orientalist' Ravi Varma whose paintings achieved great popularity, extolled as matching western style. By the time Varma died in 1906, however, many rejected what they regarded as a slavish attachment to European models. The resurgence of a distinctively Indian art became an essential component of the 'swadeshi' or boycott movement of Indian nationalism. Indian magazines and art journals were founded to discuss this development, which started with a fresh appreciation of Indian crafts initially stimulated by British commentators such as Sir George Birdwood and John Lockwood Kipling.[99] E.B. Havell, Superintendent of the Madras School of Industrial Arts 1884–92 and Keeper of the Calcutta School of Art 1896–1906, became a notable proponent of Indian fine arts. A.K. Coomeraswamy did the same for Sinhalese art, seeking out the medieval roots of a non-materialist and mystical vision, the special characteristic of the East.

While Bombay painters tended to continue to aspire to a western realistic tradition, artists in the Punjab (led by M.A. Rahman Chughtai) and Bengal adopted a new nationalist course. The great Bengali philosopher and poet Rabindranath Tagore was himself an artist, a talented amateur who expressed the timeless spiritual depths of India, seeking to distil the essence below surface reality. His nephew Abanindranath Tagore was a founder of a new Calcutta school and influenced an entire generation of painters. They returned to the fundamentals of Indian design, historical and spiritual life. No fewer than fifty-six of their paintings were exhibited at Wembley in 1924 and by then a fully fledged Indian nationalist tradition had emerged, led by such figures as Jamini Roy and Nandalal Bose. Western artists and critics like William Rothenstein, Roger Fry and Eric Gill, influenced by Coomeraswamy, came to appreciate Indian art and sought to employ some of its techniques.[100] This revaluation by western art critics served to overturn the earlier tradition of high regard for Indian crafts contrasting with a less favourable view of Indian art.[101]

While Indians thus had a long and diverse tradition of creating a fusion between European and Indian arts, indigenous arts elsewhere moved from the concern of anthropologists into the artistic mainstream.[102] The long and manifold traditions of indigenous art in Canada emerged as the truly characteristic national form. Artists of European settler ethnicity were quick to recognise this and adopted motifs and techniques from indigenous colleagues. The tradition of intricate Inuit carving on stone, bone, ivory and antler, often as decoration on practical objects, was of long-standing and such items had been bartered with whalers. Inuit even began to produce items specifically for this trade. Carvings of animals and hunting scenes came to be appreciated by western artists and motifs were imitated and adapted. From the 1940s, various Arctic Inuit developed new and flourishing traditions of sculpture, drawing and printmaking, with notable examples entering the National Gallery of Canada.[103] In the case of other First Nations, museums had been gathering totem poles and other wooden sculptures from the early days, but for ethnographic galleries rather than assemblages of supposedly canonical art.[104] In modern times a notable revival of First Nations carving has contributed to the re-creation of 'totem poles' in British Columbia.[105] Carving is important in many indigenous cultures and artists from Anglophone and Francophone traditions now often create a distinctively hybrid Canadian art by reconciling aspects of the European and local. First Nations carving and artistic motifs have entered the mainstream and indigenous artists have rediscovered creative pride and dignity, while artists from western traditions have come to see such arts with fresh eyes.

This development is paralleled throughout the former territories of settlement. In Australia, Aboriginal art remains a living tradition of an antiquity now regarded with considerable awe. Its role in Aboriginal 'Dreaming' and ceremony constitutes a continuous living tradition, handsomely acknowledged in the catalogue of the Royal Academy 2013 exhibition.[106] Today Aboriginal painters still decorate rocks with modern versions of the art of ancestors. Others transfer Aboriginal designs to various fabrics, securing eager customers. In the twentieth century, Aboriginal and western arts established a confluence through interests in abstraction and geometrical designs. Yet different indigenous artistic traditions sent the arts of former settler territories into diverging streams. In Aotearoa (Maori: 'Land of the Long White Cloud', symbolic of awareness of the country's environment and meteorology), magnificent carvings of Maori canoes or gloriously decorated churches produced by Maori builders and artists in the mid-nineteenth century (the best example at Otaki created 1851) have been revalued. Meeting houses and other examples of Maori carving, collected by New Zealand museums as ethnographic curiosities, took on a new role as long-standing traditions representing the artistic essence of the country. At the end of the nineteenth century, Maori legends were collected by Jessie MacKay and European painters started to respond to Maori material culture. In modern times New Zealand art has been fusing international movements with Maori motifs.

In South Africa the great tradition of San (Bushman) rock painting remained principally the concern of archaeologists until well into the twentieth century.[107] It was however rediscovered in the inter-war years by Walter Battiss for whom it became something of an obsession.[108] Battiss had already begun his career as an abstract painter in the 1920s, but rock art helped to develop his style. Large numbers of his paintings constitute an imaginative re-evocation of San art, and the pigments, figures and motifs of rock art were brought together in fresh conjunctions with modern meanings. Soon African artists were beginning to be accepted and encouraged on their own terms. A Pedi artist from northern Gauteng (former Transvaal), Gerard Sekoto, was exhibiting in the 1930s and went to Paris for further study. By the 1950s an entire school of painting had emerged in Johannesburg associated with the Polly Street Art Centre. A tradition known as 'township art' developed, creating new contexts for African designs and ways of looking at the world, sometimes influenced by social and economic realities of the urban setting. A similar movement occurred in Salisbury (Harare) where a school of African artists and sculptors achieved international significance through the association of their work with reinterpretations of Cubist and expressionist models. Africans were thus feeding into European traditions new insights derived from the long-standing abstract core of African art. Moreover, apartheid in South Africa stimulated the art of resistance, which in turn fed into the post-apartheid art of today. The visual arts have also been involved in refocusing the historical memory, reorientating public culture and debates about the past.[109] These developments in southern Africa were long preceded by a renewed interest in African art by western artists in the early twentieth century. Post-impressionists like Georges Braque and Pablo Picasso became enthralled by the representational, geometric and spiritual character of the African mask and sought to incorporate some of its characteristics. Great examples of African sculpture and metal work, often looted in colonial campaigns and then relegated to western museum 'ethnographic' collections, came to have new significance for western art trying to escape from its realistic cul-de-sac.[110] Nevertheless, although forms of western representational art, albeit in highly modernist idioms, have survived both in Europe and the former British Empire, imperial art had come full circle. Artists had struggled to depict the exotic in a variety of different techniques and styles, but once overtaken by newer technologies like photography, supposedly offering more realistic representations, they discovered that the best way of creating a new art was in fusing with the formerly discounted arts of indigenous peoples. Such a fusion offered opportunities to reject the arts of empire altogether, creating new traditions from the wreck of attempts at forms of imperial unity. In South Africa, this revolutionary sense was galvanised by political repression and, later, revolution.

In India and Africa the rediscovery of the wellsprings and integrity of native art forms constituted a vital part of political re-awakening. Such artistic developments have in some cases heightened political controversy and the deep sense of resentment on the part of indigenous peoples for the loss of land rights and other colonial acts of exploitation. But a fresh appreciation of their arts has undoubtedly helped in major re-orderings of cultural priorities, including approaches to museum and gallery display. The old distinctions between the supposed European mainstream and 'ethnographic' traditions have been broken down. Significantly, indigenous peoples were pulled into the wider audience with the realisation that their arts, a continuing part of their lives throughout, were a key component in the creation of distinctive national cultures emerging from the break-up of empire. If pictorial art had contributed to a sense of pride in empire for the dominant people, it now joined with other cultural forms, including crafts, music and dance, to play a key role in the creation of national ideologies in a modern multicultural world. Art as a significant cultural factor in the history of the British Empire has been ignored for a long time, both because it did not fit the dominant political/economic paradigm and because work on art history in each territory was largely overlooked by more generalist imperial or even art historians until relatively recent times. Now it is apparent that the art histories of the different components of empire can be brought together into an overall model of convergence and divergence, reflecting contemporary political, economic, social, cultural and intellectual developments between the eighteenth and twentieth centuries.[111]

1. Algernon Talmage R.A., *The Founding of Australia by Capt. Arthur Phillip R.N., Sydney Cove, Jan. 26th, 1788.* This reveals the twentieth-century fascination with mythic moments in settler history, creating images of a legendary past to help justify the present.

2. Ceremony of swearing fidelity to the British government at the Court of Select Audience of the Asante Kingdom of West Africa, later Ghana; illustration published in 1824: the British representative sits to the left of the platform.

3. Roderick Dempster MacKenzie, *The State Entry into Delhi*, at the Durbar 1903. MacKenzie was a British artist who spent many years in the United States. He was commissioned by the Viceroy Lord Curzon to paint events at the Durbar.

4. Frederick Christian Lewis, *Darbar at Udaipur, Rajasthan, 1855*. The Maharana of Udaipur receives the British representatives led by Colonel Henry Lawrence.

5. King George and Queen Mary showing themselves to the multitude, the Delhi Durbar 1911. The newly crowned emperor and empress on the ramparts of the Red Fort in Delhi with young Indian princes in attendance. Published as a postcard.

6. Justinian Gantz, *The Ootacamund Hunt Meeting at Mr. Chalmers' House at Gindy, Madras, 1845. The Jackal Pack.* 'Ooty' in the Nilgiri hills became famous for hunting, but here the hunt had come down to Madras in pursuit of jackals.

7. Adelaide Hunt Club meeting at 'The Brocas', Woodville, Adelaide, 15 August 1870. 'The Brocas' was one of the grand country houses of Adelaide, built in 1840.

8. Thomas Daniell R.A., 'The Assembly Rooms on the Race Ground, Near Madras' in the 1790s. Racing in India quickly became a significant means of socialising for the British.

9. The 12th Bengal Cavalry polo team, winners of the Peshawar Tournament 1898. The team here included an Indian, Jemadar Futteh Khan. Polo became a significant setting for mixing British and elite Indians.

By permission of Messrs. E. Hawkins & Co., Brighton.

New Song.

WORDS AND MUSIC BY ——

C. T. West.

2/- Net.

10. Song sheet 'Ranji' (1896), dedicated by special permission to H.H. Prince Ranjitsinhji (H.H. Jam Saheb Shri Sir Ranjitsinhji Vibhaji of Nawanagar). Words and music by C.T. West. This was indicative of the considerable popularity of the princely Indian cricketer.

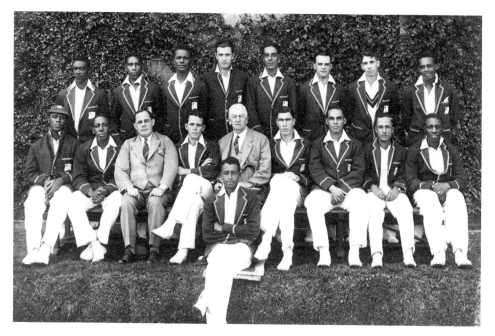

11. West Indies cricket team, Australian tour 1930–31 (photographed 1930). Although this was a mixed-race team, the management was strictly European. The first Black captain for an entire test series was not appointed until 1960.

12. Melbourne cricket ground on 1 January 1864. The popularity of cricket is well demonstrated by the extensive settler audience, including spectators in the trees.

13. Hockey team of the 4th Battalion, 1st Punjab Regiment, 1923. The team included Dhyan Chand who became a major hockey hero in India and captained the team that won the gold medal in the Berlin Olympics of 1936.

14. Football team of conscripted African drivers serving with the King's African Rifles, Kenya, 1939. Football was to become the most popular sport in Africa.

15. Edward Lear, *Kangchenjunga from Darjeeling.* The painting reveals Lear's Romantic enthusiasm for mountain scenery, the trees of India, and brightly dressed local people. Lear visited India between 1873 and 1875 at the invitation of the Viceroy Lord Northbrook.

16. Cornelius Krieghoff, *Settler's Log House*, 1856.
This painting illustrates artists' fascination with the climate of Canada and the rugged conditions experienced by the settlers.

17. Paul Kane, *Indian Encampment on Lake Huron*, 1848–50.
Kane was an Irish-born artist who was particularly enthralled by the
First Nations people of Canada. He often subordinated accuracy
to his search for the dramatic picturesque in his paintings.

18. Samuel Thomas Gill, *A Bendigo Mill 1852*.
The 'mill' apparently refers to a fight among prospectors engaged
in the gold rush in the colony of Victoria, Australia.

19. Augustus Earle, 'War Speech'. In *Sketches illustrative of the Native Inhabitants and Islands of New Zealand from original drawings by Augustus Earle Esq, Draughtsman of HMS Beagle*. This painting was lithographed and published in 1838 'under the auspices of the New Zealand Association' shortly before the annexation of New Zealand by Britain in 1840.

20. Thomas Baines, *Wagon Crossing a Drift, Natal*, 1874. This painting illustrates the characteristic ox-drawn wagon (here with a team of a dozen oxen) which was the principal mode of settler transport in the pre-railway age.

21. Lt Humphrey John Julian, *The Admiral's House, Simon's Town, Cape of Good Hope, 1844.* The Cape Station at Simon's Town on False Bay became an important British naval base for the Indian Ocean and South Atlantic.

22. Memorial to Capt. George Nicholas Hardinge R.N. by John Bacon the younger, St Thomas's Anglican (now Church of North India) Cathedral, Mumbai (Bombay). This memorial by a leading London sculptor indicates the extensive imperial trade in such monuments and their considerable quality to be found in Indian cathedrals.

23. National Women's Memorial (Nasionale Vrouemonument), Bloemfontein, South Africa. This monument, by the Pretoria architect Frans Soff and sculptor Anton van Wouw, commemorates some 27,000 women and children who died in British concentration camps during the Second Anglo-Boer War. It was unveiled in 1913.

24. Statue of King Emperor George V and obelisk marking the focus of the 1911 Coronation Durbar, Coronation Park, Delhi. This statue, originally in a central point in New Delhi, was relegated to the park on the edge of the city.

25. Bourne and Shepherd photographers at the Delhi Durbar, 1902–3. The Durbar marshalled all the media of the age. Here the photographers of the celebrated firm of Bourne and Shepherd, which had various studios in British India, are shown in their camp.

26. This newspaper photograph shows the large crowd which assembled outside the *Cape Times* office, Cape Town, on hearing news of the relief of Kimberley (11–15 February 1900).

27. 'Egypt in 1882 … introducing the Bombardment of Alexandria …', Canterbury Theatre of Varieties, Westminster Bridge Road, London. This poster from 1883 demonstrates the manner in which contemporary imperial events were featured in popular entertainment forms.

28. Robert Melville Grindlay, 'Scene in Bombay', 1826. The buildings around central Bombay Green are the office of the governor's secretary, the Court of Appeal, with the prominent theatre on the right.

29. Capt. George Francklin Atkinson, lithographed by R.M. Bryson, 'Amateur theatricals on a British station – preparing for a performance by lacing up corsets, applying make–up etc.', from *Curry and Rice*, 1860, a satirical image of British social life in India.

30. A publicity poster for the Argyle Theatre of Varieties, Birkenhead, week commencing 29 January 1912, advertising the showing of the innovative Kinemacolor pictures. This reveals the entertainment potential of the tour of the King and Queen in India for the Durbar of 1911.

31. 'How London sees the Durbar day-by-day', Hippodrome Theatre, London, from *Black and White* magazine, January 1903. Drawing by Joseph Finnemore. A well-dressed audience in the theatre watches film of the Durbar shortly after the event.

32. The Colonial Film Unit on location, West Africa, 1946. The production of colonial films for purposes of health and social instruction of Africans, as shown here by the presence of mothers and babies, resumed after the Second World War.

5
STATUARY AND SCULPTURE

C. RUDD'S NEW VIEWS OF MELBOURNE.

THE MEMORIAL STATUE OF GENERAL GORDON.—Ceremony of Unveiling by Sir Wm. Robinson (Acting-Governor), June 26, 1889.
[*Instantaneous.*]

Unveiling of the statue of General Charles Gordon by Acting Governor Sir William Robinson, Melbourne, Australia, 26 June 1889.

Apart from buildings, the most visible of the arts of empire was perhaps statuary and other forms of sculpture, readily displayed in streets, squares, parks and other public places, sometimes on and within buildings. Such sculpture has been seen as the preferred art of empire, based on the growing cult of memorials in Westminster Abbey and cathedrals, on the appearance of statues in squares and streets of London and other cities. Key buildings in London were duly adorned with figures associated with exploration and empire: the Foreign Office façade in Whitehall has busts of Cook, Drake, Franklin, Livingstone and (for humanitarianism) Wilberforce, while the Royal Geographical Society concentrates on Livingstone and Shackleton. Statues of imperial heroes, explorers and military figures can be found in most British cities, for example Glasgow.[1] This fascination with statuary and memorials duly swept both the British and other empires.[2] In visualising individuals (usually in a heroic or idealised manner), statues encapsulate in a very solid form the ideology of an age. They constitute what has been described as 'the state's memory of itself', a heightened phenomenon in an imperial setting.[3] Like ceremonial, they were highly masculinist in terms of subjects, with the obvious exception of Queen Victoria and the female personifications of the alleged qualities of justice and authority. Women were usually commemorated only in death, in imperial graveyards where they often received highly sentimentalised memorials. Statues can be interpreted as conscious constructions of the language of power, transforming the city into an imperial text. They also symbolise dominance and exclusion, the marginalisation of indigenous peoples and minorities.[4] Emblematic of the state's authority, they inevitably became objects of attack when such power waned. They are additionally representative of an aesthetic tradition in a long tradition of sculptural fine arts reaching back into the Ancient world.[5] Yet, paradoxically these plastic arts were often little noticed. They become part of an urban landscape that is both there and not there. Few people had much interest in their aesthetic characteristics – or the lack of them – and even fewer paused to read the plinths. Ironically, their significance was only fully recognised at the point at which they were unveiled or inaugurated and again at the end of empire when they invariably became symbolic of a dying and rejected ideology representing an unacceptable regime.[6] The latter reaction was mainly restricted to India and the dependent empire, although there were also outbreaks of hostility to some statues within Britain itself.[7]

Sculptural arts in the empire

There was undoubtedly an elite fascination with sculptural arts throughout the British Empire, perhaps filtering down to other white sojourners or settlers. This occurred whether statues were in stone or cast in bronze, whether free-standing or part of architectural compositions. In India, we can go further and describe it as a positive mania, a passion which in many places infected elite Indians – wealthy entrepreneurs in the cities and the rulers of princely states – as well as the British. Occasionally, a writer in the 'native' Indian press took notice and ridiculed it. There is an excellent example from 1893 when riots broke out in Bombay and a particularly unsympathetic governor, Lord Harris, whose principal passion in life was cricket, scarcely took any notice and remained in his residence at Poona (Pune). A journal in the town of Satara, inland from Bombay commented that: 'As for Lord Harris, he appears to be an inert marble statue with stuffed ears, holding in his hands a bat and ball.'[8] A statue thus became a symbol of indolence. Indians now embarked on an era of resistance to imperial statuary and it ceased to be easy for the British to commemorate their governors. In 1918, a proposal to erect a memorial to Lord Willingdon after he had ceased to be governor of Bombay met with nationalist resistance from both Hindus and Muslims, though loyal Parsis supported the idea.[9] Willingdon was later governor of Madras and governor general of India, and his statue in the latter role has now been removed from its central position in Delhi. Nationalists were already engaged in projects to erect memorials to their leaders, for example to the liberal constitutionalist Gopal Krishna Gokhale, who died in 1915.[10]

There seems to be a number of reasons for this extraordinarily prolific cultural phenomenon. The eighteenth century was an era when empire became much more prominent in British elite consciousness and, increasingly, that of a wider public. Empire had now become inextricably bound up with national status and with Britain's economic and political wellbeing in a highly competitive world. Such statues, however, were comparatively rare in Britain until the second half of the eighteenth century when the fashion for the creation (after some initial reluctance) of monuments and statues in the United Kingdom and the American and West Indian colonies developed rapidly, representing an 'elision' of nation and empire.[11] This conjunction was particularly fostered by colonial trade and was developed by private and public agencies eager to commemorate individuals who symbolised particular turning points and successes in the imperial enterprise. The earliest vandalising of monuments in the British Empire occurred when American revolutionaries tore down busts and statues of George III.[12] These political statements would only be matched by nationalist resistance in the twentieth century. Both outbreaks of iconoclasm reflected the fragility of monuments intended to be symbolic of the supposed permanence and stability of empire. Joan Coutu has pointed out the close relationship between the stone and metal of monumental commemorations and the printed word, in the pressure for their erection, in debates about their form, invitations to sculptors and occasionally the organisation of competitions, in reviews of the result, and in descriptions in the press and elsewhere of the erection and inauguration.[13] In India, statue iconoclasm had a long history. As early as 1907, during the Punjab disturbances of that year, it was alleged that a statue of Queen Victoria on the Lahore maidan was tarred and mutilated, the crown and part of the head knocked off.[14]

The loss of thirteen colonies on the eastern seaboard of North America seemed to increase the importance of empire elsewhere, which was seen as worth extending and protecting. Hence the urge to safeguard West Indian colonies and develop territories in the East became more pronounced, developments with significant cultural effects. Resulting imperial wars produced heroes, their heroism seemingly heightened by the exotic locations of their exploits. This effect emerged, if hesitantly, through the succession of eighteenth-century wars, including the major engagements and imperial acquisitions of the Spanish and Austrian succession crises. Although Admiral Vernon had been hailed as a hero earlier in the century, it was the Seven Years' War, 1756–63, which produced the first real group of imperial heroes, such as General Wolfe in Canada and Robert Clive in India.[15] In the American Revolutionary War, the victory of Admiral Rodney at the Battle of the Saints (1782), widely seen as 'saving' the British Caribbean possessions, emphasised the tradition of naval heroes which was to culminate with Nelson. Both Rodney and Nelson were honoured with well-known statues in the Caribbean, the former in the impressive Rodney memorial in Spanish Town, Jamaica, the latter in the former Trafalgar Square (now National Heroes Square), Bridgetown, Barbados.[16] The Nelson column also survives in Montreal in a former French colony, apparently erected with subscriptions from both Anglophone and Francophone citizens since Napoleon was not particularly popular in Quebec.[17] The celebration of heroic figures was to develop further during the nineteenth century, particularly for those associated with warfare, but also with exploration and sometimes missionary endeavour. In this period, statuary was increasingly devoted to monarchs and senior imperial administrators, the latter surrogate heroic figures representing the personification of power and individual moral worth, symbolising the virtuous authority of the state and its right to rule. The cult of heroes continued to sanctify vital turning points in the nation's history, perhaps also a key means of socialising the young into the values of empire. The growth of nineteenth-century print capitalism and its associated technological advances ensured that printed material became available in every home, with heroes occupying sources such as popular juvenile literature and didactic school text books.[18] Statuary in public places was similarly designed to transmit notions of exemplary authority to a wider public. For this reason, the scale of statues was enlarged to something above life-size, emphasised by elevation on plinths, on columns or under sculpted canopies, distancing the royal or heroic figure from the common run of people viewing them. They were thus rendered literally larger than life.

The development of the fascination with Ancient history and archaeology became a key aspect of intellectual and cultural approaches to the British Empire, unlocking messages from the past to explain and justify the present. This fed into the initial notion, resurrected later, that classical styles of architecture were suitable for imperial rule. It also influenced sculpture and the depiction of prominent imperial figures as sometimes dressed (particularly in the eighteenth and early nineteenth centuries) in Ancient garb such as togas, reflecting the belief that the British were emulating the alleged civilisation of Greeks and Romans.[19] Lessons from the Ancient world transmitted the notion that power and its supposed corollary, moral ascendancy, were best advertised and articulated through forms of material culture, a grandeur of which architecture and statuary were a constituent part. It may however have been the case that there was less interest in sculpture as representative of the perfect human physique as displayed by deities like Apollo or Athena, by athletes or by female personifications of virtue. At any rate, statuary associated with imperial cityscapes contributed to the 'narrative of progress' central to imperial ideology. Statues of individuals, as well as abstract personifications (including 'Progress' itself, as well as 'Agriculture', 'Engineering' and so on) demonstrated the key concept of an innovative and progressive civilisation. Statuary and sculpture became self-congratulatory, a key source of self-confidence. Although intended to impress the moral worth of rulers upon ruled, such statuary was ultimately more important in flattering and encouraging the elite that engendered it. In other words, statues boosted the imperial ego, with sculptors pandering to (and perhaps sharing) the narcissism and fantasies of superiority of an imperial culture.

This outburst of sculptural activity accompanied the development of the practice of sculpture in Britain. In the earlier period most sculpture had been undertaken by foreign nationals who came from a European tradition.[20] But after the foundation of the Royal Academy of Arts in London in 1768 and the appointment of a professor of sculpture in the early nineteenth century, training in sculpture was inaugurated and a stream of British sculptors emerged. Contemporaries surmised that the development of academic training in sculpture might produce works of great quality to vie with the admired examples from Greek and Roman worlds. Parallel with this was the emerging imperial power of the East India Company and the increasing recognition by some of its directors that its status required architectural and artistic expressions.[21] The Company thus became a major patron, often spending surprising amounts on architecture, sculpture and statuary, although it was also alarmed when employees, like Wellesley in India, took this too far. However, in these respects it often ran ahead of the state itself. As McAleer has shown, the Company directors became increasingly concerned that their headquarters in London should reflect the growing political significance and imperial pomp of their economic activities in the East. By the end of the eighteenth century the Company had a magnificent headquarters in Leadenhall Street in the City of London, which incorporated major rooms such as the Directors' Court Room and the General Court. The former had already been consciously transformed into a picture gallery of works portraying the route to India, the subcontinent itself and other Asian locations. The architecture of the General Court Room (also known as the Sale Room) had been provided with wall niches for the accommodation of statues of significant heroes and rulers of the developing Indian Empire. Statues of Admiral Sir George Pocock, Major General Stringer Lawrence and Robert Clive were commissioned from the sculptor Peter Scheemakers in 1760.[22] Sir Eyre Coote, Lord Cornwallis and later Warren Hastings joined this Valhalla.

By then statues were appearing in large numbers in India and by the end of the nineteenth century there were literally hundreds of them.[23] Indeed, it has been suggested that there were more statues and monuments in Bombay than in Glasgow and Manchester combined, while those of Calcutta vied with London.[24] It would seem that statuary had become so important in Bombay that James Douglas devoted a whole section of his 1900 book on the presidency city to them.[25] Moreover, the quality of the work was in no way inferior to the metropolitan examples. The most notable of British sculptors were highly active in satisfying this imperial market, which must have greatly contributed to their incomes and therefore to the maintenance of the growing cadre of nineteenth-century practitioners. These included John Flaxman, Sir Francis Chantrey, John Bacon father and son, Sir Richard Westmacott and many others. Occasionally, Scottish sculptors such as John Mossman, who had a major business in Glasgow, and Sir John Steell of Edinburgh were pulled in. None of them visited India, but often used portraits and prints, later photographs, to produce a likeness of the subjects. There can thus be little doubt that the opportunities afforded by empire contributed to the development of British sculptural expertise, just as it had greatly benefited the emergence of the considerable and wide-ranging school of artists supplying demands for portrait and landscape art. It may be that prestigious imperial commissions (both in Britain and overseas) also helped to transform the status of sculptors from artisans into artists, symbolised by the fact that several acquired knighthoods.

The extraordinary numbers of statues can be placed in a clear hierarchy. At the top were those of British monarchs, then those of successive governors general and, after 1858, viceroys. Governors of Bombay and Madras, and lieutenant governors of Bengal and other provinces were also commemorated with statues as were leading military figures. The most notable might be honoured with the enormously expensive bronze equestrian examples. One Secretary of State for India, Edwin Montagu, was surprisingly honoured twice (in both Calcutta and Bombay), presumably because of his role in the introduction of the

Montagu-Chelmsford reforms in 1918, prompting the Government of India Act of 1919. This act started the processes of constitutional advance in the subcontinent, though at a much slower rate than nationalists demanded, particularly as it was combined with events like the Amritsar Massacre and repressive legislation. Apart from administrators and politicians, a number of standing and seated statues were devoted to scholarly and literary figures, some to judges and lawyers, a few to clergymen (particularly bishops) and missionaries, and, at the lower end of the scale, there were busts of engineers, doctors, railway directors and various officials. Statues were also erected to Indian entrepreneurs, mainly Parsis, who made large fortunes and earned honours because of their philanthropic donations. One First World War Indian soldier, Khudada Khan, who received the Victoria Cross, was commemorated in a statue in Karachi, no doubt symbolising his exemplary loyalty and bravery.

Statues of monarchs and members of the British royal family were relatively rare until the reign of Queen Victoria. Her cultural power was such that literally hundreds were produced for distribution around the empire. Steggles suggests that more than fifty were created for India alone, twenty-five of them after her death.[26] It may be that this personification of empire in a female figure was intended to soften the masculine, military character of imperial rule. At any rate, Victoria prompted a major sculptural industry and eventually almost all significant cities and towns everywhere in the empire possessed the obligatory statue of the Queen.[27] This became almost a competitive obsession. Many of these survive, in the Seychelles and Malta for example, as well as throughout Canada, Australia and New Zealand. Beyond the empire, the British residents of Siam (Thailand) erected a statue to Victoria in Bangkok, where it became a good luck talisman for many Thai people, as apparently it remains.[28] Statues of Victoria were often standing figures (sometimes a good deal taller than life-size, as outside the provincial legislature in Victoria, British Columbia), occasionally equestrian, and often seated. The larger cities in India had multiples. The extraordinary numbers are reflected in the surprising line-ups of them in the museum in Lucknow, to which they were removed after independence. Victoria's successors, Edward VII and George V appeared both standing and in equestrian form. Consorts, including Prince Albert, Queen Alexandra and Queen Mary, were honoured, the latter two often with crowns and coronation robes. A few other women were commemorated, including Ladies Frerc and Reay, both wives of Bombay governors.

Many of the statues were highly formulaic in character. Their (male) subjects tended to be transformed into idealised romantic figures, taller than real life, with perfect classical musculature (as in exposed legs), and with highly stylised poses and gestures. The first statue of a governor general, that of Lord Cornwallis sent to Madras in 1800, was dressed as a Garter knight, starting a tradition.[29] Subsequent viceroys were generally depicted in court dress or Garter robes, providing a strikingly antique appearance distancing them from their flesh-and-blood presence. Other governors appeared in the equivalent Star of India regalia. This obsession with robes was very convenient structurally, providing stability to heavy statues and obscuring anatomical detail. Many of them were funded by 'public' subscription, which was code for donations from members of the elite, with notable contributions from Indian maharajahs and wealthy businessmen. The tradition of the provision of a statue for each outgoing viceroy continued almost down to the Second World War, with one for Lord Irwin unveiled in 1934 and Lord Willingdon in 1936. In the twentieth century, new sculptural forms ensured that a combination of greater realism and a heightened sense of individual character was introduced (good examples are the Edwin Montagu statues, the 1924 Bombay one by Riccardi and the 1931 Calcutta version by Kathleen Scott are particularly striking), but it became increasingly apparent that the age of imperial statuary was ending, relatively long-lasting as it had been. This occurred because of the rapid decline in confidence of imperial ideology, along with indigenous opposition and a more cynical awareness of the hopelessness and ultimate irrelevance of these expensive gestures in stone and bronze.

In any case, the costs of such statues were becoming more difficult to justify. The expense of some, particularly those of Queen Victoria, could be simply staggering in modern terms. A seated marble statue for the Victoria and Albert Museum in Byculla, Bombay (now Bhau Daji Lad Museum) was said to have cost £18,500, which would translate into well over half a million pounds today.[30] Another for Rajkot in Gujerat cost £3,300 while that designed to go with the Frere Hall in Karachi cost £6,000. The Bombay Flora Fountain, devoted to spring in a bizarrely inappropriate evocation of Italy, intended as an icon of the city and dedicated to Sir Bartle Frere, cost £9,000.[31] Bronze equestrian statues could be even more expensive. One commemorating the visit of the Prince of Wales to Bombay in 1875–76 cost £12,500. It was paid for by the son of the Sephardic Jewish businessman, David Sassoon, revealing just how far this entrepreneurial class would go to demonstrate loyalty to Crown and empire. Moreover, the transportation of these statues by sea to India must have created notable logistical problems, not least in requiring heavy lifting gear and awkward transportation to and from the docks. However, although many statues imply successful commemorations, not all schemes prospered. When the former Viceroy Curzon proposed a new memorial to Robert Clive, this was opposed by his successor Minto. Given the state of nationalist activity at this particular time, not least among Muslims, it was considered inopportune, even inflammatory, to embark on such a project.[32] This resistance to an autocratic viceroy accustomed to getting his way demonstrates the political sensitivity of statuary at a time of rapidly changing British fortunes.

Audience reactions

As with so many aspects of propagandist culture, it is extremely difficult to ascertain the reactions of indigenous people to these dramatic gestures. If they were designed to overawe Indians and other 'natives', transmit a sense of moral authority, or represent in sculptural form the heroic history of imperialism, then they surely failed. There are some instances of damage to statues or of their being coated with tar or paint during the imperial period, but generally they were simply ignored. There can be little doubt that their audience was essentially the citizens of the imperial power itself, the expatriates and settlers who were supposed to be impressed by the evidence of the great achievements of their 'race'. Yet even this constituency may have largely ignored them. They represented a form of imperial piety, easy to respect in passing, but equally easy to forget. The enclosed monuments in cathedrals, churches and burial grounds, however, have been more durable, and perhaps more noticed by worshippers and visitors. They spanned a larger range of class and gender. The levelling effect of death produced commemorations that drew upon both the heroic and the meek, though almost all white (and literally so when sculpted in white marble). Some such monuments included Indians, servants or soldiers mourning the departed, sometimes learned figures supporting a British scholar (all of them became honorary whites). But the hierarchy and patterns of dominance were always abundantly apparent. Many other sculptures survived in their original settings, for example in more significant cemeteries like the two in South Park Street, Calcutta.[33] The tombs there are perhaps grander than equivalents almost anywhere else in the former British Empire, illustrating the manner in which the British sought to honour those whom they regarded as the heroic dead in the cause of alleged progress. They constituted in India a climatic and epidemiological martyrology as much as an imperial one. While there are some dedicated Catholic cemeteries, for example in India and Malta, the sculptures in many imperial and colonial ecclesiastical and funerary contexts can be seen as connected with the rise of a Protestant sensibility, reflecting a desire to display spiritual and moral qualities, courage in the face of adversity, war or illness.[34] Some of the greatest collections of church statuary can be found in cathedrals. For example, St Thomas's Cathedral in Bombay is filled with memorials, some of very high quality.[35] These include the magnificent memorial to Captain George Hardinge, R.N., by John Bacon the younger (c.1808) (see Plate 22).[36] There are many others in St Paul's, Calcutta, St George's, Madras, and churches throughout India. While commemorative tablets in stone or wood are common everywhere, both the elaboration and the quality of ecclesiastical sculptures are largely unique to India.

Statues in other colonies

An interesting case of large numbers of statues surviving into the postcolonial period is in Port Louis, capital of Mauritius. These strike the visitor as almost excessive.[37] There are statues of British colonial governors and members of the royal family, but there are also examples from the French period before the British conquest in 1810. Statues of modern Mauritian politicians, some of whom helped achieve independence, have joined these mementoes of two successive empires. Perhaps it is this overlaying of different regimes that has ensured the survival of such multifarious memorials. Removal of British examples would have suggested the need also to destroy the French, but the Creole culture of an island with a highly polyglot population might have ensured respect for the Francophone past. Indeed, the statue to Bertrand-François de la Bourdonnais, the French governor after 1735, was erected in the British period. The inscription, in Creole French, suggests that a committee was established in 1853 and the statue inaugurated in 1859 under Governor Stevenson. La Bourdonnais was honoured as a founder of the modern history of the island.[38]

Nevertheless, the British were relatively sparing in erecting statues in the dependent empire, generally concentrating on monarchs. In the territories of settlement, most cities spawned statues, but seldom with the exuberant extravagance of India. This symbolises the essential difference between the nature of British power in the subcontinent and its equivalent in the colonies that became Dominions. In Sydney, New South Wales, for example, one of the first statues to be erected was of Governor Richard Bourke in 1842. As in India, its inauguration was accompanied by processions and a major unveiling ceremony, with shops and banks closed on the day.[39] Prince Albert followed in 1866, Captain Cook in 1878, Thomas Mort, an industrialist in 1879 and Queen Victoria in 1888. There were additionally four statues of Lachlan Macquarie, celebrated governor of New South Wales. The Lands Department building was provided with statues of Australian explorers, clearly symbolising increasing knowledge of the continent. In 1890, a statue of the celebrated Scottish (fiercely anti-Catholic) minister, John Dunmore Lang, was unveiled by his widow. The Catholic Church responded with various statues of clerics and other symbolic figures. If Lang was highly controversial, statues of other Scots were less so and might help to maintain a sub-British ethnic identity. Eight statues of Robert Burns appeared in Australia between 1883 and 1935, nine in Canada and four in New Zealand. There were also commemorations of Walter Scott, William Wallace, Robert the Bruce, Mary Queen of Scots and Charles Edward Stuart.[40] These statues, however, were focused in very specific ways, representing Scots as Unionists and empire loyalists. More statues appeared in Australia in the twentieth century, including monarchs and the English literary icon Shakespeare in Sydney in 1926 (another one in Stratford, Ontario), but soon the developing mores of the country were reflected in the appearance of various sportsmen. Favourite places for statues were Macquarie Street, Hyde Park, the Royal Botanic Gardens in Sydney, and the areas around cathedrals. Examples appeared across Australia, New Zealand and various Canadian provinces. Colonial, federal and provincial legislatures invariably acquired collections of statues, of monarchs and of leading politicians, and sometimes indigenous people. In the twentieth century, the focus shifted from imperial to national, towards constitutional change in the colonial territory.

The dual white ethnic history of South Africa helped to create an alternative tradition. The sculptor Anton van Wouw (1862–1945) migrated from the Netherlands to South Africa in 1880. It took him a while to become established, but once he received commissions he became, in effect, the sculptor to Afrikaans nationalism, to some extent at any rate in opposition to British imperialism. He produced statues of Paul Kruger, Jan Hofmeyr and Martinus Steyn, all for prominent public positions in the former Boer republics. He sculpted the figures on the National Women's Memorial outside Bloemfontein, designed to commemorate the suffering and deaths of women and children during the Anglo-Boer War, unveiled to considerable controversy in 1913, since it seemed to cut against the policy of reconciliation then being pursued (see Plate 23). He also sculpted a Boer woman with children for the Voortrekker Monument of the 1930s. He depicted indigenous figures, particularly of the Shangaan people, portrayed with a dignity surprising in the racial contexts of the time. His more famous indigenous sculpture is of a Bushman or San hunter of 1902, the model for which, Korhaan, had actually been his servant for a year. This exists in many reproductions. Van Wouw has a museum dedicated to his work in Pretoria.[41]

Fate of statues

Public statues which had been largely ignored suddenly came under scrutiny by nationalists in the postcolonial era. Throughout Africa, most British statues were either destroyed, put into storage, or repatriated. An example is the Sudan, which returned two notable statues to Britain in 1957 following the Suez crisis. These were the equestrian Lord Kitchener, already transferred from Calcutta (erected 1914) to Khartoum in 1920, and the celebrated example of General Gordon on his camel. The British themselves removed the statue of Lord Delamere from Nairobi in 1963 just ahead of independence. Other transfers included the highly sensitive one of the brutal John Nicholson (whose death in 1857 ended his violent responses to the revolt) trans-ferred from outside the Nicholson Cemetery in Delhi to the British High Commission in 1947 and then to the grounds of his former school in Northern Ireland. The damaged effigy of Governor General Lord Auckland, dating from 1847, was sent to the eponymous city in New Zealand. The twentieth-century example of Viceroy Lord Reading was sent to Reading in Berkshire. A bronze equestrian statue of Edward VII, erected in Calcutta in 1919, was relocated to Toronto in 1969, the considerable cost covered by a Canadian businessman.[42] Once again, we see a striking difference between the dependent empire, India and the Dominions. The latter seemed to enhance their imperial sentiment by accepting such statues, but in reality the subject matter of their public sculptures was extended by modern abstract examples, as well as depictions of previously ignored indigenous peoples. These changes reflected the development of cultural nation-alism in Canada, Australia, New Zealand and South Africa.

Although the Indian government has generally been sensitive about the survival of statues, particularly during the prime minister-ship of Nehru, both external and internal political relationships have ensured that they have been a source of controversy. In external diplo-macy, the relationship with Britain has had some ups and downs, while the connections between the central government and those of the Indian states have also affected the fate of statues.[43] Nevertheless, some were decapitated or otherwise damaged (arms and hands cut off for example) in the aftermath of independence or at key emotional moments, such as the hundredth anniversary of the Indian Revolt of 1857. It is an irony that statues, for example at the Victoria Memorial in Kolkata, may now be noticed more as an intriguing aspect of cultural heritage.[44] It is also surprising that the Marxist government of West Bengal has been more sympathetic to British statues than the administrations of other states, partly in an attempt to encourage investors, partly to develop tourism.[45] In the case of Pakistan, all statues were removed into museums or storage in view of the Islamic ban on the representation of the human form. Nevertheless, one significant memorial survives in Karachi: the Merewether clock tower, an impressive 102 feet high built between 1884 and 1892 to commemorate the Commissioner of Sind, Sir William Merewether, and designed by municipal engineer James Strachan in a Gothic revival style.[46] In India, many Calcutta statues were taken to Barrackpore, the former holiday residence of the viceroy. Others were moved into the Victoria Memorial where some in the grounds survived (and in some cases were returned from exile at Barrackpore), including that of Queen Victoria in a prominent position in front of the building.[47] Curzon, by F.W. Pomeroy, still stands near the entrance. In Bombay, a number of statues, several of them damaged, were moved to the area behind the Bhau Daji Lad Museum in Byculla. The New Delhi examples, largely erected in the dying years of imperial rule, were transferred to Coronation Park on the Ridge, where the successive durbars had taken place. These include the elongated statue of George V, originally under a *chhatri* on the Rajpath, with the sceptre and the hand holding it destroyed (see Plate 24).[48] It was removed from its original position in 1968. There are also four statues of viceroys (Lords Hardinge, Chelmsford, Willingdon and Irwin), partly mutilated. Some went into storage. Examples in Central India were moved into the museum in Lucknow.

Statues had a better chance of survival in Madras (Chennai). Cornwallis is now in the Fort Museum, along with Wellington (whose early career was in India), while the superb equestrian statue of Sir Thomas Munro by Francis Chantrey still stands in its original position.[49] The statue of George V survives in a car park near the courts complex.[50] The statue of Victoria which used to be situated outside the Victoria Memorial Hall has now been moved to the grounds of Madras University.[51] The ubiquity of statues of Victoria ensures that their condition ranges from protection to neglect. One example is the statue in the port of Visakhapatnam in Andhra Pradesh which is in very poor condition in its pavilion. Many locals not unnaturally react to this with indifference while 'heritage lovers', as one press article described them, are concerned about its state.[52] Yet the fact is that nationalists were eager to take up the equivalent use of statuary for propaganda purposes. Statues of those who resisted imperial rule began to be erected in relatively large numbers, with statues of Gandhi appearing in various locations in India (and there is also one in Pietermaritzburg, KwaZulu-Natal), as well as other leading politicians, including Subhas Chandra Bhose, who founded the Indian National Army to collaborate with the Japanese to eject the British.

Sculptures on buildings and war memorials

Monumental sculpture was a characteristic of elaborate buildings. Many allegorical figures, sometimes forming groups supporting a major statue, also embellished law courts, railway stations, banks and commercial establishments. Victoria Terminus in Bombay, the masterpiece of F.W. Stevens, was the classic example, with a large statue of 'Progress' on top of its dome with additional sculptures symbolising Engineering, Science, Commerce and Shipping, as well as medallion heads of railway company directors set into its walls. This riot of sculpture was continued within the building itself. Few other buildings inscribed the imperial ideology of progress more explicitly. Such architecture with its sculptures and the plethora of imperial statuary contributed to the 'illusion of permanence' which seized the ambitions of imperialists in India and elsewhere.[53] All empires seek to 'stop time' in favour of the survival of their ideologies and the strength and supposed durability of material culture contributed to this universal fantasy.[54] A striking example of sculptures indicating the function of a building is the extraordinary work incorporated into the Crawford Market in Bombay. Created by John Lockwood Kipling they constitute deeply incised and realistic panels representing agriculture and a market, with a dedicatory panel to Arthur Crawford. Nearby is the market fountain with a menagerie of sculpted animals.[55] Two architectural styles lent themselves to the integral addition of sculptures, one the Arts and Crafts, the other Art Deco, though they generally moved on from imperial subjects. On another continent, the parliament buildings of the Canadian Confederation in Ottawa are a major site of sculptures both externally and internally.

The most significant sculptural phenomenon of the twentieth century was the creation of war memorials throughout the empire. This had not been particularly significant in the nineteenth century, but in the twentieth the appearance of such memorials became almost an obsession. Many Anglo-Boer War memorials appeared in Britain, which Peter Donaldson has described as a transition period in the commemoration of the casualties of war.[56] After the First World War, commemorations became universal in every city, town and village throughout the British Isles (although more problematic in Ireland where Eire still has to come to terms with the involvement of men on the British side). Such memorials became a prominent part of the street furniture throughout the British World, part of the material culture of empire. Three key questions arise. The first is why memorialising became so important in this period; the second is how the momentum was generated; and the third is how far the apparent objective of an imperial patriotism was satisfied and maintained. The answer to the first may lie in changes in class structure. The casualties of earlier wars were often, putting it brutally, nameless cannon fodder from the lower classes (although many graveyards record the deaths of veterans of battles such as Trafalgar or Waterloo). Generally it was officers and members of upper-class families who were commemorated.[57] By the twentieth century, developing democratic institutions meant that it was more difficult to sustain anonymity. In any case, deaths were carefully recorded in local papers and elsewhere: a literate public was reading a ubiquitous press, and many casualties were volunteers and not members of a professional regular army.

So far as the momentum in imperial territories is concerned, there is a record of an intriguing moment. During the empire tour of the

Duke and Duchess of Cornwall and York in 1901, the Duke proposed in Perth, Western Australia, that there should be Anglo-Boer War memorials wherever colonial troops were recruited for South Africa. Having enthused about the bravery and the riding abilities of Australian troopers, he went on:

> I should like to see throughout the land memorials, no matter how humble in design, bearing the names of those whom they commemorate, not only as tribute of honour to the individual, but as emblems of patriotism, self-sacrifice and brotherhood, round which in the hour of danger the youth and manhood of succeeding generations might rally in the resolve to follow the noble example of those who have given their all, their lives, for King and country.[58]

This may have merely encouraged a developing trend, for memorials were already appearing in the settlement territories. Perhaps one of the most striking is in Invercargill on the South Island of New Zealand. This astonishing monument cost £2,000 and was designed by a Dunedin architect, Newton Vane. Planned in 1902, constructed in Aberdeen, Scotland, and shipped out to New Zealand, it was unveiled in 1908. Consisting of a double-height four-sided temple design, with a statue of a trooper on top, it stands on a roundabout in the middle of the intersection of Clyde and Tay Streets and cannot be missed by any visitor to the town.[59] In fact, there are some forty Boer War monuments in New Zealand, most of them in streets or parks, but commemoration took a further architectural form in the Veterans' Hospital in Auckland, built in a classic colonial style with prominent verandas, financed from fund-raising by the Governor Lord Ranfurly. Australia also has a number of Boer War memorials, including one inaugurated as recently as 2017 on Anzac Parade in Canberra. In both Australia and New Zealand, the Boer War has a special resonance since it is regarded as the first overseas war (as opposed to internal wars against indigenous people) and constituted a vital point in the emergence of these countries on the world stage. But they reflected a significant tension between imperial loyalty to a supposedly just empire and the growing sense of national identity.[60] These monuments and the many others that followed, commemorating the two world wars of the twentieth century, the Korean War and, where appropriate, campaigns in Malaya and Vietnam, as well as more recent conflicts as in Afghanistan, represented solid evidence of key stages in the development of national pride.

Canada is a rather different case. The war of 1812 against the United States was partly fought on Canadian soil and there were also several rebellions that involved internal military action, including those of Louis Riel leading the Métis in Manitoba (the Red River Rebellion) in 1869–70 and the North-West rebellion in Saskatchewan in 1884–85. Canadian *voyageurs* were also involved in the Sudan campaign of 1884, though as civilians and not as enlisted troops. In Ottawa, the Peace Tower of the Canadian parliament buildings has a shrine devoted to memorials and books listing the names of casualties, including those in the Sudan and the second Boer War. Parliament Hill in fact became the location for the construction of a pantheon of Canadian heroes in war and peace.[61] As well as a Boer War memorial in Ottawa's Confederation Park, there are commemorations of figures important in the creation of Canadian Confederation, particularly including Quebecois, perhaps to counter a separatist nationalist movement in Quebec.[62]

All of the former settlement territories have large numbers of monuments to the casualties of the twentieth century world wars. Major centres include national memorials, such as the War Memorial Museum in Auckland and the striking war memorial carillon adjacent to the Dominion Museum in Wellington. The Anzac memorial in Hyde Park, Sydney, is a monumental Art Deco structure completed in 1934, designed by C. Bruce Dellit and with sculptures by Rayner Hoff. The Canadian national memorial in Ottawa stands in a traffic island in Confederation Square along the road from the parliament buildings. It was designed by Vernon March with various allegorical sculptures, and contains the tomb of the unknown soldier. Inaugurated by George VI in 1939, it was re-dedicated to include the Second World War in 1982. The situation in South Africa was more complex, given the major Afrikaans rebellion in 1914 and the position of the majority African people. There is, however, a cenotaph on Heerengracht Street in Cape Town, designed, like the Ottawa one, by the sculptor Vernon March. In India, it has been suggested that the creation of New Delhi was in many respects 'a Great War story', and the erection of the All-India War Memorial, the monumental arch astride the Rajpath commemorating Indian troops killed in the war, became a central element of Lutyens' design.[63] All the names of those killed are inscribed on its walls. The Indian government cleverly converted this into a monument to the nation state, renamed India Gate. The nearby, now empty, chhatri, which formerly sheltered the statue of George V will become associated with a war memorial museum proposed for the adjacent site.[64] There are also impressive Commonwealth War Grave cemeteries and memorials in, for example, Kranji in Singapore and two in Burma, one of which at Taukkyan north of Yangon commemorates the death of the Marquess Dufferin in 1945, ironically the grandson of the viceroy who added the name of the ancient capital Ava to his title after the conquest of Mandalay.[65]

Commemorations of war have of course been highly controversial in the case of Ireland. Colonial Ireland is not included in this book, but it is perhaps unavoidable to notice the ways in which Ireland offered so many precedents in the contestation of the material presence of memorials and statuary. This happened even before the end of British rule, for example in tributes to the Irish Rebellion of 1798.[66] Resistance to monumental commemorations was very much part of the Irish nationalist pursuit of independence.[67] After Irish independence in 1922, such transformations inevitably accelerated, not least in respect of the statues of British monarchs.[68] The influence of Irish nationalism on the development of Indian and other nationalist movements in the British Empire was profound, and this was matched by reactions to monuments, memorials and statues in the imperial and postcolonial landscape.[69] Such reordering of urban sculpture in Dublin continued into modern times with the 1966 blowing up of Nelson's Pillar, a column reminiscent of the one in London's Trafalgar Square, inaugurated in 1809 and around which Trafalgar Day ceremonies had taken place during the British period. Given the removal of so many other royal and imperial statues, this was regarded as inevitable, although it was carried out by a maverick republican group.[70] It was replaced in 2003 by a tapering spire, symbolically three times the height of the pillar, representing the autonomy of the city of Dublin.

Other foci of the national identities of India and the former Dominions are to be found in the war commemorations in France, such as the Villers-Bretonneux Australian memorial near Amiens, the Canadian equivalent at Vimy, and those of New Zealand at Longueval and Le Quesnoy. There are also memorials to South African troops at Delville Wood and to Indian soldiers who fought in the First World War at Neuve Chappelle. The major irony is that such memorials, originally intended as symbolic of the unity of the British Empire, representing loyal citizens and subjects coming to the aid of the so-called mother country, in fact became vital emblems in the march towards constitutional independence. The wars were reinterpreted as having been fought for the particular objectives of Canada, Australia, New Zealand, South Africa and India.

Postcolonial memorials

Perhaps nothing better symbolises the expiry of the British Empire than the appearance of Gandhi memorials in Britain. There are at least two in London, one in Parliament Square and another in Tavistock Square. The former is close to that commemorating Nelson

Mandela, both of them not far from Churchill, a fact which might have infuriated the former imperialist. Other Gandhi memorials include at least two in Natal, one in Canberra and another in Edinburgh (others are in the USA and Buenos Aires). If Gandhi and Mandela embody universal values of peace, non-violence and heroic resistance, they are still essentially anti-imperialist. In Winnipeg, Manitoba, a museum dedicated to human rights has a statue of Gandhi, a representative fighter for values of common humanity. Standing outside the museum, it is at ground level, a recognition of Gandhi's commitment to the equality and rights of passing viewers.[71] Thus sculpture and statuary have charted the rise, elite commitment to, and then the demise of the British Empire. Nationalists throughout India, the former Dominions and colonies have ever been eager to replace the grandiloquent effigies of empire with those of national resistance. Equestrian statues are now less common, though those devoted to the seventeenth-century warrior king of Maharashtra, Chhatrapati Shivaji are an exception. Several Shivaji statues have appeared in the west of India, but surprisingly one of the first had its foundation stone laid by the Prince of Wales (future Edward VIII) in 1921. On his visit to Poona (Pune), the Prince was invited to perform the honours at what was described as the Shivaji Memorial:

> The actual ceremony followed the course of such affairs at home, but it differed beyond all comparison in the vivid picturesqueness of its setting. The structure, when finished, will consist of a stately equestrian statue of Shivaji, around which will be grouped schools and hostels for Mahratta boys. It will be a worthy memorial to the great seventeenth-century Maharaja who, as the Prince said, 'not only founded an Empire, but created a nation'.[72]

That nation was not India, but Shivaji was an icon of western Indian nationalism, thereby perhaps confirming the British accusation of Indian disunity. The ceremony was one of two at the site of the palace of the *peshwas*, the principal ministers of the Mahratta Empire. The Prince was also laying the foundation stone for the memorial to soldiers of the Mahratta regiments who had died in the First World War. The Maharajah of Kolhapur delivered a speech about the warrior tradition of the Mahrattas, symbolised by Shivaji. The two events were thus linked as a joint celebration of the Mahratta (anti-Muslim) warrior tradition.[73] In fact the Prince faced many nationalist demonstrations, Gandhian *hartals* (strikes and market closures) and even riots during his tour. It may be that his participation in the ceremony at Poona, far from turning aside resistance by showing sympathy for an Indian figure of the past, heightened the Congress movement's ambitious search for unity. At any rate, the statue still stands in Pune, bearing a sword and sometimes a flag. Shivaji continued to be highlighted as a symbol of localised nationalism in Maharashtra, with many statues unveiled since independence. Particularly grand is the heroic equestrian one unveiled on Indian Republic Day in January 1961, on Bombay's Apollo Bunder, adjacent to the Gateway of India. In this way, an epic historic figure, promoted to the status of proto-nationalist, is consciously juxtaposed with a British imperial symbol. Even more dramatically, Shivaji is projected to be commemorated on a prancing horse with outstretched sword, a statue that will be the tallest in the world (192 metres high), on an artificial island off the coast of Mumbai. The Indian Prime Minister Narendra Modi laid a foundation stone (in the sea) in December 2016.[74] Shivaji's resistance to the Mughal Empire ensures that he is hardly a unifying figure for Muslims in the highly polyglot Mumbai but he still constitutes a strenuously anti-imperial gesture. Elsewhere in India, statues have become significant in celebrating modern politicians such as the chief ministers of states. This is particularly common in Tamil Nadu and Karnataka, but the phenomenon can also be found, for example, in Shimla. These effigies are cheap, generally composed of cement, often painted in gold or black.

In the former Dominions, there has been a distinct shift in the subject matter of sculpture and statues. In Canada, the celebration of individuals now avoids concentration on royalty and politicians. In Vancouver, a central area of the city boasting bohemian restaurants, bars and galleries is known as Gastown and a statue unveiled in 1970 commemorates the character who gave his name to the area: 'Gassy Jack', John Deighton (1830–75), an adventurer born in Hull, who pitched up in British Columbia in 1867 and opened the 'Globe Saloon' in the area now bearing his nickname. In 2022 the statue was toppled by demonstrators objecting to his relationship with an under-age First Nation girl. Elsewhere there is a sculpture known as 'Indian Head' in Saskatchewan, while the Chinese Railroad Workers' Memorial was inaugurated in Toronto in 1989 to commemorate the 17,000 Chinese who worked (and many of whom died) on the Canadian Pacific Railroad, so vital to Canada's history and nationhood. Another sculpture honours the heroism of Terry Fox, the cancer victim and amputee, who set out to run across the continent to raise money for charities and died in 1981 at the age of 22. The wildlife conscience of the country is assuaged by a sculpture of the Great Auk, the bird which was hunted to extinction.[75] In Australia there have been passionate debates about statues of James Cook, Lachlan Macquarie and others, mainly in respect of the mistreatment of indigenous people resulting from their arrival.[76] It has also been inevitable that in areas where there was a notable indigenous sculptural heritage, for example among the Maori of New Zealand and the West Coast First Nations of Canada (in both cases in wood), such aesthetic traditions should be revived and celebrated as a counterpoise to the imported modes of white people and as a means to furthering the national identity of the modern nation. Perhaps few figures are more associated with the development of pride and identity than sportsmen. This has become so apparent that it has stimulated a project to record and enumerate the number of sporting statues around the world. Cricketers have been particularly visible. In Australia over twenty cricketers have been honoured. Cricket has been vital in the development of West Indian nationalism and at least three cricketers, George Headley, Gary Sobers and Viv Richards have been celebrated there. Modern geopolitics are neatly symbolised by the fact that the Viv Richards cricket stadium in St John's Antigua, opened for the 2007 World Cup, was largely paid for by a Chinese grant. In India, another nationalist cricketing territory, there are several, including K.S. Ranjitsinhji, Shute Banerjea, C.K. Nayudi and D.B. Deodhar.[77]

Nothing better represents sensitivities about imperial statuary than the Rhodes Must Fall movement. This emerged in the University of Cape Town in March/April 2015 and was regarded by its proponents as a central facet of the 'decolonisation of education' and the purification of South Africa institutions by the removal of racism. It was particularly directed at a seated statue of Rhodes by Marion Walgate erected at the university in 1934. The resistance was so strenuous (including some violence) that the university council resolved to remove it. Various other statues attacked in Cape Town included those of Jan Smuts and of an early female graduate of the University, Maria Emmeline Barnard Fuller, who was a women's rights activist. The Rhodes Memorial at the foot of the Devil's Peak is a powerfully classical structure by Sir Herbert Baker intended to glorify the ambitions of Rhodes with a dramatic equestrian statue *Physical Energy* by George Frederick Watts. It was inaugurated in 1912 and features a bust of Rhodes, which was attacked, with the nose knocked off and signs of an attempt to behead it. It has now been restored. Protests also broke out at the universities of Stellenbosch and Pretoria in 2016, although these were mainly directed at language issues, demanding the removal of instruction in Afrikaans, seen as a language of oppression. The statue of Paul Kruger in Pretoria was attacked as was that of Louis Botha outside the parliament building in Cape Town. Boer War memorials were defaced, bizarrely including one commemorating the horses that suffered in the conflict. More understandably, a statue of George V at the University of KwaZulu-Natal also came in for opprobrium. The Rhodes Must Fall movement also appeared in Oxford, where there were demands for the removal of a statue in Oriel College, of which he was a major benefactor.[78] Initially resistant, the college relented later. In an article in *The Guardian* Amit Chaudhuri pointed to the much wider context of which the Rhodes Must Fall movement was merely a symbol: the decline of multiculturalism; the continuing gross inequalities, both social and economic, across racial lines; the strange resurrection of imperial nostalgia in Britain, and much else.[79] In these ways, an entire worldview could be encapsulated in the hatred of statues that seemed to symbolise the origins of such inequalities. Richard Drayton has also discussed the role of statues and monuments as 'forms of rhetoric' and considered the arguments for and against removal.[80] This animosity towards statues has additionally surfaced in Glasgow in respect of the statue of Lord Roberts. A Glasgow resident of Asian origin has demanded the removal of 'this racist, colonial statue' and started a petition to secure support.[81]

In these ways, a new era of iconoclasm and anti-imperial reaction emerged in the early twenty-first century.[82] Statue destruction, however, had a tendency to cut in various directions. Statues of Marxist theorists of the past and leaders of more modern times were destroyed in some places. In another former empire, in Odessa, the statue of the Empress Catherine of Russia was replaced in the Soviet era by one of Karl Marx, later by a monument commemorating the 1905 mutineers on the battleship *Potemkin*. However, the Catherine the Great statue had survived and was reconstructed and returned to its position in 2007, a curious reversal to the commemoration of an imperial age. This development met with some resistance: members of the modern revived Cossacks contingent demonstrating against this Ukrainian decision.[83] Megalomaniac rulers like Saddam Hussain were famously dethroned. There was a religious dimension too. The ancient statues of the Buddha, dating from some 1,700 years ago, at Bamyan, Afghanistan, a UNESCO World Heritage Site, were destroyed by the Taliban in 2001. It has been suggested that they might be restored but this seems unlikely now that Taliban rule has returned.[84] Meanwhile, if the postcolonial distaste for Rhodes – and even Roberts – seems relatively easy to explain, it is more surprising to find that Mahatma Gandhi has also been controversial. His statue was unveiled at the University of Ghana in 2016, but by 2018 had become a source of dispute because it was pointed out that when Gandhi resided in South Africa, he had resented the fact that Indians had been bracketed with Africans in the racially discriminatory policies of the day, even suggesting that this was inappropriate since Indians were more civilised.[85] Thus he appeared to endorse the racial hierarchy of the age. There was a similar controversy about a Gandhi statue in Johannesburg in 2003. But the Ghanaian incident also reflected the extent to which a statue could play a role in modern diplomatic affairs. Ghana had close diplomatic relations with India and there was some anxiety that the Gandhi controversy would cause an unhelpful rift between the two countries. It was agreed that the statue should be re-erected in a significant location in Accra since the Ghanaian government felt that 'the issue should not be allowed to derail partnership'.[86] It had been countered that Gandhi had inspired the resistance of Kwame Nkrumah, the founder of modern Ghana. Statue iconoclasm was resurrected in June 2020 in the wake of the killing of George Floyd by the Minneapolis police and the energising of the Black Lives Matter movement. The Bristol slave trader Edward Colston's statue was toppled and thrown into the harbour. Once again, a considerable controversy arose, with some people arguing that statues should be retained, despite the fact today's movement is merely a continuing historical reaction as cultures, like the Roman and indeed the British Empire, have fallen. In a continuing movement, the statue of Egerton Ryerson, nineteenth-century Methodist minister and educator, was destroyed in Toronto in June 2021 in protest against his residential school system in respect of First Nations children. Thus, statues, and to a lesser extent other forms of sculpture, have powerfully encapsulated ideologies, which is perhaps inevitably reflected in their acceptance in one age and their rejection in another.

6
PHOTOGRAPHY

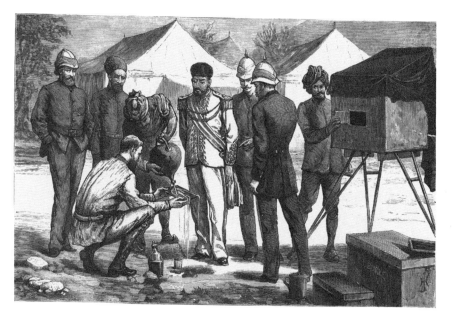

'Ameer Yakoob Khan' watching the process of fixing a photographic negative at Gandamak at the end of the Afghan War, 1879.

From art to photography

By the 1850s a great shift took place from art to photography, from drawing and painting to the camera. The new technology proceeded to sweep the empire with astonishing speed. Naturalistic (and supposedly objective) images now became available through a new technology which rapidly improved its effectiveness. The daguerreotype process was invented by Louis Daguerre in 1839 while Fox Talbot announced his calotype process in 1841, having been experimenting during the 1830s. While photography did not replace the practice of art, it did act as an auxiliary and sometimes influenced artists' work.[1] Some practitioners operated in both media. Occasionally, photography was even abandoned in favour of a return to painting, perhaps to reintroduce colour. For example, the celebrated photographer in India, Samuel Bourne, changed to deploying watercolours after returning to Britain in 1885.[2] William Armstrong of the Canadian commercial photographic company Armstrong, Beere and Hime, was a civil engineer, watercolourist and briefly photographer. The celebrated East African explorer James Augustus Grant abandoned photography for sketching, presumably because of the technical difficulties of the former.

Yet the camera became one of the key technologies of the century, as significant in its own way as steam power, the telegraph and more accurate weaponry. Indeed, the art of photography seemed ideally suited to the conditions of empire and the ideology of imperialism. Professionals like surveyors, engineers, geologists, architects and particularly the military, who had used topographical art, now turned to the camera. All used photography as a significant adjunct of their work. Moreover, war photographers became a feature of campaigns, sometimes encouraged by the authorities. A profession well represented among colonial amateur photographers was that of doctors.[3] The connection with chemistry, optics and other aspects of science is apparent. A few colonial officials also adopted the camera, intrigued by the regions and peoples among whom they worked.[4] Missionaries became assiduous in creating images relevant to their work of proselytisation. Humanitarians harnessed photography to their campaigns against the most brutal aspects of empire. There were also harrowing photographs of famine victims in India, though how far these were circulated or stimulated authorities into action is unclear.[5] Explorers and travellers, keen in the past to have artists depict the

results of their endeavours, now began to use photographs to illustrate the extraordinary places and cultures they visited. Photography
also took over older techniques like magic lantern slides and the
stereoscope (the juxtaposition of two images viewed through a
binocular device giving the illusion of three-dimensional depth) and
was powerfully democratised through the picture postcard.[6]

In the inter-war years, imperial images constituted significant
content of poster art and of advertising.[7] If sales propaganda
developed an imperial resonance, photographic images became
important in promoting overseas settlement, travel and transport,
forms of tourism, and also in fund-raising for organisations like
Christian missions. Press photographers captured imperial ceremonial, particularly connected with royal tours. Lavish albums of tours
were produced as mementoes for royal travellers and some found
their way into public collections, for example the Royal Tour of India
1905–6 and that of the Commonwealth, 1953–54.[8] While there had
indeed been many amateurs in the nineteenth century producing
photographs for private satisfaction, the invention of the Eastman
Kodak camera in 1888, followed by the box Brownie and easy-to-use
film in the early twentieth century put photography into the hands
of countless people. They filled up family albums, some of which
have been found to have historical value.[9] There were also aristocratic
amateurs, perhaps the most celebrated being the wife of the governor
general of Canada, the Countess of Aberdeen, who published
Through Canada with a Kodak in 1893 as a pictorial record of gubernatorial journeys across the continent.[10] Still photography was in
turn overtaken by moving film in the early twentieth century and by
the inter-war years cine cameras had turned such filming into an
amateur pastime recording imperial travels and family events.[11]

All these developments have been much studied.[12] A surge of
publications from the 1980s reflected both scholarly and popular
interests, a recognition of the extent to which photographs provide
much visual evidence as well as exposing ideologies embedded in

images.[13] This emergence of a vital field of study has been reflected in workshops and conferences, including discussions of the significance of photographs as historical sources, all ensuring the proliferation of publications.[14] Much of this research and discussion has considered key issues, such as the extent to which the camera became another weapon of imperialism, the images conveying political, social, religious and gender biases of the time, as well as promoting the objectification and subjugation of indigenous peoples.[15] But the camera also unveiled the emotional narratives of empire, including empathetic and humanitarian concerns.[16] In all these ways the camera became an instrument of globalisation, a creator of commercial opportunities, and an aesthetic form stimulating theoretical debate.

Early photography in empire

Information about the new medium spread remarkably quickly across the empire. News of the daguerreotype process arrived in South Africa as early as 1839, when Dr Atherstone and F.W. Barber returned to the Cape bearing reports of Daguerre's invention. Atherstone became an early amateur enthusiast.[17] Another instance comes from the life of Julia Margaret Cameron, herself later a distinguished photographer. Born and brought up in Calcutta, she continued to have close connections with the empire throughout her life, particularly after she married Charles Hay Cameron, a high-ranking Company official in Calcutta who also owned coffee estates in Ceylon. When convalescing at the Cape in the 1830s (a common resort for residents of India), Julia met the distinguished astronomer and scientist Sir John Herschel who kept her up to date with scientific developments, including his experiments in photography. In 1842, he sent her examples of photographs and informed her of the different techniques that had emerged.[18] Cameron later wrote that the arrival of such information in Calcutta was like 'water to the parched lips of the starved'.[19] Yet it has been suggested that photography arrived in India as early as 1840.[20] The East India Company Court of Directors quickly spotted its potential and suggested in 1845 that scientific and educational institutions in Bombay might introduce training in the art.[21] By the 1850s, photography, even when still using awkward equipment with long exposures and complex chemistry, was regularly entering the correspondence of military figures in the subcontinent.[22] In 1857 Robert Shebbeare, who won the Victoria Cross during the Revolt, recorded his intention to send new photographs of Delhi to his relatives at home. Later, in January 1858, he asked his sister to get one of her friends 'to do you in photograph again' since he had lost likenesses of her in camp at Rohtuck. In February of that year, he wrote home that he had received the photograph of granny and asked for more of his family. In 1860, he was posted to China for the opium war and in early July of that year he was writing home from Camp Talien Hwan in Manchuria that 'Signor Beato [is] here in nearby village' and 'wants to take my portrait for his volume of Indian celebrities'. He was intending to go down 'in all my war paint' this afternoon or tomorrow.[23] Shebbeare was then involved in the battle of the Taku Forts and Beato was on hand to photograph the resulting damage and Chinese casualties. As a result of injuries Shebbeare subsequently died at sea, but his correspondence reveals the extent to which photography had become almost a commonplace for officers on campaign. His encounter with the Italian-born photographer Felice (or Felix) Beato reflects that figure's extraordinary travels and early campaign photography.[24]

Having spent time in the Mediterranean (including the British imperial possession of Malta), working with the photographer James Robertson, Beato went to the Crimea and photographed the results of the war there. During this Mediterranean, Crimean and Middle Eastern period, he developed a technique of taking multiple contiguous exposures that could be joined together such that the highly popular and long-standing public attraction of the panorama could be turned into photographic form, albeit on a smaller scale. In 1858 he went to Calcutta and initiated travels throughout northern India to photograph the results of the 1857 Revolt, including the destruction wrought to the city of Lucknow.[25] He seems to have developed a macabre fascination with corpses (of non-European people) and ensured that human remains appeared in some of his photographs, as in his celebrated image of the Sikander Bagh palace in Lucknow, for which the bodies had actually been disinterred.[26] After the 1860 Opium War in China, he spent time in Japan before being invited to join the Wolseley expedition to Khartoum to rescue General Gordon. Now firmly established as a war photographer he went on to Burma for the ending of the third Burmese war, in which the British completed their conquest, and stayed there for some years. In these ways, images of colonial campaigns, at least of the results of the fighting, became available.[27] It may be that it was Victorian society's fascination with war which proved to be a major fillip to the development of photography world-wide.[28] Moreover, as photographic reproduction became easier later in the century, Beato's work came to illustrate many war and travel accounts as well as articles in the illustrated newspapers, such that his images of the East and of colonial campaigns became standard. He published two photographic albums, *Native Types* and *Views of Japan* in 1868.[29] In the twentieth century, interest in Beato, as with most early photographers, grew tremendously and many books were published about his colonial exploits.[30] If Beato tended to view the results of wars, others photographed on the spot during campaigns. A good example is John McCosh, an army surgeon who took photographs in Burma during the second Burmese war in 1852.[31] A military man with an unlikely name, Captain Linnaeus Tripe, accompanied Arthur Phayre's mission to the court of King Mindon in Ava in 1855 and took many photographs on the journey up the Irrawaddy.[32] Photographers from the firm of Bourne and Shepherd visited Burma in the late 1860s and early 1870s, with a particular interest in photographing its peoples, an opportunity occasioned by imperial war and conquest.

Early photography and India

The itinerant Beato was followed by large numbers of practitioners who opened up businesses in India. Just as the subcontinent inspired many travelling artists, photographers were also highly mobile, attracted by India's unique combination of rich and extensive cultural history, remarkable architectural traditions, fascinatingly diverse peoples and opulent princely lifestyles. Like artists, photographers were captivated by striking topographical characteristics, including great mountain ranges, forests and the diversity of flora and fauna.[33] While professional photographic studios were established in cities and towns to satisfy the considerable market for portraits of expatriates and elite Indians, as well as (later) postcards and other images, some photographers set off on travels. John Burke and William Baker were Irishmen who both left the military in India and established a commercial photography business in Peshawar in 1861.[34] But the lure of the frontier and Afghanistan was appealing and they set out to photograph the region as well as chronicle incidents of the 'Great Game' between the rival empires of Russia and Britain. They were also on hand to photograph wars in Afghanistan.

Perhaps the most famous photography business in India was that of Samuel Bourne and Charles Shepherd. Although the origins of that company are complex, partly connected with studios founded in Agra and Simla from about 1863, the partnership existed by 1864 and their most celebrated studio had already been opened in Calcutta, eventually with branches throughout India as well as in London and Paris. Despite the company being in its infancy, Samuel Bourne chose to go on a series of photographic journeys into the Himalayas between 1863 and 1866. He wrote extensive letters to the *British Journal of Photography* and delivered lectures about his travels. These have been published and offer striking details of the conditions he faced.[35] He took well over 2,000 photographs on these journeys. The other notable photographic studio in Calcutta was Johnston and Hoffman, opened in 1882 and positioned in a key location on Chowringhee Road. They opened branches in Darjeeling and Simla in the 1890s, then one in Rangoon. They were prominent in issuing postcards, starting in 1898. A later example is Fred Bremner who went to India in 1882, apprenticed himself to Lawrie's of Naini Tal (Lawrie, who also had a studio in Lucknow, was his brother-in-law) before establishing a studio in Karachi, and later in Quetta, Lahore and Rawalpindi, and finally Simla from 1910.[36] A good deal of Bremner's business was with the Indian army as his published works reveal. In 1895 he produced an album of sixty photographs, *Types of the Indian Army*, in a limited edition of around fifty copies. Other albums, generally dealing with the service of regiments, were published in Quetta and Lahore. He also photographed Indian princes, whom he treated very sympathetically. His wife photographed the Begum of Bhopal and was permitted to photograph ladies of the *zenana* of Muslim princes.[37] The Riddell Collection of photographs in the Scottish National Portrait Gallery contains many photographs of India from Bremner, as well as from Bourne and Robertson (one of the incarnations of that company), and L.H. Wilson.[38] Apparently, these include images of trades and occupations ranging from:

A fruit market in Quetta to a laboratory in Nepal; carpet designers and makers of brassware in the Punjab and metalworkers in Bombay; writers and bankers in Delhi and Benares. There are vendors of Kashmiri woodcarving and Mooltan pottery; bazaars in Udaipur; snake charmers and flower sellers in Bombay.[39]

Photographers were clearly fascinated by Indian crafts and associated commercial activity.

The global spread of commercial photographers and indigenous practitioners

Bremner's photographic practice survived into the 1920s. He was one of a wave of commercial photographers who illustrate the astonishing globalising power of empire in facilitating the rapid appearance of photographic companies. Within scarcely a decade of the invention of photography, commercial photographers from an extraordinary range of ethnicities were opening premises on every continent. It is difficult to establish which was the earliest of these, but it seems that Robert Hall set up a studio in Currie Street, Adelaide as early as 1846. It has also been suggested that Hall introduced photography to Western Australia in the same year, when he took the first portraits in Perth.[40] This must have been partly on the strength of the daguerreotype camera he bought from the artist S.T. Gill at this time. William Johnson, who was an uncovenanted member (that is in the clerical rather than administrative branch) of the Indian Civil Service set up a daguerreotype studio in Bombay in 1852 and moved on to calotype technology in 1854. John Nicholas opened a studio in Madras around 1858. In 1846, William Syme, a coppersmith in Cape Town, advertised for daguerreotype apparatus and is known to have begun producing photographs shortly afterwards. In 1854 he went to Britain to study the collodion process and was soon using it in his business in Cape Town.[41] James Robertson, who had teamed up with Beato for a period, opened a photographic business in Pera, Istanbul, in 1854, but abandoned it in the 1860s when he returned to his profession as an engraver at the mint.[42] Some well-known photographers were employed by existing firms before setting up their own establishments. Examples include Charles Nettleton who arrived in 1854 and opened his studio in Melbourne in 1858 after employment with a firm known as Durea and McDonald. Given Melbourne's status as the gold boom city, it is perhaps not surprising that it was also a major centre of photography. John Nicol Crombie, originally an engineer, arrived there in 1852 and became assistant to photographers Meade Brothers, before moving to New Zealand in 1854 and starting businesses in Nelson and Auckland. Later in the century, Thomas Mathewson opened a luxurious studio in Brisbane, Queensland.[43] James Bragge emigrated to South Africa and became a photographer in the 1860s, then moved to New Zealand and opened a celebrated studio in Wellington, also using a mobile dark room to travel extensively taking topographical images.[44] The celebrated William Notman emigrated from Scotland to Canada in 1856 and immediately opened his studio in Montreal.[45] Further west, Frederick Dally, an immigrant to British Columbia from London, set up a photographic gallery in Victoria in 1866 which was active until 1870.[46] He travelled around British Columbia, photographing landscapes, settlements, the Cariboo gold rush, and First Nations people.[47] The Colonial Office commissioned photographs from him and he accompanied the governor on a voyage round Vancouver Island and along the coast. His photographic albums are highly regarded and one he presented to Queen Victoria is in the Royal Collection.[48]

James Bruton's studio opened in Port Elizabeth in 1858 before he moved to Cape Town. Robert Harris also had a business in Port Elizabeth from 1880 and was active in supplying photographs for books of South African scenery. But photography was not an exclusively male profession. Many studios employed women as assistants, some of whom worked on the technical side or became photographers themselves. Notman appointed women to his printing room.[49] A studio in Colombo, Ceylon was very much the business of a woman, known as Madam Del Tufo, operating between 1914 and 1930. Inez Maria Gibello was born in India, the daughter of an Italian merchant. In 1895 she married Innocenzo del Tufo who had studios in Bombay, Bangalore, Ootacamund and Madras. They opened a Colombo branch in 1900, with Inez operating independently from 1914.[50]

All these examples come from the major colonial cities, but there were similar photographic establishments in every colony, including Caribbean and Pacific islands,[51] Singapore, Malaya and African territories acquired later in the century. Strikingly, non-Europeans seized upon the technology and rapidly established themselves as expert practitioners. In India, the most famous is Lala Deen Dayal who attended the Thomason engineering college in Roorkee, initially joined government service, but attracted the attention of the Maharajah of Indore and British officials, securing photographic commissions. He photographed the tour of the governor general in Central India in 1867 and then the visit of the Prince of Wales to India in 1875.[52] He had studios in Indore, Secunderabad and Bombay, later in Hyderabad after he had been appointed court photographer to the Nizam in 1885, where he photographed the exterior and interior views of the palaces. He also accompanied Curzon on his viceregal tours.[53] He was one of the photographers of Curzon's 1903 Delhi Durbar and took as many as 400 images, of which 100 were chosen for an album, though it was not a commercial success. Dayal's work has been seen as offering an 'alternative modernity', images that can be seen as subtly subverting the Durbar while apparently depicting its events.[54] Many of his glass plates have survived and are in a public collection in New Delhi, while the business was continued by his descendants. Many Indian photographers followed, some commercial professionals, others from among the princely rulers. One of these was Maharajah Sawai Ram Singh II of Jaipur who, under the tutelage of the photographer T. Murray, became enthralled by the medium and worked in wet collodion plates and sensitised albumen paper.[55] All photographers, European and Indian, were supported by Indian assistants in a variety of roles.[56] When Violet Jacob visited the Maharajah of Dhar in 1897, she and her husband 'were photographed, by order of His Highness' by a 'Hindu whom he had sent for the purpose, for he is interested in collecting the portraits of all his English guests'.[57]

Further east, the most celebrated Chinese photographer in Hong Kong was Lai Afong, who was already well established when the traveller and photographer John Thomson opened his studio there after 1868.[58] Thomson was an admirer of Lai Afong's work, which he extolled in his book *The Straits of Malacca, Indo-China and China*.[59] Lai was superior to all other Chinese photographers he had seen, his photographs being well executed and 'remarkable for the artistic choice of position'. His clientele was clearly a mixed one since he 'kept a Portuguese assistant to wait on Europeans'. Other Chinese photographers included Mee Cheeung who developed a business in Hong Kong in the 1890s. The East African island of Zanzibar, a key centre for exploration and slavery suppression in the region, had a celebrated photographic business, A.C. Gomes and Son (the family may have been from Goa), perhaps as early as 1868,[60] though it has been suggested that the business started in Aden in 1869 and moved to Zanzibar soon afterwards.[61] Gomes took official and semi-official photographs in Aden with his son A.F. taking the first photographs of the Uganda Railway. A.F. opened a studio in Dar-es-Salaam during the British mandate in the former German colony in 1929. W.D. Young had a business in Nairobi c.1908. In West Africa, the Freetown-born members of a Creole family, the Lisk-Carew brothers, Alphonso and Arthur, established themselves as the pre-eminent photographic studio in Sierra Leone from 1905. This studio continued to operate for some fifty years.[62] Later, a notable African photographer was Solomon Osagie Alonge (1911–94), a Nigerian who was official photographer to the court of the two successive *obas* (kings) of Benin. He made a remarkable record of the pageantry, clothing, regalia and rituals of the royal court, as well as recording receptions for members of the British royal family, governors general and others.[63] Trained in Lagos, he opened the Ideal Photo Studio in Benin City and maintained the historical record of the Benin court and capital city when active between 1926 and 1989. Photography additionally created opportunities for people of one colony to work in another. We have already seen the example of the Gomes family. Burma offers others since the British conquest created opportunities for commercial photographers in Rangoon and later Mandalay, including Indian immigrants. D.A. Ahuja was a Punjabi photographer whose business was first known as Kundan Dass in 1885, but became Ahuja of Sule Pagoda Road, Rangoon in 1890. He bought the rights to images of Beato and Klier (though he was sued by the latter) and took over the studio of Watts and Skeen.[64] Many decades before the Japanese invasion, there were also Japanese photographers at work in Burma. Although Tibet was never part of the British Empire, despite being invaded and photographed by the British (as in the Younghusband expedition of 1903–4), the thirteenth Dalai Lama (in office 1879–1933) apparently took up photography.[65] Other photographers used the camera differently. Rajendra Lall Mitra was a Calcutta polymath, a figure of the Bengal Renaissance, who adopted it as an aid to his study of antiquities.[66]

Albums, societies, exploration, ethnography, lantern slides and postcards

Many commercial photographers published albums of pictures, entering the publishing field as well as running a studio. An example is J. Watson's *Queensland Album of Photographic Scenery* of 1873, while John Caire, whose studio in Adelaide opened in 1867, produced *Views of Bendigo* (1875), *Views of Victoria* (1877–79), *Views of Sydney Harbour and New South Wales* (c.1877), *Victorian Scenery* (c.1883) and *Gippsland Scenery* (c.1866). Some were ethnographic 'types' as with William Johnson's *The Oriental Races and Tribes, Residents and Visitors of Bombay* (2 vols, 1863 and 1866), representing the characteristic colonial reduction of the identity of individuals to stereotypes. Even department stores found it profitable to produce and sell such albums, for example Whiteaway, Laidlaw and Co. of Rangoon, although they could be expensive.[67] This explosion in the numbers of photographic studios indicated the extent of demand for portraits and topographical views. Many studios additionally issued series of stereoscopic slides relating to travel and colonies. The London Stereoscopic Company sold well over 2 million, while the Notman company in Montreal started issuing stereoscopic views of Canada in 1859.[68]

As photography swept the empire, societies and institutions organised themselves for the dissemination of information, good practice and social contact for amateurs and professionals. The

Bombay Photographic Society was founded in 1854 and equivalents followed in Calcutta and Madras in 1856.[69] Similar societies sprang up around India and elsewhere in the colonies.[70] This was a technology which inspired clubability in the exchange of technical and aesthetic ideas. Somewhat later, the first Camera Club in South Africa appeared in Kimberley in 1890 with another created in Cape Town in the same year.[71] Meanwhile, the significance of photography for the military, and hence for imperial and national enterprises, had already been recognised when the photographic section of the telegraph school of the Royal Engineers at Chatham was formed in 1856. A separate School of Photography and Chemistry was founded in 1874 and was combined with the Survey School in 1904. This training activity was charged with preparations for Boundary Commissions, Middle Eastern Surveys and military campaigns in north-east Africa. There is a photograph of the North-West Frontier of India survey group of 1865 in the Riddell Collection of the Scottish National Portrait Gallery, which identifies both British and Indian members by name. Indians were indeed closely involved in such surveys.[72]

From the mid-nineteenth century, the camera became a vital adjunct of all exploratory expeditions and the publications arising from them. The lifetime of the most high-profile explorer of the nineteenth century, David Livingstone (1813–73), was punctuated by the invention of photography. By the time he was planning his Zambezi expedition in 1857 he was aware of its significance and appointed his brother as the project's photographer. Charles Livingstone was a failure in this role, but John Kirk, significantly a doctor, produced some useable photographs. The symbiotic relationship between photography and exploration was neatly illustrated by the inclusion of a section on photography in the Royal Geographical Society's (RGS) *Hints to Travellers* of 1864, while the RGS also assisted explorers by loaning cameras and providing other services.[73] For the RGS, photography was to be used mainly as an aid to cartography.[74] In the early twentieth century, photography was important in expeditions to the final frontier in the Antarctic.[75]

Exploration was closely connected with ethnographic photography, including anthropometric physical anthropology which became a key aid to the development of the racial theories of the period. Anthropological photography existed in various forms. On the one hand, it was intended to produce a complete record of the peoples of empire, in some cases because it was imagined that, in a Darwinian way, they could be categorised on a scale of primitiveness in which some were doomed to disappear. Photography could provide an archival record of their existence and their appearance, as well as of their culture. Anthropometry on the other hand constituted the science of the physical measurement of humans. This was designed to indicate the supposed relationship between such physical measurements and physical, intellectual and even psychological characteristics. It was thus essentially a racial tool, a means to the production of putative race hierarchies, particularly developed after 1869 when a systematic grid was introduced against which subjects could be photographed.[76] It constituted the racialised version of photographs taken in European prisons that were designed to show the physical and physiognomic features that could allegedly indicate criminality. By extension, prisoners in the colonies constituted a captive and non-resistant group among whom such techniques could be used. Hence photography became a prime tool of racial theory and practice of the period, initially encouraged by the RGS and the Ethnological Society of London. In subtly different ways this was a tradition which continued into the twentieth century, not only through the work of anthropologists, but also such figures as the explorer, traveller and photographer Wilfred Thesiger.[77] Exploration was also closely connected with the phenomenon of the magic lantern slide. Livingstone was himself celebrated for using the magic lantern to captivate – and sometimes terrify – his audiences in Africa (although his slides were generally not photographic). Famously, he called it his 'valuable travelling friend', the 'oxy-hydrogen light of civilisation'. This was emblematic of the lantern's apparent represen-

tation of the superior culture of Europeans through its striking technology. While the concept of the projected slide through a machine
with a light source goes back to the seventeenth century, it was only
in the middle of the nineteenth that it became inseparably connected
with photography. Although it remained shackled to the notion of
'magic' acquired in the first two centuries of its use, it now became a
supposedly more rational vehicle for the projection of the emotional
narratives of empire.[78] The images projected underlined this by
revealing so much about the world. In an illuminating exercise, Jack
Thompson analysed the subjects represented in the slide sets that
survive in the missions of northern Malawi and in collections in
Edinburgh. He demonstrated the ways in which Africans were
inducted into the notion that the civilisation of Britain was transparently 'advanced' through the material presence of buildings, transport
systems and images of fighting power. The lantern shows thus
asserted that here were cultures of such power and physical presence
that it was useless to attempt to defy the inexorable forces they represented. Missionary propaganda set out to reveal the power of the
Christian faith through biblical scenes, and above all through depictions of people transformed by conversion. In Britain, such 'before'
and 'after' effects could also prove valuable in securing emotional and
financial support for missionary work, as would images of the most
celebrated missionaries, depicted as heroes coping with alien natural
environments, disease, wild animals and indigenous people supposedly sunk in inter-tribal warfare and alien moralities. This tool was
of great value both 'home' and 'away', with special biographical sets
on sale. An excellent example is the set of forty hand-coloured slides
for use in lectures, 'The Life and Work of David Livingstone',
published by the London Missionary Society about 1900.[79]

As Thompson and Ryan have demonstrated, the immensely
popular lantern-slide performances purported to be an entertainment and educational medium, yet contrived to propagate imperial
ideologies, including empire geographies and relationships, visions

of the natural world, exotic topographies, built environments and peoples, as well as concepts of social and religious improvement.[80] The Church Missionary Society created a Lantern and Loan Department in 1881 and in 1898 there were almost 3,000 requests for the loan of slides.[81] This was perhaps the most potent visual medium between the eras of the panorama and the cinema. While slide series based on photographs were used from at least the 1850s, it was only after the invention of the dry plate gelatin photographic process, and its development in the 1870s, that images could be translated more readily into slides. Hence, the real heyday of the slide series lasted from the 1880s to the 1920s. Commercial manufacturers and sellers of slides occasionally employed photographers to travel the world to bring back suitable images. Among these companies were Newton of London, G.W. Wilson of Aberdeen and Scott of Glasgow.[82] To demonstrate how extensive such materials could be, Newton had a catalogue of some 200,000 slides on the eve of the First World War. The point about the lantern was that as well as projecting images from photographs taken around the world it was sufficiently portable to be taken to relatively remote regions. Slides could be shown to quite small audiences of African villagers out of doors after dark, or to thousands assembled in spaces like London's Royal Albert Hall, as in H.M. Stanley's mass audiences for lectures about his African explorations. A set of sixty-three slides used by him is in the collections of the African Museum in Tervuren, Belgium.[83] Thus it was flexible enough to convey ideologies and emotions in an entertaining way both in the metropole and at the colonial 'periphery'.

Secular organisations also used slides to project social messages. These included Barnardo's boys' homes, the Salvation Army, the Band of Hope and other temperance associations all of which used the 'before' and 'after' technique to drive their points home. This drew some criticism since some saw the images, for example of homeless boys before they were 'saved' by Barnardo's, as overdrawn and demeaning, especially since these were necessarily 'faked' as in the case of similar missionary slides. The first Barnardo's home was set up in 1870 and in 1891 the organisation was already establishing a relationship with Australia when A.R.E. Burton, Secretary of the Victorian Scripture Instructional League, was sent to the Antipodean colonies to give lantern-slide lectures about social problems in Britain and their effects upon the young.[84] This fund-raising operation was highly successful, with Burton's lectures attended by large audiences. The Australian Anglican missionary to Aborigines, John Brown Gribble, had already taken up the technique to raise both profile and funds for his mission, Warangesda in western New South Wales. In these ways, Burton operated 'telescopic philanthropy' (so often criticised by Charles Dickens and others) in reverse, seeking Australian support for the disadvantaged 'waifs' of London while Gribble sought funding for his work with Aborigines. These contrasting operations established the background to the later efforts to migrate (involuntarily) some of the orphans to Australia, while the Australian policy of removing children (particularly of mixed race), later known as the Stolen Generations, was connected with the kind of images presented by Gribble of the supposedly degraded lifestyles of Aborigines.[85] Slides were also marshalled for one of the relatively rare instances of official propaganda, the operations of the Colonial Office Visual Instruction Committee founded in 1902.[86] This organisation sent Hugh Fisher as 'official artist/photographer' to India to compile images, although it was sometimes suspected that he was more interested in art than in photography. Nevertheless, sets of slides depicting aspects of the Indian Empire were produced and used.

From the end of the nineteenth century, however, photography took a new and more democratic turn.[87] This was with the invention of the picture postcard and its progressive acceptance by the Post Office as a postal item. So-called smaller 'court cards' were issued between 1895 and 1899, but the long-running standard size began to be issued in the latter year. Initially, messages had to be written on a small blank space on the pictorial side with the reverse reserved for the address. In 1902, the Post Office relented and postcards with divided backs appeared, enabling a message to be written on the left and the address on the right. It is really from this point (including the impetus of the Anglo-Boer War) that literally millions of them were printed and transmitted from colony to metropole and across the web of imperial territories. In their Edwardian heyday they were issued in both black and white and early coloured versions. But they became much more than simply the conveyors of messages. Large numbers of recipients were attracted by the fascination of readily available images of colonial places and soon a major collecting craze was in full swing with albums of postcards created in many homes. Postcards additionally became an important advertising medium often using imperial images: emigration societies saw them as a cheap way of projecting propaganda while shipping lines and companies selling imperial products (such as Lipton's tea) used them to advertise services and products. Missionary societies sold them at missionary exhibitions regularly held in Britain. The great industrial exhibitions also became a source of countless postcards, both as images of their own temporary architectural splendours and as propaganda from their many exhibitors. The related cigarette cards offered another marketing technique.

Colonial postcards have become a source of serious study in modern times since their images have considerable historical value, not only in revealing past urban and rural topographies but also for ethnography and the ideologies encapsulated within them.[88] An early example of a work utilising postcards was Alloula's celebrated *The Colonial Harem*, which revealed the strikingly gendered attitudes and erotic sexual stereotyping of women in those sold in Algeria.[89] These images, assembled as *scènes et types*, which were popular and regularly sent through the post, distorted the lives and cultural manners of women in North Africa, denigrating them in the process. Further evidence of scholarly interest comes in the work of Gilles

Teulié, who has also examined the racial aspects of postcards illustrating women and their significance in popularising empire.[90] Another is Beukers' *Exotic Postcards* covering the stereotyping, racial (and racist) ethnographic gaze, and again the mainly demeaning and erotic presentation of women in many places in the world.[91] In an entirely different league, valuable postcard illustrations as empirical evidence include the officially inspired joint publication of the National Archives of both Malaysia and Singapore, *Reminiscences of the Straits Settlements through Postcards*, which largely features buildings and urban and rural scenes.

Many commercial photographers increased their commercial range, and presumably their incomes, from the issue of such cards. Since there are literally innumerable examples, West Africa illustrates the phenomenon well. The Lisk-Carew studio issued large numbers of cards of Sierra Leone, as did other Freetown photographers such as Greensmith (who proudly exhibited the warrant of HRH the Duke of Connaught because they photographed his visit to West Africa), W.S. Johnston, Pickering and Berthoud, and Paris and Co., all of them operating early in the twentieth century.[92] In addition, cards of imperial territories were produced in Europe by the celebrated Raphael Tuck company in London (which began producing postcards on a large scale from 1899–1900) and Thies of Hamburg.[93] Jacob Vitta of Tarkwa in south-west Gold Coast produced cards for this colony, while H. Sanya Freeman (probably another Sierra Leonean Creole) of Lagos described himself as 'photographer-in-chief' to the governor of Nigeria.[94] Missionary societies additionally produced postcards for the commercial market, with images that were not necessarily connected with proselytisation. Three West African examples were the Basel Mission, which published cards of the Gold Coast, the Methodist Book Depot for Cape Coast (issuing cards of the Ashanti War and the Siege of Kumasi in 1900) and the Church Missionary Society in Lagos. This was just an additional money-making venture illustrating missionary signing up to imperial exploits. This extensive market continued to grow until the inter-war years, and these West African examples can be multiplied countless times in relation to other parts of Africa, India, South-East Asia, the Caribbean and territories of white settlement.[95] In the case of India, vast numbers of cards were produced with a ready market among expatriate Britons and travellers.[96] These included lengthy series depicting the range and specific roles of Indian servants, a tradition starting with early cards in the late 1890s, demonstrating the notoriously large numbers of domestic staff underpinning the lives of Europeans.

Such runs of cards popularly reflected the more serious ways in which photography became the ideal auxiliary for the Victorian passion for categorisation, dividing and subdividing peoples in racial, cultural, physical and religious ways, as well as in relation to their physiognomies and clothing. The most celebrated example was the eight-volume study by John Forbes Watson and John William Kaye, *The People of India*, published between 1868 and 1875 and containing 468 photographs to illustrate the alleged range of ethnicities and tribes.[97] This project, inaugurated by the Viceroy Canning, who had encouraged officers of the government to take photographs, was followed by other examples. This approach to the peoples of India became central to British theories of rule in the subcontinent.[98] Such British ideological passions have been usefully linked to the Orientalism debate initiated by Edward Said, and extended to New Zealand and the Pacific.[99] This underpinning of imperial theory can be found in the extraordinarily diverse and prolific series of 'ethnic' postcards issued in India and elsewhere.[100] This tradition of 'types', exhibiting a great diversity of peoples continued into the inter-war years, projecting a principal British justification for their rule. Large numbers of postcards of peoples of Burma were issued which, while extending the notion of manifold ethnic heterogeneity illustrative of past conflict, also present a remarkable amount of evidence for textiles, clothing, crafts and carving, embracing materials and structures that have often disappeared.[101] Large numbers of cards illustrated the principal cities and towns, demonstrating the expansion of an alleged European civilisation. Cards thus operated as souvenirs, vehicles of communication, transmitters of justificatory ideology, collectables, and now sources for research.[102]

Photography, imperial ideologies, missionaries and humanitarianism

If photography became deeply instrumental in embedding imperial ideologies in global culture, it also became a vehicle for Christian missionary endeavour and humanitarian efforts. Photographers were never neutral, all their images being concerned to project particular messages, while missionary photographers had a very specific focus: to expand the kingdom of the Christian God. It is noticeable that many who have written about missionary photography have been practising Christians sharing, at least in part, the vision of the missionaries themselves.[103] A sense of this is perfectly conveyed in an editorial in the *International Bulletin of Missionary Research*:

> Hans Rollmann demonstrates that missionary photographs from Labrador some 130 years ago constituted much more than simply visual proof of the legitimacy of the Moravians' work and their worthiness of financial support. They served a profoundly theological purpose as well, reinforcing the Moravian Church's self-definition as a mission church, and reaffirming each congregation, however remote, as part of a wider entity.[104]

When missionaries photographed indigenous people among whom they worked, they were concerned either to demonstrate the extent to which missionary endeavour was required to 'bring light on darkness' or were anxious to reveal the transforming effect of conversion. Missionary ethnic photographs thus set out to reveal either strange and barbaric practices or the transformation of converts through clothing, interest in the gospels and the attributes of Europeans, as in western buildings or crafts such as printing. The heroism of missionaries in alien and dangerous environments was rewarded in the commitment of converts taking holy orders and making the great leap of both faith and culture. Mission stations, churches, schools, hospitals and the proffered industrial and agricultural training supplied further attractive images. Another group of heroes were the doctors, nurses and artisans who offered routes to conversion via good works, overturning supposedly primitive methods in warlike societies. Printed in missionary publications and magazines, or the great wave of popular missionary biographies of the late nineteenth and early twentieth centuries, such images achieved wide circulation to stimulate the support of the Christian constituency at home, not least in the provision of funds. What is striking is that such material was slotted into the wider imperial tradition of adventure and heroism.[105] In these and other ways, the synergy between missionary and imperial objectives becomes obvious, if 'imperial' is interpreted as meaning the supposedly visionary and transcendental objectives of idealists.

Among the proponents of such an agenda, missionaries were often in the forefront of humanitarian campaigns, supplying photographs to expose the atrocities that stirred the conscience of the liberal public at the turn of the twentieth century. The most celebrated example was the Congo Reform Association (CRA) active between 1904 and 1913 and co-founded by E.D. Morel. This organisation set out to expose atrocities perpetrated in the Congo Free State, the private fiefdom of the Belgian King Leopold II. The CRA based its campaign on evidence provided by missionaries of the Congo Balolo Mission, a Baptist missionary organisation active in the Congo from 1889. The key figures were the Rev. John Harris and his wife Alice, who arrived in the Congo in 1898, and later Roger Casement, the British Consul in the Congo. Casement travelled widely in the territory and prepared a report for the British Foreign Office in which he exposed the campaign of violence, enslavement, torture and mutilation imposed by Leopold's officers in pursuit of rubber extraction.[106] The report was published in 1904. The Harrises then became involved in the CRA although Morel would have preferred the organisation to remain essentially secular. Nonetheless, he came to accept their hugely effective methods in publishing photographs and delivering lantern-slide lectures around Britain and the USA. The shocking photographs emerging from the Congo, showing mutilations suffered by people failing to supply their requisite quota of rubber or who had, in the eyes of the brutal regime, transgressed in other ways, now brought photography to the fore as a weapon of supposedly anti-imperial propaganda.[107] A number of missionaries had been involved in taking atrocity photographs and Grattan Guinness (a founder of the mission) and Casement were couriers who brought these back from the Congo for wider distribution.[108] Many were printed in missionary publications. The Harris lantern-slide show collection can be found in the National Museums, Liverpool. Paradoxically, this campaign led to the extension of direct European imperialism, since international outrage ensured that Leopold was forced to hand over the Congo to the Belgian authorities in 1908. This outcome no doubt pleased the missionaries since they always opposed the exercise of imperialism by proxy, as in the late nineteenth-century British chartered companies.

In Australia at a later date there were some photographers who sought to show the complexities and variety of Aboriginal societies and also reveal the justice of their causes, for example in relation to land rights.[109] Other examples of such Australian photography have been charted by Jane Lydon who has demonstrated that there were humanitarian networks across the British Empire, bound together by the extensive print and visual culture of missionary associations. Thus missionaries sought to oppose the cultural denigration and physical brutalising of Aboriginal peoples by white stockholders and settlers by creating, partly through photographs, a greater sense of sympathetic understanding of the dignity of the people and of their capacity to imbibe Christianity and therefore western 'civilisation'. One means of doing this was by photographing Aborigines in western clothing, sometimes as couples to illustrate the redeeming power of the conjugal relationship.[110] It can therefore be said that humanitarian photography in this period, while setting out to mitigate the racial attitudes and accompanying violence of imperial rule, did so within the strict bounds of imperial ideology. Thus, while such photographs sought to prompt outrage at specific conditions, they were nonetheless invariably designed to demonstrate that imperialism could create uplifting opportunities within the context of the hierarchical structures and sense of cultural superiority of the dominant (white) people. Humanitarianism cannot therefore be separated from its imperial contexts. Seldom overtly anti-imperial, photography was directed more towards the creation of ethical empire. This was very much a liberal and idealistic concept of the time, although some today consider it an oxymoron.

Photography simultaneously constituted a likeness, a tool and a weapon of imperialism. It was the likeness of empire in that photography established its own imperial surge and global dynamic, offering vast numbers of images of imperial places and people to the readers of books, magazines and illustrated journals. Far from wiping out the sense of the secret and the hidden, these seemed, for western peoples, to enhance the supposed heroic adventure and romance of imperial and colonial places. What seemed like an objective likeness offered the opportunity for all to enter the territories of empire and become part of the supposed excitement of the imperial mission. Hence the camera established its own territory, not least after the emergence of the postcard and the opportunity to capture empire in the albums of collectors, many of them ordinary people, who might not have possessed more expensive photographs. This likeness also encouraged the critics of empire through offering visions of the brutality and destructiveness of imperial campaigns while also providing evidence for those following a religious or humanitarian ambition of improvement of the human condition. In consciously creating negative images and sensations, the camera both stimulated opposition to the enterprise and suggested the possibility of progress and improvement, the allegedly positive side of the imperial drive.

It was a tool that helped to fashion the growth and development of imperial rule, from the point of view of continuing military conquest, increasing settlement patterns, and technical and economic developments. Governments quickly recognised that photography was a vital auxiliary to empire. From the middle of the nineteenth century, almost every event was made available to policy makers and the inhabitants of the British World. The events and settings of empire were accessible to all, even if most only noticed those within their immediate experience and needs. Few places continued to be unknown, even if romantic conceptions ensured that some had to be. Photography was the essential tool of explorers, geographers, geologists, engineers of railway lines and canals, as well as of agricultural, industrial and other major developments. It became the key device of advertisers in the great commercial and consumption boom of the last decades of the century. It was a crucial instrument of missionary endeavour, supporting the essential drive to blend Christianity with the 'civilising mission'. This included city improvement and the creation of better sanitary and domestic conditions in the twentieth century. The camera provided photographic evidence for slum conditions and overcrowded living spaces leading to the prevalence of diseases and social problems. The resulting slum clearance was based on positive ambitions, but often produced negative results.[111]

Cameras 'shot' people and scenes, turning them into tools of imperialism, for Brenda Croft 'the most abusive of colonial weapons'.[112] Many indigenous peoples, not surprisingly, saw the parallelism with the gun, between the 'barrel' and the 'lens', and deeply suspected it as a result, particularly if their religious sensibilities saw the capture and depiction of the human form as being dangerously unacceptable. They saw it as potentially an instrument of death and to a certain extent their fears were justified. Many in the West saw the camera as 'capturing' declining cultures, some of them doomed to extinction. As the alleged 'preserver' the camera was also the destroyer, precursor of the failure of preservation. Moreover, as war photographers followed the military, they often captured the corpses of the defeated, the individual remains of what seemed to be dying peoples and systems. Military photographers were also capable of being insensitive. Colonel W.W. Hooper, who spent forty years in India and was active as a photographer both there and in Burma, was the subject of censure for his callous handling of his efforts to photograph the execution of dacoits after the third Burma War.[113] He had also been unfeeling in the manner in which he had arranged victims of the 1876–78 Madras famine for the sake of his photographs.[114] The camera thus encouraged powerful sensations of racial difference in its relentless depictions of 'otherness', supposedly backward, sometimes quaint, occasionally threatening, and even at times amusing. It became the framer of aspects of modern racism, the key component of the sense of superior dominance of imperial peoples. Sometimes it was possible for these effects to take the opposite course, a turn that was to rise to predominance towards the end of empire and in the postcolonial period.

This makes the camera the agent of all that was negative and even destructive in empire. But there can be no doubt that photography also succeeded in capturing images, as never before, of antiquities, buildings, even natural phenomena doomed to disappear as modernity (in technological developments or agricultural and industrial changes) rolled relentlessly on, or as seismic and meteorological events took their toll. Even here, however, modern scholars have suggested that the extensive photographing of Indian architecture was part of the British project to codify and control the cultural heritage of India.[115] Nevertheless, in Burma, a territory particularly afflicted by destruction, photographs have retained a record of countless buildings, religious and secular, that were destroyed by British, Japanese and other attackers during the Second World War. These included monasteries, temples and stupas, the palace in Mandalay, and much more.[116] The products of the camera have become research tools in the present, not just for the ideologies inherent in their framing of the world, but also for the images of buildings and antiquities, textiles, crafts and other achievements which they preserved.

But importantly, the camera ceased to be merely the implement of dominant imperialists. The supposedly oppressed seized it with enthusiasm, sometimes because it presented commercial opportunities and the possibilities of making a living, even a fortune. The camera became a global device, valued by peoples outside as well as embroiled in the imperial nexus. New practitioners brought fresh visual concepts to bear, linking the photographic medium to a diversity of cultures. They also set out to mediate their relations with imperial rulers, with their own people, nationalist politics and modernism generally.[117] Throughout the empire, indigenous photographers took over the camera to preserve images of themselves, as well as both kin and kind. In Madras, for example, commercial photography reached the bazaars by the 1880s and much cheaper photographs became available.[118] The camera could become a tool of ordinary people as well as of aristocrats and rulers. Soon the gaze was reversed and the subalterns of empire set about photographing the personalities and places of imperialists. Significantly, it became the weapon of nationalism, projecting the achievements and talents of people seeking a new political dispensation, transmitting likenesses of nationalist leaders into more remote areas, thus disseminating news and sympathetic support. An early example is Neils Walwin Holm, a photographer in Lagos from the 1890s to 1910. Holm was a lawyer involved in the Pan-African movement who set about undermining 'the ideologies of scientific racism and primitivism' partly by creating a photographic and postcard archive revealing the modernism and cosmopolitanism of Lagos.[119] A remarkable example has been explored by the historian John

McCracken.[120] He rescued the reputation of Mungo Murray Chisuse, a Malawian printer who visited Scotland twice and, in 1897, seems to have taken lessons in photography from a notable practitioner, Francis Caird Inglis, as well as spending some months in the printing shop of the publisher Nelson. Returning to Malawi, Chisuse became discontented with the manner in which the Blantyre mission had become intent on racial separation and set himself up as a professional photographer, famously taking photographs of John Chilembwe who led the revolt against the colonial power in 1915. He took many other photographs of Africans, including associates of Chilembwe, but mercifully escaped implication in the revolt and therefore avoided execution. He gave his sitters a dignity and individuality often absent from colonial photography. Much later, the South African nationalist Robert Sobukwe took photographs both in and out of prison designed to reveal the courage and grace of those resisting apartheid, furthering the cause of Black rule.[121] Thus, whereas the camera had been the ideal weapon of imperialism, it became ammunition in the hands of the nationalist cause. However, it must be said that alarmingly it sometimes stirred up communal tensions and political dissent. It also recorded the horrors of decolonisation events, such as the disastrous partition and withdrawal from India in 1947. In other words, the camera has been a many-headed instrument. Jack Thompson clearly expressed its twin effects in colonial circumstances by seeing it as potentially 'liberating and affirming', expressing individual identity and making its subjects more widely known. But it could also be 'an act of violence against the other, an invasion of personal space and a stealing of identity'.[122] Now, in the days of the ubiquity of mobile phone cameras, vast numbers of images are everywhere, often integrating owners through the phenomenon of the 'selfie'.

7
THE PRESS

INSIDE THE PRINTERS' SHOP, LOVEDALE

Inside the printer's shop, Lovedale Mission, South Africa, illustration in a book published in 1909.

News and information throughout the empire were disseminated by new print media, which were originally thought to enhance the cultural unity of the British world. By the twentieth century, however, they were progressively (and rapidly) breaking it down. Newspapers and journals constituted the earliest form of such publications, but their conveyance of news from the metropole and concern for the imperial relationship became increasingly contested. The invention of the telegraph and the international network of undersea cables by the middle of the nineteenth century seemed to promote the integration of imperial press and information systems, particularly with the creation of agencies to gather and disseminate news.[1] These arrangements seemed to reach a climax at the time of the First World War, but the sense of unity they supposedly engendered has been overdrawn. After the Great War, the colonial press scarcely reflected empire connections. From the 1920s international and local affiliations, together with the new medium of radio, became more important than imperial affinities. Of all the cultural transfers of empire, the press thus constitutes a phenomenon where results diverged most strikingly from intentions. Initially, it seemed to the rulers of empire that the printing press and its products could be a valuable handmaiden of imperialism by transmitting information, laying down regulations, as well as propagating the dominant language and ideas of European civilisation. But the result was akin to the tale of the Sorcerer's apprentice whose inadequate magic created the means of fetching quantities of water to save him work, but was then threatened by a destructive flood through his inability to cancel the spell.[2] Similarly the press ultimately overwhelmed imperial rule by stimulating forces menacing its very existence.

It is true that newspapers and journals conveyed British characteristics round the world, not least in the spread of the English language. They disseminated forms of print culture only recently developed in Britain itself, soon generating wider functions than offering news and advertising. They also carried traditions of political disputation in respect of governing institutions like representative and responsible government, as well as issues relating to education and the Christian religion. They spread habits of dialogue, debate and argumentative responses which became the mark of a free society, particularly instrumental in leavening and ultimately breaking autocratic tendencies. They also helped to distribute Enlightenment ideas through news of literary, scientific and other cultural and intellectual societies. Hence they became vehicles for both new forms of

knowledge and contested concepts of social progress, soon demonstrating that imperial controls were inadequate to suppress dissent.
In territories of settlement they were concerned with the stimulation
of migration and the creation of appropriate social and cultural
conditions for migrants, together with economic policies and
commercial developments. Newspapers invariably carried features
listing the arrival and departure of ships, the most significant oiling,
as it were, of the colonial societies and economies in the period. They
charted the spread of railway lines and the appearance of great
resource 'windfalls' such as gold and mineral strikes. They were of
course dependent on the global spread of printing presses (a repeated
phenomenon as the technology improved) and of metal movable
type in various forms, stimulating their manufacture in Britain.
Skilled printers became prized immigrants. Missionary societies and
their far-flung stations were assiduous in spreading such presses
and printers, also training indigenous people.[3] It was not long before
'print shops' were an essential feature of towns almost everywhere,
concerned with printing visiting cards, invitations, posters and all
the other items so culturally essential in the nineteenth century. As
representative institutions, cultural societies, sports and clubs proliferated across the world, printing became vital in producing agendas,
minutes, laws and regulations, programmes, educational syllabi and
texts, all vital to their smooth running. Since printing presses, as in
their earliest days, became the source of libel, scurrilous disputation
and opposition to authorities, they constituted a major focus of social
and political tensions. Easily identifiable, they were subject to attack,
destruction or confiscation. Moreover, like so many other technological developments, colonialists found it impossible to maintain
the exclusivity of printing. Printing presses were destroyed during
the Indian Revolt in 1857 and the resisters themselves used printing
in North India for their own propaganda purposes.[4] By this time it
can be said that the printing press had become truly Indian, so extensive was its use.[5]

Wherever newspapers appeared, they were dependent on several preconditions. As well as a press and the printer, they needed paper, premises and relative freedom from official intervention. There had to be means of newsgathering and a literate readership hungry for reports and information gleaned from announcements and advertisements. Costs had to be recovered, initially from subsidies for publishing official notices, later from the purchase price (to be kept as low as possible to ensure wide circulation) or, more importantly, advertising. Progressively, the flow of news was transformed. At first information was brought by pedestrians and riders, even by carrier pigeons.[6] Trans-oceanic news was conveyed by ships on journeys that, in the age of sail, could take weeks or months, particularly in the case of Asia. This was greatly speeded up by the steam ship, the railway, and then, from the later 1850s the cable, notably undersea lines. These became more numerous and sophisticated and by the early twentieth century had embraced most of the world, a system largely controlled by Britain. But in the years before the First World War, wireless telegraphy began to show its potential, a means of faster transfer of information, providing an opportunity for other states to break the British hold upon global systems, and ultimately a rival for the press itself. Such diversity was extended by computerisation and satellite communications later in the twentieth century. The various colonies of the British Empire reflected the similarities and differences inherent in these revolutionary changes.

The writing of newspaper history has tended to focus on political and economic content. Less attention has been paid to the ways in which the imperial and colonial press came to reflect cultural phenomena, the extent to which the readership secured news of sports, entertainments and other material reflecting colonial interests and local identities. Newspapers exhibited and took pride in the opening of new educational institutions, museums and art galleries, as well as both amateur and professional theatrical and musical performances. The role of the press in developing cultural forms promoting local and national identities cannot be ignored. This chapter will assess the extent to which the non-political columns of selected papers revealed an emphasis on the cultural unity of the empire or served to underpin growing local affinities and forms of consciousness. The latter became increasingly prominent, for example as sporting encounters became more common between metropolitan and colonial teams, as well as among fixtures in neighbouring territories or on an international basis. These certainly aroused as much passion and adherence to newly formed identities as national politics. The rest of this chapter will examine the phases in the development of a colonial press, although diverging political affiliations in the growing print sector are not considered since these are largely irrelevant to the focus on cultural material.

The printing press and early newspapers

In Britain, the *Oxford*, later *London*, *Gazette* was founded in the 1660s Restoration era primarily to disseminate government information, while newspapers in their relatively modern format began to appear in the early eighteenth century.[7] These succeeded the unofficial, often one-off and sometimes libellous broadsides, poems and posters, which were used by individuals to disperse information, unveil scandals (as they saw them) and score points off enemies. Famously, Elizabeth Mallet founded the *Daily Courant* in London in 1702, the earliest daily paper, which survived until 1735. Sometimes notable events gave a colonial newspaper a considerable fillip. Still in Europe, the *Gibraltar Chronicle* was first issued in 1801 and (edited by a Royalist Frenchman) was the first to carry the news of the Battle of Trafalgar and the death of Nelson in a supplement which appeared in both English and French. It became a daily in 1821 and is still publishing today.[8] But daily publication was initially rare. What distinguished newspapers was their regularity (usually weekly), semi-official status and identifiable premises, ensuring that governments (and sometimes mobs) could identify their source. At the same time, a colonial press appeared in the thirteen colonies on the North American seaboard. Newspapers were founded in Boston in 1704 (with a rival appearing in 1719), Philadelphia also in 1719 and Virginia in 1736. By 1775, there were thirty-seven papers in the colonies, all of them weeklies. The influence of such press developments was soon felt further north. The first newspaper in what became Canada was the *Halifax Gazette* which appeared in Nova Scotia in March 1752, produced by John Bushell an immigrant printer from Massachusetts, the printing press having been imported a little earlier.[9] Although Bushell's business was always precarious and he died insolvent, he continued to produce the weekly double-page *Gazette*, generally with the help of a subsidy from the colonial government (but for a gap in the 1760s) until 1867, so that there was a semi-official organ for the publication of announcements and laws.[10] The first issue of the *Gazette* survives and reveals that the paper reprinted excerpts from British and European publications, from the American and Caribbean colonies to the south, as well as government proclamations, ship movements, crime reports and information about 'runaway' slaves.[11] About a quarter of this material related to Nova Scotia. This is an interesting mix of news from the metropolis, the hemisphere (including West Indian plantations) and useful announcements regarding travel, import and export arrangements, as well as crime. The latter was to become a central feature of newspapers, no doubt designed to induce a frisson in their readership. The *Gazette* soon had competition from the *Halifax Chronicle* (1780–1837) and the *Halifax Journal* (1781–1870). The bilingual *Quebec Gazette* was first published in 1764, clearly a vital government-sponsored (and censored) paper appearing just a few years after the British occupation. This was a new development because the authorities in New France had refused to permit the operation of printing presses before the Seven Years' War. The *Montreal Gazette* story is interesting for the relationship with the American Revolution.

In 1779, Fleury Mesplet published *La Gazette du Commerce et Littéraire*, but his sympathies with the American Revolution led him to fall foul of government and he was imprisoned. However, the British needed a printer and he was released as the only skilled person in the city. From 1782 he was permitted to publish the bilingual *Montreal Gazette*. Meanwhile, the *Upper Canada Gazette*, in what was to become Ontario, appeared in 1793 on the assumption that this was a loyal colony.[12]

Several of the early Canadian journals were published by loyalist printers migrating from the newly independent United States. The relationship with colonial administrations was to be a key characteristic of all the eighteenth-century colonial newspapers, including the *New Brunswick Royal Gazette and Advertiser* of 1785, and the *Prince Edward Island Royal American Gazette and Weekly Intelligencer* (1787) started by James Robertson who was a step migrant from Scotland to New York and then Prince Edward Island. The *Canadian Courant and Montreal Advertiser* appeared in 1807, with the *Kingston Gazette* following in 1810. Sometimes the early gazettes survived until modern times as the official organs of the provinces of the Canadian Confederation. The repeated, but not universal, use of the name *Gazette* revealed the extent to which these journals followed the early British example. The other name, *Advertiser*, reflected a principal objective of such papers, vital for revenue, for the development of colonial commerce and as a means of exchange for private citizens. Such papers rapidly spread westwards across Canada.

Early papers in other colonies took a parallel form to those in North America. The content of the *Jamaica Gazette* of 1788 was similar to its Halifax equivalent.[13] Sometimes, they were entirely government-inspired, as in the case of the *Cape Town Gazette and African Advertiser* issued in 1800 during the first period of the British occupation of the Cape after the invasion of 1795. Printed in both English and Dutch, it was designed to be the mouthpiece of the administration and to encourage commerce through advertising. A

241

primitive printing press apparently arrived in New South Wales with the first fleet in 1788 but lay unused until transported convicts with some printing experience took it on. It printed government announcements and regulations until the more regular *Sydney Gazette and Advertiser* was issued in 1803. This was particularly valuable for the locals in offering advertisements for the sale of land and properties, a basic requirement of colonial settlement. By the early decades of the nineteenth century, weekly papers were almost universal in the colonies and were supplemented by various monthly magazines and other occasional publications.

In India, there was an extraordinary growth of English-language journals in the late eighteenth century. Perhaps no fewer than twenty-four weeklies or monthlies appeared in Calcutta between 1780 and 1800.[14] The first of these was *Hicky's Bengal Gazette or the General Calcutta Advertiser* founded by James Augustus Hicky in January 1780. He had imported his printing press in 1777 and there were already three to five presses in Calcutta in the 1780s, and between seven and ten in the following decade, an astonishing growth of printing activity.[15] His initial proposals for the paper contained twenty-two objectives, many related to the usual announcements. But it is interesting that the fourteenth in the list was the publication of 'Playbills and Notice of Public Assemblys', evidence of the lively theatrical and social life in the East India Company capital.[16] From the first edition it was apparent that it would adopt a different tone from its North American counterparts. William Hickey, the diarist, recorded that *Hicky's Gazette* was redolent of the low wit of its founder, who also doled out 'appropriate nicknames' and related 'satirical anecdotes'. It increasingly became filled with 'personal invective and the most scurrilous abuse'.[17] This was directed against the leading figures of the East India Company, including Warren Hastings and Chief Justice Sir Elijah Impey. Hicky was soon arrested and imprisoned, his type seized and the paper closed down in 1782.[18] The *India Gazette* appeared in 1780, published by two Company employees, supportive of the administration, and inevitably this more complaisant paper survived. The *Bengal Hurkaru* was first published as a weekly in 1795, but importantly became a daily in 1819.[19] By absorbing *The Scotsman in the East* in 1825 and the *Bengal Chronicle* in 1827, it revealed the extent to which papers had proliferated in Bengal. It continued to be published as the *Bengal Hurkaru and Chronicle* until 1866.[20]

In Ceylon, the first newspaper, the *Colombo Journal*, was founded in 1833 by the governor, Wilmot Horton, who wrote for it under a pseudonym. But in 1834 the London authorities ordered him to close it and the independent *Observer* was founded by merchants. Later several newspapers were founded by different interests, including from 1846 *The Times* and *The Examiner*, each taking contrasting positions on race, education, political and economic issues.[21] Meanwhile, the speed of dispersal of newspapers is reflected in the manner in which Hong Kong acquired them after the occupation in early 1841, just before China was forced to cede it in the Treaty of Nanking ending the opium war. The colony soon had three newspapers, taking opposing stances on the great issue of the day, the opium trade. *The Friend of China*, founded by an American Baptist missionary and an Englishman, took an anti-opium stance. *The Canton Register*, founded in 1827 by James Matheson of the powerful Jardine Matheson Company to influence the Far Eastern merchant community, now moved into Hong Kong having sat out the war in Portuguese Macao. It inevitably favoured the opium trade, while the *China Mail*, established in 1845, was partly financed by the Jardine Matheson rival, Dent's.[22] Moving south, *The Straits Times and Singapore Journal of Commerce* of 1845, initially an eight-page weekly, was designed to offer information for the commercial sector. Much later, the *South China Morning Post* was founded in 1903 by a combination of Hong Kong Chinese and British interests, with its content designed to appeal to this double readership, offering a mix of sports and mercantile news.[23] It offers an interesting example of British linguistic discrimination since it was never censored, while the

Chinese press in Hong Kong was always subjected to the censor's scrutiny.[24] As we shall see, this became particularly true of all publications in indigenous languages.

Press censorship, repression and struggles for press freedom

Although the early colonial newspapers were often government-inspired or subject to control through reliance on subsidies, still an opportunity was created for resistance. They sometimes became a major source of dissidence for administrations increasingly alarmed by the conflict of ideologies inherent in the American and French revolutions and subsequent wars. Hence newspapers were quickly subject to attempts at legal controls. In the early nineteenth century, particularly in the settler territories, papers began to achieve a degree of independence through the growth of advertising revenue, which helped to encourage a more radical approach. In India and South Africa, however, such journalism prompted renewed censorship.

The nervousness of the East India Company was well demonstrated in the actions of the autocratic and ever-suspicious Governor General Wellesley, anxious about the war, revolutionary Jacobinism, and the possibility of French publications in India. He imposed a Censorship of the Press Act in 1799. Moreover, paranoia about press criticism was reflected in the number of times proprietors or editors were deported, a convenient weapon the Company could wield against its enemies. These included William Duane, editor of *Indian World*, in 1793; Charles Maclean (controversial doctor and student of plague and contagion), who had been expressing his opposition in the *Bengal Hurkaru*, in 1798; John Silk Buckingham, a particularly virulent critic of the Company and editor of the *Calcutta Journal*, then C.J. Fair, editor of the *Bombay Gazette*, both in 1823.[25] This could, however, be a two-edged sword since the result was that these articulate journalistic critics often continued their opposition in Britain. Perhaps because of the early Calcutta conflicts with the

Company, papers in Madras and Bombay often seemed careful to maintain good relations with the administration since their survival depended on it. Wellesley's was the first of a number of censorship acts during British rule. In 1823, Acting Governor General John Adam introduced licensing arrangements which had the effect of controlling papers. By this time, a Bengali press had appeared and the celebrated Hindu reformer Rammohun Roy closed down his Persian paper in protest at the new regulations. However, relative press freedom, within a registration regime, was declared by Acting Governor General Charles Metcalfe in 1835. This aroused anxiety on the part of the Company directors and was far from being the end of press censorship in India.

Careful government supervision of political activities and all forms of information transmission occurred in many colonies during the Revolutionary and Napoleonic Wars.[26] Such restrictions often continued in the post-war years, particularly where governors were former senior military men. But this time of repression may have stimulated the emergence of more radical politics, well reflected in the affiliations of the press. In Canada, the control of colonial governments tended to be in the hands of local oligarchies such as the 'Family Compact' in Ontario or the *Château Clique* in Quebec, and pressures built for a more representative system to be set up. While there had been elected assemblies of an advisory nature in Nova Scotia from 1758 (with other Canadian colonies following in succeeding decades), 'responsible government' represented a greater degree of local control. One proponent of press freedom, William Lyon Mackenzie, emigrated to Canada from Scotland in 1820. He had been involved in shop-keeping and continued in that role, somewhat more successfully than in the depressed post-war economy of Britain. In 1824, however, he changed tack and founded a newspaper, the *Colonial Advocate and Journal of Agriculture, Manufactures, and Commerce.* He issued this from his printing base in Queenston, Ontario and rapidly emerged as a major news editor, reprinting material from around the world and exchanging copies of his paper with editors in Canada, the United States and Britain. Promoting himself as entrepreneur, publisher and editor, he declared that he was devoted to furthering the economic development and improvement of his new homeland. He soon claimed to be printing a thousand copies a week and moved to the provincial capital of York (later Toronto).[27] Mackenzie's career as a radical politician prospered here and he joined both provincial assembly and town council, becoming mayor in 1834. Emerging as a fierce controversialist, he led an abortive rebellion of 1837 and was driven into exile in the United States when it was brutally suppressed. He returned with a free pardon in 1849 when responsible government had been granted. It was perhaps his upbringing as a Presbyterian secessionist which helped to develop his frequently scurrilous radicalism.[28]

Mackenzie was not the only radical journalist in Canada in this period, although few were so extreme or favoured the American political model as he did. These included Joseph Howe of the Halifax *Novascotian* newspaper (from 1824), George Brown of *The Globe* in Toronto, and Amor de Cosmos, founder in 1858 of *The Colonist* in Victoria, British Columbia. Cosmos (born as the more prosaic William Alexander Smith) was a strong proponent of responsible government and of British Columbia joining the Canadian Confederation after 1867. Other radical journalists in Quebec and Manitoba were representative of the clamour of political activity of the period, a ferment which the Durham reforms of 1839 were designed to divert from the revolutionary line taken by the American colonies in the previous century.[29]

If the press in Canada was reasonably free of government restrictions (although Mackenzie's enemies encouraged the raiding of his premises and the destruction of his press), this was not true of other colonies. The press in the Cape Colony, conquered by the British for the second time in 1806, was inevitably subject to tight controls both during and after the war years. Journalists here were soon determined to overthrow what they saw as gubernatorial despotism. The South

African case reveals the extent to which more was at stake than just press freedom. It is a complex story, but the bare bones suggest that the desire for a free press at the Cape was part of an intellectual turmoil transferred to Cape Town, particularly from Edinburgh.[30] This involved the creation of literary and scientific societies inspired by the European Enlightenment, and was also connected with missionary endeavour and educational provision. It additionally related to developing white migration, frontier policy and even the attempt at more liberal policies towards slavery emancipation or at least the amelioration of the conditions of Black people, though consistent with the tight boundaries of the age. But the proponents of liberating the press went further since, for them, it was bound up with economic freedoms in the creation of banking, insurance and commercial sectors. The leading figures in this movement, far from being a homogeneous group in the detail of their views and ideas, were George Greig, an experienced printer who imported a press to the Cape, John Fairbairn and Thomas Pringle, who were close friends and migrants from the Edinburgh literary world, and John Philip, the influential London Missionary Society superintendent at the Cape. Pringle and Fairbairn initially tried to allay the fears of the imperious governor, Lord Charles Somerset, by insisting that their sole desire was to establish a literary periodical.[31] But it was fairly obvious that this was designed to be a Trojan horse for wider concerns. Nevertheless, the *South African Journal*, after intervention from London, was founded in 1823. In the same period Greig published the *South African Commercial Advertiser*, the new smokescreen being supplied by supposedly uncontroversial economic matters. Pringle and Fairbairn took this on and there ensued a struggle with the governor which continued until he departed in 1826. The *Advertiser* was closed for several years, but after lobbying an ordinance was passed in 1829 establishing limited press freedom and the paper reappeared. Somerset was a Tory Anglican aristocrat who saw the forces ranged against him as being religious dissenters, Scots and

Whigs, all anathema. But he could not resist the breaking up of the despotic logjam. Pringle, regarded as the founder of South African poetry in English, returned to Britain and became Secretary of the Anti-Slavery Society.

Printing in indigenous languages

In India, journalistic endeavours in Indian languages quickly became the norm, starting around 1818 in Bengali, with others to follow. By the1830s, the genie was truly out of the bottle and a prolific Indian-language press was in existence, the first indigenous, non-English press in the empire. In the final decades of the century, this had tied up with growing nationalist activity, causing fresh headaches for the imperial authorities and stimulating renewed efforts at censorship. In Ceylon, newspapers in Sinhala and Tamil appeared from the 1840s, growing in numbers in the 1860s.[32] African examples, generally with missionary help, began to appear soon after those in South Asia. Missionaries imported printing presses mainly to print African-language translations of the Bible, but also to distribute Christian materials, mission notices, newspapers and magazines. One of the first was in Xhosa, an Nguni language of the Eastern Cape, issued in 1837 under the influence of the Glasgow Missionary Society and the Wesleyan Methodist mission.[33] This was called *Umshumayeli Wendaba*, appropriately translated as 'Preacher of the News'. It lasted only until 1841 and was followed by two more short-lived Xhosa papers in the 1840s and 1850s, with various others following until the 1930s. In West Africa, a Yoruba-language paper appeared in Nigeria in 1859. Its shortened title was *Iwe Irohin Fun Awon* and it survived until 1867.[34] Many more indigenous-language papers appeared in West Africa, but their survival was often precarious because the growing educated elite invariably preferred to read in English. In the British colonies in South-East Asia and the Far East, papers in Chinese appeared soon after English equivalents. In these ways the printing press was taken over by indigenous peoples, independently in India and elsewhere in Asia, often as a result of the print needs of Christian missions in Africa and usually under tight controls. It was soon apparent that here was a technology invaluable for twentieth-century nationalist movements. Hence the printing press became another weapon in the hands of the enemies of empire. In India and the dependent empire, papers reflected both verbal struggles between imperial rulers and nationalist resisters and the cultural concerns of readerships.

Proliferation of newspapers in the nineteenth century

The later nineteenth century saw a massive expansion in the colonial press, as every city acquired additional and sometimes rival papers, while many smaller towns also began to produce their own. Weeklies became dailies and evening editions, or separate evening papers, appeared. In India, English-language papers continued to expand in numbers and influence, the most famous example being the *Bombay Times and Journal of Commerce*, which first appeared in 1838. Initially twice-weekly, it became a daily in 1850. After taking over the *Bombay Standard*, it established a relationship with Reuters and became the first Indian news agency. Renamed *The Times of India* in 1861, it established itself as India's paper of record. Throughout its existence, it had both British and Indian editors and proprietors, and the readership reflected this mix. This duality was symbolised in a 2013 Indian commemorative postage stamp in which a reader was depicted with a trouser on one leg and a *dhoti* on the other.

Although India is regarded in the Anglophone world as the first great cockpit of the press outside Europe and the Americas, the speed of dissemination of printing presses and papers seemed unstoppable. In Canada, daily papers took off in the 1840s, sometimes on a seasonal basis. By 1873 there were forty-seven dailies in Canada, aided by cheaper prices for paper and the growing sophistication of printing.[35] This had risen to a peak of 143 in 1911, a tremendous expansion reflecting population growth, rising literacy and continuing urbanisation which, together with the railways, aided distribution. Revenue also grew with advertising constituting 80 per cent of income, the purchase price only 20 per cent. Many other magazines and journals were founded, with an increasingly diverse content – sports pages, articles about entertainment and cultural events, and from 1882 the first women's section.[36] A similar growth was to take place in Australia, with multiple papers in major cities and local ones in most smaller towns. In South Africa, the *Cape Town Mail* was founded in 1840 and the *Natal Witness* in 1846.[37] Imperial developments also contributed to press expansion. *The Royal Gazette and Sierra Leone Advertiser* first appeared in Freetown in 1817, produced by a printer from Nova Scotia.[38] Charles McCarthy, governor of the Gold Coast settlements, started issuing the short-lived *Gold Coast Gazette and Commercial Intelligencer* in Accra in 1822. Thus, as elsewhere, the desire of colonial administrations to issue information to the people they ruled was the initial driver of newspaper creation. But African journalists in West Africa also desired to issue a journal in English. Charles Bannerman, sometimes regarded as the first African newspaper editor, started the *Accra Herald* in 1858. This was handwritten and copied for its subscribers, Bannerman's promised press having allegedly been lost in the Liverpool docks.[39]

The Scramble for Africa ensured that newspapers continued to appear as soon as colonies were created in East and Central Africa. A year after the British South Africa Company set about the conquest of the region between the rivers Limpopo and Zambezi in 1890, a handwritten, cyclostyled weekly paper, the *Mashonaland Herald and Zambesian Times* was produced, printed from 1892 and later a daily, the *Rhodesia Herald*. After the conquest of Matabeleland in 1893, the *Bulawayo Chronicle* appeared. These two papers catered for white settlers and displayed little interest in the majority African population. Similar developments occurred in East Africa, with newspapers rapidly founded in Kenya and Uganda. The *Uganda Argus* was one of several East African English-language papers, while in the 1920s others were published in Luganda, a key language of the colony.

The 'imperial press system', international news, and content analysis

By the time these papers appeared, an imperial press system had emerged, particularly embracing the Dominions.[40] This apparently centralised system was dependent on the development of agencies as the prime means for the collection and dissemination of news, a service ideally suited to the operations of the electric telegraph and international cables. The most celebrated was Reuters, founded by Paul Julius Reuter, a migrant from Germany via France after the European revolutionary activity of 1848.[41] Arriving in Britain in 1851, Reuter started a telegram company and a news service for the banking and financial sector. In 1858 this attracted its first newspaper client and thereafter built up a major international network serving British colonial papers. Cabled messages were expensive and it therefore made sense to 'bundle' these through an agency. Although Canada often received its news from the United States, London became a clearing house for cabled news from around the world. There were inevitably tensions in these developments, for example between the big metropolitan dailies and supposedly disadvantaged provincial papers, although many of the latter were soon being collected into combines. The South African press was accused of being in the pockets of the great mine owners, although the situation was more complex than this would suggest. Meanwhile, Australian and New Zealand papers set about establishing their own news agencies. For international news at least, the system worked and circulations grew, though there may have been other reasons for this.

Such an arrangement encouraged and was dependent upon the increasingly expansive capitalist press, seeking more capital and greater revenue potential. By 1900 the press had become big business, owned by major capitalist concerns, the ownership of which was regarded by many wealthy businessmen as a route to power and influence. Their intervention, together with many takeovers, ensured that groups of papers were formed in all the major territories. A classic case was the Argus group in southern Africa. This was also dependent on the continuing development of print technologies, reduced costs in some areas, and circulation growth. A major technological improvement was the invention of the linotype machine in the 1890s.[42] This paralleled the considerable expansion of the journalist profession, through migration both into and out of Britain and by the local training of more printers and journalists. Press institutes were founded, such as the Australian Institute of Journalists in Melbourne in 1892 and the Australian Journalists' Association in 1911.

Although this imperial system seemed to last to the First World War and beyond, by this time the colonial press had come to satisfy increasingly local needs, mirroring the growing emergence of national rather than imperial sentiment in the settler territories. While the Dominions were going their own way, in the 'dependent' empire new nationalist movements set out to advance their cause by creating their own press mouthpieces. Hence, the system was breaking apart by the end of the Second World War. The press now reflected the global structure of nation states as well as competition from the cinematic newsreel and universal radio transmission. Later, television with tentative origins in the 1930s exploded in its incidence and influence in the post-war period, particularly after the appearance of colour and the near universality of access to televisions.

The influence of the so-called imperial press system has been somewhat exaggerated. In many press studies, historians have concentrated on politics and diplomacy, providing a slanted view of the significance and content of newspapers. This is 'top-down' and any examination of colonial newspapers soon reveals how relatively unimportant it was. For this study, a number of issues were examined to assess the significance of cultural content. This material may be defined as anything relating to sports, amusements and entertainment to religious and educational news, and, more rarely, to literary events. The papers surveyed were *The Times of India*; in Australia the *Mercury* (of Hobart, Tasmania) and the *Sydney Morning Herald*; in New Zealand *The Auckland Star*; in Hong Kong the *Daily Press*; in Singapore *The Straits Times*; and in Canada the *Montreal Gazette*. Three years were chosen for sampling, 1895, 1908 and 1923, selected to avoid the imperial 'hot spots' of the second Anglo-Boer War and the First World War to indicate content in more 'normal' times. The political affiliations of the papers are irrelevant to the objectives of the content analysis. The selection is mainly influenced by availability of these papers on the web.

One observation is that, with the exception of the Montreal example, no longer an official publication despite the name *Gazette*, all these papers look remarkably similar, generally with classified advertisements on both first and last pages, dense texts on narrow columns, sometimes provided with content headings.[43] In each case, the newspapers grew in size, sometimes dramatically, between 1895, 1908 and 1923, while the price often remained the same. The focus of advertisements changed over time, not least because of the development of new entertainment and transport technologies. The prime examples are the appearance of the gramophone and the marketing of brands for sale as well as records to play on them, the emergence of the motor car and motor cycle, and particularly the development of moving film and the cinema. It is quite clear from an examination of these newspapers that international and British 'cable news' constituted a small proportion of the material offered to readers. This is true (in a rough computation of the number of columns) in all the papers as indicated in Table 7.1.

It is apparent from Table 7.1 that foreign and British imperial news constituted a relatively small proportion of the offerings, that a combination of sporting and entertainment news (and advertisements) always exceeded such material, and that local news was always

Table 7.1: Content analysis of selected colonial newspapers

Approx. number of columns given to the following subjects:	Foreign news	Sport	Culture and enter't[44]	British/ imperial	Local news	TOTAL no. cols
Times of India						
Tue 5.3.1895 (LVII/55, 8pp, 7c)	3.8	0.8	1.3	3.5	21.4	30.8
Thu 15.10.1908 (LXXI/247, 12pp, 6c)	4.6	3.0	3.7	4.5	21.0	36.8
Sat 17.11.1923 (LXXXVI/256, 16pp, 6c)	1.5	3.7	8.5	6.2	25.7	45.6
TOTAL	**9.9**	**7.5**	**13.5**	**14.2**	**68.1**	**113.2**
Mercury (Hobart)						
Wed 12.6.1895 (LXV/7887, 4pp, 9c)	2.15	0.4	3.6	2.4	8.05[45]	16.6
Tue 15.9.1908 (XC/12011, 8pp, 8c)	2.55	4.8	5.15	6.5	21.8	40.8
Sat 10.2.1923 (CXVIII/17270, 16pp, 8c)	2.45	8.1	27.6	2.05	16.45	56.65
TOTAL	**7.15**	**13.3**	**36.35**	**10.95**	**46.30**	**114.05**
Sydney Morning Herald						
Thu 10.10.1895 (No.17960, 8pp, 8c)	0.5	1.95	4.1	2.0	31.1	39.65
Sat 10.2.1908 (No.21861, 12pp, 8c)	1.7	12.5	10.15	3.2	30.7	58.25

	1	2	3	4	5	6
Wed 14.3.1923 (No.26579, 22pp, 8c)	2.2	4.35	10.8	5.0	27.25	49.6
TOTAL	**4.4**	**18.8**	**25.05**	**10.2**	**89.05**	**147.5**
Auckland Star Sat 9.3.1895 (XXVI/58, 8pp, 8c + supp.)[46]	1.7	7.3	25.75	4.55	11.65	50.95
Wed 14.10.1908 (XXXIX/246, 12pp, 9c)	3.9	6.3	26.05	6.5	20.50	63.25
Tue 20.3.1923 (LIV/68, 14pp, 8c)	1.1	6.3	11.2	3.35	19.10	41.05
TOTAL	**6.7**	**19.9**	**63.0**	**14.4**	**51.25**	**155.25**
Daily Press (*Hong Kong*) Fri 15.11.1895 (No. 11782, 4pp, 7c)	3.45	0.0	2.7	1.3	7.1[47]	14.55
Tue 29.9.1908 (No. 15740, 8pp, 6c)	2.4	2.0	1.6	3.1	14.1	23.2
Sat 6.10.1923 (No. 20360, 12pp, 6c)	1.85	3.75	2.7	3.5	16.2	28.0
TOTAL	**7.7**	**5.75**	**7.0**	**7.9**	**37.4**	**65.75**
Straits Times Fri 4.10.1895 (No. 18739, 4pp, 7c)	1.1	1.75	1.85	1.4	6.85[48]	12.95
Thu, 12.3.1908 (No. 22597, 8pp, 6c)	1.9	3.0	7.9	7.15	10.75	30.7
Sat 14.4.1923 (No. 27225, 16pp, 6c)	3.75	0.95	8.45	4.45	12.65	30.25
TOTAL	**6.75**	**5.7**	**18.2**	**13.0**	**30.25**	**73.9**

Approx. number of columns given to the following subjects:	Foreign news	Sport	Culture and enter't[44]	British/ imperial	Local news	TOTAL no. cols
Montreal Gazette						
Mon 2.9.1895 (CXXIV/210, 8pp, 7c)	6.9	13.20	3.4	3.1	11.5[49]	38.10
Fri 1.5.1908 (CXXXVII/105, 14pp, 7c)	7.8	5.3	4.1	2.75	34.8	54.75
Wed 14.2.1923 (CLII/39, 22pp, 8c)	12.9	14.4	18.4	13.0	44.5	103.2
TOTAL	**27.6**	**32.9**	**25.9**	**18.85**	**90.8**	**196.05**
GRAND TOTAL	70.2	103.85	189.0	89.5	413.15	865.7

Sources:
India: ProQuest Historical Newspapers *Times of India* database, https://about.proquest.com/en/products-services/pq-hist-news/
Australia: National Library of Australia TROVE online portal, https://trove.nla.gov.au/newspaper/
New Zealand: National Library of New Zealand, https://paperspast.natlib.govt.nz/newspapers
Hong Kong: Hong Kong Public Libraries, https://mmis.hkpl.gov.hk/web/guest/old-hk-collection
Singapore: NewspaperSG, National Library Board Singapore https://eresources.nlb.gov.sg/newspapers/
Canada: https://news.google.com/newspapers

more important. These effects became more pronounced with time, the 1920s reflecting such proportions particularly strongly. Content relating to sport, entertainment and other forms of cultural activities was clearly significant in the colonies of white settlement, rather less so in territories strongly devoted to commerce. However, in almost all examples, the number of columns devoted to the cultural category far exceeded those on political and international affairs.

Late nineteenth-century newspapers have been seen as illustrating a new form of journalism. This was not particularly represented in the appearance of papers, except in some instances by the inclusion of photographs, but a new sensationalism manifested itself in the reporting of imperial and related events, particularly as transmitted by special correspondents either well known in other fields or to be so later. Such writers included G.A. Henty, H. Rider Haggard, Joseph Conrad and Winston Churchill, all of whom have been seen as transferring elements of the imperial adventure tradition into the reporting of contemporary events.[50] While this is certainly true of Britain, it is perhaps more problematic to find it transferred into the colonial press, except in rare instances of reprinting or syndicating such material. However, nothing improves the sales of newspapers more than war and the greatest stimulus to the imperial press system was perhaps the outbreak and conduct of the Anglo-Boer War of 1899–1902 (see Plate 26).[51] Colonial newspaper readers were hungry for war news, particularly once Canadian, Australian and New Zealand military contingents were involved, a development raising the international profile of these colonies. This perhaps created the one notable moment when the press reported that the hearts of colonial settlers seemed to beat in unison. The Relief of Mafeking in the Anglo-Boer War in May 1900 prompted parallel public celebrations and ceremonies in many colonies. A survey of papers reveals the extent to which this was strikingly true. An excellent example comes from Western Australia, where it was reported that jubilation in Perth on Saturday and Sunday, 19–20 May, was extraordinary, with the 'generally restrained people of Perth' going 'almost mad with intoxicating excitement', while those in Fremantle were 'equally fervent'. The government declared the day a holiday and there was a procession through the port by mayor and councillors with the Fremantle 1st Infantry band, the Infantry and Artillery Corps, the Locomotive Workshops Band and employees, as well as the harbour employees and trade union members. Large numbers assembled for the speeches, patriotic songs and instrumental music.[52] Similar press reports described celebrations elsewhere in Australia and in Otago in New Zealand[53] and Halifax, Nova Scotia.[54] In the latter, a design was submitted for a processional arch and striking public events were organised.[55] It has been argued, however, that in Melbourne the main celebrants were the lower middle class and youths.[56] They may have been the most obvious, but the press examples given here seem to suggest that wider sections of the population were involved. Marching bands, music and mass singing were particularly alluring. Critics of these examples of patriotic frenzy seem to have been drowned out by the general air of rejoicing.

Perhaps it was these events which led imperial figures like Alfred Milner to imagine that the power of the press had great potential in influencing public opinion. Thus the need for successful news management seemed apparent. However, there is a world of difference between patriotic events in a war and support for the ambitions of political pressure groups. Some committed figures thought there was a fair wind for various imperial projects, including closer cooperation and tariff reform. But the idea of imperial federation was long dead and colonial sentiment seemed unlikely to be seduced afresh. Renewed attempts in the post-war reconstruction period to manipulate the press for 'constructive imperialism' and imperial preference were no more successful, while efforts to create a joint defence system tended to take more national than imperial forms.[57] Individual colonial sentiment ensured that such projects were always likely to be subordinated to the specific interests of particular colonial populations, pursuing overriding economic concerns and geopolitical anxieties, for example relating to Japan. The First World War was to produce renewed calls for colonial support which were by and large successful, but only the economic crisis of the Great Depression seemed to encourage any desire for joint action. Nevertheless, the dream of an empire united by the press persisted. Press baron Lord Northcliffe went on an empire tour in 1921–22 and returned convinced of the need for a 'world newspaper as an organ of the English-speaking peoples'.[58] He saw himself as an apostle of a global order based on empire. It was all an illusion.

These failures place the notion of a successfully centralised press system into context. The evidence suggests that newspapers and their readers were more focused on local interests and cultural and sporting opportunities. Increasingly, features for women and children also became more prominent. Such items had greater immediacy for the readership since they took place in familiar environments involving people with a profile in their own communities. Taken together, such content was likely to have more positive effects on sales than imperial or international news. It may be, however, that international news became progressively more important than British and imperial material, particularly in the inter-war years.[59] This effect developed further in the 1930s, both because of the major global depression and in view of anxieties about the possibility of another war. Moreover, by this time it was clear that settler colonial populations had begun to view the First World War in negative terms. In the 1930s they were undoubtedly supporters of appeasement.

The press and nationalism in India and Africa

Just as the white settler populations of the Dominions were increasingly interested in local affairs and the cultural and sporting content of their lifestyles, so were the indigenous populations of India and Africa focused upon the development of cultural and political nationalism.

Given the anxiety about the potential for criticism in the vernacular press, imperial rulers had to ensure that mechanisms for translation were in place for monitoring and censorship. It was however a line that was increasingly impossible to hold. Fresh censorship was imposed in India in 1878 (the Gagging Act), 1881, 1908, 1910 (the latter two repealed in 1921), and again in 1931. If these measures were intended to suppress nationalist activity, in fact they tended to ratchet it up. While the Indian press had provided some limited support for Britain in the First World War, partly because of the involvement of large numbers of Indian troops and of Gandhi's ambulance corps, it was increasingly firm in its support for the nationalist cause, albeit fractured by the development of communalism. Moreover, cultural confidence grew through increasing emphasis on Indian philosophy, literature, art and music. Indian nationalists, such as Gandhi and Nehru, were assiduous in establishing their presence in the press, which of course had the dual effect of propagating their ideas and making their names more widely known.

The importance of the press for the dissemination of the message of African nationalism had long been recognised. Early South African nationalists John Tengo Jabavu and John L. Dube were involved in editing papers in the Cape and Natal in the 1880s and early in the twentieth century. Jomo Kenyatta, future president of Kenya, edited a Gikuyu language paper in 1925. Nationalism also took up residence in English-language papers. The Nigerian nationalist Nnamdi Azikiwe edited the *African Morning Post* in Accra after his return from education in the United States, then moved to Lagos and founded the *West African Pilot* in 1937. As usual, the British attempted censorship. The primary excuse was fear of communism, a convenient smokescreen for attempts to control nationalist agitation, although British ambivalence ensured that this was never particularly effective.[60] Another control technique was the cultural reinvasion of West Africa by British newspaper interests. In 1947, the London *Daily Mirror* group established a newspaper in Lagos and also moved into Freetown and Accra, opening the *Daily Graphic* in the latter in 1949. These became known as the 'White Press' and were quite successful because of their professionalism and slick presentation. Also in 1949, the Ashanti Goldfields Corporation started publishing the *Ashanti Times*, a capitalist invasion into the field which had sufficient success that it survived after independence until 1970.[61] Even so, it became apparent that the postcolonial press in many parts of Africa was going to be generally even less free than in the imperial period. In 1981, both the Salisbury (Harare) and Bulawayo newspapers were taken over by the Zimbabwean state, and considerable difficulties were placed in the way of the creation of an opposition paper such as the *Zimbabwe Independent*. Sadly, Zimbabwe had become the classic case of the already apparent shift of the African press moving from colonial to postcolonial persecution.[62] While the press had been important in promoting the decline of empire, it remained vulnerable in territories where more dictatorial regimes established themselves. In South Asia it remained a vigorous and prolific sector, although in Myanmar and Hong Kong its independence tended to be compromised. Meanwhile, in the territories of white settlement, its political and cultural diversity became a key means of securing its independence, while also establishing the primacy of national interests. It additionally came to reflect changing attitudes, for example to indigenous people.

8
THEATRE

The amateur cast of Gilbert and Sullivan's *Pirates of Penzance* (1879) performed by the British community at Simla, India, date unknown.

Theatrical performances, whether plays, variety shows or musicals, were among the flagship cultural events of the British Empire from the eighteenth to the twentieth centuries. The performers might be either professional paid actors, comedians and singers, or amateurs seeking to entertain restricted social groups. The professionals were part of a tradition of touring which enabled large numbers of actors, initially often from Britain, to visit various parts of the empire repeatedly to present their productions, providing them with additional opportunities for work and incomes. However, the necessary travel costs and the moving of sets and costumes greatly reduced their potential earnings. Nevertheless, they continued from the nineteenth century until at least the 1920s, and they constituted an extraordinary inter-colonial network, promoted by the convenience of steam ships and the extension of railways. This globalisation of contemporary western theatre conventions prompts consideration of a complex of analytical themes, including the influence of transport forms and commercial conditions, the provision of repertoire and actors, changing fashions in play popularity, contemporary theatre aesthetics and architecture, audience social and racial relationships, local politics, and norms of respectability. It also intersected with migration histories and with aspects of financial success, risk and failure. In recent scholarship, it has additionally become the subject of network theory, in the provision of productions and the connections of writers, producers and actors. Such performances were perhaps one of the most striking ways in which imperial culture ran on largely common lines throughout the British World. For much of the time, the United States can be seen as part of such an entertainment world, since touring companies inevitably combined appearances there with visits to Canadian cities, sometimes before moving on to other territories such as Australia. The importance of both professional and at least some amateur performances was that, unlike sports and other cultural activities, they generally (with some exceptions) involved women as well as men. They were directly connected with the metropolitan stage, with the same plays, musical comedies or performing acts appearing around the colonies. Audiences enjoyed very similar theatrical fare everywhere, even if topical allusions might have been different according to location (see Plate 27). The tours also developed business opportunities and entrepreneurship with complex partnerships; sometimes they were even involved in colonial construction projects.

The resulting web of inter-colonial networks was capable of becoming locally self-sustaining.

The other originators of theatrical performances were the military. Wherever regiments were stationed or naval vessels based, garrison theatres became common. A more hard-headed approach to leisure might have been expected from a profession whose business was war and defence, yet there can be no doubt that 'garrison theatricals' were a characteristic of military life, associating such drama with the mailed fist of imperial power. An officer corps from an urbane and self-consciously cultured class was keen both to entertain themselves and to find yet another means of keeping other ranks away from more dangerous pastimes. Moreover, theatricals became a means by which the military and naval forces were able to ingratiate themselves with colonial settlers and expatriates. In providing an attractive public face, the military reassured white colonists about the presence of offensive and defensive warlike forces while also suggesting their essentially civilising effects. Sometimes men or young soldiers played female parts, as at the dawn of theatrical events in early modern Britain. At other times, women were drawn in from surrounding settler or expatriate society, a practice not without its dangers in stimulating romance. At any rate, such military commitment ensured that theatrical events were both popular and encouraged in the empire, despite occasional efforts at control by civil authorities and the anxieties of churches about alleged immorality. The Roman Catholic Church sometimes became concerned about plays that criticised or satirised its precepts.

Rehearsals and performances were certainly a means of alleviating boredom, but they were also an opportunity to bring settlers or sojourners together into satisfyingly sociable and culturally familiar experiences. There is evidence that they were prepared to travel long distances to reach the performances. If such events were, like sports, nostalgic reminders of home, instances of a culture apparently only temporarily lost, they also produced a reassuring sense of an enriching and distinctive ethnic aesthetic. In some places they were another means of transplanting cultural forms into seemingly alien environments, one where the maintenance of racial exclusivity might be important. Like all performance arts, they were also a means of escape from the often gruelling business of life, conjuring up the realm of the imaginary and the different lives of characters in the plays or personalities in variety shows, recreating memories. The fact that such performances were particularly popular in hill stations in India and elsewhere is illustrative of the leisured escapism the theatre offered.

Performances might be mounted in many different locations, in wooden shacks and tents, in town, school or other local halls, thus any available space. Through the growth of larger centres they moved into dedicated theatres, an architectural form symbolising a global common culture spreading rapidly in the territories of white settlement or colonies with considerable expatriate groups as in India. Such provision was highly responsive to infrastructural developments and economic change. The spread of railway lines created fresh areas of settlement stimulating the appearance of new towns, for example in the prairies of Canada. But it was the 'windfall', unexpected engines of economic change that galvanised the creation of further theatrical opportunities. Gold 'rushes' were perhaps the most energising, but the discovery of other minerals or the development of significant agricultural monocultures might have the same effect. Colonial wars could result in the movement of regiments and their concentration in encampments and barracks. While campaigns clearly occupied the time of troops and naval personnel, the threat of war or its aftermath could present periods of relative inactivity and boredom in which theatricals might flourish. The rest of the chapter will examine amateur and professional dimensions of theatre culture in the British World, including the range of performances of classic and modern plays, of vaudeville, variety and comic shows.[1] While amateur theatricals were almost universal, the professional activities involved theatre managements, specialist agents, the building of theatres often on the London model, and the growth of the bourgeois public sphere. But none of this took place in a theatrical vacuum.

Indigenous theatre

Almost all indigenous peoples have traditions of theatrical performance. The theatrical recounting or the active recreation of myths and legends are common in many societies. Significant religious and spiritual material is often projected in such performances as well as in the characteristic processions of many cultures. These usually involve ruling and royal elites and can be seen as a form of theatre. There is a good deal of visual evidence in the great temples of Bagan and elsewhere in Burma of a long tradition of dance and of court entertainments. Theatrical troupes entertained King Thebaw and Queen Suphayarlat and other Burmese rulers in the nineteenth century.[2] Elsewhere in Asia, for example in the Malay peninsula, puppet theatre was (and remains) common (stimulating the artistic creation of the elaborate puppets), while shadow theatre has long been practised in India and China.[3] Chinese plays and operas followed the diasporas of Chinese people into various areas of settlement in the British Empire. For example, a Chinese United Dramatic Society began to perform lavish versions of Cantonese operas in Toronto as early as 1933.[4] In Canada, the theatrical pow wows resurrected (after repression) at the end of the nineteenth century also constituted cultural performances and became increasingly popular in modern times. The same was and remains true of Aboriginal corroborees in Australia, where almost every aspect of indigenous life and the socialisation of the young is performance-based. Theatrical events lie at the very heart of Aboriginal notions of the past, the environment, spiritual relations and much else. In Africa too, dance and related theatrical performances lay 'at the crossroads of the religious and the secular', and constituted a long pre-colonial tradition which continued after the arrival of Europeans.[5] In southern Africa, Khoisan theatre traditions are said to be of great antiquity.

In India, the dramatic arts were of ancient origin, in some cases preceding those of Greece.[6] 'Theatre in India is a composite art form in the harmonious fusion of elements from dance, music, pantomime, epic and ballad recitations, graphic and plastic arts and ritual.'[7] Generally, these dramatic traditions became regional, connected with the different languages of the subcontinent. Hence Indian theatre was extensive in its range of material, performance styles and chronological depth. In modern times, some forms of ancient Indian theatre were revived and often coexisted with the arrival of western theatre, while hybrid forms of theatre blending Indian tradition with western conventions also developed. A classic case of the latter was Parsi theatre, which introduced the proscenium arch and adapted European moving scenery to historic spectacle, with songs, dancing and pantomime elements. A Parsi group, the Victoria Theatre Company, toured Burma in 1881 and other examples were taken to Ceylon, the Malay States and Singapore. The company arrived at the Colonial and Indian Exhibition in London in 1886 to show its wares to the English, but its resounding success in South-East Asia was not matched in London, where it was much criticised in the press.[8]

In the many global examples of indigenous theatre the historical and cultural cohesion of peoples was performed and re-created, phenomena which have invariably survived the arrival of western drama. Indigenous theatre upheld the maintenance of the social order and of hierarchies of power and authority, underpinning the spiritual and historical traditions designed to create a sense of ethnic identity and distinctiveness. There was clearly an educational role, theatrical events serving to socialise the young into the combined secular and spiritual pasts and presents of the society into which they had been born. But there were also invariably spaces for either subtly subversive or openly satirical performances which could help to produce flexible reactions to outside influences.

In many places in colonial times indigenous theatre might take on the Shakespeare canon, and the question arises whether this constituted an invasion of cultural colonialism influenced by mission and other schools, or whether it developed into a genuine fascination, not least if the material resonated with elements of traditional stories. Missionaries were also keen to develop a culture of conversion in the performance of biblical stories or key moments in the life of Christ. They often recognised that this could be particularly effective if such presentations were rendered as consistent with elements of traditional religious or philosophical belief. Some missionaries in the Far East, for example, tried to reconcile their Christian message with aspects of Confucianism. However, the development of lighter dramatic forms in the later nineteenth century, such as farce, burlesque, revue and musical comedy might offend missionaries and other 'improving' agencies. They also served, it may be argued, to drive a wider racial wedge between cultures. The rest of this chapter will explore the development of western theatre in Canada and other territories, with separate sections on professional touring companies and amateur theatre.

The arrival of European theatre

Theatre travelled with the earliest settlers, with theatrical events becoming significant cultural moments in all settlement territories in the British Empire. Inevitably, Canada was in the vanguard, initially through the French-speaking settlers of New France. The first western theatrical performance in Canada is said to have taken place in 1606 near Port Royal in Acadia, the French colony in the areas which later became the maritime provinces.[9] It was of a light-hearted play by Marc Lescarbot, a writer who visited Acadia and wrote the first *Histoire de Nouvelle France*. French theatre developed more seriously after 1640 in Quebec, although the Catholic Church was not happy about such performances. It is said that the plays, performed entirely by amateurs since there were no professionals, were successes from Paris by Corneille, Racine and Molière. But Molière's play *Tartuffe* was to bring this French colonial theatre to a grinding halt. The bishop objected to the play because it attacked religious hypocrisy and proceeded to ban all further performances. Ironically enough, theatre only resumed in Quebec after the British (Protestant) conquest in 1759. Plays, mainly by Molière, were staged by British garrisons in Montreal and Quebec City. In the late 1770s, a French immigrant resurrected theatrical performances, though still facing Church opposition. In 1825, a Theatre Royal opened in Montreal and in the same year another of the same name appeared in Quebec City. Plays were produced in both English and French and the first known professional company in Canada commenced performing, though again encountering Church displeasure. Dramatic societies were later founded in both Montreal and Quebec City and these dominated the middle decades of the century. The next revolution occurred with the laying down of the railway lines and the development of the steam ship. Now touring companies could reach eastern Canada from the USA and some of these were from France. Church and stage continued to be at odds, but throughout the region the touring system continued to develop with celebrated international actors performing with cheaper local players, a successful means of attracting audiences.

Just as the soldiers resurrected a theatrical tradition in Quebec, so it was the military in garrisons in Halifax, Nova Scotia and Kingston, Ontario, who were most active in maintaining stage performances. The quantity of theatrical activity in Halifax from the early days of the foundation of the town has been described as 'astounding'.[10] Some of these theatrical offerings provide an impression of the dramatic material produced for Canadian audiences in the period. The New Grand Theatre opened in 1789, while the Theatre Royal in Spring Gardens was the most important playhouse between 1846 and 1867. In 1819, Halifax Theatre reopened with a performance of

Macbeth and 'the grand military spectacle of the death of General Wolfe' (presumably a tableau), seen for the first time there and directed by Mr Betterton from London.[11] Amateur groups, players from the Mechanics' Institute and, inevitably, the garrison soldiers all performed. While the military preference was for works by Sheridan and Shakespeare, there were also occasional appearances by professionals and travelling companies performing vaudeville. Touring troupes began to come from Boston and New York, and performances took place in the Temperance Hall which later became the Lyceum Theatre.[12] Residents of Halifax were subsequently made aware of events elsewhere in the British Empire by 'The Great Exhibition of India and the Sepoy Rebellion, a panorama nightly at the Temperance Hall'.[13] In 1858, the celebrated play *Jessie Brown and the Relief of Lucknow* by Irish playwright and actor Dion Boucicault (also active in the United States) ran for a week with capacity audiences in the Lyceum.[14] This was one of several 'Mutiny' dramas and events of spectacular equestrian theatre that were considerable hits in London, and no doubt went on tour to other Canadian cities. *Jessie Brown* has been described as part of a 'global republic of performance' which, with news stories, ballads, songs, lectures and dramatic reconstructions carried an alleged incident of the Indian revolt to many quarters of the British Empire.[15] In the Victorian era, by which time most towns had theatre buildings, Gilbert and Sullivan became extremely popular, together with pastiches based upon the operettas introducing local characters and issues. The navy also took plays to the colonies: a play by E.T. Coke, *A Subaltern's Furlough*, was performed by the officers of HMS *St. George* in Halifax on 18 September 1861.[16] The garrison theatres injected a taste for light-hearted revues, and in 1889 Canadian military theatricals took a new turn with the appearance of a musical, *Leo, the Royal Cadet*, in the Kingston Royal Military College, which introduced an inter-colonial adventure and romance tradition. It involved a young Canadian going to South Africa to fight the Zulus, who were apparently portrayed as both fierce and noble, even contributing their own song to the performance. The climax involved a romantic and heroic return to Canada.[17] Thus audiences were being offered imperial theatre similar to that mounted in Britain.[18] In the high Victorian period, the press became the inevitable adjunct of theatrical events, in printing advertisements, as well as reviews and even extracts.

On the other hand, there were major ups and downs in the development of a local writing tradition. Canadian playwrights produced short satirical dramas, but with improvements in transport, foreign touring companies began to predominate, often bringing melodramas from Britain. International stars such as Sir Henry Irving and Sarah Bernhardt began to visit Canada, the latter touring nine times between 1880 and 1917. She also visited Quebec, where the bishop continued the anti-theatrical tradition by warning Catholics against attending her performances. Irving appeared in Toronto with his Lyceum Company in February 1884, one of his visits to eastern Canada that were extensions of lucrative tours to the United States.[19] Such popular theatrical events inhibited the development of a local writing tradition, although a combination of the First World War and the rise of the popularity of American cinema partly reduced the opportunities for touring companies. Amateur theatrical clubs became significant in the inter-war years and with the development of Canadian radio and the founding of the Canada Council, particularly with increased arts funding after the Second World War, homegrown Canadian productions as well as new traditions of play-writing became more significant. In the same period, Quebec theatre in French flourished with a new play-writing tradition. The Anglophone stage was maintained and strengthened by the first productions of Shakespeare plays in a summer festival in Stratford, Ontario in 1953. This Stratford Festival was conceived by local businessman Tom Patterson, and the plays were first performed in a concrete amphitheatre under a tent, directed by Tyrone Guthrie and with Alec Guinness as its first star. It quickly became an international success, growing considerably once the new theatre was built in 1957 and remains one of the most notable theatrical fixtures in Canada.[20]

Inevitably, eastern Canada was early in its theatrical offerings, but the prairies and western Canada soon connected with these introduced theatrical traditions. In the prairie colonies (later provinces after 1867), amateurs introduced western theatrical traditions as the immigrant population grew, while in British Columbia the Royal Navy was inevitably important. Educational institutions and student performers were everywhere active in presenting plays. The 1860s gold rush in British Columbia helped to stimulate this, with amateur dramatic societies in Victoria on Vancouver Island from 1862 and in New Westminster, near the modern Vancouver, in 1866. Interior towns also spawned such societies and settlers were able to access theatrical performances, often produced in taverns. After a period when plays were performed in a converted ice rink, Vancouver began to acquire dedicated theatres, such as the Opera House of 1891, the York (1912) and the Orpheum (1927). It is intriguing that the polite tenor of theatre in Victoria seems to have been disrupted by a race riot in 1860, when seats reserved for white patrons were invaded by Black people.[21] This reflects the early racial tensions in the province, but also suggests a particular desire of people experiencing discrimination to see the play.

Meanwhile, populations in the prairie provinces were tiny with only a handful of people living in wooden shacks where the city of Winnipeg would later grow. Nevertheless, as early as the 1840s the military garrisons at Upper and Lower Forts Garry presented dramatic performances.[22] The First Ontario Rifles created a space they called the Theatre Royal and regularly performed farces and burlesques. Meanwhile the Quebec Rifles also put on productions. Later, an amateur dramatic society was formed in 1867 and performances began in the somewhat fragile wooden Red River Hall, which burned down in 1874. Other makeshift theatre spaces included the Manitoba Hall, later called the Opera House, the Second Theatre

Royal, the Dufferin Hall (made from the frame of a church which was caught in a cyclone). The Winnipeg Literary and Dramatic Society was formed in 1877 and it was said that settlers travelled long distances to see their comedies. A theatre was created out of the top storey of the first city hall and an early touring company arrived from the east in 1878. The McDowell Theatre Company presented favourites such as *East Lynne*, *The Shaughraun*, *Our Boys*, *Colleen Bawn*, *Mary Warner*, *The Two Orphans* and *Uncle Tom's Cabin*. The theatre, however, came in for some stick from the temperance lobby because of the ready availability of liquor. The first true theatre, the Princess Opera House, with an audience capacity of nearly 1,400, opened in 1883 with a visiting American opera company staging Flotow's *Martha*. Soon afterwards the theatre's respectability was demonstrated by the mounting of a 'Grand Shakespearian Event' consisting of *Richard III*, *Othello*, *Hamlet*, *Macbeth* and *The Merchant of Venice*, featuring Thomas W. Keene, the popular tragedian. But after this promising start, the Princess Opera House was completely destroyed by fire in 1892, the fate of so many theatres. Performances continued in the Bijou Opera House, the later Grand Opera House, and plays and other offerings were presented in the Winnipeg, Dominion and Walker Theatres, the latter inaugurated in 1907 and described as 'absolutely fireproof'. Further theatres were opened before the First World War, but the first classic period was to come to an end with the overwhelming popularity of the cinema in the 1920s. In Saskatchewan, itinerant entertainers apparently made visits to the province as early as 1833. There were the usual amateur companies, but surprisingly there was a fully professional company in the province in 1887. Theatres were built in Saskatoon and Regina, and theatrical presentations followed a similar pattern to those elsewhere in Canada. Throughout this period, the fare continued to be highly conservative, with productions which would have been recognisable to audiences in Britain. Theatre in its more national Canadian guise was only fully developed on the prairies as elsewhere after the Second World War.

While Canada constituted an early example of western theatrical dispersal, theatres also opened in other territories early in the era of British rule. The eighteenth century saw a number of theatres opening in the principal cities of India in the East India Company period. In Calcutta, western theatre had its origins in the mid-eighteenth century and the first dedicated theatre appeared in the 1770s.[23] There may even have been an earlier one in the Lalbazar in 1745, while the New Playhouse opened in 1775 with popular Shakespeare and Restoration plays. The Calcutta stage was not, however, reserved for English drama. The first Bengali plays were produced in Lebedeff's Theatre in 1795.[24] Later, in the nineteenth century the Pomeroy Dramatic Company performed at the Corinthian Theatre. In Bombay, there was a theatre on the green in 1770 (see Plate 28), which was repaired by Charles Forbes's Company after 1818. Theatres rapidly appeared in cities throughout India. In Lahore (now Pakistan), plays were performed in the Lawrence Hall, but modern theatres soon developed. In the Shah Almi district of the city the tradition of popular Indian theatre was maintained with companies soon appearing at the Mahabir Theatre near the Shah Almi gate.[25] The second half of the nineteenth century was a rapidly developing age of western theatre building, with Royal or Grand Opera houses appearing in the principal cities. Theatres also opened in railway towns. Touring troupes, as we shall see, regularly performed in India in this period.

The First Fleet to New South Wales in 1788 conveyed the tradition of theatricals as well as people. In 1789, George Farquhar's *The Recruiting Sergeant* of 1706 was performed by convicts.[26] In 1800, the first Shakespearean play, *Henry IV*, was produced in a makeshift theatre in Sydney.[27] The building of modern theatres soon proceeded apace in the Australian colonies, starting with the Royal in Hobart in 1837, the Melbourne Athenaeum (1839) and Queen's, Adelaide (1841), while the gold rushes of the 1850s produced a considerable boom in such building. An interesting case study is the colony of

Western Australia which was in effect founded in 1827. In March 1833, the theatrical tradition surprisingly started with an indigenous performance: Swan River and King George Aborigines (already identified with colonial geographical names) held a corroboree in the yard of Mr Purkiss and the lieutenant governor with several ladies present.[28] The 'native' Yagan introduced it and it was described as an 'amusing diversion'. In 1839 a local paper announced that private theatricals had been held in a private house, with a temporary stage and painted scenery. Despite a local describing this as the 'acme of licentiousness', such amateur performances took a tentative hold with more in Hodges' Hotel in 1842. Later the Amateur Dramatic Company performed in the hall of the Mechanics' Institute during race week, indicating the manner in which different forms of entertainment fed off each other. But Western Australia was far from being a theatrical paradise: in 1868 the *Fremantle Herald* was complaining that nowhere else would it be so difficult to fill an amusements column. Nevertheless, a Fremantle Amateur Dramatic Society was active by 1869, while Geraldton, 263 miles north of Perth, had an Amateur Club by 1882 and was the first town to have a Gilbert and Sullivan production. By the end of the century, many drama clubs were in operation, including that of the Church of England Young Men's Society with men playing female roles. Already travelling companies were arriving from the East, including that of Mr and Mrs George Case in 1867, and in the following year the Theatre Comique turned up before leaving for Shanghai. Many travelling companies appeared in the 1870s and 1880s, while in the 1890s Williamson and Musgrove promoted plays in Perth Town Hall, opened in 1870. Other venues were St George's Hall of 1879, and the Cremorne Gardens from the 1890s. The first true theatre was the Theatre Royal in Hay Street of 1897, with His Majesty's, the first one in concrete and steel, following in 1904. There had been a plan for a 1,200-seat theatre in Kalgoorlie, but such developments were highly sensitive to economic forces and this project came to nothing with the end of the gold boom.

A criterion of civilisation in Australia highlighted the manner in which theatre performances were received by audiences, calming down from the boisterousness of the early days. Moreover, it seems that grand opera was a highly popular interest when promoted by William Saurin Lyster and his Royal Italian and English Opera Company between 1861 and 1880, while melodrama and pantomime represented the 'lower' end of theatrical offerings.[29] Lyster also took his company to New Zealand where an extraordinary range of grand operas, including works by Donizetti, Bellini and Wagner, were performed starting out in Dunedin.[30] A high point in Australasian theatre came in 1855 when the Irish actor/manager Gustavus Brooke performed Shakespeare on a tour of no fewer than 22 Shakespeare plays and 200 performances.[31] Brooke was drowned when his ship foundered on another journey to Australia in 1866. In New Zealand's Canterbury province, the first production took place in Lyttelton Town Hall in 1857, and Christchurch's new music hall became the Royal Princess Theatre in 1863, with a resident company performing a mix of farces, Sheridan and Shakespeare. The Bard's plays remained the favourites for some time, particularly under the influence of actor-managers William Hoskins and Florence Colville. In the 1870s, visiting stars included Mrs Scott Siddons and George Rignold.[32] Another sign of sophistication was the appearance of Shakespeare Societies. The Shakespeare Society in Melbourne, for example, was founded in 1884 and there were equivalents in Geelong, Bendigo and in New Zealand Dunedin. Some of these later disappeared, but the Melbourne one survived with quite a considerable membership (largely male, middle-class and Anglo-Saxon, although a few women participated) which enjoyed a fare of readings, papers and lectures.[33] There was even a fund started for a Shakespeare Memorial Theatre in Melbourne, but that came to nothing. Shakespeare's reputation was infinitely malleable, even to the extent of supporting colonial expansion and confirming the patriotism of the First World War. For the members, Shakespeare was the true touchstone, much preferred to what was seen as the anti-intellectualism of the popular forms of the day, spectacular theatre, musicals and melodrama. The first party of Australian theatrical entertainers turned up in Hong Kong in 1842, only a year after the British occupation of the island. They seem to have been all male, since it was said that the female parts would be taken by men, appropriately dressed and made up. Already there seems to have been a plan to build a theatre in the colony.[34] Audiences there were soon ethnically mixed.

Racial exclusiveness, however, was common in most territories of both settlement and sojourning, although this was eventually overturned in India. In many places, the economics of seat prices were enough to maintain racial social distance. In slave societies, however, the situation was inevitably different. In the West Indies, slaves would never be permitted into the theatres except to perform the most menial tasks or sometimes to hold seats or boxes for their so-called masters. The theatre was thus both a symbol of imperial power and of racial oppression in a particularly reprehensible form. In these societies, the theatre was susceptible to fears of legislative change and economic decline, for example in the period leading up to and after emancipation, not least because of the falling numbers of the white population. This even affected the choice of plays since tragedies became unpopular. It took some time for the theatre to recover and an even longer period for Black people to access it fully.[35] This apparent insistence on racial exclusiveness in performances was replicated in different ways in colonies in southern and eastern Africa. This was highly ironic since the plays of Shakespeare had been translated into African languages throughout the continent and have sometimes constituted, in adapted forms, one of the foundations of modern African theatre.

Amateur drama

We have already seen how important amateur performances were in Canada and other colonies, and it is true that amateur theatricals were everywhere one of the passions of the expatriate colonial condition. E.M. Forster combined such amateur drama with the club, the key colonial social centre, in his novel *A Passage to India*. The visiting mother of the magistrate, Mrs Moore, finds that the third act of *Cousin Kate* was well advanced by the time she re-entered the club building. 'Windows were barred, lest the servants should see the mem-sahibs acting, and the heat was consequently immense.'[36] Discomfort had to be borne for the sake of racial exclusiveness. *Cousin Kate* was a play by Hubert Henry Davies, which had been produced by Charles Wyndham at the Theatre Royal, Haymarket in 1903, so a classic case of a transfer into amateur dramatics. The other significant location of such activity was in schools, where plays offered educational, confidence-building and performance experience. The hall of the Bishop Cotton School in Bangalore actually had fly mechanisms and other backstage features normally found in a professional theatre, although these were later destroyed during a misguided renovation.[37] In such schools, teachers were often appointed for their abilities in producing plays and acting.

As in Canada, the military were important propagators of amateur drama. The tedium of military life in India was alleviated by sports and theatricals. Each military station had its theatre, however makeshift, and plays were produced everywhere, from significant administrative centres like the Fort in Madras or the great military cantonment in Bangalore down to the smallest of 'stations'. There was a garrison theatre in the cantonment at Matunga near Calcutta, later abandoned when the area was incorporated into the city.[38] A striking theatre was built in the cantonment at Fatehgar near the Company station of Farrukhabad, painted (both exterior and interior) in 1815 by Sita Ram.[39] Military theatricals had their origins in the East India Company period and, as always, there was a complex of motives. Finding substitutes for excessive drinking or other vices was one, and maintaining a certain degree of surveillance was another. There was even a hint of an educational purpose for troops. Theatricals were time-consuming:

men built temporary stages and painted the scenery. At times it formed a convenient link between the military and local expatriates.[40] Europeans would form part of the audience and local white women sometimes 'made up' the men who were supposed to be playing women. This was a welcome extension of amateur theatricals in expatriate life. In some places, troops were also able to see travelling professional companies. The celebrated Wheeler Company, for example, performed for soldiers and charged half-price for seats at the back, no doubt hoping that they would not be too rowdy and disturb other patrons.[41]

Garrison theatre was also very important in maintaining western theatrical traditions in South Africa. There is evidence that the first Shakespeare performance, *Henry IV, Part I*, was presented by troops in a new theatre opened in Cape Town in September 1800. This was subsequently used by Dutch, French and German dramatic societies, evidence of a rich amateur tradition at the Cape. During an outbreak of Puritanism, the theatre was sold in 1838 and became a church.[42] If opposition to theatre in Quebec came from the Catholic hierarchy, in South Africa it originated with the Calvinist Dutch Reformed Church. Nevertheless, drama had been kept alive by garrison performances, not restricted to the British. Both Dutch and French soldiers had performed at the Cape in the eighteenth century and in 1807, Captain W. Frazer introduced Sheridan and Goldsmith. Amateur societies were founded in Cape Town in 1829, then Grahamstown (1837) and Stellenbosch (1838).[43] In Grahamstown amateur players performed Andrew Geddes Bain's Dutch play *Kaatje Kekkelbek or Life among the Hottentots* in 1838, a play featuring the Grahamstown prison from the perspective of a Khoi woman.[44] Amateurs kept theatre alive until professional companies appeared and formal theatres were once again constructed. The first Cape Town theatre burned down in 1839 and a new Victoria Theatre (later known as the Drury Lane Theatre) opened in 1846, followed by theatres opening in Grahamstown, Port Elizabeth, Pietermaritzburg and elsewhere. The Dutch (Afrikaans only emerged as a literary language later in the century) were also active and became more critically engaged as the century wore on. Amateur dramatic societies were inevitably racially exclusive, which was also true of the settler colonies in East and Central Africa. Indeed, amateur societies in Southern and Northern Rhodesia and Nyasaland, often founded in the 1930s, remained whites-only right up to independence. In East Africa dramatic 'skits' sometimes satirised the Swahili language.[45] They have been described as 'ego-boosting attempts at culture regeneration', designed to 'give colonialists a sense of identity and consolidate their myth of superiority'.[46] In such territories, Africans were introduced to western drama and perhaps encouraged to produce their own hybrid versions in mission schools, not least because translations of Shakespeare into African languages were common. There were, for example, translations into Tswana by Sol Plaatje, a nationalist who worked as a court translator.

In many places, amateur theatricals amounted almost to a passion. In the New South Wales town of Parramatta, amateur performances were already active in 1833 and later the Cumberland Amateur Dramatic Society and the Cumberland Opera Society became significant components of cultural life.[47] There are countless examples throughout Australia. Amateur dramatic performances spread western theatre to New Zealand in the 1840s, soon after the foundation of the colony, with performances taking place in pubs before theatres were built. Troops arriving for the Maori Wars between the 1840s and 1870s also brought garrison theatricals to New Zealand. Within a few decades, all the major New Zealand towns had theatres, though many built in wood were vulnerable to fire.[48] Major societies were founded later, for example in Wellington in 1880, amalgamating with the Amateur Operatic Society in 1891.

Perhaps the supreme example of such drama was the Amateur Dramatic Club of the most celebrated Indian hill station, Simla (see Plate 29). 'Doz', the *nom de plume* of the author of a lively early twentieth-century book, suggested that the performers of the Amateur

Dramatic Club were professionals who happened to have government or military posts as pastimes![49] Their devotion was such that no professional touring companies were ever allowed to make any inroads into the town.[50] The tradition had a long history. When Emily Eden visited Simla in 1838, she found 'a little sort of theatre, small and hot and something dirty'. A Captain N set out to put on six plays for the aid of famine relief, but the actors fell out and when the gentry withdrew, the clerks of the uncovenanted service took over, some of them of mixed race. Members of the social 'quality' refused to watch them, but Lord Auckland and his party did and they acted well, including one man nicknamed 'Sophia' for successfully playing female roles. Auckland also lent his band.[51] In 1839, tableaux and charades, organised by the governor general's aides-de-camp, were performed on a temporary stage at Annandale, the sports ground downhill from Simla.[52] Later the tradition was maintained in the theatre in the Royal Hotel (later Lawries) or in various drawing rooms at houses such as Snowden, Kennedy, Oakover, Abbeyville and even the mansion used as viceregal residence, Peterhof. The Viceroy Lytton (1876–80) was himself a playwright and produced his own play. Once the new Viceregal Lodge was built, Lord Lansdowne ordered a stage to be built in it.[53] The signal for the start of the golden age of Simla theatricals, however, was the opening of the Gaiety Theatre in 1887 (there was also a railway theatre there).

The Simla Amateur Dramatic Club was socially as well as racially exclusive, with senior military officers mainly constituting the executive committee, although it became more democratic in the twentieth century. The club produced as many as twenty different plays in the season from April to October, which declined to six or seven in the 1930s. Plays were financed by auctioning off the rental of the boxes, which could be expensive. Serious plays and Shakespeare were seldom performed, the favourite fare being farces, burlesques, comedies, satires and musicals.[54] For the larger performances, it was often necessary to fill leading roles by recruiting at down-country stations.[55]

Occasionally, there were upper-class Indian participants, though the local Indian dramatic society had mixed fortunes in securing access to the theatre. Today the foyer displays photographs of the productions between 1894 and 1905, including Gilbert and Sullivan operettas (*The Mikado*, *The Yeomen of the Guard* and *Iolanthe*), at least two plays by Oscar Wilde (*An Ideal Husband* and *The Importance of Being Earnest*), and, surprisingly, Mascagni's *Cavalleria Rusticana* in 1901, which must have placed considerable musical demands upon the cast.[56] But Simla was not of course alone among the hill stations in having amateur dramatics at its cultural core. This was also true of Mussoorie and the celebrated Ooty (then Ootacamund).[57] If amateur performances were often exclusively British, Indians were employed for menial tasks such as scene changing and other roles. Yet another location of amateur dramatic activity was the universities, which provided opportunities for the involvement of women. A Canadian example is the Women's Dramatic Club of University College Toronto, active from 1905.[58]

Professional theatrical troupes touring the empire

If amateur theatricals offered the main fare for many colonial populations, nevertheless professional companies were soon appearing throughout the colonies. It may be said that western theatre in this period, as in others, rejoiced in a combination of the supportive and the subversive, if expressed in mainly covert, though sometimes overt ways. The satirical potential of performance was in evidence in the seventeenth and eighteenth centuries, sometimes arousing the suspicion of political and ecclesiastical authorities (as in Quebec). Much of nineteenth-century theatre can be analysed in terms of its conformity with the ideologies and social mores of the day, as well as the comic potential of sending them up, though without undermining them. For imperial audiences these tensions constituted a central part of the entertainment. Shakespeare was a common theme throughout, but as the nineteenth century progressed other examples of early modern, Restoration and eighteenth-century drama declined in significance. There was an increasing emphasis on modern plays as well as on a combination of more light-hearted material with the presentation of increasingly overt imperial tableaux and contemporary works dealing with heroic events. This raises the interesting question as to why the high point of imperialism apparently coincided with less demanding theatrical fare. It was surely one of the consequences of more apparent ideological commitment, although Shakespeare always survived.

This was very much the kind of material which touring companies carried to so many corners of the British World. The actors in such companies led forms of transnational lives.[59] They invariably toured with plays recently produced in London as well as musical comedies which both celebrated and sent up the characteristics of the contemporary world, including perhaps some of the elements that colonials might be missing. They carried with them European ways of acting and therefore of audience watching and responding, described as 'another link of kinship'.[60] The elements of that kinship and social familiarity included the creation of stereotypical figures, forms of gendered narrative and various notions of political and professional relationships that linked to the social inheritance of the audience. In these ways, a cultural 'bubble' was created that escaped being pierced even when the 'Other' was portrayed, since non-European peoples were generally depicted in racially specific ways that confirmed rather than undermined the stereotypes, thus appropriating non-Europeans rather than creating opportunities for cross-cultural exchange. Hence the touring companies contributed to a sense of racial 'cultural globalisation'.[61] Some of the tours started earlier in the century in primitive conditions, but they later became a central theatrical characteristic of colonial entertainment. Australia and, by extension, New Zealand were key locations for travelling companies. In South Africa, theatre performances were given a new lease of life when such companies arrived from the mid-1850s, invariably travelling between Britain and Australia. These included Sefton Parry in 1855 while in 1886, Luscombe Searelle was persuaded to stay in South Africa to conduct his opera repertoire and remained for six months. He added Gilbert and Sullivan to his offerings and ended up controlling theatres in Kimberley, Pretoria, Pietermaritzburg and Durban. He also toured to Southern Rhodesia and Mozambique. Another impresario, Harry Stodel, brought music hall in 1891. Theatres in Cape Town and Johannesburg burned down, but Cape Town acquired new 'houses' in the shape of the Opera House in 1893 and the Tivoli in 1903. With the arrival of Leonard Rayne's productions of farces (with the occasional Shakespeare for ballast) in 1895 escapist colonial theatre took off in South Africa. Meanwhile in the later nineteenth century Canada enjoyed touring companies including those of Sir Johnston Forbes-Robertson, E.H. Sothern, John Barrymore, Maude Adams, and Harley Granville Barker offering Shakespearean and other classic material.

By this time, satire was enshrined as a central theatrical motif. Gilbert and Sullivan operettas became phenomenally popular and the D'Oyly Carte company had three troupes which toured Britain, the US and colonies. London musical comedy hits with long runs went round the empire. These included *A Gaiety Girl*, which developed the convention of gaiety girls as chorus and dancers. Its satire of upper-class social conventions, of the military (Guards officers) and of the predilections of a hypocritical judge and a clergyman caused considerable irritation and it was later cleaned up to a certain extent. It toured the US and Australia in 1894 and had further productions around the empire. Many other such comedies followed. *Our Miss Gibbs*, involving the adventures of a shop girl, had an even longer run at London's Gaiety Theatre and similarly travelled round both Britain and the world, starting in several cities of South Africa and Southern Rhodesia in 1910, India and the Far East in 1911, Australia and New Zealand in 1912. An example of a local touring company was the Australian troupe established by Alfred Woods and Maud Williamson. Woods had created a career out of appearing opposite imported stars, but he and Williamson got together in Sydney to create their own company. In 1901, they were billed as being about to perform for eight days in Launceston, Tasmania, with a play called *Boy Jim*, adapted from Conan Doyle's *Rodney Stone*, as well as *The Gates of Bondage*, *Hands Across the Sea* and a version of Marie Corelli's *Barabbas*.[62] The Woods-Williamson company also turn up performing at the Grand Theatre in San Francisco in 1905, indicating the manner in which Australian theatre connected with the USA at this time.[63] Maud Williamson apparently delighted audiences with her performance in *The Gates of Bondage*. There was an all-women troupe, managed by Miss Victoria Loftus, which toured extensively (including Ceylon) calling themselves the British Blondes Burlesque. They got into trouble, however, in the always strait-laced Dunedin in 1879 for a high-stepping dance sequence which, according to a local paper, shocked ladies in the audience and attracted the 'dirty minded'![64] Another Loftus travelling troupe seems to have performed safer Gilbert and Sullivan. Individual woman performers also toured the empire and even performed in the Chattar Manzil, the former palace in Lucknow which became emblematic of violence in the 1857 Revolt. In 1868 Grace Egerton delivered her 'impersonations' there while touring all the significant Indian cities with her husband George Case.[65] The Cases subsequently created one of the many touring theatrical troupes. A blackface Christy minstrel troupe toured the empire, which had a certain insulting irony about it, but must have confirmed many settler and expatriate prejudices.[66] To add to the diversity, there was even a skating troupe which reached India from Cape Town.

There were so many travelling companies that it is impossible to list them. One that has been well documented was founded by William John (W.J.) Holloway and continued by his son John.[67] This company first appeared in Ballarat in Victoria in 1880 (with Lytton's play *Richelieu*). W.J. Holloway emigrated to Australia in

1856 and, in common with many other touring actors, had to turn his hand to other jobs before and after performing. But his fascination with theatre developed when he heard many of the great actors of the day performing in Sydney, perhaps 'star' performers towards the end of their careers. Taking to the stage himself, he tied up with others like Walter Montgomery and George Coppin and initially toured to Brisbane and Adelaide. Having founded his company, he took it to various Australian cities and to New Zealand, the normal pattern being to perform Shakespeare followed by more modern plays. He also visited London to see how things were done in the West End and look for fresh repertoire. At this period, South Africa, formerly regarded as a graveyard for touring companies, provided opportunities for aspiring actors. When Lilian Braithwaite shocked her middle-class family by announcing that she wished to move on from amateur dramatics to the professional stage, she made her debut in Durban in 1897.[68] She later became a noted fixture of London's West End. Meanwhile, Holloway decided to take on the challenge of South Africa where audiences turned out to be highly receptive, but his tours had a habit of encountering periods of political turbulence. For example, his tours coincided with the 1895 Jameson Raid into the Transvaal (to support an attempted revolution by the 'Uitlander' gold miners); a gold slump later in the decade; the Second Anglo-Boer War; and later with a violent white workers' strike in 1913 when there were serious armed clashes and many deaths in the streets. There was, however, a highly successful tour in 1911 on their way to South Asia and the Far East, though in 1922 another led by John Holloway coincided with the most serious of all the Rand strikes resulting in a loss of £4,000. Touring could indeed be financially precarious. Nevertheless, tours kept actors in work and provided extended opportunities for star actors whose careers were fading, and they sometimes made profits, set against the hardships of travel, less than comfortable accommodation, poor weather and the considerable problems of moving stage scenery, props and costumes. This

was, after all, an era when theatrical audiences' expectations of realistic, even spectacular backdrops and other stage business were high,
very much part of the dramatic experience. The touring companies'
approach to personnel was also very hierarchical. They attempted to
have a 'name' to pull in the crowds, particularly for Shakespeare, but
there was a sharp drop in income for the other principal players and
an even greater one for those who supplied the 'bit' parts.

Yet touring remained extraordinarily extensive. It embraced North
America, the West Indies, South Africa, India, South-East Asia and
the Far East. The successful Holloway tour of 1911, with Matheson
Lang as star, had a ten-week season in South Africa, starting in
Johannesburg's His Majesty's Theatre in much more settled and civilised conditions (for white people) than earlier visits. It proceeded to
Pretoria, Kimberley, Durban and Cape Town, with command performances involving the governor general of the new Union, Lord
Gladstone, who greatly approved of their activities. After a hazardous
voyage across the Indian Ocean, the company arrived in Bombay,
where *The Times of India* hailed the arrival of Lang by announcing
that his South African tour had 'eclipsed all records'.[69] The company
opened in the Bombay Royal Opera House, where the Indian passion
for Shakespeare, particularly among students, ensured capacity
houses and almost riotous attempts to secure tickets.[70] Here they
played to multi-racial audiences which were entirely unheard of in
South Africa. They moved on to Calcutta, Rangoon, Singapore and
Hong Kong (two weeks each in the latter two, where the audiences
were racially mixed). The treaty port of Shanghai was regarded as
'the best theatre date in Asia' for travelling companies and they
performed there for a month.[71] The Caledonian Society insisted on
getting *Macbeth*, which was not in the company repertoire, so the
actors had to learn it hurriedly and create appropriate scenery and
costumes. The Caledonian Society booked the theatre for three
nights. The tour moved on to Manila in the Philippines. Lang
became fascinated by China, touring there again in 1914, which is

why he took on the play *Mr. Wu*, by Harold Owen and Harry Vernon, one of his greatest successes in London and elsewhere.

Such touring was 'developed to a scale that was unprecedented' by Maurice Bandmann (1872–1922), the son of a German-American Shakespearean actor, Daniel Bandmann, and a British actor mother, Millicent Farmer.[72] Bandmann, who Anglicised his name by removing the final 'n', became the most energetic travelling theatrical entrepreneur, creating a multiplicity of troupes (40–50 throughout his career) taking plays and musical comedies to North and South America, the West Indies, South Africa, the Mediterranean, India, the Far East, Australia and New Zealand. He eventually established his headquarters in Calcutta, where by 1907 he was sole lessee of the Theatre Royal and was building the Grand Opera House. He later added the notable empire, modelled on London's Gaiety, and proudly proclaimed that the Viceroy Hardinge was a patron.[73] Also active in Bombay, he built a corrugated iron theatre there until his Royal Opera House could be completed.[74] He had an Armenian partner in Calcutta and a Parsi in Bombay, cross-cultural entrepreneurship matched by his occasional employment of Indian and Anglo-Indian actors and dancers. As well as operating in Ceylon, he created an extensive touring circuit by connecting with the Australian Tivoli management and the African Theatre Trust of South Africa.[75] His touring Opera Company apparently had a repertoire of thirty musicals and a dozen plays.[76] While this activity reflected the common cultural relationships of empire, it also spread into China, Japan, Java and the Philippines. Bandmann even negotiated an opportunity to enter Siam, where the king had become used to British theatre when a midshipman in the Royal Navy's Mediterranean fleet. Clearly this extension constituted an informal cultural imperialism, not least since the offerings were in English. The material performed was essentially conservative, although Gilbert and Sullivan provided apparently subversive elements in the presentation of contemporary politics and society. Yet none of this was immediately killed by the popularity of cinema, continuing in some form into the 1920s and beyond. But Bandmann hedged his bets by developing cinemas, proclaiming that he had an arrangement to take Charles Urban's Kinemacolor technique to the East. In many respects it was not until the 1950s that new contemporary forms of theatre, more cross-cultural, more local, more hard-hitting began to emerge in, for example, the settlement territories of the former empire.

Travelling companies had a last hurrah during the Second World War when, for example, the Kendal family were recruited by ENSA (Entertainments National Service Association) to perform for troops in India Command and elsewhere. They took a familiar repertoire of Shakespeare as well as Sheridan's *The Rivals* (1775) and Goldsmith's *She Stoops to Conquer* (1773). It was this experience which led Geoffrey Kendal to develop touring in India after the war and independence.[77]

In all these ways, imperial theatre may have supplied psychological uplift for settlers and sojourners and an educational experience for the young and indigenous people. But it went further as a guard against boredom and providing a sense of cultural connection to ethnic origins. While Shakespeare maintained his authoritative and patriotic function, it is intriguing that supposedly 'serious' theatrical offerings gave way to light comedy and musicals in the late nineteenth and early twentieth centuries. This may have held up the development of a modern, more searching theatre exploring key social, racial, gender, ethnic and political themes until after the Second World War. But the emergence of a true theatrical renaissance at the end of empire was remarkable. Just as art discovered new roots in indigenous traditions, so did theatre begin to draw on a much greater range of inspirations, a development symbolising the substitution of challenging national forms for a supposedly homogeneous imperial theatre. Modern theatrical experiences in former Dominions and colonies reveals the extent to which this is true. In many ways, it certainly involved the development not just of self-reliance, but also a significant rediscovery of indigenous forms. But to draw a distinction between hegemonic imposition in the imperial period and cultural formation in the postcolonial is too simple. Both were enmeshed in various ways throughout the history of theatrical dispersal and adaptation.[78]

However, on the way to these modern transformations, Shakespeare presents a particular problem. It has been argued that the teaching of Shakespeare to Indians in the schools of the Raj was designed as part of the civilising mission, such that Indians would be turned into 'quasi-Englishmen'.[79] Moreover, particular editions of the texts were produced for India, including serious revisions to *Othello* and the re-slanting of *The Tempest* to give it a pro-imperial twist.[80] Such views, however convincing, are based upon textual evidence. The record of performance reveals that Shakespeare was so popular that some other forces were at work, that Shakespeare struck particular chords in both Indian and African cultures, quite separately from cultural imperialism. Although there can be little doubt that Shakespeare was edited and interpreted for all colonial contexts, often to produce specific inflections of female roles or make racial points (as in *Othello*), even to emphasise patriotic and apparently imperial themes, still Shakespeare seems to have continued to cross cultural and ethnic barriers. Even in the post-independence period, the Kendal acting family continued to perform Shakespeare with their company, 'Shakespeareana', throughout India and the Far East from the late 1940s until the 1970s.[81] They appeared to considerable acclaim in the hill stations, in the former princely states, in schools and colleges, but also in the major cities, though it is true that they suffered increasingly from tight finances and discovered that interest was waning in the later period. Felicity Kendal put this down to the decline of princely patronage and also the interest of schools, and perhaps because the imperial-inspired fascination with the Bard was beginning to wear off. In the 1965 Merchant/Ivory film *Shakespeare Wallah*, loosely based on the Kendal family's experiences, with a screenplay by Ruth Prawer Jhabvala, the main culprit is depicted as the tremendous rise in popularity of the products of Bollywood. This seems convincing, but there are clearly complex cross-currents at work. That neatly sums up the lengthy experience of colonial theatre in its various guises, both serious and light, until dramatically modernised and nationalised in the modern era.

9
FILM AND RADIO

The Electric Picture Palace, Mussoorie, northern India, c.1916, from a contemporary postcard.

Given more advanced travel technologies, moving film spread across the British Empire even faster than photography. The Lumière brothers' firm in Lyon is credited with inventing the first practical camera for moving images in 1894–95 (although others were experimenting and creating rival systems). Their first film was then shown in Paris in December 1895. The Lumière system crossed the Atlantic with the first demonstration of the Cinématographe in

Montreal in June 1896, followed by showings in Ottawa (of the American Edison Vitascope) in July 1896, in Toronto at the end of August in the same year and reaching Vancouver two years later in December 1898.[1] Very quickly, the rival companies, Lumière and Edison, the latter using various names, were touring the world with their shows. It has been suggested that the moving film camera appeared in Africa soon after its invention in France.[2] Films were shown in the Empire Theatre, Johannesburg, South Africa in May 1896.[3] The first film was seen in Melbourne, Victoria in August or October of 1896.[4] In Perth, Western Australia, there was a demonstration in the Cremorne Gardens in 1896 and films were soon being shown in vaudeville theatres with open-air cinema shows in Perth's gardens by the Esplanade from 1905.[5] There was a private showing of an early system in Auckland in 1895, with the first public Kinematograph display taking place in the Auckland Opera House during Charles Godfrey's vaudeville show in 1896.[6] The *New Zealand Herald* described the excitement this caused and predicted that there would be crowded houses 'even though the machine were the only attraction'. Moving film duly spread to other New Zealand cities and became a feature of the 1898 Otago Jubilee Industrial Exhibition (commemorating the white settlement in Otago in 1848), the programme (entry one shilling) to include 'Faust Up To Date or the Haunted Castle', billed as the 'longest and most expensive film ever shown in the colonies'. Additionally, nineteen shorts were listed, including 'The London Fire Brigade', 'Train through the Mountains', 'Dragoons Swimming their Horses', 'Tower Bridge, London', 'Piccadilly Circus' and 'Railway Station Scene'.[7] Thus the titles celebrated new technology and prominently featured London. Across the Pacific, the first screening in Singapore of a system called the Ripograph was in the Adelphi Hall in May 1897.[8] This possibly had an open-air showing in Hong Kong in the same year.[9] Thus moving images swept round the empire within two or three years of its invention. Initially, it was seen as a novelty, part of more conventional theatre performances. The technology, however, developed with extraordinary speed and had already reached a higher degree of sophistication, with longer pieces of film, in the years before the First World War. A 'home' cine camera was produced in 1921 and the private production of 'movie' film then accelerated rapidly. Thus, early in the century settlers were familiar with the medium, the numbers of practitioners had grown exponentially and silent feature films, documentaries and newsreels had become virtually universal.[10] It was perhaps a little slower to reach parts of Africa and South-East Asia and in many places it remained an elite interest for some time.[11]

Approaches to cinema history in the British Empire

Among themes in the history of imperial cinema, we need to consider not only its effects upon imperial culture but also the extent to which this innovative technology had an ideologically conservative influence or helped to advance the emergence of new identities and political affiliations. The impact of film can be charted through the almost explosive production of both feature films (fictional material) and the supposedly factual documentaries.[12] Features were made from the earliest days, but the limitations of the technology ensured that initially they were always 'shorts', each reel not much more than a minute long. It was generally not until the inter-war years that they reached the kind of length recognisable in modern times, even in silent format. After the advent of sound, full-length features began to be made. This increasing length and entertainment potential were matched by the provision of dedicated buildings. Whereas films were initially shown along with other performances in existing theatres, halls or exhibition buildings, cinemas of growing size and sophistication soon appeared. The more informal film shows continued in remoter areas, in tents, even out of doors, or from travelling vans or railway trains, but the major cities had dedicated cinemas (initially created from existing theatres) by the First World War. New buildings were constructed in the inter-war years with multiple cinemas, often with audience capacity of a thousand people, in all the larger cities. At the end of the First World War, there were already five cinemas in Singapore while later in the 1920s there were twenty-one in Bombay and twenty-three in Calcutta, some in new architectural styles like Art Deco.[13] Cinema culture took off in Hong Kong at the same time, often shown in Chinese opera theatres, mirroring the economic growth of the colony and the developing (western and hybrid) cultural awareness of its Chinese citizens.[14] By this time cinemas (often more modest in scale and style) were also appearing in many other towns in India and the colonies. In the larger centres, they became genuinely palaces of entertainment, increasingly elaborate, including additional social spaces in their foyers, with opulent decoration and even early air-conditioning. This encouraged and responded to the vast growth of audiences at a time when the scale of urbanisation continued to balloon, albeit occasionally checked by economic slumps.[15] Thus film-going became both the perquisite and the symbol of a supposedly sophisticated and modernising population even as rural migrants joined this 'club', swelling urban numbers. However, as Burns suggests, although cinema became a global phenomenon, it did not necessarily represent a globalising one.[16] In other words, films could mean contrasting things to different audiences while, in addition, there were conscious attempts to impede the power of the American product. Moreover, the viewing of films continued to be a highly diverse experience with older films still shown in some places and 'silents' surviving into the 'talkie' era. Older forms of projection continued in use and, for many colonial audiences, the plush dream palaces of the major cities remained just that: dreams.[17]

This diversity in the spread of film and in access and experience, perhaps particularly apparent in Africa and other remoter colonies, could also be a characteristic of the territories of white settlement. In Canada and Australia, First Nations and Aboriginal people experienced little of this until modern times. The presence of small Maori communities in New Zealand towns and cities, together with a relative lack of racial discrimination, marked out that territory as distinctive. In the West Indies, film-going started out as predominantly a white pursuit but was soon taken over by Black and Asian populations. In West Africa films made a relatively slow start. Meanwhile, in southern Africa and in some colonies in East and Central Africa, white minorities faced a dilemma. Should film be used as a means of surveillance of Black residents, distracting them from what white people regarded as more dangerous social activities (like drinking in beer halls), while acting as an anaesthetic for political and social discontents? But the anaesthetic could all too readily be suspected of turning into a stimulant and this led to the almost universal exercise of censorship in colonies with non-white populations. Initially in the reluctant hands of the police, boards were established by the later 1920s to censor both the films themselves and the posters. These boards were made up of officials and their wives but could also include missionaries and local residents.[18]

South Africa had a censorship act from 1931 and banned all films with racial interaction during the apartheid era. Northern Rhodesia had an African member on its censorship board by the 1950s, a practice apparently recommended as early as 1930.[19] In such colonies there was also racial discrimination in the provision of cinemas. Africans were not permitted to enter 'white' cinemas in towns but might be able to experience films in a highly controlled or censored form in mining compounds, Black 'locations' or mission stations. Elsewhere discrimination might be exercised through ticket pricing, ensuring that white expatriates could be segregated into the most expensive part of the auditorium.

The advent of film produced a strange amalgam of exaggerated expectation and an inflated sense of panic among imperial administrative elites and dominant white groups. The optimism was based on the notion that this was a medium so hypnotic in its power over audiences that it could be used to disseminate uplifting messages of religious significance and educational import in respect of hygiene and health, as well as of environmental and productive (for example agricultural) improvement. Films had the capacity to modernise what were conceived to be backward populations. It was even thought that rural film shows might halt the socially and politically dangerous population drift to towns.[20] If uplift was expected from factual films with a high propagandist content, panic was associated with features. Film fear took many different forms, all based on perceptions of the immensely suggestive power of moving images. Might indigenous peoples not find evidence that white supremacy was not as invincible as local assumptions about power might suggest? If Black boxers could defeat white opponents, as in the celebrated case of the world heavyweight championship bout between the African American John (Jack) Johnson and the white James J. Jeffries in 1910, then the expectation (and terror) of Black physical superiority might be transferred into other spheres. The overwhelmingly racial content of such boxing matches, universally available through newsreels, caused major anxiety in white-dominated territories. Moreover, if Black and Asian people could be depicted in films as having qualities of personal courage, moral power and even military capacity, might this not stimulate resistance and revolt? Equally, if a non-white audience could encounter images of political dissent and worker and trade union demands for better conditions, might not this be translated into reality? Was it possible that historical revolutionary activity (even if in North America or France in the eighteenth century) might inspire ideas in Afro-Asian peoples in contemporary times? D.W. Griffiths' celebrated 1915 film *The Birth of a Nation*, while epoch-making in the history of productions because of its epic length (three hours) and powerful orchestral score, caused great alarm, not just for re-creating the assassination of Lincoln and the American Civil War, but for its degrading depiction of African Americans and elevation of the Ku Klux Klan into a heroic force.[21] It seemed decidedly inappropriate for Black audiences, having caused violence and riots in the USA. Even worse, because more immediate and less theoretical, if such audiences were confronted with films of gangsters and violent cowboys (particularly in conflict with the hopelessly heroic resistance of North American native peoples) might this not be translated into the conditions of modern colonial society? Would the tension and excitement of the early thrillers have excessively stimulating effects upon the allegedly ever-suggestible 'natives'? And if the males in such audiences were confronted with images of scantily clad or otherwise alluring white women, might this not excite (in the outrageous racial attitudes of the day) their naturally lascivious natures, encouraging erotic desire and the increasing prevalence of rape? This was a particularly potent anxiety in southern Africa, where woefully racist double standards applied: white rape upon Black women went relatively unpunished while its opposite could lead to a sentence as draconian as the death penalty.

Other forms of panic centred on the cultural predominance of American films. Fear of the US film industry developed particularly intensively during the First World War and continued into the inter-war years. This fear took three forms: first it was thought that American films were so appealing (and so prolific) that they would overwhelm any production in Britain. But it went deeper than this: it was thought that the display of American material culture could have significant effects upon trade, colonial peoples (both settler and indigenous) being induced to prefer American products to British. Second, after the advent of 'talkies' in the late 1920s, it was feared that the slang and accents of North America would begin to constitute the norm for English language teaching and usage. Inevitably, such fears were particularly prominent in the West Indies and in Canada, but were also evident throughout the British Empire in Africa, Asia and Australia/New Zealand.[22]

Another route into the colonial history of film is to examine the business dimensions, the emergence of cinema production and distribution as a major capitalist phenomenon, as well as the more local provision of the interface with the consumers, namely the renting of films, the supply of seats and the selling of tickets. Although a British film industry made a tentative start in the early years, growing considerably in the 1930s, it has been pointed out that the British took little part in the supply and showing of films in the colonies. The cinema industry was often pioneered by immigrants in territories of white settlement, while elsewhere entrepreneurs tended to be Parsis in India, Chinese in South-East Asia and the Far East, and Jewish businessmen in South Africa and the Caribbean.[23] It is interesting to speculate why this was the case: whether British colonials had, as they thought, larger economic fish to fry, lacked the interest or expertise in the film industry, or whether there was a certain amount of snobbery at work with cinema regarded as a form of low culture. Nevertheless, there were other areas of entrepreneurship, in retail trades and the opening of hotels, where immigrant groups like Syrians in West Africa and Armenians in South-East Asia tended to be active.

Topical films

The situation was rather different in respect of films supplying news or providing religious, medical, moral or educational messages where the British were more likely to be involved in the supply of these 'respectable' products. In the case of 'news' content, wars were a tremendous fillip to the expansion and influence of the medium which is reflected in the considerable importance of film in presenting images of soldiers departing for the Anglo-Boer War from Britain, Canada, Australia and New Zealand.[24] Here was a medium capable of arousing patriotic and imperial loyalties. It was, however, more difficult to display the actual events of the war, although some cameramen were active in South Africa. The primitive and unwieldy nature of early cameras predictably led to faked sequences (as would happen again in the First World War). Nevertheless, filmed material in the Great War was more convincing and by the Second World War the sequences were a good deal more graphic and comprehensive. Dramatic international events, including European conflicts with global consequences, could be conveyed with some immediacy to audiences throughout the empire.

During the early decades of the twentieth century, newsreels became the principal vehicles of topical content, if in highly selective forms. In 1908, various shorts were put together by Pathé to form an early newsreel, a technique formalised when Pathé's British newsreel started in 1910. Others followed, the important ones being the Animated Gazette, Gaumont Graphic and Topical Budget, the latter taken over by the War Office in 1917 as an overtly propagandist vehicle. The Empire News Bulletin and British Movietone News appeared in the inter-war years, in 1926 and 1929 respectively. By this time, British newsreels had become highly popular additions to British cinema programmes, though audiences were shielded from content that might prove politically controversial or encourage social or labour dissent. The military remained a popular subject, even in times of peace, as did examples of modern technology (with flight a new exciting and adventurous frontier), successful examples of resource extraction and trade, and inevitably sporting events, particularly inter-colonial and international ones. Although it might seem that the value of news would be diminished by delays in transmission as the stock was carried by sea and rail to its destination, a problem only overcome by the development of air transport, nevertheless images of remarkable events remained fresh for new viewers. Hence British news material seems to have gone round the empire. Examples in the earliest days would include a short film of the funeral procession of Queen Victoria in 1901, followed by the funeral of Cecil Rhodes, still regarded as an imperial hero, in Cape Town a year later. In 1903, the Canadian Ireland brothers were showing film of the coronation of Edward VII in the Prince's Building Trinidad on 23 and 24 February 1903 (the delayed coronation actually took place on 9 August 1902, reflecting the time it took the film to reach the West

Indies).[25] The Ireland brothers continued to show films of notable American and British personalities for some years. Another example is the remarkable films of the 1911 Delhi Durbar in which George V and Queen Mary crowned themselves emperor and empress of India (see Plates 30 and 31). Showings were a tremendous success in Britain, filling cinemas and receiving plenty of press comment. The film apparently appeared in three different versions (in terms of length) not only throughout the British Empire, but also in the USA, Germany and France.[26] The Anglo-American film-maker Charles Urban produced a two-and-a-half-hour epic of the same event which he issued in Kinemacolor, entitled *With Our King and Queen through India or The Delhi Durbar*, using an early colouring technique. Only a small section of this film survives, but, despite a soft focus, it undoubtedly has surprising immediacy, with marching British and Indian troops, a dramatic gallop of cavalry and gun teams, the firing of salutes and the display of a princely camel corps.[27] Newsreels covered British royal occasions throughout the inter-war years, including the tours of the Prince of Wales (later Edward VIII), his brother Prince George (Duke of Kent), the Jubilee of George V, his funeral, and the coronation of his successor, George VI. Interestingly, material relating to other royal families and rulers in Africa and India was also prominent. An excellent, high-profile example is the coronation of Ras Tafari Makonnen as the Emperor Haile Selassie of Ethiopia in November 1930, replete with many sequences of visiting dignitaries, with one version showing shots of the film cameramen themselves, as well as of the Emperor unveiling a remarkable equestrian statue of his predecessor, Menelik.[28]

Local newsreels included the highly prolific Indian News Parade and Indian Movietone News.[29] Major territories of empire issued their own newsreels, including the African Mirror in South Africa, later taken over by African Film Productions. This company also attempted to enter the commercial film market to counter the influence of the American product. It is apparent that while feature films, so often American, would have provided the most prominent and popular cinema fare, the showing of newsreels (despite having international content) must have been a constant reminder of the imperial connection. The production, distribution and programming of newsreels turned film into a major supplier of news, though dependent on the willingness of distributors to adopt them for their circuits. In the days of sound, the British examples became famous for the distinctive voices of their commentators, using a dramatic, almost exaggerated form of staccato standard English, though it would have been possible to dub them into local accents. Hence newsreel became a means of public participation in events, as well as creating a binding effect through unveiling major national, often royal, occasions, both in Britain and in tours of empire.

Documentary and 'uplift' films

The Salvation Army was involved in the making of experimental films as early as the 1890s and had apparently made some thirteen in India by 1906.[30] Missions became important partners in the provision of supposedly factual and uplifting films, using the medium as potentially an effective means of conversion and an aid to spirituality and worship. There were films devoted to the life of Christ and to biblical stories while the mission societies also set out to illustrate their adherence to the principle of conversion by works, the notion that spiritual objectives would be achieved through the pursuit of western medicine and, for example, scientific approaches to agronomy. J. Merle Davis called it 'Christian social work'.[31] A number of societies became involved including the Methodists, the Church Missionary Society, the Church of Scotland Missions and particularly the London Missionary Society. David Livingstone had worked for the latter, at least in the early part of his career, and this may explain its involvement in modestly helping to finance the making of M.A. Wetherell's film *David Livingstone*, planned in 1923 and released in 1925. This 90-minute silent feature, filmed on location in Zanzibar, East and Central Africa, had been promoted at a London lunch hosted by the proprietor of the *Daily Telegraph*, Lord Burnham, and was supported by key members of the British Establishment, including Sir Frederick Lugard (architect of Indirect Rule and later British representative at the Mandates Commission of the League of Nations), W.G. Ormsby-Gore, under-secretary for the colonies, clergymen including the Bishop of London, and *The Times*. These generally emphasised the moral and educational content of the film, the attractions of its exotic locations and wildlife, and the fact that it was a British film, supposedly countering what were seen as the more pernicious aspects of American films.[32] It was filmed on a major expedition extensively reported in the press and regarded as matching in geographical terms that of Livingstone himself. The explorer was portrayed as 'the epitome of "British character"' in a way intended to 'instil in the young courage, perseverance, devotion to duty, self-sacrifice, patriotism and pride in empire'.[33] Such high seriousness might be expected to detract from its entertainment value, but it did recoup its costs and was shown widely in cinemas as well as religious outlets, although it was refused release (presumably on commercial grounds) in the USA and South Africa.

The earnestness of this film was matched by various other projects, including British Instructional Films, which was created to provide documentaries, some features and news material. This operated between 1919 and 1932 and in the middle of the 1920s produced films that featured almost all the colonies.[34] Missionary efforts at film making continued, together with those that became semi-official Colonial Office products. Indeed, there was an interesting mutual engagement with film by both missions and officials. Even so, inter-war attitudes towards film tended to alternate between enthusiasm and scepticism. This resulted from the different agendas of the leading players.[35] One was the usual anxiety about the growing dominance of American films and their allegedly negative influence upon British imperial culture and consequently on colonial subjects, a concern shared by King George V himself.[36] Another was doubts about the loyalties of indigenous peoples and therefore the necessity for engineering their economic and moral 'uplift'. This included situations in which Africans were sucked into working in growing capitalist enterprises in West, Central and South Africa, producing major (and politically and morally dangerous) social disruption.[37] International Christian organisations and British missionary societies inevitably saw continuing efforts at Christian conversion as one solution. In southern Africa, the main focus of American missionary interest was the mine 'compounds' of the Rand and Northern Rhodesia. Given that these were unisex male living areas, with families left in rural villages, here was clearly a potential seedbed for various forms of alleged anti-social behaviour. Davis saw the cultural and educational potential of film as presenting an antidote, to be used to depict the better qualities of European and African cultures. In this the missions should be fully involved, with 'a moving picture outfit' constituting a significant addition to the 'equipment of every African mission'. If too costly, then several missions should collaborate, perhaps following the advice of the experienced American Congregational Board.[38]

While colonial officials seemed to sign up to these ideas, not least as a route to the maintenance of labour relations and civil peace, their overriding concern was that films should have positive effects upon the economic development and commercial value of colonies. The colonial conferences of both 1927 and 1930 considered the potential utility of film and the Colonial Secretary L.S. Amery appointed a film committee in 1929. But while the Colonial Office was alert to the significance of film and its potential for 'uplift' and the projection of imperial ideas, individual colonies faced with financial stringency were a good deal more cautious. This was true in the East African territories of Kenya, Uganda and Tanganyika, where colonial budgets were particularly stretched by the collapse in raw material prices of the period. These economic concerns ensured that colonial film-making was placed in the hands of the Empire Marketing Board (EMB), the body designed to pull the empire together into a more effective trading unit. A few films were made, but although the EMB was wound up in 1932 its lasting significance was as a training ground for documentary film-makers who took their skills to other organisations, including the General Post Office and Imperial Airways.[39]

Nevertheless, with some hesitation and pressed by the missionaries, the Colonial Office agreed to the setting up of the Bantu Educational Kinema Experiment (BEKE), which made some thirty-five films between 1935 and 1937, concentrating on colonies in East and Central Africa. Such films have been described as representing 'the political economy of community development'.[40] They tried to advance the modernisation process, for example in setting out to demonstrate the alleged dangers of following 'witchdoctors', and they used the 'Mr. Wise and Mr. Foolish' format to demonstrate how recommendations on education, finance and health could work for those wise enough to adopt them.[41] Despite all these efforts, including the setting up of the unsuccessful British United Film Producers Ltd in 1931 to distribute British films of all types to the colonies, there was a sense that Britain was failing in efforts to use film. In the late 1930s, Lord Hailey lamented that so little had been done to produce suitable films for African audiences. His work betrayed the attitudes of the age, namely that films suitable for Europeans were not necessarily so for Africans, that the supposedly 'primitive' mind had difficulties in following filmic narrative, yet conceding that films could have considerable social and educational value for non-literate audiences.[42]

Despite some scepticism, missionary societies maintained their confidence in the power of film. As revealed in the London Missionary Society journal *The Chronicle*, the society continued its film-making efforts, with no fewer than thirty films made between 1930 and 1940 archived in the British Film Institute.[43] Finally, attempts were made to use film as a means of education and modernising propaganda, for the teaching of children about the imperial relationship and the nature of the societies and economies in which they lived, but also in pursuit of health (notably with respect to tropical diseases) and agricultural improvement.[44] Racial ideas were central to these productions. Films were almost exclusively produced by whites for the supposed enlightenment and uplift of non-whites, all based on the notion of mental and cognitive differences between white and Black viewers. Ethnic films were designed to show exotic places and the diversity of peoples, generally to emphasise primitiveness and the technological gap.

The colonial era and some of its attitudes were perpetuated in various film units which, in some respects, continued to influence productions after independence (see Plate 32). Two examples were Jamaica and the Nigerian Federation.[45] In the latter case, film-making continued to concentrate on documentaries and newsreels, following the practice of the Nigerian Federal Film Unit created in 1950. There was little attempt to produce feature films until the development of video technology.[46] However, the colonial tradition continued most prominently in the region of Africa where white supremacy survived for the longest period, in South Africa, the Central African Federation and Rhodesia. It was here that colonial ideas and methods survived into the postcolonial era. Films there 'were remarkable for their simplistic style, demeaning images, and paternalistic messages'.[47] Discriminatory censorship between white and Black audiences was maintained. Educational and propaganda films designed for African audiences continued to be made by the Central African Film Unit and from 1957 a newsreel was issued specifically for Africans.[48] After the winding up of the Central African Federation in 1963, when Northern Rhodesia and Nyasaland moved into independence as Zambia and Malawi, the Rhodesia Front regime in Rhodesia continued with such films until it collapsed in 1980. The white population, constituting 4 per cent of the whole, continued to attempt to control the information fed to Africans, to prevent movement to towns to keep Black people restricted to crowded and environmentally degraded reserves or 'tribal trust lands', and to shield them from what the white administration regarded as the dangerous ideas inherent even in American cowboy movies.[49] This constituted the final doomed attempt by white people to control what Africans were allowed to see. Everywhere localised feature film production was inhibited by the colonial preference for documentaries and would only emerge in many places after independence.

Talkies

A number of consequences followed the shift from silent films to 'talkies'. Silent films had been universal with actions comprehensible to all, though in some performances helped by commentators, often using the language of the audience. With sound, films became language-specific and if subtitled required a degree of literacy. Despite the enormous power of the American film industry, local film industries had sprung up almost from the earliest days, but sound ensured that such local production would become more significant. In settlement territories, film soundtrack could now reflect the distinctive accents of Canadians, South Africans, Australians or New Zealanders. A developing contrast became apparent between the standard English that imperial rulers and educationalists would rather disseminate and American and other forms of English, including accent, distinctive idiom and slang. But now there was additionally an opportunity to use national and regional languages in many colonial territories, a development particularly significant in India where film production began to use Hindi and other tongues from the 1930s. Thus the 'vernacular press' was matched by 'vernacular cinema'. This had wider ramifications. Imperial rule had encouraged several diasporas, including Chinese workers moving to colonial territories and, more importantly, Indians (often from western India) to Pacific and Indian Ocean islands, South and East Africa, and the Caribbean. Such dispersed language groups were able to access films that culturally renewed their ties to their place of origin, confirming their sense of ethnic identity and knowledge of historical migrations. Films had the power to emphasise trans-oceanic associations cutting across national political alignments.

Empire feature films

So far as features were concerned, the 1930s saw a wave of films set in empire contexts and invariably reflecting imperial ideologies. The cult of Livingstone ensured that he continued to be the subject of films, including British ones of 1933 and 1936, and the lavish sound version of *Stanley and Livingstone* issued by 20th Century Fox in 1939.[50] The heroic spotlight now inevitably fell on Stanley, the American citizen, instead of Livingstone. The Hungarian immigrant Alexander Korda founded London Film Productions in 1932 in a conscious attempt to match the scale and magnificence of the Hollywood product. Korda was joined by his brother Zoltan and together with the producer Michael Balcon they had links with Establishment figures and the Conservative party. Their films proved to be such box office successes, combining patriotism with profit and displaying the essence of the imperial adventure tradition which had infused so much juvenile and other forms of literature, that the genre was also pursued in the USA where a number of such imperial epics were produced.[51] Thus, the adventure tradition influenced a cultural mix of journalism, some popular art, then film. Among British films were *Sanders of the River* (1935), *The Drum* (1938) and *The Four Feathers* (1939) while Hollywood produced an earlier *Four Feathers* (1929), *Clive of India* (1935), *King of the Khyber Rifles* (1929), *Lives of a Bengal Lancer* (1935), *Stanley and Livingstone* (1939) and *The Rains Came* (1939–40). All these have been the subject of increasingly sophisticated analysis in recent years.[52] Prem Chowdhry has examined the examples set in India in terms of their imperial, racist and gender content. She has argued that far from merely resurrecting late nineteenth-century imperial ideas, they represent contemporary attitudes. They were in short 'designed to sustain imperialism, subvert growing nationalism, establish relations of domination, lay claims to legitimacy, and undermine the demand for self-government and democracy in India'.[53] The American films in the genre both represented American ambivalence towards empire and nationalism while still subscribing fully to the 'cultural outlook that located heroes and villains in racial stereotypes'.[54]

Cinema had started out by reflecting central themes of contemporary media, namely warfare, royal events, exotica of all sorts, the drama of modern technology, not least in its application to the economic resources of empire, as well as the escapism of melodrama and romance or the thrill, sometimes terror, of adventure and criminal genres. Were they, however, influential in the maintenance of imperial culture and identities? Were they central to the dissemination of imperial ideas in Britain, shoring up the essentially atavistic character of empire?[55] Grieveson has suggested that 'the cinematic image' and documentaries were 'bent towards the fantastical maintenance of a dying dream of economic and geopolitical dominance' and 'to mummify change'.[56] Judged in terms of resisting the onward march of the dynamic of history, films were clearly failures, but they may well have influenced the consciousness of contemporaries, particularly white people, as well as the attitudes of the 'movers and shakers' of imperial culture and policy. They were significant in reaching out across the wider Anglophone world, perhaps reassuring white settlers that the adventure tradition, with its 'emphasis on masculinity, aggression and penetration in relation to the colonial' domain continued to justify their presence in exotic global contexts.[57] Yet they must sometimes have met a degree of growing scepticism as local identities moved towards disrupting the British Empire's cultural homogeneity. Cinematic features dominated by the American product constituted the primary threat to imperial identity and the focus upon a metropolitan-led culture maintaining hegemonic and racial stereotypes. The cinema's impact may have been variable, but certainly contributed to the loosening of the British cultural grip.

In territories of white settlement and in India, films would chart the development of local identities and shift the identity of the personnel of cultural leadership. After all, Canada, South Africa, Australia and New Zealand all developed their own cinema industries. These early films, sometimes by amateurs, set out to depict the landscape and products, as well as the ethnic character, of their territories. The British 'Quota Act' of 1927, renewed in 1938, was designed to protect British and Commonwealth film-making from American dominance, though in a very limited way.[58] Independently, in this period some documentary film-making in the Dominions was beginning to be more highly organised. The celebrated documentary film-maker John Grierson reported on the Canadian situation in 1938, and the National Film Board of Canada was established in 1939, later to be the Canadian Film Development Corporation of 1967.[59] There were similar developments in Australia. In each case, these efforts resulted mainly in the making of documentaries. In Canada, the most vigorous feature film-making was in Quebec, inevitably influenced by France and promoted by the needs of a French-language population. The origins of this lay in the era of imported silent films, enthusiastically shown in Quebec and viewed by one scholar as the basis of a culture countering both dominant English-speakers and the Roman Catholic Church.[60] After the Second World War, it was thought that the trade imbalance (and consequently payments problem) with the USA would help to stimulate the film industries of countries seeking import substitution, but in reality this produced relatively little effect. In the case of each Dominion film industry it was not until the 1960s and beyond that feature films began to be made, a few securing an international reputation. Through being shown, and winning prizes, at film festivals such as Cannes, they found a wider global audience, even if they never fully succeeded in standing up to the American behemoth.

India constitutes the single case of national film production which came to rival the American industry in terms of investment, numbers of films made and extent of distribution. Short films were made in India from the earliest days, with the first full-length silent feature in 1913. The industry developed considerably after the First World War, particularly with the advent of sound. Just as Quebec developed its own language film tradition, it was the opportunity to produce films in multiple Indian languages that ensured the industry's growth. Bombay became the centre of production, although there was also a good deal of regional film-making. The creation of 'Bombay Talkies' in 1934 proved to be a significant landmark while some English-language Indian films began to secure an international reputation from the 1950s.[61] 'Bollywood' (a term which some dislike as detracting from the originality of the Indian product) was to explode from the 1960s, with films in Hindi, distinctive story lines and celebrated song and dance routines. With heavy investment, lavish productions and celebrated stars, Bollywood began to establish a global appeal, not only among the Asian diaspora on every continent, but sometimes with western audiences. This ensured the survival of cinema-going in dedicated buildings in India when competition from television was closing cinemas in many countries. National film-making traditions also developed in many other places. A well-documented example is Ceylon (Sri Lanka), where film production vigorously emerged, initially in Madras and later in Ceylon itself. The leaders of this were the Tampoes, father and son, R.M.S and Robin, the latter giving up a career at the bar.[62] Influenced by Indian directors from North and South India, Tampoe produced a corpus of Sinhala feature films which laid the foundations of a significant national industry.

Radio

Of all the news and information media, radio required the greatest technical and scientific knowledge to understand and create its 'wireless' transmissions.[63] The telegraph, cable and telephone had required wires, radio mysteriously did not. While it was used for the transmission of messages, for example in a maritime context, in the years before the First World War, it was only later that the medium was available for home information and entertainment. However, neither those creating radio news and programmes nor the audience required technical understanding, although in the early days of a simpler technology there were amateurs active in organising trans-mitters and receivers. Nevertheless, after some early experiments and a rush to secure licences, the position in Britain was regularised with the founding of the British Broadcasting Company in 1922, later transformed into a Corporation. As radio became increasingly important in British national life between the wars, the administra-tion of the BBC under John Reith took great pains to take an Establishment line, a policy which involved supporting the central ethos of the British Empire.[64] Reith took an almost mystical view of the power of his organisation in national and imperial life. He saw the opportunity to broadcast the bells of Big Ben and the King's speeches (such as at the opening of the Wembley Empire Exhibition in 1924) and, from 1932, Christmas messages to the empire, with associated programming, as being central to such a mission. As with other media, radio swept rapidly round the empire. The BBC was influential in this imperial expansion when it founded the empire Service in 1932, initially broadcasting only in English.[65] From 1938, the service started broadcasting in other European languages and with technical advances adding more world-wide transmission, transforming itself into the highly influential World Service in 1965. The Empire Service had several audiences: white colonial expatri-ates, the inhabitants of the Dominions and English-speaking non-white people in the colonies. Increasingly, as it morphed into the World Service, the objectives changed. Instead of pulling together Anglophone colonial populations, it became a propaganda service enhancing Britain's diplomatic and security interests. The thrust of maintaining imperial cultural ties was thus diluted by anxieties about international affairs up to the Second World War.

As this indicates, the major significance of radio lay in the fact that it knew no borders. The very nebulousness of radio transmission ensured that it could be a means of resistance and propaganda across frontiers, exposing populations to what administrations might regard as dangerous cultural and political influences, both external and internal. In another form, listeners in Asian colonies often found Dutch short-wave radio broadcasts in English from the Netherlands more appealing in entertainment value.[66] Nevertheless, there is a considerable paradox in the development of radio around the British Empire. On the one hand, the BBC established a model largely followed elsewhere, sometimes with a very similar name and acronym as in CBC in Canada and ABC in Australia. But despite the Empire and World services of the BBC retaining their authority in news broadcasting, Dominions' radio stations were vital in the creation of national identities, celebrating the linguistic and ethnic diversities of their populations, although indigenous ethnicities continued to be culturally suppressed until relatively modern times. In Canada, just as the tremendous power of American films had caused alarm, so were those involved in Canadian broadcasting (originally in the hands of various organisations such as the Canadian National Railway) anxious about the influence of America. Partly to counter this, the Canadian Radio Broadcasting Commission was created in 1932 and was transformed into its present form as the CBC in 1936. In Canada and elsewhere, radio stations often had local and informal origins, even starting from broadcasting clubs of enthusiasts. In New Zealand a professor of physics at Otago University began broadcasting in 1921. But there was a tendency towards rationalisation in the 1930s. Similar broadcasting organisations were founded in Australia (Australian Broadcasting Company in 1929 becoming the Australian Broadcasting Commission in 1932), and the New Zealand Broadcasting Board, also 1932. Broadcasting in South Africa began in 1923 and early companies (including South African railways) were merged into the African Broadcasting Company of I.W. Schlesinger, already powerful in the cinema industry. This later became the South African Broadcasting Corporation in 1936. Canadian and South African radio systems were at pains to broadcast respectively in both English and French and English and Afrikaans, while New Zealand broadcasters also created a Maori language service. It may be that such broadcasting was significant in developing linguistic autonomy and cultural identity among South Africa's Afrikaans people, influencing future political behaviour in the post-Second World War period.[67] In Ceylon an engineer in the telegraph department began broadcasting in 1923; Radio Colombo was active in 1925 and later became Radio Ceylon. Broadcasting in India also began with the activities of radio clubs, but the private Indian Broadcasting Company was created in 1927, incorporated into an Indian State Broadcasting Service in 1932, later All-India Radio (1936). The rulers of the Indian Raj had now secured a higher degree of control over broadcasting than had been possible in the case of the press. Moreover, Indian broadcasting was turned to propagandist geo-political purposes when a Pushtu service was created in 1939 to counter German propaganda on the borders of the subcontinent. Nevertheless, some independent radio stations continued to broadcast in India.

Radio in Africa was treated by the British colonial authorities as another means of transmitting information and modernising ideas to the indigenous populace. This was aided by the invention of the relatively simple 'frying pan' radio (or saucepan radio) and the development of battery-operated models that could be taken to the villages. But for colonial powers in Africa, the cross-border receipt of programmes and news broadcasts could be regarded as destabilising. The different rates of nationalist advance ensured that ideas about aspirant post-colonial freedoms could be broadcast, a phenomenon particularly true in the last redoubts of white power in Central and southern Africa, which were susceptible to radio broadcasts from adjacent newly independent states. The attempted controls of the dying colonial empire tended, however, to be inherited by postcolonial states in their search for stability and political compliance.[68] Writing more generally with regard to the former Dominions, Simon Potter wrote that 'Commonwealth collaboration in radio in the 1950s might . . . be interpreted as a doomed rear-guard action, fought using the weapons of a bygone age'.[69] Thus radio turned out to be as ineffectual in maintaining imperial culture as the documentary films of the same period.

CONCLUSION

Removal of the statue of Cecil Rhodes (sculptor Marion Walgate) from the University of Cape Town, South Africa, 9 April 2015.

The dominant elite of the British Empire, in common with other historic empires, had a yearning for a unified imperial culture propagated through a whole range of cultural forms. These constitute the ambitious expression of the cultural imperialism required to underpin the social, political and military thrusts central to imperial expansion. For the rulers and protagonists of empire, such cultural instruments represent the allegedly civilised essence of empire. Yet it has long been the case that historians have generally concentrated on political and administrative, economic and military aspects of imperial history. This book has directed attention towards the cultural economy, with the associated themes of cultural capital, traffic and the dissemination of skills and ideas. All of these are never static phenomena, but dynamic processes that have produced significant permutations in the imperial and colonial environment. They were beamed towards the migrants and expatriates of the imperial society as well as the indigenous peoples of both settler territories and the colonies of rule. But efforts at creating an imperial culture out of the multiple proselytising components of cultural imperialism were seldom successful over time. On the contrary they tended to engender striking adaptations in which the hoped-for uniform culture of empire was ultimately transmuted into cultures of national identities, even if sometimes retaining trace elements from the imperial source. The nation-state order that succeeded empire continued to show features of the imperial cultural system, but each society had converted such raw material into new combinations expressing unique identities.

The cultural economy required considerable capital inputs. Ceremonies cost money, in the labour of the organisers, the marshalling of peoples, the erection of decorations, the deployment of animals, bands and so on. The grandest of ceremonials also stimulated international travel for both participants and spectators. In the case of the sporting passions of empire, large blocks of land were required for racecourses or for land-intensive sports like polo or golf, while plots had to be bought or acquired for the fields on which team sports could be played. Stands had to be built, as well as club buildings, stables where appropriate, and pavilions for socialising. Sports generally require accessories: cricket bats, wickets, footballs, polo sticks and so on. These became part of imperial commerce until colonies began to produce them for themselves. A lively trade in horses and hounds developed from the eighteenth century onwards. Horses were originally used for other purposes, for transportation, as cavalry mounts, for shepherding and herding in pastoral lands, and

317

for carriages for the elite, but as new technologies performed some of these functions, horses and ponies became more specialised for ceremonial and the cavalry, as well as in the pursuit of sports, polo, forms of hunting, above all racing. Both military and civilian sporting interests produced a considerable international trade, particularly after jockey clubs and bloodstock controls began to command the racing world. The more specialised hounds could become a highly lucrative trade as demand grew when hunting with hounds became more fashionable in India, Australia and other colonies. Elephants and camels were the subjects of highly specialist markets trading them in India and elsewhere. The creation of rules and regulations and the founding of institutions to administer these sports were all part of a global cultural traffic. The transcontinental movements of teams, bloodstock, jockeys and trainers were all encouraged by new steam technologies at sea and on land.

The development of arts in the empire also stimulated much cultural traffic, in trade in materials, as well as transfers of ideas, techniques and practitioners. In these ways western artistic endeavour was relocated into a wider world. In turn, considerable architectural projects were inaugurated. Art galleries developed as one of the institutions required by the colonial bourgeois sphere, while various other art organisations, academies and institutes were required to bring artists together, train them and regulate the profession. All these usually needed buildings, another stimulus to colonial construction activity, and professions such as surveying and architecture as well as building contractors. Some of these buildings, particularly as architectural styles moved on beyond the classical, required sculptural embellishments. Statues became a necessary part of the street furniture in many colonies, supposedly emblematic of artistic sophistication, but also of the common stock of royal and heroic figures (sometimes local and political personalities) that contemporaries thought should be commemorated. This became an essential aspect of imperial propaganda. In the early nineteenth century, the supply of statues became a significant part of imperial trade often enhancing the income of a growing number of sculptors in Britain. Such statuary led to a remarkable seaborne trade in heavy stone and bronze sculptures from metropole to colonies. Given contemporary customs and attitudes in respect of death, seemingly heightened in imperial contexts, large numbers of memorial tablets and sculptures were required for cathedrals, churches, chapels and other Christian institutions. Many of these were produced locally, developing new trades and arts. On a smaller scale, photography stimulated its own commerce, enhanced in a growing and progressive way by rapid developments in technologies. The appearance of photographic businesses throughout the empire ensured a rapidly developing traffic in materials and personnel. Photographic premises became a vital component of every self-respecting town in the empire, such that the proliferation of print shops was matched by the supply of photographic studios. A considerable trade in cameras, photographic paper and chemicals, later in film, emerged to satisfy both commercial professionals and the vast numbers of amateurs among settler and expatriate populations. Here, cultural traffic jumped very effectively across ethnic lines as indigenous people adopted the art and associated trades in large numbers.

The press was one of the longest standing and most significant of the elements of an imperial culture: initially relatively primitive in its technology and capital requirements, this changed by the later nineteenth century. Technology became increasingly sophisticated; papers grew in size and numbers and were joined by many other publications, magazines, newsletters and the like. Many of these were illustrated. With these developments, the physical plant to accommodate presses and journalists proliferated. As we have seen, the extensive print culture of the colonies required 'print shops' to be available in almost every town. Printing presses themselves were a significant factor in trade, constantly requiring renewal as technologies developed. Moreover, the dramatic growth in the numbers of journalists, mirroring that of artists and photographers, ensured the existence of a mobile migrant profession which developed important transcolonial and continental exchanges. The press was dependent on the rapid transfer of items of news, a requirement increasingly satisfied by the telegraph, undersea cables and more advanced modes of transport. Organs of the press became a vital means of promoting and advertising other cultural occasions, including those in sporting and performance fields, as well as church services and various musical events. Theatrical shows needed posters and programmes. More than any other agency, the press was significant in spreading the English language and British ideas, rapidly establishing a fever chart for British imperial developments. But the content analysis of newspapers reveals the extent to which local and national interests took over. For white newspaper readers, local sporting and cultural material became dominant, except perhaps in wartime and the lead-in to wars. But in their different ways, in settler territories, India and the 'dependent' colonies, there was a parallel shift towards national identities and nationalist politics. The press ceased to act as the prime agent of the imperial connection, not least when it became an equally potent vehicle for nationalist politics and demands for independence and the break-up of empire. But its importance has been recognised by some postcolonial regimes equally anxious to establish controls and bend it to their will.

Finance capital was required in the construction of concert halls, theatres and later cinemas, with beneficial consequences for colonial construction industries, invariably employing non-white labour. In the course of the nineteenth century the possession of elaborate, high-capacity theatres became a matter of civic pride in every colony, as was to be the case with cinemas in the twentieth. Hence the different forms of human, social and cultural capital had to draw on finance capital familiar in other colonial operations. In the effort to make such entertainment conform as far as possible with the metropolitan models, there was also a necessary trade in musical instruments, even in stage machinery and scenery, particularly as part of the complex logistics of the travelling troupes. The cinema stimulated fresh trades as well as striking entrepreneurship and, once again, mobility of materials and people. Such cultural capital had the capacity to be a significant psychological support for both settlers and expatriates in empire, although it was a system which, in being self-generating, was open to modifications and hybridities that produced alternative variants contributing to new identities. Many such buildings have continued to be used in the postcolonial period, sometimes adapted to fresh needs.

Cultural capital and investment hence lubricated the flow of cultural traffic. The conveyance of all the elements of an imperial culture around the globe operated as the material content of such traffic and, over some time and at varying speeds, aspects of import substitution appeared in many places. Yet the homogeneity and exclusiveness of such cultural processes became increasingly faulty and limited. Empire set up many professional webs and networks of cultural practitioners. While artists, journalists, printers, writers, together with actors and other entertainers honed their skills and reputations through their imperial journeys, they also inspired the development of competitors and colleagues originating in the colonies. Thus cultural traffic increasingly became multi-directional. Such networks operated at a number of different levels, the local both in the metropole and the colonies, the macro in forming intercontinental and inter-colonial bonds, and perhaps the meso in creating the cross-over lines that connected them. Above all, sportsmen of great skill emerged in many colonies and they began to ensure that the traffic took multiple directions, both between colonies and reciprocally with the metropole. It can be said that the practice of medicine, the study of various sciences and the operations of missionary educators were all influenced by experiences at the so-called imperial periphery. Some may suggest that these patterns had a regressive effect, for example in the feeding back of the fascination with royal tours or in the enhancement of ceremonial ideas in Britain, but generally the reciprocal effects of these colonial-inspired influences could be fructifying. Yet these same cultural experiences fed the search for new identities and the sense of distinctiveness of so many colonies. If in the earlier period cultural phenomena created significant support systems that made colonial and emigrant lives bearable for military and administrative personnel, settlers, planters, urban dwellers and those involved in proto-industrial and trading activities, they later took on a new role in creating local identities and loyalties. Instead of being, as perhaps they were intended to be, the trappings of white settlers and expatriates, even symbolic accoutrements of their exclusive lives, they developed wider audiences. In many cases (cricket is an excellent example) it was imagined that they would have no interest at all for indigenous people. But this assumption was rapidly proved wrong. Almost all aspects of a supposed imperial culture were taken over by indigenous people, modified and bent to their own purposes. In the case of ceremonial, display, relationships with environments and spiritual observance, as well as theatrical performance, there were rich indigenous precedents. These survived right through the imperial period, even when there were attempts to suppress them. Others blended with cultural imports to create powerfully hybrid forms. The twentieth century was an era in which Europeans rediscovered and revalued these indigenous traditions. In the case of art they became the central content of new and divergent artistic formations around the former colonies. In these ways the breaking and modifying of cultural forces that were supposed to create an overall imperial culture produced significant modifications and variations to such an ambitious design. While many aspects of cultural globalisation cannot be gainsaid, nevertheless Canada, Australia, New Zealand, South Africa, India and many other colonies in the Caribbean, Africa and Asia each produced fragmented responses in which local cultures reasserted themselves, reaffirming a whole range of cultural distinctions vital to their own sense of nationalism. This even occurred in the adaptation and further enriching of the English language. Thus efforts at imperial cultural globalisation were doomed to break up into proudly heterogeneous patterns. Cultural traffic became trans-ethnic in many enlightening ways.

Moreover, new twentieth-century technologies had a notable capacity to break down old boundaries, both literally and metaphorically. One of the most striking of these was radio which, by its very nature, both leapt over frontiers and rapidly produced colonial alternatives to metropolitan offerings. Radio was superseded in turn by television, not covered in this book, but demonstrating some of the same combination of national developments and international offerings. Film helped to propagate an American cultural imperialism, which was much feared, but still swept a good deal before it. Nevertheless, there were national responses to this new empire of the arts and fresh cinematic models appeared in many colonies, in the form of documentaries, newsreels and even feature films. India's so-called Bollywood was the most successful of these, but there were many other manifestations of such an effect. By this time, the indigenous peoples of empire, often intended as a potential audience and receptacle for an imperial culture, had created a mosaic of national cultures, even if in many places some of the controls exercised by imperial authorities came to be reimposed by postcolonial states.

It is also important to consider the reciprocal effects of empire upon Britain. Imperial ceremonial, for example, was a notably theatrical phenomenon in which ritualised performances created an illusion of power played out on clearly demarcated stages, from which audiences took a variety of different meanings. It has been suggested that the particular propensity, and alleged capacity, for ceremonial and pageantry on the part of the British may have lacked full acceptance and justification until modern times.[1] But in the imperial setting such events had a longer history and were invariably inflated, not least when they involved the overawing of indigenous people. There may therefore be a case for suggesting that the British fascination with ceremony and pageantry came as much from the empire as from metropolitan sources. The global setting emphasising the complexities and varied layers of meaning of such ceremonial performances ensured the British ceremony and pageantry were as much formed at the periphery as in Britain itself.[2]

Despite much criticism, ceremonial was memorable and perhaps fortifying for participants and spectators, particularly when captured in photographs and film. Yet despite being ephemeral and insubstantial, it was instrumental, a constant assertion of power and group allegiances, even a means of diverting attention from the real world of empire, from the acts of resistance, the horrors of violence and famine, from social deprivation, labour unrest and other aspects of the imperial condition. It can also be seen as supplemented by the formal ceremonies of the Christian churches which, both within and outside physical ecclesiastical buildings, were a key part of public ritualised formalities. All such stylised events unveil cultural forms that provide insights into the imperial condition.

It is perhaps inevitable that one of the most visible expressions of imperial ideology, statuary and sculpture, should have become a focus for dispute in a postcolonial age. Such works were not only striking symbols of conquest, power and dominance, but in their glorification of (largely male) individuals were also intended to convey the alleged moral power of the imperial condition. In many places they remain as mute expressions of the values of an age, but in others have stimulated considerable hostility. Statues so provocatively displayed in squares and prominent public spaces have aroused negative and vehement reactions as controversial symbols of the racism and violence of their age.

Films often represented the apparently paradoxical combination of a new technology conveying conservative content. Originally feeding off existing entertainment forms, films grew to consume them, yet they were also open to penetration by nationalism. They could ultimately unveil a wider world community to colonial peoples as well as increasing awareness of geographic, cultural and ethnic borders of their own territory, enhancing their sense of identities, both local and national. In African and Asian colonies, films could promote a sense of difference, perhaps contributing to new nationalist forms, helping to impel these territories in the direction of independence, albeit in various conflictual ways.[3] Cinema was also capable of bringing out what Hailey described as 'the apparent contrast between our political liberalism and our social exclusiveness', in other words the disjuncture between aspirant political forms and discriminatory social practice. Both resided in different ways within the physical construction of the cinema and its products. However, it may be too glib to see the influence of film as carrying major instrumentality in respect of nationalist developments. After all, some (perhaps most) historical accounts of the rise of nationalism and the emergence of postcolonial territories in a global nation-state order have barely mentioned the influence of film, except perhaps in its newsreel form. This may reflect scholarly biases, but it might also be symptomatic of the fact that populations received their impressions from many sources, including newspapers, education, and vast public gatherings.

Both film and radio, in common with other media like the press, illustrated the manner in which it became progressively impossible for imperial authorities to 'hold the ring' in the pursuit of a common empire culture in the twentieth century. Separate colonial identities in both the so-called Dominions and in territories of the 'dependent empire' became unstoppable. These modern media interacted with the development of political nationalism to secure the global breakup of the imperial connection. All of this constitutes a plea for the inclusion of cultural themes in imperial studies. We also require a good deal more quantitative understanding of the economic significance of cultural traffic. The cultural dimensions of empire can illuminate many other themes and will repay much further study.

NOTES

Abbreviations

CUP   Cambridge University Press
EUP   Edinburgh University Press
IBMR   *International Bulletin of Missionary Research*
IJHS   *International Journal of the History of Sport*
JICH   *Journal of Imperial and Commonwealth History*
MUP   Manchester University Press
OUP   Oxford University Press
UP   University Press
YUP   Yale University Press

Introduction

1. The phrase 'who died for civilisation' is common on Belgian colonial memorials. Matthew G. Stanard, *The Leopard, the Lion and the Cock: Colonial Memories and Monuments in Belgium* (Leuven, Leuven UP, 2019), passim. The use of this phrase belies the violence and brutality of the Leopold II regime in the Congo, for which a prime justification, central to the alleged *mission civilisatrice*, was supposedly to free Congolese people from the so-called Arab slave trade. The British in Africa also highlighted this motivation.
2. For the cultural significance of the built environment, see John M. MacKenzie, *The British Empire through Buildings: Structure, Function and Meaning* (Manchester, MUP, 2020).
3. For a comparative examination of many of these imperial myths, see John M. MacKenzie, 'Empires in world history: characteristics, concepts, and consequences', introduction to the Wiley-Blackwell *Encyclopedia of Empire* (Malden, MA, Wiley-Blackwell, 2016), pp. lxxxiii–cx, particularly cv–cvii.
4. J.R. Seeley, *The Expansion of England* (London, Macmillan, 1883), p. 51.

5. Under this treaty, Scotland retained Presbyterianism as the dominant religious denomination, as well as its banking, legal and educational systems. Seeley failed to note that this survival of Scottish civil society was key to the maintenance of a distinctive Scots identity, a failure still prevalent today.

6. See for example John M. MacKenzie with Nigel R. Dalziel, *The Scots in South Africa* (Manchester, MUP, 2007), p. 260.

7. From the standpoint of the twenty-first century, it is apparent that the project to forge a nation of Britons, as charted in Linda Colley, *Britons: Forging the Nation 1707–1837* (New Haven, CT, YUP, 1992) achieved only limited success.

8. This may also have been the case in Belgium, where the Flemish and Wallonian elements of the population (Dutch in the north and French in the south) may have been pulled together through the joint project of empire after the country took over the Congo in 1908. This binding effect was lost after decolonisation in 1960. Stanard, *The Leopard, The Lion, and the Cock*, chapter 1.

9. The conventional demarcation of the ethnicities of the British Isles into English, Irish, Scottish and Welsh itself constitutes a relatively crude set of categories. These can be sub-divided into regional ones, such as Highlands, Lowlands and Borders of Scotland. 'British World' publications include Carl Bridge and Kent Fedorowich (eds), *The British World: Diaspora, Culture, Identit*y, special issue of *JICH*, 31, 2 (May 2003); Kate Darian-Smith, Patricia Grimshaw and Stuart McIntyre (eds), *Britishness Abroad: Transnational Movements and Imperial Cultures* (Melbourne, Melbourne UP, 2006); Kent Fedorowich and Andrew S. Thompson, *Mapping the Contours of the British World* (Manchester, MUP, 2013). See also James Belich, *Replenishing the Earth: The Settler Revolution and the Rise of the Anglo-World, 1783–1939* (Oxford, OUP, 2009).

10. Saul Dubow, 'How British was the British World? The case of South Africa', *JICH*, 37, 1 (2009), pp. 1–27.

11. John M. MacKenzie, 'Irish, Scottish, Welsh and English worlds? The historiography of a four-nations approach to the history of the British Empire', in Catherine Hall and Keith McClelland (eds), *Race, Nation and Empire: Making Histories, 1750 to the Present* (Manchester, MUP, 2010), pp. 133–53; MacKenzie, 'Irish, Scottish, Welsh and English worlds? A four-nation approach to the history of the British Empire', *History Compass* (online journal), 6, 5 (2008), pp. 1244–63.

12. John M. MacKenzie, 'Heroic myths of empire', in John M. MacKenzie (ed.), *Popular Imperialism and the Military* (Manchester MUP, 1991), pp. 109–38; Berny Sèbe, *Heroic Imperialists in Africa: The Promotion of British and French Colonial Heroes, 1870–1939* (Manchester, MUP, 2013).

13. These words have become highly pejorative, remaining so for many nationalists and postcolonial historians, but here they are intended to describe those who were (generally voluntarily) co-opted into the imperial enterprise, no doubt securing personal advancement and often economic security as a result.

14. Duncan Bell, *Reordering the World: Essays on Liberalism and Empire* (Princeton, NJ, Princeton UP, 2016), pp. 143–4 and passim. This is a theory which, in the British case, supposedly applied principally to the colonies of white settlement. For greater detail, see also Duncan Bell, *The Idea of Greater Britain: Empire and the Future of World Order, 1860–190*0 (Princeton, NJ, Princeton UP, 2007).

15. It is noticeable that during the Canada 150 celebrations in 2017, the origins of the country within the British Empire were generally played down.

16. John Darwin, *After Tamerlane: The Global History of Empire* (London, Allen Lane, 2007), p. 212. Darwin's more recent *Unlocking the World: Port Cities and Globalization in the Age of Steam 1830–1930* (London, Allen Lane, 2020) constitutes a magnificent survey of the economic, social and cultural significance of port cities on a strikingly global scale. This includes the significance of the conditions that facilitated their rise and prompted their decline and sometimes demise, including some comment on their

role in cultural dispersal. There is comparatively little, however, on the cultural forms that constitute the focus of this book.

17. Stewart J. Brown (ed.), *William Robertson and the Expansion of Empire* (Cambridge, CUP, 2008) contains discussion of Robertson's ideas concerning the Spanish Empire, empire in the Americas, and on 'stadial theory'.

18. Kathleen Wilson, *The Sense of the People: Politics, Culture and Imperialism in England, 1715–1785* (Cambridge, CUP, 1995).

19. The Society for the Promotion of Christian Knowledge was founded as early as 1698, initially to issue religious tracts and pamphlets, but also to proselytise in the Highlands of Scotland and in the American colonies. This was followed by the foundation of the Society for the Propagation of the Gospel in Foreign Parts in 1701 and by the Scottish Society for the Promotion of Christian Knowledge in 1709. For early religious connections between Scotland, America and Christian proselytisation, see Colin G. Calloway, *White People, Indians and Highlanders: Tribal Peoples and Colonial Encounters in Scotland and America* (Oxford, OUP, 2008).

20. Daniel R. Headrick, *The Tools of Empire: Technology and European Imperialism in the Nineteenth Century* (New York, OUP, 1981); Headrick, *The Invisible Weapon: Telecommunications and International Politics 1851–1945* (New York, OUP, 1991); Michael Adas, *Machines as the Measure of Men: Science, Technology and Ideologies of Western Dominance* (Ithaca, NY, Cornell UP, 1989).

21. Douglas J. Lorimer, *Colour, Class and the Victorians* (Leicester, Leicester UP, 1978) and Lorimer, *Race, Race Relations and Resistance: A Study of the Discourse of Race in Late Victorian and Edwardian Britain, 1870–1914* (Manchester, MUP, 2013).

22. Belich, *Replenishing the Earth.* The 'Anglo-World' referred to in Belich's subtitle perhaps suggests a linguistic definition since this 'Anglo World' was also Irish, Scottish and Welsh, as well as English. For Scotland, see T.M. Devine, *To the Ends of the Earth: Scotland's Global Diaspora 1750–2010* (London, Allen Lane, 2011) and John M. MacKenzie and T.M. Devine (eds), *Scotland and the British Empire* (Oxford, OUP, 2011).

23. T.M. Devine, *The Scottish Clearances: A History of the Dispossessed* (London, Allen Lane, 2018).

24. C. Hagerman, *Britain's Imperial Muse* (Basingstoke, Palgrave Macmillan, 2013).

25. Martin J. Wiener, *English Culture and the Decline of the Industrial Spirit, 1850–1980* (Cambridge, CUP, 1981, 2nd edn, 2004).

26. David Cannadine, *Ornamentalism: How the British Saw Their Empire* (London, Allen Lane, 2001). See also Robert Aldrich, *Banished Potentates: Dethroning and Exiling Indigenous Monarchs under British and French Colonial Rule, 1815–1955* (Manchester, MUP, 2018).

27. John M. MacKenzie, 'Orientalism in Arts and Crafts revisited: the modern and the anti-modern, the lessons from the Orient', in Ian Richard Netton (ed.), *Orientalism Revisited: Art, Land and Voyage* (Abingdon, Routledge, 2013), pp. 117–27.

28. Donald Worster, *Nature's Economy: A History of Ecological Ideas* (Cambridge, CUP, 1977), p. 2.

29. Mark Bradley (ed.), *Classics and Imperialism in the British Empire* (Oxford, OUP, 2010). Frank Turner has written of the centrality of classicism in the intellectual experience of an educated Victorian elite in his *Contesting Cultural Authority: Essays in Victorian Intellectual Life* (Cambridge, CUP, 1993), p. 284. Thomas Arnold's *History of Rome*, 3 vols (London, Fellowes, 1838–43) spread information about Rome and its empire to further generations. Extracts in the *Penny Magazine* reached a wider audience.

30. John M. MacKenzie, 'Empires of travel: British guide books and cultural imperialism in the 19th and 20th centuries', in John K. Walton (ed.), *Histories of Tourism: Representation, Identity and Conflict* (Clevedon, Channel View Publications 2005), pp. 19–38 and John M. MacKenzie, 'Empire travel guides and the imperial mind-set from the mid-

nineteenth to the mid-twentieth centuries', in Martin Farr and Xavier Guégan (eds), *The British Abroad since the Eighteenth Century* (Houndmills, Palgrave Macmillan, 2013), vol. 2, pp. 116–33.

31. J.G.A. Pocock published several volumes under the common title *Barbarism and Religion*. See particularly *Barbarism and Religion*, vol. 4: *Barbarians, Savages and Empires* (Cambridge, CUP, 2005). For an excellent examination of the connections between Ancient and British concepts of barbarism, see Norman Etherington, 'Barbarians ancient and modern', *American Historical Review*, 116, 1 (February 2011), pp. 31–57.

32. Henry Morton Stanley, *Through the Dark Continent* (1878) and *In Darkest Africa* (1890). The phrase was repeated in many books in the late nineteenth century, for example in Stanford's *Compendium of Geography*. Sir John S. Keltie referred to the 'barbarous continent' on page 1 of his *The Partition of Africa* (London, Edward Stanford, 1893).

33. According to *Hobson-Jobson*, the Hindi word *pukka* means ripe, mature or cooked, consequently substantial or permanent, interestingly sometimes used of buildings to mean made of brick and mortar rather than mud, matting or timber. Henry Yule and A.C. Burnell, *Hobson-Jobson: An Anglo-Indian Dictionary* (Ware, Herts, Wordsworth Editions, 1986, first published 1886), p. 734.

34. Ramachandra Guha, *A Corner of a Foreign Field: the Indian History of a British Sport* (London, Picador, 2002), p. xiv.

35. Darwin's *After Tamerlane* has been a notable exception. Where empires have been examined in comparative ways, as in Jane Burbank and Frederick Cooper, *Empires in World History* (Princeton, Princeton UP, 2010), Timothy H. Parsons, *The Rule of Empires* (Oxford, OUP, 2010), or Dominic Lieven, *Empire* (London, Pimlico, 2003), the approach has invariably been political. Sometimes a comparative approach has been introduced in order to 'exceptionalise' the British Empire. See my critique of this in MacKenzie, 'The British Empire: ramshackle or rampaging? A historiographical reflection', *JICH*, 43, 1 (March 2015), pp. 99–124.

36. Mary Beard unveiled significant aspects of Roman social life through gravestones. See: www.eagle-network.eu/story/putting-ancient-inscriptions-in-the-limelight (accessed 25 October 2019).

37. MacKenzie, 'The British Empire: ramshackle or rampaging?'.

38. Of the six volumes the two most relevant to this work are the *Age of Empires, 1800–1920*, edited by Kirsten McKenzie, and *The Modern Age, 1920–2000*, edited by Patricia Lorcin (London and New York, Bloomsbury, 2018–19).

39. Peter Burke, *What is Cultural History?* (Cambridge, Polity, 2004).

40. For a classic survey of the emotional economy of empire, see Joanna Lewis, *Empire of Sentiment: The Death of Livingstone and the Myth of Victorian Imperialism* (Cambridge, CUP, 2018).

41. The lines of this debate were drawn between Jean Comaroff and John Comaroff, *Of Revelation and Revolution: Christianity, Colonialism, and Consciousness in South Africa*, 2 vols (Chicago, University of Chicago Press, 1991 and 1997) and Andrew Porter, *Religion versus Empire? British Protestant Missionaries and Overseas Expansion, 1700–1914* (Manchester, MUP, 2004).

42. Ronald Hyam, *Britain's Imperial Century 1815–1914: A Study of Empire and Expansion* (London, Batsford, 1976), pp. 129–134 and 150–164. A.P. Thornton also made some pioneering excursions into cultural history in his *For the File on Empire* (London, Macmillan, 1968).

43. Ronald Hyam, *Sexuality and Empire* (Manchester, MUP, 1990). Also Hyam, 'Empire and sexual opportunity', *JICH*, 14, 2 (1986) and 'Concubinage and the Colonial Service: the Crewe circular', *JICH*, 14, 3 (1986). Other works on sexuality have been published more recently.

44. Jan Morris, *Pax Britannica, The Climax of an Empire* (London, Faber, 1968); *Heaven's Command: An Imperial Progress* (London, Faber, 1973); *Farewell the Trumpets: An*

Imperial Retreat (London, Faber, 1978); and *The Spectacle of Empire* (London, Faber, 1982); with Simon Winchester, *Stones of Empire: Buildings of the Raj* (Oxford, OUP, 1983). Morris once expressed her credo to me as being that the British Empire was a dreadful phenomenon only redeemed by its 'style'.

45. Geertz's concept of 'thick description' has been influential. See his 'Thick description: towards an interpretive theory of culture', in his *The Interpretation of Cultures: Selected Essays* (New York, Basic Books, 1973), pp. 3–30; Nicholas Thomas, *Entangled Objects: Exchange, Material Culture and Colonialism in the Pacific* (Cambridge, MA, Harvard UP, 1991); Nicholas B. Dirks (ed.), *Colonialism and Culture* (Ann Arbor, Michigan UP, 1992), Nicholas B. Dirks, Geoff Eley and Sherry B. Ortner (eds), *Culture/Power/ History: A Reader in Contemporary Social Theory* (Princeton, NJ, Princeton UP, 1994); Nicholas B. Dirks, *The Scandal of Empire: India and the Creation of Imperial Britain* (Cambridge, MA, Harvard UP, 2006); Bernard S. Cohn, *Colonialism and its Forms of Knowledge: The British in India* (Princeton, NJ, Princeton UP, 1996).

46. Edward W. Said, *Culture and Imperialism* (London, Chatto and Windus, 1993). Catherine Hall's edited collection *Cultures of Empire: A Reader* (Manchester, MUP, 2000) is also useful, but adopts a different meaning to the concept of culture from this book.

47. Said, *Culture and Imperialism*, pp. 71–2.

48. Nicholas Thomas, *Colonialism's Culture* (Princeton, NJ, Princeton UP, 1994), introduction and pp. 64 and 168. Thomas pointed out that colonialism's objectives were often 'faulty and limited'. Thomas mainly dealt with language and texts, offering a more nuanced argument than that of Said.

49. Frederick Cooper and Ann Laura Stoler (eds), *Tensions of Empire: Colonial Cultures in a Bourgeois World* (Berkeley, University of California Press, 1997). Leila Tarazi Fawaz and C.A. Bayly (eds), *Modernity and Culture* (New York, Columbia UP, 1998) compared phenomena in the British and French empires.

50. Martin Evans (ed.), *Empire and Culture: The French Experience, 1830–1940* (Houndmills, Basingstoke, Palgrave Macmillan, 2004).

51. Wilson, *The Sense of the People: Politics, Culture and Imperialism in England, 1715–1785*; Antoinette Burton (ed.), *After the Imperial Turn: Thinking with and through the Nation* (Durham, NC, Duke UP, 2003); Philippa Levine and Susan R. Grayzel (eds), *Gender, Labour, War and Empire: Essays on Modern Britain* (Basingstoke, Palgrave Macmillan, 2009); Philippa Levine (ed.), *Gender and Empire* (Oxford, OUP, 2004); Angela Woollacott, *Gender and Empire* (Houndmills, Palgrave, 2006); Wendy Webster, *Englishness and Empire 1939–1965* (Oxford, OUP, 2005). For a general survey, see Barbara Bush, *Imperialism and Postcolonialism* (London, Routledge, 2006).

52. Sarah Stockwell (ed.), *The British Empire: Themes and Perspectives* (Oxford, Blackwell, 2008); and A.G. Hopkins, 'Back to the future: from national history to imperial history', *Past and Present*, 164 (August 1999), pp. 198–243 and particularly C.A. Bayly, *The Birth of the Modern World, 1780–1914* (Malden, MA, Blackwell, 2004), chapters 5, 6, 9 and 10.

53. Maya Jasanoff, *Edge of Empire: Conquest and Collecting in the East, 1750–1850* (London, Fourth Estate, 2005) and Holger Hoock, *Empires of the Imagination: Politics, War and the Arts in the British World 1750–1850* (London, Profile, 2010).

54. Ashley Jackson, *Mad Dogs and Englishmen: A Grand Tour of the British Empire at its Height 1850–1945* (London, Quercus, 2009); Jackson and David Tomkins, *Illustrating Empire: A Visual History of British Imperialism* (Oxford, Bodleian Library, 2011); Jackson, *Buildings of Empire* (Oxford, OUP, 2013); Tristram Hunt, *Ten Cities that Made an Empire* (London, Allen Lane, 2014).

55. John M. MacKenzie, *Propaganda and Empire: The Manipulation of British Public Opinion, 1880–1960* (Manchester, MUP, 1984); MacKenzie (ed.), *Imperialism and Popular Culture* (Manchester, MUP, 1996); Catherine Hall and Sonya O. Rose, *At Home with the Empire: Metropolitan Culture and the Imperial World* (Cambridge, CUP, 2006);

Kathleen Wilson (ed.), *A New Imperial History: Culture, Identity and Modernity in Britain and the Empire, 1660–1940* (Cambridge, CUP, 2004); Bernard Porter, *The Absent-minded Imperialists: Empire, Society and Culture in Britain* (Oxford, OUP, 2004) offers the controversial alternative view. Sathnam Sanghera, *Empireland: How Imperialism Has Shaped Modern Britain* (London, Penguin, 2021).

56. These sources will appear in the appropriate places in the following chapters.

57. Barry Crosbie and Mark Hampton (eds), *The Cultural Construction of the British World* (Manchester, MUP, 2016) and Ruth Craggs and Claire Wintle, *Cultures of Decolonisation: Transnational Productions and Practices* (Manchester, MUP, 2016).

58. Stephanie Barczewski, *Country Houses and the British Empire, 1700–1930* (Manchester, MUP, 2014) and Charles V. Reed, *Royal Tourists, Colonial Subjects and the Making of a British World, 1860–1911* (Manchester, MUP, 2016). On royal tourism, see also Robert Aldrich and Cindy McCreery (eds), *Royals on Tour: Politics, Pageantry and Colonialism* (Manchester, MUP, 2018), which deals with a number of comparative examples in European empires and also indigenous rulers.

59. Examples include Jonathan F. Vance, *A History of Canadian Culture: From Petroglyphs to Product, Circuses to the CBC* (Don Mills, Ont., OUP, 2009); Hsu-Ming Teo and Richard White (eds), *Cultural History in Australia* (Sydney, New South Wales UP, 2003). A pioneering work was Pierre Berton, *Canada from Sea to Sea* (Ottawa, Department of External Affairs, 1958). For New Zealand, see James Belich, *Making Peoples, a History of the New Zealanders: From Polynesian Settlement to the End of the Nineteenth Century* (London, Allen Lane, 1996) and Belich, *Paradise Reforged: A History of the New Zealanders from the 1880s to the Year 2000* (London, Allen Lane, 2001).

60. John C. Mitchem, *Race and Imperial Defence in the British World, 1870–1914* (Cambridge, CUP, 2016).

61. Carl Berger, *The Sense of Power: Studies in the Ideas of Canadian Imperialism, 1867–1914* (Toronto, Toronto UP, 1970).

62. John Griffiths, *Imperial Culture in Antipodean Cities, 1880–1939* (Basingstoke, Palgrave Macmillan, 2014); S. Jackson, *Constructing National Identities in Canadian and Australian Classrooms* (Basingstoke, Palgrave Macmillan, 2018).

63. Annie E. Coombes, *History after Apartheid: Visual Culture and Public Memory in a Democratic South Africa* (Durham, NC, Duke UP, 2003); Steven C. Dubin, *Transforming Museums: Mounting Queen Victoria in a Democratic South Africa* (London, Palgrave, 2006). See also A. Coombes, *Reinventing Africa: Museums, Culture and the Popular Imagination in Late Victorian and Edwardian England* (New Haven, CT, Yale UP, 1994).

64. There is a considerable and growing literature on India. The pioneering work was Abdullah Yusuf Ali, *A Cultural History of India during the British Period* (New York, AMS Press, 1976, first published 1945); see also Om Prakash, *A Cultural History of India* (New Delhi, New Age International Publishers, 2004).

65. Sujit Sivasundaram, *Islanded: Britain, Sri Lanka and the Bounds of an Indian Ocean Colony* (Chicago, University of Chicago Press, 2013).

66. Jack Goody, *The Culture of Flowers* (Cambridge, CUP, 1993) and idem, *Food and Love: A Cultural History of East and West* (London, Verso, 1998). Goody has pointed to specific cultural areas that can be taken up by imperial historians.

67. Considerable insights into the Chinese treaty port of Shanghai are offered in Robert Bickers, *Empire Made Me: An Englishman Adrift in Shanghai* (London, Allen Lane, 2003). See also Bickers (ed.), *Settlers and Expatriates* (Oxford, OUP, 2010). A fascinating account of the British community in a South American city is Michelle Prain (ed.), *The British Legacy in Valparaiso* (Santiago, Ril Editores, 2011). Also D. Rock, *The British in Argentina* (Basingstoke, Palgrave Macmillan, 2019).

68. MacKenzie, *Propaganda and Empire*.

69. In the French case, see Pascal Blanchard, Sandrine Lemaire, Nicolas Boncel and Dominic Thomas, *Colonial Culture in France since the Revolution*, trans. Alexis

Pernsteiner (Bloomington, IN, University of Indiana Press, 2014) and Pascal Blanchard, Nicolas Boncel, Gilles Boetson, Eric Deroo, Sandrine Lemaire and Charles Forsdich (eds), *Human Zoos; Science and Spectacle in the Age of Colonial Empires* (Liverpool, Liverpool UP, 2008). For Germany, see Eric Ames, Marcia Klotz and Lora Wildenthal (eds), *Germany's Colonial Pasts* (Lincoln, NE, University of Nebraska Press, 2005), covering a range of cultural and racist forms during the brief German experience of colonialism. For Belgian *lieux de memoires*, see Stanard, *The Leopard, the Lion and the Cock*. The essays in John McAleer and John M. MacKenzie (eds), *Exhibiting the Empire; Cultures of Display and the British Empire* (Manchester, MUP, 2015) make some attempt to deal with influences both within and beyond Britain.

70. Elizabeth Buettner, *Europe after Empire: Decolonization, Society and Culture* (Cambridge, CUP, 2016).

71. John M. MacKenzie, 'Art and the empire', in P.J. Marshall (ed.), *The Cambridge Illustrated History of the British Empire* (Cambridge, CUP, 1996), pp. 296–316.

72. For a comparative examination of these phenomena, see many of the entries in the Wiley-Blackwell *Encyclopedia of Empire*.

73. Niall Ferguson, *Empire: How Britain Made the Modern World* (London, Allen Lane, 2003); Gary B. Magee and Andrew S. Thompson, *Empire and Globalisation: Networks of People, Goods and Capital in the British World, c. 1850–1914* (Cambridge, CUP, 2010).

74. Robert Ross, *Clothing: A Global History or, The Imperialists' New Clothes* (Cambridge, Polity Press, 2008).

75. Significant country traders in Penang, like James Scott and David Brown, following Indian precedents, adopted local dress and acquired multiple partners, in the course of making considerable fortunes. But later administrators began to express disapproval of such behaviour, producing change in notions of 'respectability'.

76. A recent, one-dimensional, book stressing the violence of empire to the exclusion of all else is Richard Gott's *Britain's Empire: Resistance, Repression, Revolt* (London, Verso, 2011).

77. The classic instance is the 'beni' dance forms of eastern Africa. Terence O. Ranger, *Dance and Society in Eastern Africa, 1890–1970* (London, Heinemann, 1975). See also John M. MacKenzie, 'Scottish diasporas and Africa', in Angela McCarthy and John M. MacKenzie (eds), *Global Migrations: The Scottish Diaspora since 1600* (Edinburgh, EUP, 2016), pp. 63–80, particularly pp. 73–4.

78. John M. MacKenzie, *The Empire of Nature: Hunting, Conservation and British Imperialism* (Manchester, MUP, 1988).

79. William Beinart and Lotte Hughes, *Environment and Empire* (Oxford, OUP, 2007) provides a useful overview.

80. Dane Kennedy, *The Magic Mountains: Hill Stations and the British Raj* (Berkeley, University of California Press, 1996).

81. 'Neo-Europes' was a concept used by Alfred W. Crosby in his *Ecological Imperialism: The Biological Expansion of Europe, 900–1900* (Cambridge, CUP, 1996).

82. Tanja Bueltmann, *Clubbing Together: Ethnicity, Civility and Formal Sociability in the Scottish Diaspora to 1930* (Liverpool, Liverpool UP, 2014).

83. For Australia, see Eric Richards, *Destination Australia: Migration to Australia since 1901* (Sydney, University of New South Wales Press, 2008).

84. Melvyn Bragg, *The Adventure of English: 500 AD to 2000: The Biography of a Language* (London, Hodder and Stoughton, 2003).

85. Estimates inevitably vary, but the first language figure lies between 360 and 400 million, the second between 1.5 and 2 billion.

86. Bell, *Reordering the World: Essays on Liberalism and Empire*.

87. Antoinette Burton, *The Trouble with Empire* (Oxford, OUP, 2015).

Chapter 1 Imperial Ceremonial

1. A.H.M. Kirk-Greene, 'The thin white line: the size of the civil service in Africa', *African Affairs*, 79, 314 (1980), p. 58.
2. William Shakespeare, *Henry V*, Act iv, scene 1.
3. This was commissioned by the Australian Pioneers' Club.
4. A postcard exists of the departure of Governor Sir Frederick Cardew from Sierra Leone (c.1900), showing troops, officers, dignitaries on the jetty at Freetown under a farewell banner, with the ship lying offshore. It was issued by local photographer, W.S. Johnson, and others were issued by Lisk-Carew Brothers.
5. Simon Deschamps, 'Freemasonry as a connective force of empire', *e-Rea*, online journal, 14, 2 (2017), https://journals.openedition.org/erea/5853, and 'James Burnes – freemason and empire builder', in press.
6. In India, Christian clergy were less prominent to avoid offending Muslim and Hindu subjects of the British.
7. Basil Johnston, *Ojibway Ceremonies* (Lincoln, NE, University of Nebraska Press, 1990); Basil Johnston, *Manitous, the Spiritual World of the Ojibway* (St Paul, MN, Minnesota Historical Society Press, 1995); Blair Stonechild, *The Knowledge Seeker: Embracing Indigenous Spirituality* (Regina, University of Regina Press, 2016).
8. For Maori ceremonial, Anne Salmond, *Hui: A Study of Maori Ceremonial Gatherings* (Wellington, Reed, 1977); Anne Salmond, *Tears of Rangi: Experiments across Worlds* (Auckland, Auckland UP, 2017).
9. Thomas Keneally, *Australia* (London, Royal Academy of Arts, 2013), pp. 116 and 84.
10. For Anishinabe, Crown Treaties and mutual interpretations, see Aimée Craft, *Breathing Life into the Stone Fort Treaty* (Vancouver, UBC Press, 2013). The Stone Fort Treaty is Treaty One of 1871 in Manitoba.
11. Such encounters could be turned to the advantage of the indigenous chief. In Northern Rhodesia (Zambia), Mrs Anderson, the wife of the rural district commissioner of Ndola told me that she and her husband had arrived at the village of a Bemba chief in a hot and thirsty state. The chief provided them with the local beer, which was many times stronger than the European equivalent. They drank copiously and almost literally passed out, postponing the actual encounter by several hours.
12. See: www.thecanadianencyclopedia.ca/en/article/indigenous-regalia-in-canada (accessed 8 March 2020).
13. Anon., *The Prince of Wales' African Book: A Pictorial Record of the Journey to West Africa, South Africa and South America* (London, Hodder and Stoughton, 1925), 'Gold Coast and Ashanti' chapter, no pagination; Charles Turley, *With the Prince Round the Empire* (London, Methuen, 1926), p. 131, said 40,000 participated.
14. G. Ward Price, *Through South Africa with the Prince* (London, Gill, 1926), pp. 178–87.
15. A.A. Frew, *Prince George's African Tour* (London, Blackie, 1934), pp. 96–8. In an extraordinary gesture, he presented walking sticks to the chiefs.
16. Turley, *With the Prince Round the Empire*, p. 125.
17. Terence Ranger, 'Making Northern Rhodesia imperial: variations on a royal theme, 1924–1938', *African Affairs*, 79, 316 (1980), pp. 362–5.
18. For interpretations of such dancing, see John M. MacKenzie, 'Scottish diasporas in Africa', in Angela McCarthy and John M. MacKenzie (eds), *Global Migrations: The Scottish Diaspora since 1600* (Edinburgh, EUP, 2016), pp. 73–4.
19. The picture was backdated to at least 1861 in order to include Prince Albert who died in that year.
20. Lynda Nead, 'The secret of England's greatness', *Journal of Victorian Culture*, 19, 2 (2014), pp. 161–82.
21. Neil Parsons, *King Khama, Emperor Joe and the Great White Queen: Victorian Britain through African Eyes* (Chicago, University of Chicago Press, 1998).

22. Hugh Macmillan, 'Lewanika' (c.1842–1916), *Oxford Dictionary of National Biography*, https://org/10.1093/ref:odnb/75928, published online 24 May 2007 (accessed 4 November 2019). See also C.W. Mackintosh, *Coillard of the Zambezi* (London, Fisher Unwin, 1907), p. 430.

23. Yeta's secretary, Godwin Mbikusita, published an account of the ruler's visit to Britain, which is full of admiration for the British and for the rituals of the coronation while still being conscious of the Lozi king's status. Godwin Mbikusita, *Yeta III's Visit to England* (Lusaka, 1940).

24. Ham Mukasa, *Uganda's Katikiro in England* (introduction by Simon Gikandi) (Manchester, MUP, 1998).

25. Terence Ranger, 'Invention of tradition in colonial Africa', in Eric Hobsbawm and Terence Ranger (eds), *The Invention of Tradition* (Cambridge, CUP, 1983), p. 240.

26. Martin R. Doornbos, *Regalia Galore: The Decline and Collapse of Ankole Kingship* (Nairobi, 1975).

27. Adrian Greenwood, *Victoria's Scottish Lion: The Life of Colin Campbell Lord Clyde* (Stroud, History Press, 2015), pp. 91–2.

28. Andrew Gailey, *The Lost Imperialist: Lord Dufferin and Mythmaking in an Age of Celebrity* (London, John Murray, 2013), p. 146.

29. Alister McCrae and Alan Prentice, *Irrawaddy Flotilla* (Paisley, James Paton, 1978), p. 165. The last Burmese king was quick to acquire steam vessels for himself.

30. Sir William Foster, 'British artists in India', *Journal of the Royal Society of Arts*, 98, 4820 (May 1950), p. 523. Lewis was the brother of the more famous Orientalist painter John Frederick Lewis.

31. Dennis Kincaid, *British Social Life in India 1608–1937* (London, Routledge, 1938), p. 10.

32. Philip J. Stern, *The Company State: Corporate Sovereignty and the Early Modern Foundations of the British Empire in India* (Oxford, OUP, 2011).

33. William Dalrymple, *The Anarchy: The East India Company, Corporate Violence and the Pillage of an Empire* (London, Bloomsbury, 2019) has many examples.

34. J.P. Losty (ed.), *Sita Ram's Painted Views of India: Lord Hastings's Journey from Calcutta to the Punjab, 1814–1815* (London, Thames and Hudson, 2015).

35. This is presumably the British regimental band rather than the King of Oudh's English band, which he was reported as having recruited from Indian musicians in his state. Ferdinand Mount, *Tears of the Rajahs: Mutiny, Money and Marriage in India 1805–1905* (London, Simon and Schuster, 2015), p. 267.

36. General Godfrey Charles Mundy, *Journal of a Tour in India* (London, John Murray, 1858, 3rd edn), pp. 9–10.

37. Illustrated in J.P. Losty, *Delhi 360 Degrees: Mazhar Ali Khan's View from the Lahore Gate* (New Delhi, Roli Books, 2012), pp. 8–9.

38. Henry Yule and A.C. Burnell, *Hobson-Jobson: An Anglo-Indian Dictionary* (Ware, Hertfordshire, Wordsworth Editions, 1996, first published 1886), p. 941.

39. Mary Lutyens, *The Lyttons in India: Lord Lytton's Viceroyalty* (London, John Murray, 1979), p. 26.

40. Ibid., p. 30, quoting Lytton's own diary.

41. *Hobson-Jobson* defines a *shigram* as 'a kind of hack palankin carriage', often drawn by camels in North India.

42. Lord Beveridge, *India Called Them* (London, Allen and Unwin, 1947), p. 356.

43. Violet Jacob, *Diaries and Letters from India* (Edinburgh, Canongate, 1990), p. 49.

44. Gailey, *Lost Imperialist*, p. 142.

45. The first sheriff of Calcutta was appointed in 1775. See: https://en.wikipedia.org/wiki/Sheriff_of_Kolkata (accessed 7 November 2019).

46. See: https://en.wikipedia.org/wiki/Sheriff_of_Mumbai for sheriffs of Bombay (accessed 7 November 2019). An early incumbent was Sir George Birdwood.

47. For the proclamations of Edward VIII and George VI in Toronto, see YouTube news-reels on www.youtube.com/watch?v=N6iZcSYZm0g (accessed 7 November 2019).

48. John M. MacKenzie, *Propaganda and Empire: The Manipulation of British Public Opinion 1880–1960* (Manchester, MUP, 1984), pp. 231–2.

49. The army in India recognised four denominations for chaplaincies: Anglican, Church of Scotland, Methodist and Roman Catholic.

50. George W. Clutterbuck, *In India or Bombay the Beautiful* (London, Ideal Publishing Union, 1899), p. 49

51. Ibid., pp. 174–5.

52. Donald James Mackay, Lord Reay was born in the Netherlands where his father had been a government minister and was only naturalised as a British subject in 1877.

53. Clutterbuck, *In India*, pp. 82–5.

54. Martin Gilbert (ed.), *Servant of India: A Study of Imperial Rule 1905–1910 as told through the correspondence and diaries of Sir James Dunlop Smith, Private Secretary to the Viceroy* (London, Longmans, 1966), p. 29.

55. Ibid., pp. 77–8.

56. Craig Murray, *Sikunder Burnes, Master of the Great Game* (Edinburgh, Birlinn, 2016), pp. 89–92.

57. See the striking descriptions in Field Marshal Lord Roberts of Kandahar, *Forty-one Years in India: From Subaltern to Commander-in-Chief* (London, Richard Bentley, 1897), vol. 1, pp. 454–68.

58. Bernard S. Cohn, 'Representing authority in Victorian India', in Hobsbawm and Ranger (eds), *The Invention of Tradition*, pp. 165–210.

59. For Lytton's durbars, see Lutyens, *The Lyttons in India*, pp. 45, 62, 70. For the Imperial Assemblage, see Roberts, *Forty-one Years in India*, vol. 2, pp. 91–8; also Lutyens, pp. 74–87. The grand events had local manifestations. The 1858 Proclamation by Queen Victoria indicating the end of the East India Company and the advent of Crown rule was announced in ceremonies throughout India. The durbars of 1903 and 1911 were reproduced around the subcontinent.

60. The durbars did a good deal more than 'serve to nationalize a local ceremonial idiom'. David Cannadine, *Ornamentalism: How the British Saw their Empire* (London, Allen Lane, 2001), p. 109.

61. Thomas R. Metcalf, *Ideologies of the Raj* (Cambridge, CUP, 1995), pp. 78–9. Much of global imperial rule was shot through with such ironies.

62. Cohn, 'Representing authority', pp. 179–83.

63. Ibid., pp. 184–5.

64. Over 300 ceremonies were held all over India on the day of the proclamation in 1877, ensuring the wider dissemination of the meaning of the Assemblage. Cohn, 'Representing authority', p. 207.

65. Ibid., p. 204.

66. These quotations come from *The Scotsman*, on various dates in January 1877 and after. For more details see John M. MacKenzie, 'Exhibiting empire at the Delhi Durbar 1911: imperial and cultural contexts', in John McAleer and John M. MacKenzie (eds), *Exhibiting the Empire: Cultures of Display and the British Empire* (Manchester, MUP, 2015), pp. 194–219, particularly p. 200.

67. *The Scotsman*, 31 January 1877, p. 4; 6 March 1877, p. 3; 3 December 1877, p. 7.

68. Cohn, 'Representing authority', pp. 189 and 200.

69. For example, H. Talboys Wheeler, *The History of the Imperial Assemblage at Delhi, held on 1st January 1877 to celebrate the Assumption of the Title of Empress of India by HM the Queen, including historical sketches of the Indian Princes, Past and Present* (London, Longmans Green, 1877). This was matched in 1903 by Stephen Wheeler, *A History of the Delhi Coronation Durbar held on 1st January 1903 to Celebrate the Coronation of His Majesty King Edward VII, Emperor of India, Compiled from Official Papers* (London,

John Murray, 1904). Curzon, always interested in publicity, was critical of this work since its text is as ponderous as its title.

70. These census figures are provided in Murray's *A Handbook for Travellers in India, Burma and Ceylon* (London, John Murray, 1919), pp. cxxxii–cxxxviii.

71. *The Times*, 18 December 1911, p. 8, columns 1–2.

72. Dr Minoti Chakravarty-Kaul delivered a paper on this destruction at the Manchester Metropolitan conference on the 1911 durbar held in 2011, and reported in the *Bulletin of the German Historical Institute*, 34, 1 (2012), pp. 165–8. See also David A. Johnston, *New Delhi: The Last Imperial City* (Basingstoke, Palgrave Macmillan, 2015), chapter 8; Cohn, 'Representing authority', p. 195.

73. Press Association (PA) report from Delhi 4 December 1902, quoted in *The Scotsman*, 29 December 1902, p. 8.

74. Chandrika Kaul, *Reporting the Raj: The British Press and India, c. 1880–1922* (Manchester, MUP, 2003), p. 105.

75. *The Scotsman*, 13 November 1902, p. 5. The report also suggested that, although the 1903 event might cost double this, eastern history was full of examples 'of the inestimable value of prestige among tributary races'.

76. *The Scotsman*, 13 November 1902, p. 5, and 30 December 1902, p. 4.

77. Kaul has indicated the extent to which Reuters and the other agencies lavishly covered the durbars, as well as the number of major Fleet Street figures sent out by newspapers to report on them: *Reporting the Raj*, pp. 43, 61, 63, 77, 109.

78. *The Scotsman*, 29 December 1902, p. 8.

79. *The Scotsman*, 30 December 1902, p. 4.

80. For the media and empire, see Simon J. Potter (ed.), *Newspapers and Empire in Ireland and Britain: Reporting the British Empire c. 1857–1921* (Dublin, Four Courts Press, 2004) and Chandrika Kaul (ed.), *Media and the British Empire* (London, Palgrave Macmillan, 2006).

81. Mortimer Menpes, *The Durbar* (London, Adam and Charles Black, 1903); Lovat Fraser, *At Delhi* (Bombay, Times of India, 1903). As well as Stephen Wheeler's book, there were also Valentia Steer, *The Delhi Durbar of 1902–3: A Concise Illustrated History* (London, Marshall, 1903) and John Oliver Hobbes (Mrs Pearl Craigie), *Imperial India: Letters from the East* (London, Fisher Unwin, 1903).

82. For an extensive collection of photographs, see Julie F. Codell (ed.), *Power and Resistance: The Delhi Coronation Durbars* (New Delhi, Alkazi Collection of Photography and Mapin Publishing, 2012).

83. Ibid., pp. 36–7, 42, 47, 55–7, 62, 75, 76, 126.

84. Julie Codell's introduction to *Power and Resistance*, p. 17. See also Jim Masselos for an extended discussion of the reactions of the crowds at the various durbars, 'The Great Durbar crowds: the participant audience', in Codell (ed.), *Power and Resistance*, pp. 176–203.

85. All these events, and much else, are detailed in the 388-page *Official Directory with Maps, Coronation Durbar 1911* (Delhi, Government Printing, 1911), a modern reprint. The chapters include: 'The programme of state ceremonies'; 'The state entry', 'Receptions in the Fort and in the Ridge Pavilion', 'Reception of ruling chiefs', 'Unveiling of King Edward Memorial', 'Military church parade', 'Presentation of the colours', 'The durbar', 'The state reception', 'Presentation of volunteer and Indian officers', 'State garden party', 'Review', 'Investiture', 'Review of police', 'Departure of their Imperial Majesties', 'Sports and games'. For sporting events, see chapter 3 on 'Team sports'.

86. MacKenzie, 'Exhibiting empire at the Delhi Durbar', p. 205.

87. Ibid., pp. 206–12.

88. Anne de Courcy, *The Fishing Fleet: Husband-hunting in the Raj* (London, Weidenfeld and Nicolson, 2012), pp. 24–5.

89. *Coronation Durbar Delhi 1911: Official Directory*. For a recent history of the honours system and its social and cultural significance, see Tobias Harper, *From Servants of the Empire to Everyday Heroes: The British Honours System in the Twentieth Century* (Oxford, OUP, 2020).

90. The Imperial Hotel in New Delhi, an Art Deco survivor from the construction of the capital, is entirely themed with images of the Durbar. Heritage, perhaps with an eye to tourism, is something of an obsession in independent India.

91. When I visited in February 2020, a group of youths were enthusiastically playing cricket by the obelisk marking the spot of the crowning. Symbolically, the place of imperial ritual had become devoted to an imported sport.

92. For imperial dimensions of youth organisations, see MacKenzie, *Propaganda and Empire*, pp. 240–48; John O. Springhall, *Youth, Empire and Society: A Social History of British Youth Movements* (Brighton, Croom Helm, 1977); John O. Springhall (ed.), *Sure and Stedfast: A History of the Boys' Brigade, 1883–1983* (London, Collins, 1983).

93. Robert Baden-Powell's *Scouting for Boys* (London, Cox, 1908) remains the best source for the foundation of the movement and its professed ideals. See also Allen Warren, 'Citizens of the empire: Baden-Powell, scouts and guides and an imperial ideal', in John M. MacKenzie (ed.), *Imperialism and Popular Culture* (Manchester, MUP, 1986), pp. 232–56.

94. Warren, 'Citizens of the empire', p. 249.

95. Ranger, 'Making Northern Rhodesia imperial', pp. 366–8.

96. Turley, *With the Prince Round the Empire*, p. 71.

97. Anon., *The Prince of Wales' African Book*, no pagination. Later in the tour he reviewed a march of Chilean boy scouts in Santiago, demonstrating the penetration of the scout movement into extra-imperial zones.

98. Frew, *Prince George's African Tour*, illustrations, p. 76, frontispiece, p. 160, respectively. He also visited a camp of white scouts drawn from throughout Natal. Ibid., p. 94.

99. Ranger, 'Invention of tradition in colonial Africa', p. 235, quoting John Lonsdale on the celebrations of the colonial state in Kenya. Lonsdale also pointed to the carniva-lesque entertainments that took place even in this remote corner of East Africa.

100. Ibid., p. 246. While the date may represent the influence of the First World War, still the association of the missions with order and discipline certainly stimulated such approaches.

101. Ibid., pp. 230–6.

102. Charles V. Reed, *Royal Tourists, Colonial Subjects and the Making of a British World, 1860–1911* (Manchester, MUP, 2016), pp. xxv–xxvi.

103. For the encounters between the Prince of Wales and the Indian princes, along with the extraordinary amount of present-giving, see Kajal Meghani, *Splendours of the Subcontinent: A Prince's Tour of India 1875–6* (London, Royal Collection Trust, 2017).

104. Sir Percy Sykes, *Sir Mortimer Durand, a Biography* (London, Cassells, 1926), pp. 58–9. 'Middies' were midshipmen, who must have been bemused by their new roles.

105. This was the first time that the wife of such a senior royal accompanied her husband, as she continued to do in future tours and ceremonies.

106. Donald Mackenzie Wallace, *The Web of Empire: A Diary of the Imperial Tour of their Royal Highnesses the Duke and Duchess of Cornwall and York in 1901* (London, Macmillan, 1902), pp. 121, 135, 163, 274. Wallace was appointed assistant private secretary to the prince to keep the diary of the tour. Lists of medals and of the recipients of honours were included in appendices. The mileage of the entire tour is on p. 441. In Montreal, the royal party stayed in the home of Donald Alexander Smith, Lord Strathcona, an indication of its size and opulence. Strathcona, founder of the Canadian Pacific Railway, made many philanthropic donations to hospitals, McGill University and the Presbyterian Church.

107. St John's Cathedral, Brisbane, replaced an earlier pro-cathedral and was partially completed in 1910. The original architect was John Pearson and his son Frank reworked the designs after his death.

108. St George's Cathedral, designed by Herbert Baker, was not fully completed in its present form until 1936.

109. Wallace, *Web of Empire*, pp. 125–6. The Exhibition Building still stands, a UNESCO World Heritage Site.

110. Ibid., pp. 73, 99 and 128.

111. Robert Aldrich and Cindy McCreery (eds), *Royals on Tour: Politics, Pageantry and Colonialism* (Manchester, MUP, 2018). The essays here deal comparatively with the ceremonial and pageantry of other countries (European and non-European) and monarchies.

112. The *Illustrated London News* issued magnificently illustrated supplements for the Prince of Wales's tour of India in 1875–6 and illustrated journals in the respective colonies followed this custom.

113. *The Times of India*, 21 November 1921, p. 7.

114. Reed, *Royal Tourists*, passim.

115. Ibid., p. 37.

116. As the efficacy of tours declined, as nationalist resistance increased, and as the participants (particularly the Prince of Wales, future Edward VIII, became more racist and bored), the travels seemed to become ever more extensive, followed by many publications. A selection would include St John Adcock, *The Prince of Wales' African Book*; Sir Percival Phillips, *The Prince of Wales' Eastern Book: A Pictorial Record of the Voyages of HMS Renown, 1921–1922* (London, Hodder and Stoughton, 1923); Ward Price, *Through South Africa with the Prince*; Turley, *With the Prince Round the Empire*; Frew, *Prince George's African Tour*; King George's Jubilee Trust, *Their Majesties' Visit to Canada, the United States and Newfoundland, 1939* (London, Macmillan, 1939).

117. V.C. Scott O'Connor, *The Empire Cruise* (London, printed privately for the author), 1925. Was it privately printed because not expected to have commercial prospects? This may also have been true of some of the privately produced royal tour books.

118. The purposes of the cruise were laid out on pp. 13–14 of O'Connor's book.

119. O'Connor, *The Empire Cruise*. For numbers visiting the ships, p. 275; for desertions, p. 228.

120. The interview is in ibid., pp. 248–9.

121. John M. MacKenzie, 'Lakes, rivers and oceans: technology, ethnicity and the shipping of empire in the late nineteenth century', in David Killingray, Margarette Lincoln and Nigel Rigby (eds), *Maritime Empires: British Imperial Maritime Trade in the Nineteenth Century* (Woodbridge, Suffolk, Boydell Press, 2004), pp. 111–27; and R.V. Kubicek, 'The role of shallow-draft steamboats in the expansion of the British Empire, 1820–1914', *International Journal of Maritime Research*, 6, 1 (June 1994), pp. 85–106.

122. For the wider context of the empire cruise, see Daniel Owen Spence, *Colonial Naval Culture and British Imperialism, 1922–67* (Manchester, MUP, 2015).

123. Pamela Mountbatten, *India Remembered: A Personal Account of the Mountbattens During the Transfer of Power* (London, Pavilion Books, 2007), pp. 42–50, 220–31.

124. Martin Shipway, '"Transfer of destinies", or business as usual? Republican invented tradition and the problem of "independence" at the end of the French Empire', in Robert Holland, Susan Williams and Terry Barringer (eds), *The Iconography of Independences: 'Freedoms at Midnight'* (Abingdon, Routledge, 2010), pp. 101–2.

125. Cannadine, *Ornamentalism*. Cannadine contributed an essay to the *Iconography of Independence* book: 'Independence Day ceremonial in historical perspective', pp. 1–17.

126. Philip Murphy, 'Independence Day and the Crown', in Holland, Williams and Barringer (eds), *Iconography*, pp. 20–7.

127. Ibid., p. 25.

Chapter 2 Equestrian Sports

1. The pioneering book was J.A. Mangan, *The Games Ethic and Imperialism: Aspects of the Diffusion of an Ideal* (London, Frank Cass, 1988). This is particularly concerned with the dissemination of the sports ethic through the schools founded in the empire, including those created by missionaries. See also the collection of essays: J.A. Mangan (ed.), *The Cultural Bond: Sport, Empire, Society* (London, Frank Cass, 1992). The field of sports history grew dramatically in the 1980s and 1990s, with large numbers of articles relating to the imperial dimensions of the phenomenon published in the *International Journal of the History of Sport* (*IJHS*), founded in 1984, and other journals. It is impossible to encompass all this material.

2. A pioneering article retained an air of national pride: Harold J. Perkin, 'Teaching the nations how to play: sport in the British Empire and Commonwealth', *IJHS*, 6, 2 (1980), pp. 145–55. A more substantial article was by Brian Stoddart, 'Sport, cultural imperialism and colonial response', *Comparative Studies in Society and History*, 30, 4 (1988), pp. 649–73.

3. Jeffrey A. Auerbach, *Imperial Boredom: Monotony and the British Empire* (Oxford, OUP, 2018) fails to mention sports, but they were a key antidote for boredom for soldiers between campaigns, officers at hill stations, and elite colonists enjoying leisure provided by cheap labour. Natural history pursuits and the creation of museums can even be seen as the product of colonial boredom. Pre-empting Auerbach, I wrote that 'the influence of boredom upon history should never be underestimated'. John M. MacKenzie, *Museums and Empire: Natural History, Human Cultures and Colonial Identities* (Manchester, MUP, 2009), pp. 105–6.

4. J.A. Mangan, *Athleticism in the Victorian and Edwardian Public School: The Emergence and Consolidation of an Educational Ideology* (Cambridge, CUP, 1981).

5. Brad Patterson, Tom Brooking and Jim McAloon, *Unpacking the Kists: The Scots in New Zealand* (Montreal and Kingston, McGill-Queen's UP, 2013), pp. 18, 235–7.

6. Dennis Kincaid, *British Social Life in India 1608–1937* (London, Routledge 1938), p. 255.

7. The Earl of Cromer, *Modern Egypt* (London, Macmillan, 1908), pp. 253–4.

8. Anthony Kirk-Greene, 'Badge of office: sport and His Excellency in the British Empire', in Mangan (ed.), *Cultural Bond*, pp. 178–200. Kirke-Greene provided an exhaustive listing of the sporting interests of colonial civil servants and governors, and considered the manner in which appointments were conditioned by athletic and sporting ability.

9. J.D. Campbell, ' "Training for sport is training for war": sport and the transformation of the British army, 1860–1914', *IJHS*, 17, 4 (2000), pp. 21–58.

10. Ham Mukasa, who accompanied Apolo Kagwa to England for the coronation of Edward VII in 1902, expressed astonishment at the manner in which the British could play sports in the unlikely surroundings of a ship. Quoted in Kirk-Greene, 'Badge of office', p. 179. I observed this passionate tradition much in evidence on my own early voyages on the Union-Castle Line in the 1950s and 1960s.

11. The Uberoi sports equipment suppliers, originally with a headquarters in Sialkot (now in Pakistan) and with branches throughout India, claims on its website to have been founded in 1888, www.justdial.com/Kolkata/Uberoi-Ltd-Near-New-Market-New-Market/033P400893_BZDET (accessed 25 June 2020).

12. For African examples see John Blacking, 'Games and sport in pre-colonial African societies', in William J. Baker and James A. Mangan (eds), *Sport in Africa* (New York, Africana Publishing, 1987), pp. 3–22.

13. Some games claim ancient histories, with *kabbadi* originating in Maharashtra and Kho-Kho in the Punjab, but also in other regions of India and elsewhere in Asia. Both experienced something of a renaissance in the twentieth century.

14. For the New Zealand case see Patterson, Brooking and McAloon, *Unpacking the Kists*, pp. 182–91. Such games were common throughout the empire.
15. B.A. 'Jimmy' James (ed.), *High Noon of Empire: The Diary of Lt. Col. Henry Tyndall 1895–1915* (Barnsley, Pen and Sword Books, 2007), p. 76.
16. James L. Hevia, *Animal Labor and Colonial Warfare* (Chicago, University of Chicago Press, 2018).
17. Sandra Swart, 'Horses, power and settler society, the Cape c. 1654–1840', *Kronos: Southern African Histories* (University of the Western Cape), 29 (November 2003), pp. 47–63.
18. Dressage is outside the scope of this chapter. Among horse 'disciplines' it originated on the Continent and was pursued more energetically in several European countries before becoming popular in Britain. Evidence of the popularity of all horse disciplines in Western Australia can be found in Marion Hercock with Zoe Harrison, *A History of Dressage in Western Australia* (Carlisle, Western Australia, Hesperian Press, 2019).
19. Kincaid, *British Social Life*, p. 34.
20. John M. MacKenzie, *The Empire of Nature: Hunting, Conservation and British Imperialism* (Manchester, MUP, 1988), p. 169.
21. Gillian Tindall, *City of Gold: The Biography of Bombay* (London, Temple Smith, 1982), p. 161.
22. Sir Evan Cotton, *East Indiamen: The East India Company's Maritime Service* (London, Batchworth Press, 1999), p. 35. See also Robert Lindsay (1754–1836), *Anecdotes of an Indian Life*, edited by David R. Syiemlieh (Shillong, North-Eastern Hill University Publications, 1997), pp. 7–8.
23. A pipe was a butt or half a tun.
24. Cotton, *East Indiamen*, p. 35.
25. Dorothy Laird, *Paddy Henderson: The Story of P. Henderson and Company, 1834–1961* (Glasgow, Outram, 1961), pp. 104–6.
26. The significance of the Ooty hunt is well represented on the memorial tablets on the walls of St Stephen's Church Udagamandalam (Ooty, visited 2 February 2020), where Lt Allfrey, Major Heseltine (Master of the Hunt in various years from 1906 to 1919) and Captain Preston are commemorated. The latter drowned (aged 43) in the Kromund River while hunting with the Ooty Hounds in 1857.
27. Mollie Panter-Downes, *Ooty Preserved: A Victorian Hill Station in India* (London, Century Publishing, 1985), p. 68.
28. *A Handbook for Travellers in India, Burma and Ceylon* (London, John Murray, 1919), p. 565. The handbook described 'Ooty' as a sportsman's paradise, with 'varied and interesting' sport, including shooting elephants and bison, tigers (rare) and panthers, stalking for ibex and muntjacs, fishing for mahsir, shooting with shotguns for various fowl, as well as the jackal hunt. Here was the full hunting, shooting and fishing agenda. Mollie Panter-Downes gave 1844 as the year of foundation of the Ooty Hunt and described the walls of the club as being festooned with pictures of its activities: *Ooty Preserved*, pp. 67–8.
29. Helen Robinson, *Constantia and its Neighbours* (Wynberg, Houghton House, 2014), p. 120.
30. General Godfrey Charles Mundy, *Journal of a Tour in India* (London, John Murray, 3rd edn 1858, first published 1832), pp. 177, 346.
31. Emily Eden, *Up the Country: Letters written to her sister from the Upper Provinces of India*, introduction and notes by Edward Thompson (London, Curzon Press, 1978, 1st edn 1930).
32. Marion Hercock, 'A history of hunting with hounds in Western Australia', in *Early Days, the Journal of the Royal Western Australia Historical Society*, 2, part 6 (2000), pp. 695–712. Horses were also used for show-jumping and eventing.

33. The French were also a significant horse-racing society, but in some respects the passion seems to have been learned from the English. Napoleon was keen on its development and the major racecourses, like Longchamp and Chantilly, were created in the nineteenth century. It was never so prominent in the French Empire, although there is an exception in Quebec.

34. For horse racing in Britain see Mike Huggins, *Flat Racing and British Society, 1790–1914* (London, Frank Cass, 2000); *Horse Racing and the British* (Manchester, MUP, 2004); and *Horse Racing and British Society in the Long Eighteenth Century* (Martlesham, Suffolk, Boydell, 2018).

35. The racecourse at Ooty, close to the centre of town, is now somewhat dilapidated and is used only for training. The adjacent cricket ground is, however, still very active.

36. Eden, *Up the Country*, pp. 42–4.

37. See Royal Western India Turf Club website pages: www.rwitc.com/club/bequeathingLegacy.php, www.rwitc.com/club/timeline.php, www.rwitc.com/club/aboutus.php (all accessed 19 November 2019) which contain useful information about the history of the Turf Club.

38. Tindall, *City of Gold*, pp. 161–2.

39. I am grateful to racing journalist and writer Rolf Johnson for information.

40. See Royal Calcutta Turf Club website: www.rctconline.com/ShowContent. php?this=20&himg=18&SSid=0 (accessed 19 November 2019). Geoffrey Moorhouse suggested that before 1818 the heat dictated that all races were ridden before sunrise. Geoffrey Moorhouse, *Calcutta: The City Revealed* (Harmondsworth, Penguin, 1974), p. 60. There is some information on racing in Calcutta in Krishna Dutta, *Calcutta: A Cultural and Literary History* (Oxford, Signal, 2008).

41. In the early nineteenth century, there were still sunset carriage rides on the Calcutta Esplanade, where the fashionable acknowledged each other as though in Hyde Park. Joy Melville, *Julia Margaret Cameron, Pioneer Photographer* (Stroud, Sutton Publishing, 2003), p. 1.

42. Anusha Parthasarathy, 'Survivors of time: Madras Race Club – a canter through centuries', in *The Hindu*, Chennai, 2 August 2016, www.thehindu.com/features/metroplus/survivors-of-time-madras-race-club-a-canter-through-centuries/article2916420.ece (accessed 8 January 2020).

43. The picture (a hand-coloured aquatint) shows the Assembly Rooms in an impressive Georgian building, from which an outsize Union flag flies. Some Indians with cow and goats pass by in the foreground while horses are ridden behind. St Thomas's Mount is on the right of the painting.

44. This racecourse is still active, close to the city, and with owners' and public entrances near the Radisson Hotel.

45. *The Times of India*, 14 November 1921, p. 12.

46. Rudyard Kipling, *Kim*, chapter VI.

47. Francis Ingall, *The Last of the Bengal Lancers* (London, Leo Cooper, 1988), p. 50.

48. Swart, 'Horses, power and settler society', p. 60. The first Turf Club had 29 members, of whom 20 were officers in the army or the navy.

49. Robinson, *Constantia and its Neighbours*, p. 121.

50. Swart, 'Horses, power and settler society', p. 60.

51. See: www.tba.co.za/horse-racing-south-africa/ (accessed 16 December 2019).

52. These are, respectively, Kenilworth and Durbanville; Flamingo Park and Fairview; Greyville and Scottsville; Turffontein and Vaal.

53. Robinson, *Constantia and its Neighbours*, pp. 120 and 165.

54. Sir W.F. Butler, *Sir William Butler, an Autobiography* (London, Constable, 1911), p. 421.

55. Matthew L. McDowell, 'Sport and social relations in the Falkland Islands up to 1982', *JICH*, 48, 6 (2020), pp. 1078–108, particularly pp. 1088–9.

56. 'Singapore's first racecourse is built, 1842', http://eresources.nlb.gov.sg/history/events/591b55ff-5885-47f4-a3ae-8dbb5cc725b3 (accessed 12 November 2019).

57. See: www.horseracing.com/blog/development-of-horse-racing-in-malaysia/ (accessed 12 November 2019).

58. See: http://eresources.nlb.gov.sg/infopedia/articles/SIP_1069_2007-06-20.html (accessed 12 November 2019).

59. Andrew Marshall, *The Trouser People: The Quest for the Victorian Footballer who Made Burma Play the Empire's Game* (London, Viking, 2002), pp. 158–9.

60. *Rangoon Times*, Christmas number, 1912. This paper is not available on any digitised system, but I found bound copies of the Christmas numbers in the library of an Ayeyarwady river steamer in 2016.

61. Noel F. Singer, *Burmah, a Photographic Journey, 1855–1925* (Gartmore, Stirlingshire, Kiscadale Publications, 1993), p. 64.

62. Andrew Hillier, *Mediating Empire: An English Family in China, 1817–1927* (Folkestone, Renaissance Books, 2020), p. 141. Guy Hillier, Agent of the Hong Kong Bank, was a 'fearless jockey' on both courses.

63. See: https://standardbredcanada.ca/news/2-24-17/canadian-racing-celebrates-250-years.html (accessed 18 November 2019).

64. J. Thomas West, 'Thoroughbred racing', in *The Canadian Encyclopedia*, www.thecanadianencyclopedia.ca/en/article/thoroughbred-racing (accessed 19 November 2019).

65. Alec H. Chisholm, *The Australian Encyclopaedia*, vol. 4 (Sydney, Angus and Robertson, 1958), p. 537. See also pp. 537–47 for much of the material that follows.

66. Frances Pollon, *Parramatta, Cradle City of Australia* (City of Parramatta, 1983).

67. Jenny Gregory and Jan Gothard (eds), *Historical Encyclopaedia of Western Australia* (Crawley, WA, University of Western Australia Press, 2009), p. 458.

68. See National Museum of Australia website, www.nma.gov.au/defining-moments/resources/melbourne-cup (accessed 18 December 2019).

69. Greg Ryan, 'Sport in Christchurch', in John Cookson and Graeme Dunstall (eds), *Southern Capital: Christchurch, towards a City Biography* (Christchurch, University of Canterbury Press, 2000), p. 329.

70. Patterson, Brooking and McAloon, *Unpacking the Kists*, pp. 237–8.

71. John Griffiths, *Imperial Culture in Antipodean Cities, 1880–1939* (Houndmills, Palgrave Macmillan, 2014), pp. 49–50.

72. 'Racing: history – establishment and administration', from *An Encyclopaedia of New Zealand*, edited by A.H. McLintock, originally published in 1966. In *Te Ara – the Encyclopedia of New Zealand*, www.TeAra.govt.nz/en/1966/racing-horse (accessed 13 November 2019).

73. Marquess Curzon of Kedleston, *Leaves from a Viceroy's Notebook and Other Papers* (London, Macmillan, 1926), 'The cradle of polo', pp. 79–90. For the development of polo in a key era, see Patrick McDevitt, 'The king of sports: polo in late Victorian and Edwardian India', *IJHS*, 20, 1 (2003), pp. 1–27. As McDevitt shows, the princes took up polo as an opportunity for 'conspicuous consumption and lavish hospitality', a means of social interaction with the British, and therefore of legitimating their social position in India.

74. Luise Elsaesser, '"Dashing about with the greatest gallantry": polo in India and the British metropole, 1862–1914', *Sport in History*, 40, 1 (2020), pp. 1–27. For a local history of the sport, see Jaisal Singh, *Polo in India* (New Delhi, Lustre Press, Roli Books, 2007), with an introduction by Yuvraj Shivraj Singh Jodhpur.

75. For the origins of Hurlingham, see www.hurlinghamclub.org.uk/about-the-club/history/introduction-polo/ (accessed 10 November 2019).

76. In many clubs and hotels in India, photographs of polo players on the walls invariably reveal both British and Indian players in the same teams. The photograph of the winning team at the Peshawar tournament in 1898 has one Indian member, Futteh Khan.

77. See 'The Imperial Assemblage at Delhi, 1877 from the pages of *The Scotsman*'.
78. *The Scotsman*, 24 December 1902, p. 7
79. *The Scotsman*, 1 January 1902, p. 4.
80. *The Scotsman*, 6 December 1911, p. 9.
81. *The Times of India*, 6 December 1911, p. 5.
82. *Rangoon Times*, Christmas number, 1921. There were also regular horse and dog shows in Burma. By this time, the Indo-Burma Petroleum Co. had a refinery in Rangoon and the numbers of expatriates grew considerably. Oil had been extracted in Burma in pre-colonial times and the British developed the industry from the late 1880s, ultimately supplying all the needs of India.
83. Tony Mason and Eliza Riedi, *Sport and the Military: The British Armed Forces 1880–1960* (Cambridge, CUP, 2010), p. 57.
84. Winston S. Churchill, *The Story of the Malakand Field Force* (first published 1898, new edn, London, Leo Cooper, 1989), pp. 158–60. The Inter-Regimental Tournament had been founded in 1877 and there were several other tournaments.
85. Winston S. Churchill, *My Early Life* (London, Odhams, 1947), pp. 104–6, 117–18, 115–16, 204–8.
86. James (ed.), *High Noon of Empire*, p. 77.
87. Ingall, *Last of the Bengal Lancers*, p. 62.
88. Charles Turley, *With the Prince Round the Empire* (London, Methuen, 1926), pp. 110, 126.
89. See: www.britishpathe.com/video/indian-polo-championship/query/Willingdon (accessed 5 January 2020).
90. See: https://specialcollectionsuniversityofsouthampton.wordpress.com/2018/12/07/british-polo-day-lord-mountbatten-and-polo/ (accessed 5 January 2020).
91. See: www.britishpathe.com/video/lord-mountbatten-playing-polo (accessed 5 January 2020).
92. Mason and Riedi, *Sport and the Military*, pp. 57–78.
93. *The Times* reported that between 1880 and 1914 there had been thirty-six officer deaths on the polo field, mainly in India. Ibid., p. 73.
94. While polo is still played in India, it seems to be less popular in the Indian army. In Annandale, Simla, an area now militarised, the British polo ground has been transformed into a nine-hole golf course. Golf is also played at the notable military cantonment in Wellington near Ooty.
95. For polo in New South Wales, see www.nswpolo.com.au/About/History-of-NSW-Polo-Association (accessed 9 November 2019).
96. See: Sally Weedon, *Countess of Dudley Cup Tournament 1985: a short history of the polo clubs in NSW and their participation in the Countess of Dudley Cup 1910-1985* (Sydney, NSW Polo Association, 1985), available through the NSW Polo Association website www.nswpolo.com.au/Assets/Pages/22/Book_of_History_from_1985.pdf.
97. See: NSW Polo Association Polo Tournament programme for Australasian Polo Cup and Hordern Cup, Kensington Racecourse, 20-24 June 1933, available through the NSW Polo Association website: www.nswpolo.com.au/Assets/Pages/22/1933-NSWPA-Polo-Program-Scaned-LowRes.pdf.
98. See: www.singaporepoloclub.org/about/abouts/history (accessed 10 November 2019). The King's Own were an infantry regiment, so polo was not restricted to cavalry. See also an article in the *Straits Times*, 31 January 1899, on the founding of a polo club in Singapore, http://eresources.nlb.gov.sg/newspapers/Digitised/Article/straitstimes18990131-1.2.41 (accessed 10 November 2019).
99. Ryan, 'Sport in Christchurch', p. 335.
100. See: www.polo.org.nz/ (accessed 10 November 2019).
101. See: www.bbc.co.uk/news/world-latin-america-28157865 (accessed 9 November 2019).

102. See: https://theroyalselangorpoloclub.com/about-us/ (accessed 10 November 2019). See also the 'History of polo in Malaysia', https://rmpa.org.my/history/ (accessed 10 November 2019).
103. C.S. Nicholls, *Red Strangers: The White Tribe of Kenya* (London, Timewell Press, 2005), p. 170.
104. Quoted in Kirk-Greene, 'Badge of office', p. 179.
105. Marion Hercock, 'Equestrian sports', in Michelle Prain (ed.), *The British Legacy in Valparaiso* (Santiago, Ril Editores, 2011), p. 334.
106. The prolific American historian of polo, Horace A. Laffaye, has written works on polo in Britain, the USA and Argentina, as well as *The Evolution of Polo, The Polo Encyclopedia* and other titles.
107. See: www.sapolo.co.za/the-association/history-of-polo-in-south-africa (accessed 10 November 2019).
108. Ingall, *Last of the Bengal Lancers*, p. 78.
109. MacKenzie, *Empire of Nature*, pp. 186–9.
110. Hevia, *Animal Labor*, pp. 261–2.
111. MacKenzie, *Empire of Nature*.
112. J.A. Mangan and Callum McKenzie, '"Blooding" the martial male: the imperial officer, field sports and big-game hunter', *IJHS*, 25, 9 (August 2008), particularly pp. 1057–79.
113. Kincaid, *British Social Life*, p. 179.
114. For India, see Vijaya Ramadas Mandala, *Shooting a Tiger: Big-game Hunting and Conservation in Colonial India* (New Delhi, OUP, 2019).
115. For both masculinity and women hunters, see Angela Thompsell, *Hunting Africa: British Sport, African Knowledge and the Nature of Empire* (Houndmills, Basingstoke, Palgrave Macmillan, 2015).
116. John M. MacKenzie, 'Hunting in East and Central Africa in the late nineteenth century', in Baker and Mangan (eds), *Sport in Africa*, pp. 172–95, and *Empire of Nature*, chapters 8–11.
117. MacKenzie, *Empire of Nature*, pp. 48–51, 307–8.

Chapter 3 Team Sports

1. John Blacking, 'Games and sport in pre-colonial African societies', in William J. Baker and James A. Mangan (eds), *Sport in Africa* (New York, Africana Publishing, 1987), pp. 3–22.
2. Terence O. Ranger, *Dance and Society in Eastern Africa, 1890–1970: The Beni Ngoma* (London, Heinemann, 1975). See previous chapter for indigenous sports in Asia.
3. Basketball was promoted by religious and youth organisations, perhaps because it is amenable to indoor play. For its arrival in New Zealand before the First World War, see John Griffiths, *Imperial Culture in Antipodean Cities, 1880–1939* (Basingstoke, Palgrave Macmillan, 2014), p. 142.
4. Cecil Headlam, *Ten Thousand Miles through India and Burma: An Account of the Oxford University Authentics' Cricket Tour . . . in the year of the Durbar* (London, Dent, 1903), pp. 168–9.
5. Quoted in Anthony Kirk-Greene, 'Badge of office: sport and His Excellency in the British Empire', in J.A. Mangan (ed.), *The Cultural Bond: Sport, Empire, Society* (London, Frank Cass, 1992), p. 184.
6. C.L.R. James, *Beyond a Boundary* (London, Stanley James, 1993), p. 3. James's lifetime coincided with the parallel development of West Indian cricket and nationalism.
7. See Boria Majumdar, 'Imperial tool for nationalist resistance: the games ethic in Indian history', *IJHS*, 21, 3–4 (2004), pp. 384–401. Additionally, Majumdar charts the spread of football in India through the public schools.

8. The village of Freuchie in Fife won the National Village Championship at Lord's in 1985, beating a Surrey side.

9. Chuck Korr and Marvin Close, *More than Just a Game: Football v Apartheid* (London, Collins, 2008); also chapters on South Africa and New Zealand in John Nauright and Timothy J.L. Chandler (eds), *Making Men: Rugby and Masculine Identity* (London, Frank Cass, 1999).

10. A few examples suffice – 'a sticky wicket', 'a straight bat', 'up stumps', 'bowling a googly', 'a long innings', and so on.

11. Ramachandra Guha, *A Corner of a Foreign Field: The Indian History of a British Sport* (London, Picador, 2002). See also Guha, 'Cricket and politics in colonial India', *Past and Present*, 161 (November 1998), pp. 155–90, and the light-hearted *Wickets in the East: An Anecdotal History* (Delhi, OUP, 1992).

12. Guha, *Corner of a Foreign Field*, p. xv.

13. Such racial discrimination was apparent in 1925 when Jack Leslie, who had a Jamaican father and English mother, was chosen to play football for England against Ireland. His selection was rescinded, presumably on racial grounds. The first black player to appear for England was Nottingham Forest's Vic Anderson, fifty-three years later in 1978.

14. A story regarding this painting, in an article by a cricket enthusiast, is at www.thehindu.com/society/history-and-culture/madras-miscellany-a-daniell-now-in-madrasi-hands/article19251215.ece (accessed 28 November 2019).

15. Guha, *Corner of a Foreign Field*, pp. 3–4.

16. For cricket in Bombay see: https://mumbaicricket.com/mca/download/Historyofmca/The_Pre-Natal_days.pdf (accessed 29 November 2019).

17. Tony Mason and Eliza Riedi, *Sport and the Military: The British Armed Forces 1880–1960* (Cambridge, CUP, 2010), pp. 24, 29, who describe Major R.M. Poore, the army's 'W.G. Grace', as playing for regimental and civilian teams in the 1890s.

18. Violet Jacob, *Diaries and Letters from India 1895–1900* (Edinburgh, Canongate 1990), p. 87.

19. For Parsis, Simon Deschamps, 'Freemasonry and the Indian Parsi community: a late meeting on the level', *Journal of Freemasonry and Fraternalism*, 3, 1 (2012), pp. 61–72. The first Parsi Lodge, 'Rising Star' in the Scottish rite, was founded in 1843. The Parsis claimed a cultural synergy between Zoroastrianism and Freemasonry, and the Scots Lodge was always more willing to admit non-European masons.

20. Guha, *Corner of a Foreign Field*, pp. 11–15.

21. 'Gymkhana' is an Indian word which the British took over to mean a social and sporting club. In Britain it now denotes a series of competitive equestrian events, but in India it embraced all sports, including cricket.

22. Boria Majumdar, 'Cricket in colonial India: the Bombay Pentangular, 1892–1946', *IJHS*, 19, 2–3 (2002), pp. 157–88.

23. Guha, *Corner of a Foreign Field*, p. 28.

24. Ibid., pp. 69–74.

25. Harris played cricket as captain of Kent and was president of the MCC. As a powerful cricket administrator he was a highly controversial figure.

26. The incident is recounted, with the newspaper quotes, in Guha, *Corner of a Foreign Field*, pp. 64–5.

27. Satadru Sen, *Migrant Races, Empire, Identity and K.S. Ranjitsinhji* (Manchester, MUP, 2004).

28. For Indian princes, see Boria Majumdar, 'Maharajahs and cricket: self, state, province and nation', *IJHS*, 22, 4 (2005), pp. 639–48.

29. M.N.M. Badruddin, writing in the *Bombay Chronicle* under the headline 'India must give up cricket', quoted in Guha, *Corner of a Foreign Field*, pp. 255–6.

30. The Ahmedabad stadium, for 132,000 spectators, said to be the largest in the world, was rebuilt at great cost and opened in 2020.

31. Ashis Nandy insisted this was the case, quoted in Brian Stoddart and Keith Sandiford (eds), *The Imperial Game* (Manchester, MUP, 1998), p. 116.
32. Brian Stoddart, 'Cricket and colonialism in the English-speaking Caribbean to 1914: towards a cultural analysis', in Hilary McD. Beckles and Brian Stoddart (eds), *Liberation Cricket: West Indies Cricket Culture* (Manchester, MUP, 1995).
33. Frank Worral played in Lancashire during his career – a county with connections with West Indian cricket since both Learie Constantine and C.L.R. James lived there for a time.
34. Guha, *Corner of a Foreign Field*, p. 227.
35. See: www.nma.gov.au/defining-moments/resources/aboriginal-cricket-team (accessed 18 December 2019).
36. The team, who played in bare feet, was made up of members of three tribes, the Jarwadjali, Gunditjmara and the Wotjobaluk. The outstanding player was Unaarrimim, who was given the European name of Johnny Mullagh. Other team members were given demeaning names like Sixpence. Memorabilia of the tour were auctioned at Christie's in 2002: *The Guardian*, 8 March 2002, p. 12.
37. Angela Woollacott, 'Gender and sexuality', in Deryck M. Schreuder and Stuart Ward (eds), *Australia's Empire* (Oxford, OUP, 2008), pp. 312–13.
38. A recent survey of Australian cricket is Jared van Duinan, *The British World and an Australian National Identity: Anglo-Australian Cricket, 1860–1901* (London, Palgrave Macmillan, 2018).
39. Richard White and Hsu-Ming Teo, 'Popular culture', in Schreuder and Ward (eds), *Australia's Empire*, p. 352.
40. Quoted in ibid., p. 353.
41. See: https://teara.govt.nz/en/cricket/page-3 (accessed 18 December 2019).
42. Greg Ryan, 'Sport in Christchurch', in John Cookson and Graeme Dunstall (eds), *Southern Capital, Christchurch* (Christchurch, Canterbury University Press, 2000), p. 328.
43. Ali A. Mazrui, 'Africa's triple heritage of play: reflections on the gender gap', in Baker and Mangan (eds), *Sport in Africa*, p. 219. This triple heritage was black African, Islamic and European, and Mazrui considered that this had helped the emergence of African sportswomen.
44. Peter A. Horton, '"Padang or paddock": a comparative view of sport in two imperial territories', *IJHS*, 14, 1 (1997), pp. 1–20.
45. Peter A. Horton, 'The "green" and the "gold": the Irish-Australians and their role in the emergence of the Australian sports culture', *IJHS*, 17, 2–3 (2000), pp. 65–92.
46. See: www.indianmirror.com/games/hockey/History-Of-Hockey.html (accessed 20 December 2019).
47. Although the British team had won gold in 1908 and 1920, it was said that they did not take part in 1928 for fear of being beaten by India.
48. Boria Majumdar, 'The golden years of Indian hockey: "We climb the victory stand"', *IJHS*, 25, 12 (2008), pp. 1592–611.
49. Erik Nielsen, '"Indian hockey (and football) tricks": race, magic, wonder and empire in Australian–Indian sporting relations, 1926–38', *Sport in Society*, 15, 4 (2012), pp. 551–64. Nielsen analyses the racial aspects of these encounters and demonstrates the tension between them and the rhetoric of imperial unity and 'sister dominion'.
50. Ice skating is inevitably not much associated with India, but the ice-skating club in Simla was founded in 1920 and still exists.
51. Women's hockey only became part of the Olympics in 1992, and hockey generally only appeared in the Commonwealth Games in 1998. The men's tournament has been exclusively won by Australia, though the women's tournament has also been won by India and New Zealand.
52. In 1961, the Professor of Scottish History in Glasgow University taught this interesting fact.

53. He observed in his diary that they played rugby, more demanding in his view than association football, despite the climate. A keen sportsman, he also went shooting and, at Bhagalpur, his up-river station in Bengal, played rackets, badminton and tennis. He and his fellow officers went riding regularly on a flat piece of land they called the 'race-course'. Sir Percy Sykes, *Sir Mortimer Durand, a Biography* (London, Cassell, 1926), pp. 30, 36, 40–1.

54. Alister McCrae, *Scots in Burma* (Edinburgh, Kiscadale, 1990), p. 72. And, 'when the rains let up, [we] turned to tennis. The Kokine Swimming Club was the most popular mecca the whole year round and commanded a wide membership of all ages of the European community.'

55. Mason and Riedi, *Sport and the Military*, p. 34. See also pp. 32–7 for the other material in this paragraph.

56. Football was dependent on the environment. In Landi Kotal, the terrain was too rocky. Francis Ingall, *The Last of the Bengal Lancers* (London, Leo Cooper, 1988), p. 37. Instead, the main sport was field hockey, 'at which the men excelled'.

57. Jacob, *Diaries and Letters*, pp. 165–70.

58. Durand had organised this tournament in Simla from 1886. Military teams, Foreign Office clerks and townsmen participated. In 1895 the Highland Light Infantry secured the trophy (a silver football) outright, having won three years in a row. Sykes, *Durand*, pp. 175–6. There is a photograph of the Highland Light Infantry team that won the cup in 1893: Anne Buddle, 'India's associations in Scotland's national galleries', in Roger Jeffery (ed.), *India in Edinburgh* (New Delhi, Social Science Press, 2019), p. 80.

59. Guha, *Corner of a Foreign Field*, p. 244. This 1911 tournament is examined in Tony Mason, 'Football on the Maidan: cultural imperialism in Calcutta', in Mangan (ed.), *The Cultural Bond*, pp. 142–53. See also Novy Kapadia, 'Triumphs and disasters: the story of Indian football, 1889–2000', and the more sophisticated essay by Paul Dimeo, 'Football and politics in Bengal: colonialism, nationalism and communalism', both in Paul Dimeo and James Mills (eds), *Soccer in South Asia: Empire, Nation, Diaspora* (London, Frank Cass, 2001), respectively pp. 17–40 and pp. 57–74.

60. The Riddell Collection of photographs in the Scottish National Portrait Gallery contains an (undated) photograph of a Signal Company playing football with a team of Gurkhas with the title 'The Tommys' favourite pastime': Buddle, 'India's associations in Scotland's national galleries', p. 80.

61. Richard Sidney similarly described how difficult it was to persuade Malayan schoolboys at his Kuala Lumpur school to carry their own cricket bags, which was regarded as coolie work. Richard J.H. Sidney, *In British Malaya Today* (London, Hutchinson, c. 1927), p. 276. For sports in Malaya, see also Janice N. Brownfoot, '"Healthy bodies, healthy minds": sport and society in colonial Malaya', *IJHS*, 19, 2–3 (2002), pp. 129–56.

62. J.A. Mangan, 'Soccer as moral training: missionary intentions and imperial legacies', in Dimeo and Mills (eds) *Soccer*, pp. 41–56, and at greater length in his *The Games Ethic and Imperialism: Aspects of the Diffusion of an Ideal* (London, Frank Cass, 1988).

63. Rugby may always have been a marker of social tone. The cinchona planters of the Nilgiri hills revealed their British social origins by taking holidays in Ootacamund in order to play rugby. Mollie Panter-Downes, *Ooty Preserved: A Victorian Hill Station in India* (London, Hamish Hamilton, 1967), p. 64.

64. *Rangoon Times*, Christmas number, 1913. These Christmas numbers of the newspaper, originally founded as the *Rangoon Chronicle* in 1854 soon after the conquest, with its name changed to *Rangoon Times* in 1858, were quite lavish affairs, with many advertisements and articles rounding up the social and cultural events of the year for the white expatriates.

65. *Rangoon Times*, Christmas number, 1921. A round-up of sport in the colony during the year included an athletics meeting, hockey, women's tennis, all involving white expatriates.

66. Andrew Marshall, *The Trouser People: The Quest for the Victorian Footballer who Made Burma Play the Empire's Game* (London, Viking, 2002), passim.
67. Sidney, *In Malaya Today*, p. 46.
68. Ibid., p. 281.
69. One Boer officer, P.A.M. Cloete, used family contacts (son-in-law of Chief Justice Sir Henry de Villiers) and cricket skills to get himself released from prison to spend the war in England, where he was acceptable as a cricketer: Helen Robinson, *Constantia and its Neighbours* (Wynberg, Houghton House, 2014), p. 175.
70. Anthony Clayton, 'Sport and African soldiers: the military diffusion of Western sport throughout sub-Saharan Africa', in Baker and Mangan (eds), *Sport in Africa*, p. 117.
71. Ibid., p. 127.
72. Oral evidence from Alexander MacKenzie, who was a player with Inverness Thistle after the First World War and played with Africans while living in Kenya in the 1920s and early 1930s. Plate 14 shows a barefoot African team of King's African Rifles personnel in Kenya in 1939.
73. J.A. Mangan, 'Ethics and ethnocentricity: education in British tropical Africa', in Baker and Mangan (eds), *Sport in Africa*, pp. 153–5.
74. Ibid., p. 144.
75. Ibid., p.152.
76. Phillip Vasili, '"The right kind of fellows": Nigerian football tourists as agents of Europeanisation', *IJHS*, 11, 2 (1994), pp. 191–211.
77. Korr and Close, *More than Just a Game*.
78. Rugby arrived in Japan when Royal Naval officers trained Japanese counterparts in the 1870s. Later an educator spread it in Japanese schools and universities. I am grateful to Jim Hoare for information about rugby in Japan.
79. Samoans transformed cricket into *kirikiti* to convert it into a field of traditional contestation. Benjamin Sacks, 'A footnote to sport history: twenty years of cricket, conflict and contestation in Samoa, 1880–1900', *IJHS*, 34, 14 (2017), pp. 1483–500.
80. Peter A. Horton, 'Pacific Islanders in global rugby: the changing currents of sports migration', *IJHS*, 29, 27 (2012), pp. 2388–404.
81. The populations of Fiji, Samoa and Tonga are (2017 and rounded) respectively 985,000, 196,000 and 108,000.
82. David R. Black and John Nauright, *Rugby and the South African Nation* (Manchester, MUP, 1998), pp. 91–3.
83. Ibid., p. ix.
84. Roy Hay and Bill Murray, *A History of Football in Australia: A Game of Two Halves* (Melbourne, Hardie Grant, 2014).
85. Roy Hay, *Aboriginal People and Australian Football in the Nineteenth Century* (Newcastle, Cambridge Publishing, 2019).
86. See: www.britannica.com/sports/Australian-rules-football (accessed 13 March 2020).
87. *Australia* catalogue (London, Royal Academy of Arts, 2013), p. 166. The artist was the celebrated Arthur Streeton.
88. Peter A. Horton, 'Rugby Union football and its role in the socio-cultural development of Queensland, 1882–91', *IJHS*, 9, 1 (1992), pp. 119–31.
89. David Marsh, 'Rugby Union', in Jenny Gregory and Jan Gothard (eds), *Encyclopedia of Western Australia* (Perth, University of WA Press, 2009), p. 787.
90. *The Guardian*, 20 July 2017, www.theguardian.com/sport/2017/jul/21/rugby-union-has-an-image-problem-in-indigenous-australia (accessed 23 December 2019).
91. See: www.nma.gov.au/defining-moments/resources/nicky-winmars-stand (accessed 23 December 2019).
92. Terence Ranger, 'Pugilism and pathology: African boxing and the black urban experience in Southern Rhodesia', in Baker and Mangan (eds), *Sport in Africa*, pp. 196–216.

See also Shamya Dasgupta, 'An inheritance from the British: the Indian boxing story', *IJHS*, 21, 3-4 (2004), pp. 31-51.
93. See: www.rbyc.co.in/ (accessed 2 January 2020).
94. *Rangoon Times,* Christmas number, 1913.
95. It is unclear what Sonchi was in this context.
96. *Coronation Durbar Delhi 1911: Official Directory with Maps* (Calcutta, Government Printing, 1911), pp. 79-91.
97. C.S. Nicholls, *Red Strangers: The White Tribe of Kenya* (London, Timewell Press, 2005), p. 171.
98. Sidney, *In Malaya Today*, p. 12.

Chapter 4 Arts of Empire and of Nations

1. Tim Barringer, Geoff Quilley and Douglas Fordham (eds), *Art and the British Empire* (Manchester, MUP, 2007), p. 3.
2. See the multi-volume survey, David Bindman, Henry Louis Gates et al. (eds), *The Image of the Black in Western Art*, particularly vols 2 and 3 (Cambridge, MA, Belknap Press, Harvard UP, 2010 and 2011). Also David Dabydeen, *Hogarth's Blacks: Images of Blacks in Eighteenth-century English Art* (Manchester, MUP, 1987).
3. John M. MacKenzie, 'The art of the empire', in Peter J. Marshall, *The Illustrated History of the British Empire* (Cambridge, CUP, 1996), pp. 296-315, attempted to integrate aspects of the culture of empire.
4. The catalogue *The British in India* accompanied an early exhibition in the Brighton Museum and Art Gallery in 1973. A V&A exhibition catalogue was Mildred Archer and Ronald Lightbown, *India Observed: India as Viewed by British Artists, 1760-1860* (London, V&A Museum, 1982). In 2002, a small exhibition of paintings by Rudolf Swoboda displayed products of his commission by Queen Victoria, after the Colonial and India Exhibition of 1886, to travel in India to paint portraits for her; see Saloni Mathur, *An Indian Encounter: Portraits for Queen Victoria by Rudolf Swoboda* (London, National Gallery, 2002). Among the considerable attention paid to India, see also C.A. Bayly (ed.), *The Raj: India and the British 1600-1947* (London, National Portrait Gallery, 1990); Julius Bryant and Susan Weber (eds), *John Lockwood Kipling: Arts and Crafts in the Punjab and in London* (New Haven, CT, YUP, 2017). More broadly, Alison Smith, David Blayney Brown and Carol Jacobi (eds), *Artist and Empire: Facing Britain's Imperial Past* (London, Tate Publishing, 2015) contains a survey of artists; see also John M. MacKenzie (ed.), *David Livingstone and the Victorian Encounter with Africa* (London, National Portrait Gallery, 1996), particularly chapter 5, pp. 269-97; for Australia, see the *Australia* catalogue (London, Royal Academy of Arts, and Canberra, National Gallery of Australia, 2013).
5. For North America, see Abigail Tucker, 'Sketching the earliest views of the New World', *The Smithsonian Magazine*, December 2008.
6. The classic work is Bernard Smith, *European Vision and the South Pacific* (New Haven, CT, Yale UP, 1985, originally published by Oxford, Clarendon Press, 1960); also Smith (with Rüdiger Joppien), *The Art of Captain Cook's Voyages*, 3 vols (Oxford, OUP, 1985-7); William Hauptman (ed.), *John Webber 1751-1793: Pacific Voyager and Landscape Artist* (Bern, Kunstmuseum and Manchester, Whitworth Art Gallery, 1996).
7. Mildred Archer, *India and British Portraiture 1770-1825* (London, Sotheby's Publications, 1979). Other artists in India included George Willison, John Thomas Seton, Catherine Reid, Arthur William Devis, John Smart and Frederick Christian Lewis. Towards the end of the period many were painting the readily portable and fashionable miniatures. See also John McAleer, *Picturing India: People, Places and the World of the East India Company* (London, British Library, 2017), chapters 2 and 3.

8. H.J. Noltie, *Indian Botanical Drawings 1793–1868* (Edinburgh, Royal Botanic Garden, 1999); Noltie, *The Dapuri Drawings: Alexander Gibson & the Bombay Botanic Gardens* (Edinburgh, the Antique Collectors' Club in association with the Royal Botanic Garden, 2002); Noltie, *The Cleghorn Collection: South Indian Botanical Drawings 1845–1860* (Edinburgh, Royal Botanic Garden, 2016).

9. William Dalrymple (ed.), *Forgotten Masters: Indian Painting for the East India Company* (London, Philip Wilson for Wallace Collection, 2019), a catalogue of a major exhibition at the Wallace Collection in 2020 which laudably moves the focus from the commissioners of the art to the artists themselves.

10. Geoff Quilley and John Bonehill (eds), *William Hodges 1744–1897: The Art of Exploration* (New Haven, CT, Yale UP, 2004), contains material both on the Cook voyage and on India.

11. William Hodges, *Select Views of India Drawn on the Spot in 1780, 1781, 1782, 1783* (London 1785–8).

12. William Hodges, *Travels in India during the years 1780, 1781, 1782, 1783* (London, 1793). See also G.H.R. Tillotson, 'The Indian travels of William Hodges', *Journal of the Royal Asiatic Society*, third series, 2, 3 (1992), pp. 377–98.

13. Publications on the Daniells include Mildred Archer, *Early Views of India: Picturesque Journeys of Thomas and William Daniell, 1786–1794* (London, Thames and Hudson, 1980), B.N. Goswamy, *Daniells' India: Views from the Eighteenth Century* (New Delhi, Nyogi Books, 2013) and many articles in the journal *Bengal Past and Present*.

14. Many can be seen in the Fort Museum in Chennai (Madras) and on the walls of the Imperial Hotel, New Delhi.

15. J.P. Losty (ed.), *Sita Ram's Painted Views of India: Lord Hastings's Journey from Calcutta to the Punjab, 1814–1815* (London, Thames and Hudson, 2015).

16. Giles Tillotson, review of Pauline Rohatgi and Graham Parlett, *Indian Life and Landscape by Western Artists: Paintings and Drawings from the Victoria and Albert Museum, Seventeenth to Early Twentieth Centuries* (Mumbai, Chhatrapati Shivaji Maharaj Vastu Sangrahalaya in association with the V&A, London, 2008), *Journal of the Royal Asiatic Society*, 20, 3 (2010), pp. 289–90.

17. Mildred Archer and Toby Falk, *India Revealed: The Art and Adventures of James and William Fraser, 1801–1835* (London, Cassell, 1989), pp. 44–6.

18. Ibid., p. 47.

19. Sir William Foster, 'British artists in India', *Journal of the Royal Society of Arts*, 98, 4820 (May 1950), pp. 518–25.

20. Emily Eden, *Up the Country: Letters Written to Her Sister* (London, Curzon, 1978). She produced portraits of Sikhs, Afghans and members of Indian royal courts. These were published as *Portraits of the Princes and People of India with 28 hand-coloured lithograph plates* (London, Dickinson, 1844); Mary Ann Prior, *An Indian Portfolio: The Life and Work of Emily Eden* (London, Quartet Books, 2012).

21. Tobin has pointed out that some of the early portraits of military figures depicted them in a form of cross-dressing with Native American peoples. This matched the fact that the Mohawk leader Joseph Brant was depicted in the same period in a form of western dress, a search for hybridity which may have represented aspects of appropriation or of supposed reconciliation. Beth Fowkes Tobin, *Picturing Imperial Power: Colonial Subjects in Eighteenth-century British Painting* (Durham NC, Duke UP, 1999), chapter 3.

22. For the influence of the painting of the death of Wolfe, see Kathleen Wilson, *The Sense of the People: Politics, Culture and Imperialism in England, 1715–1785* (Cambridge, CUP, 1995), p. 195 and Nicholas Rogers, 'Brave Wolfe: the making of a hero', in Kathleen Wilson (ed.), *A New Imperial History: Culture, Identity and Modernity in the Empire 1660–1840* (Cambridge, CUP, 2004), pp. 239–59. See also Tobin, *Picturing Imperial Power.*

23. Glyn Williams, *The Death of Captain Cook: A Hero Made and Unmade* (London, Profile, 2008) is the most accessible of a considerable literature.

24. Another famous rendition was by Arthur William Devis, with Daniel Maclise following several decades later.
25. For a recent popular account of West, see Loyd Grossman, *Benjamin West and the Struggle to be Modern* (London, Merrell, 2015).
26. Jane Kamensky, *A Revolution in Color: The World of John Singleton Copley* (New York, Norton, 2016), charts the relationship between the artist's personal life and his response to the events of the day.
27. Painted in 1799, two years after the battle off the coast of the Netherlands in October 1797.
28. For a general survey of panoramas, see Ralph Hyde, *Panoramania! The Art and Entertainment of the All-embracing View* (London, Trefoil and Barbican Art Gallery, 1988).
29. See V&A Museum: https://collections.vam.ac.uk/item/O78231/the-storming-of-seringapatam-panorama-key-lee-john/ (accessed 6 February 2020). See also McAleer, *Picturing India*, p. 26. Ker Porter's panorama covered some 2,500 square feet of canvas and toured the country. It was shown in Edinburgh at the panorama building on the Mound, built in 1823 to show the panoramas of the inventor of the idea, Robert Barker. For Ker Porter, see Anne Buddle, 'India associations in Scotland's national galleries: from Tipu to the trenches and Simla to Surrealism', in Roger Jeffery (ed.), *India in Edinburgh* (New Delhi, Social Science Press, 2019), p. 91.
30. MacKenzie, 'Art and the Empire', p. 299.
31. The dungeon is now a tourist attraction in Srirangapatna. The picture is in the National Gallery of Scotland, www.nationalgalleries.org/art-and-artists/5685/general-sir-david-baird-discovering-body-sultan-tippoo-sahib-after-having-captured-seringapatam-4th (accessed 3 July 2020). Wilkie copied his depiction of Baird from a statue by Laurence Macdonald.
32. John E. Crowley, *Imperial Landscapes: Britain's Global Visual Culture, 1745–1820* (New Haven, CT, YUP, 2011).
33. Mildred Archer, *Visions of India: The Sketchbooks of William Simpson, 1859–1862* (London, Phaidon, 1986).
34. Gordon appeared in stained glass in the Blairgowrie Methodist Church, Perthshire, built in 1885–7, and also in the chapel of Sedbergh School in Cumbria.
35. J.W.M. Hichberger, 'Democratising glory? The Victoria Cross paintings of Louis Desanges', *Oxford Art Journal*, 7, 2 (1984), pp. 42–51. Hichberger saw this project as part of the struggle between middle classes and aristocracy for control of the army after the Crimean disasters.
36. This painting was commissioned by the *Illustrated London News* and an engraving was published in that journal.
37. J.W.M. Hichberger, *Images of the Army: The Military in British Art 1815–1914* (Manchester, MUP, 1988).
38. The *Illustrated London News*, for example, issued a lavishly illustrated supplement, priced at one shilling, to commemorate the visit of the Prince of Wales to India.
39. This painting in the collection of Glasgow Museums appears as the cover of John M. MacKenzie and T.M. Devine (eds), *Scotland and the British Empire* (Oxford, OUP, 2011).
40. For panoramas relating to the British Empire, see Denise Blake Oleksijczuk, *The First Panoramas: Visions of British Imperialism* (Minneapolis, MN, University of Minnesota Press, 2011). Ralph Hyde in *Panoramania!* suggested (p. 11), that panoramas constituted an extraordinary combination of high art and entertainment, bringing together 'art, illusion, education, and cultural presence' (p. 16). Apparently (p. 24), panoramas were admired by Sir Joshua Reynolds and Benjamin West.
41. For Lear, see Scott Wilcox, *Edward Lear and the Art of Travel* (New Haven, CT, Yale Center for British Art, 2000), pp. 111–12 and Vidya Dehejia, *Impossible Picturesqueness:*

Lear's Indian Watercolours, 1873–75 (Sri Lanka, Grantha, 1990). On arriving in Bombay in November 1873, Lear wrote ecstatically of the 'overpoweringly amazing [sights] ... colours and costumes ... myriadism of impossible picturesqueness'. Also see Jeffrey Auerbach, 'The picturesque and the homogenization of empire', *British Art Journal*, 5, 1 (spring/summer 2004), pp. 47–54.

42. J.R. Harper, *Painting in Canada: A History* (Toronto, University of Toronto Press, 1977). See also Dennis Reid, *A Concise History of Canadian Painting* (Don Mills, Ontario, OUP, 1988).

43. This survey is based upon the collections of the National Gallery of Canada in Ottawa, the Montreal Museum of Fine Arts and various other galleries and their publications.

44. The quotation comes from the caption. See also Marc Mayer, *Art in Canada* (Ottawa, National Gallery of Canada, 2017), p. 218.

45. See: www.gallery.ca/collection/artwork/the-last-of-the-hurons-zacharie-vincent (accessed 9 March 2020).

46. Ironically, the Beothuk people of Newfoundland, one of whom was the subject of Lady Hamilton's portrait miniature, really were doomed to extinction. See Kristina Huneault, 'Always there: Aboriginal people and the consolation of miniature portraiture in British North America', in Barringer, Quilley and Fordham (eds), *Art and the British Empire*, pp. 288–308.

47. R.H. Hubbard, *Antoine Plamondon (1802–1895), Théophile Hamel(1817–1870): Two Painters of Quebec / Deux Peintres de Québec* (Ottawa, National Gallery of Canada, 1970).

48. Illustrated in Mayer, *Art in Canada*, pp. 92–3.

49. This can be seen in the Montreal Museum of Fine Arts.

50. Krieghoff was partly trained in Dusseldorf, Germany. He continued to be well travelled throughout his life.

51. Illustrated in Mayer, *Art in Canada*, p. 122.

52. Ibid., p. 126.

53. Harper, *Painting in Canada*, p. 148.

54. Ibid., p. 186.

55. For example, see his *Smelter Stacks, Copper Cliff* of 1936. Ibid., p. 69.

56. Ibid., p. 217.

57. Thomson died in 1917, and the group was only fully formed and recognised after his death. They included Franklin Carmichael, Lawren Harris, A.Y. Jackson, Frank Johnston, Arthur Lismer, J.E.A. Macdonald and F.H. Varley. Although the group was entirely male, some women exhibited with them. Their last exhibition was in 1931. David Silcox, *The Group of Seven and Tom Thomson* (Toronto, Firefly Books, 2001). Joan Murray's *The Best of the Group of Seven* (Toronto, McClelland and Stewart, 1984), contains an essay by Lawren Harris on the coming together of the group.

58. There is now an extensive literature on Carr, but see Sarah Milroy and Ian Dejardin, *From the Forest to the Sea: Emily Carr in British Columbia* (Fredericton, New Brunswick, Goose Lane Editions, 2015).

59. Thomas Keneally, 'Dead heart/live heart', in *Australia* (London, Royal Academy of Arts, 2013), pp. 30–3. In this catalogue, p. 15, Allan Myers has argued that visual art was the first (presumably distinctive) Australian art form, developed well ahead of Australian literature, music, dance and theatre.

60. This painting, owned by the British Royal Collection Trust, is on permanent loan to the Parliament House in Canberra. The Royal Exhibition Building was designed by the Melbourne architects Reed and Barnes and is a rare survivor of the international exhibition movement of the late nineteenth and early twentieth centuries.

61. *Terra nullius* constituted the theory that the land of Australia was not truly owned in the western legal tradition since Aborigines were nomads. This supposedly justified the fact that there were never treaty relations with Aboriginal people to enact any supposed

transfer of ownership. These issues only began to be resolved in legal cases in tl twentieth and early twenty-first centuries.

62. See *Australia* catalogue, footnote 3. The pioneering book of Bernard Smith, *Plac and Tradition: A Study of Australian Art since 1788*, first published in 1945, remain able. The edition of 1979 (Melbourne, OUP) has a new introduction. Smith i' an extensive chronological table, passing through early colonial, colonial and romantic periods; then early Australian, academic and impressionist phases, u modern movement. See also Robert Hughes' *Art of Australia* (Harmondsworth, 1984).

63. See: http://adb.anu.edu.au/biography/watling-thomas-2776 (accessed 11 2020).

64. See: http://adb.anu.edu.au/biography/macquarie-lachlan-2419 (accessed 1 2020).

65. Jeanette Hoorn, 'Joseph Lycett: the pastoral landscape in early colonial Au *Journal*, 26 (26 June 2014), www.ngv.vic.gov.au/essay/joseph-lycett-the-pas scape-in-early-colonial-australia/ (accessed 2 April 2020). Some examples art can be found in John Turner, *Joseph Lycett: Governor Macquarie's Ct* (Newcastle, NSW, Hunter History Publications, 1997).

66. *Australia* catalogue, p. 93.

67. Jane Lydon, *Imperial Emotions: The Politics of Empathy across the Bt* (Cambridge, CUP, 2020), pp. 52–3.

68. Ron Appleyard, *S. T. Gill: The South Australian Years, 1839–1852* (Adelaid of South Australia, 1986). Also Ian Auhl and Denis Marfleet, *Australia's E Era, 1841–1851: Paintings by S. T. Gill* (Adelaide, Rigby, 1975).

69. Smith, *Place, Taste and Tradition*, pp. 77–8.

70. Donald Simpson and Peter Lyon, *Commonwealth in Focus: 130 Years History* (Melbourne, Clemenger Harvie, 1982), p. 118.

71. *Australia* catalogue, p. 296.

72. Lydon, *Imperial Emotions*, p. 112. The quotation is from the Earl c patron of the exhibition.

73. Quilley and Bonehill (eds), *William Hodges 1744–1797*.

74. Augustus Earle, *A Narrative of Nine Months' Residence in New Zeala* published 1832, a later 1909 edition from Whitecombe and Tombs has been placed on the web by the Gutenberg Project: ww files/11933/11933-h/11933-h.htm (accessed 17 March, 2020). Ea artist on the *Beagle* expedition.

75. Ibid., chapters 7 and 29.

76. Pamela Ruskin, 'George French Angas, pioneer artist', *Walkabout*, 3:

77. Michael Dunn, *New Zealand Painting: A Concise History* (Auckl Auckland Press, 2003), pp. 26–8.

78. See: www.lindaueronline.co.nz/artist/the-materials-and-techniques-((accessed 17 March 2020). See also www.lindaueronline.co.nz/arti: the-portraits-of-gottfried-lindauer (accessed 17 March 2020) and co.nz/artist/gottfried-lindauer-a-career-in-new-zealand (accessed 1;

79. Gil Docking, *Two Hundred Years of New Zealand Painting* (Me 1971), p. 62.

80. Ibid., p. 54.

81. See: www.nzafa.com (accessed 24 March 2020).

82. Christopher Johnstone, *Landscape Paintings of New Zealand: A South* (Auckland, Random House, 2006), p. 220.

83. Johnstone, *Landscape Paintings*, examines the influence of th seventy-three New Zealand painters.

84. Ibid., pp. 210 and 190.

85. Ibid., p. 138.
86. The pioneering survey is Esmé Berman, *Art and Artists in South Africa: An Illustrated Biographical Dictionary and Survey of Painters and Graphic Artists since 1875* (Cape Town, A.A. Balkema, 1974), which, with caveats about the period when it was written, offers a convenient introduction. A more modern approach is John Giblin and Chris Spring, *South Africa: The Art of a Nation* (London, Thames and Hudson, 2016). Giblin and Spring conveniently identify the many immigrant streams, including Dutch, British, Malay, Chinese and Indian.
87. Ian D. Colvin, 'South African aquatints: Samuel Daniell and his work', *The State*, 6, 6 (December 1911), pp. 557–65. Aquatints are a form of printmaking in which various tonal effects can be achieved, almost resembling watercolour. This article, and other items quoted in this chapter, was supplied in the early stages of the research by the British Library's interlibrary loan photocopying service. See also John McAleer, *Representing Africa: Landscape, Exploration and Empire in Southern Africa 1780–1870* (Manchester, MUP, 2010), p. 161.
88. The Trekboers were Afrikaner farmers who progressively moved into the interior in search of land. The Voortrekkers represent the major migratory thrust of such farmers of the 1830s.
89. McAleer, *Representing Africa*, contains much information about Baines. For older studies, see J.V. Woolford, 'Africa through the eyes of a painter-explorer', *Geographical Magazine*, March 1983; Frank R. Bradlow, 'The colourful Thomas Baines', *South African Library Bulletin*, 29 (1975), pp. 138–43; and 'Thomas Baines: his art in Rhodesia from the original paintings in the Central African Archives' (Salisbury, Central African Archives, 1956). Many of Baines's oil paintings and other images are held by the Royal Geographical Society in London, https://images.rgs.org/searchresults.aspx?S=Thomas%20Baines (accessed 19 March 2020).
90. His extensive journals of exploratory and prospecting activities were published as *The Northern Goldfields Diaries of Thomas Baines (First Journey 1869–1870; First Journey 1870–1871; Second Journey 1871–1872)*, edited by J.P.R. Wallis and containing several illustrations of Baines's art, 3 vols (London, Chatto and Windus, 1946).
. For South African artists the baobab was the equivalent of the Australian eucalypt in its role as the iconic tree of the region, presenting particular challenges in its representation.
Harper, *Painting in Canada*, p. 227. Even then, some critics from the London Royal Academy considered that Canadian art was not sufficiently Canadian, but demonstrated the extent of French influence.
Tom August, 'Art and Empire – Wembley, 1924', *History Today*, 43 (October 1993), pp. 38–44. Also Ann Davis, 'The Wembley controversy in Canadian art', *Canadian Historical Review*, 54, 1 (March 1993), pp. 48–74.
Edward Salmon and Major A.A. Longden, *The Literature of the Empire and the Art of the Empire* (London, Collins, 1924), pp. 257–88. The quotations are on pp. 257–8. This was the eleventh volume in the twelve-volume survey of empire associated with the Wembley Exhibition. The general editor was Hugh Gunn and there was an advisory committee of the imperial 'great and good'. Literature occupied a much larger space than art.
Sixty posters are in Stephen Constantine, *Buy and Build: The Advertising Posters of the Empire Marketing Board* (London, HMSO, 1986). See also Melanie Horton, *Empire Marketing Board Posters* (London, Scala, 2010).
Lord Hailey, *An African Survey: A Study of Problems Arising in Africa South of the Sahara* (London, OUP, 1938), p. 1304. This perhaps remains true as visitors to the remarkably popular Quai Branly Museum in Paris can testify.
Mildred Archer, *Company Paintings: Indian Paintings of the British Period* (London, Victoria and Albert Museum, 1992). This book covers various areas of India, as well

as Nepal, Burma, Sri Lanka and Malacca (Malaysia). More recently, Dalrymple (ed.), *Forgotten Masters*. See also Pratapaditya Pal and Vidya Dehejia, *From Merchants to Emperors: British Artists and India, 1757–1930* (Ithaca, NY, Cornell UP, 1986), p. 127. This book surveys many artists who worked in India and moves on to consider photography.

98. The paragraphs that follow are partly based upon Tapati Guha-Thakurta, *The Making of a New 'Indian' Art: Artists, Aesthetics and Nationalism in Bengal, c. 1850–1920* (Cambridge, CUP, 1992).

99. For Kipling, see the V&A catalogue of 2017: Bryant and Weber (eds), *John Lockwood Kipling*.

100. Partha Mitter, *Much-maligned Monsters: A History of European Reactions to Indian Art* (Oxford, OUP, 1977), particularly chapters V and VI. See also Mitter's monumental *Art and Nationalism in Colonial India 1850–1922* (Cambridge, CUP, 1994).

101. John M. MacKenzie, *Orientalism: History, Theory and the Arts* (Manchester, MUP, 1995), pp. 132–3. See also William Greenwood and Lucien de Guise, *Inspired by the East: How the Islamic World Influenced Western Art* (London, British Museum, 2019); Nicholas Tromans (ed.), *The Lure of the East: British Orientalist Painting* (London, Tate Publishing, 2008); and Lucien de Guise, *Beyond Orientalism: How the West was Won over by Islamic Art* (Kuala Lumpur, Malaysia, Islamic Arts Museum, 2008).

102. Barringer, Quilley and Fordham (eds), *Art and the British Empire*, barely notice these developments.

103. See: www.gallery.ca/collection/collecting-areas/indigenous-art/inuit-art# (accessed 18 March 2020). Quamajug, a new and highly innovative Inuit art centre, was opened in Winnipeg in early 2021.

104. For the extent of such collecting, see John M. MacKenzie, *Museums and Empire* (Manchester, MUP, 2009), chapters 2 and 3. See also Sarah Longair and John McAleer (eds), *Curating Empire: Museums and the British Imperial Experience* (Manchester, MUP, 2012).

105. See: www.thecanadianencyclopedia.ca/en/article/aboriginal-art-in-canada (accessed 9 March 2020). Such carving can be seen at the Museum of Anthropology in the University of British Columbia and at the Royal British Columbia Museum in Victoria, BC. Modern carvers keep the tradition alive and provide demonstrations for visitors.

106. Wally Caruana and Franchesca Cubillo, 'Country: Aboriginal art', in Thomas Keneally, *Australia* catalogue, pp. 42–89.

107. An undated example is *Rock Paintings in Africa* (Claremont, Cape Town, South African Archaeological Society). This contains examples of paintings from throughout the region, carefully copied by specialists. See also Roger Summers, *Prehistoric Rock Art of the Federation of Rhodesia and Nyasaland*, paintings and descriptions by Elizabeth Goodall, C.K. Cooke and J. Desmond Clark (Salisbury, National Publications Trust, 1959); Peter Garlake, *The Painted Caves: An Introduction to the Prehistoric Art of Zimbabwe* (Harare, Zimbabwe, Modus, 1987).

108. Walter Battiss, *The Artists of the Rocks* (Pretoria, Red Fawn Press, 1948).

109. Annie E. Coombes, *History after Apartheid: Visual Culture and Public Memory* (Durham NC, Duke UP, 2003).

110. The classic instance of the looting of great examples of African art comes from the British Benin campaign of 1897. Annie E. Coombes, *Reinventing Africa: Museums, Material Culture and Popular Imagination* (New Haven, CT, Yale UP, 1994). For the seizure of African artistic artefacts in the Congo, see Enid Schildkrout and Curtis A. Keim (eds), *The Scramble for Art in Central Africa* (Cambridge, CUP, 1998).

111. MacKenzie, 'Art and the Empire'.

Chapter 5 Statuary and Sculpture

1. See R. McKenzie, *Sculpture in Glasgow: An Illustrated Handbook* (Glasgow, Foulis Archive, 1999). The statue of Lord Roberts (described by George Frederick Watts as the finest equestrian statue of its age) overlooks Kelvingrove Park and the university in Glasgow. It has a panel listing Roberts' campaigns (original spellings) – the Indian Mutiny, Umbeyla, Abyssinia, Lushai, Afghanistan, Burmah, South Africa – and sculptured friezes of troops, including Gurkhas and Sikhs. Unveiled in 1916, after a successful public subscription, it commemorated the freedom of the city given to Roberts in 1914. It was copied by Henry Poole from the original in Calcutta by Harry Bates. Another copy in London's Horse Guards lacks the plinth, the sculptured panels and the striking location.

2. For comparative material on Belgium, see Matthew G. Stanard, *The Leopard, the Lion and the Cock: Colonial Memories and Monuments in Belgium* (Leuven, Leuven UP, 2019). Fresh demands for the destruction of statues of Leopold II were made in June 2020. For France, see Robert Aldrich, *Vestiges of the Colonial Empire in France: Monuments, Museums and Colonial Memories* (Basingstoke, Palgrave Macmillan, 2005); also Robert Aldrich, 'Commemorating colonialism in a post-colonial world', *e-Rea*, online journal, 10, 1 (2012), https://journals.openedition.org/erea/2803?lang=en (accessed 28 October 2019).

3. James E. Young, *The Texture of Memory: Holocaust Memorials and Meaning* (New Haven, CT, YUP, 1993), p. 211.

4. Iain Hay, Andrew Hughes and Mark Tutton, 'Monuments, memorials and marginalisation in Adelaide's Prince Henry Gardens', *Geografiska Annales*, Series B, Human Geography, 86, 3 (September 2004), pp. 200–16.

5. Mulualem Daba Tola, 'The historiography and values of statue construction: focus on global perspectives', *Humanities and Social Sciences*, 5, 2 (2017), pp. 53–9.

6. For the relationship between sculpture and ceremonial, see Martina Droth, Jason Edwards and Michael Hatt (eds), *Sculpture Victorious: Art in an Age of Invention, 1837–1901* (New Haven, CT, YUP, 2014), pp. 102–47. There is a list of memorials to Queen Victoria on p. 132.

7. For example, the then Mayor of London, Ken Livingstone, suggested that statues of imperial figures in Trafalgar Square and elsewhere were no longer relevant to modern Britain and should be removed: 'Mayor attacks generals in battle of Trafalgar Square', *The Guardian*, 20 October 2000. The generals in question were Sir Henry Havelock and Sir Charles Napier. There have been similar controversies about statues in Australia and Canada, largely on the grounds of violence against and dispossession of indigenous peoples. See for example an article by Paul Daley in *The Guardian*, 24 August 2017, 'Statues are not history'.

8. Quoted in Ramachandra Guha, *A Corner of a Foreign Field* (London, Picador, 2002), pp. 68–9.

9. Ibid., pp. 137–8, quoting an article by Jim Masselos.

10. Mamta Kumari, *The Life and Times of Gopal Krishna Gokhale* (New Delhi, Ocean Books, 2018), pp. 164–5.

11. Joan Coutu, *Persuasion and Propaganda: Monuments and the Eighteenth-century British Empire* (Montreal, McGill-Queen's UP, 2006).

12. In the case of one in New York, the lead used for the torso and horse (the head was removed to England by a British officer) were melted down and converted into thousands of bullets. Ibid., p. 4.

13. Ibid., pp. 7–8.

14. It is unclear where this happened, but Lahore seems most likely. B.R. Nanda, *Gokhale: The Indian Moderates and the British Raj* (Princeton, NJ, Princeton UP, 1977), p. 271. See also Gilles Teulié, 'World War Two iconoclasm: the destruction and reconstruction of memorials to Queen Victoria and Edward VII on the French Riviera', *e-Rea*, online

journal, 14, 2 (15 June 2017), https://journals.openedition.org/erea/5809 (accessed 26 February 2020), p. 10. An illustration of this event, from *La Croix Illustrée*, appears on p. 11. War-time iconoclasm comes perhaps in a different category: statues of Queen Victoria and Edward VII on the Riviera were attacked, damaged and in one case totally destroyed, by German and Italian troops during the Second World War. There were efforts to reconstruct them after the war, not just as an act of friendship in the alliance with Britain but also to help maintain the British tourist industry. Similarly, statues in Hong Kong were damaged and destroyed by the Japanese occupiers. Some of them were reproduced after the war, though a square consciously created as a royal space was later transformed into a public park with more neutral connotations. Wing Sze Tam, 'Public space and British colonial power: the transformation of Hong Kong Statues Square, 1890s–1920s', MPhil. thesis, Lingnan University, Hong Kong, 2014.

15. The development of national consciousness during such wars is charted in Kathleen Wilson, *The Sense of the People: Politics, Culture and Imperialism in England, 1715–1785* (Cambridge, CUP, 1995). For Vernon, see ibid., chapter 3. For Wolfe, see Nicholas Rogers, 'Brave Wolfe, the making of a hero', in Kathleen Wilson (ed.), *A New Imperial History: Culture, Identity and Modernity in Britain and the Empire, 1660–1840* (Cambridge, CUP, 2004), pp. 239–59.

16. There has been some controversy about this statue in postcolonial Barbados, but it survives. There is a hint that it may be regarded as good for tourism. See: https://barbados.org/lord-nelson-statue-barbados.htm#.Xlk-g0qnyUk (accessed 28 February 2020).

17. A proposal to move this to a more Anglophone quarter of the city was never carried out. Erected in 1808–9, this Nelson memorial, in common with the one in Barbados, is a good deal older than the column in Trafalgar Square. See: www.victorianweb.org/authors/dickens/montreal/7.html (accessed 28 February 2020).

18. John M. MacKenzie, *Propaganda and Empire* (Manchester, MUP, 1984); Berny Sèbe, *Heroic Imperialists in Africa: The Promotion of British and French Colonial Heroes, 1870–1939* (Manchester, MUP, 2013).

19. See for example Kostas Vlassopoulos, 'Imperial encounters: discourses on empire and the uses of Ancient history during the eighteenth century', in Mark Bradley (ed.), *Classics and Imperialism in the British Empire* (Oxford, OUP, 2010), pp. 29–53; also Rama Sundari Mantena, 'Imperial ideology and the uses of Rome in Britain's Indian Empire', in ibid., pp. 54–73. For the later period, see Virginia Hoselitz, *Imagining Roman Britain: Victorian Responses to a Roman Past* (Woodbridge, Suffolk, Boydell Press, 2007) and Sarah J. Butler, *Britain and its Empire in the Shadow of Rome: The Reception of Rome in Socio-political Debate from the 1850s to the 1920s* (London, Bloomsbury, 2012).

20. Examples of this include the East India Company employing the Dutch sculptor Michael Rysbrach to supply the extraordinary overmantel showing Britannia receiving the riches of the East for the Directors' Court Room in their headquarters.

21. John McAleer, *Picturing India: People, Places and the World of the East India Company* (London, British Library, 2017).

22. The cost to the East India Company of these statues was £600. By this time, monuments to officers who had distinguished themselves in imperial contexts were appearing in Westminster Abbey. An example is Vice-Admiral Charles Watson, who had helped to suppress piracy against Company ships. Barbara Groseclose, *British Sculpture and the Company Raj: Church Monuments and Public Statuary in Madras, Calcutta and Bombay to 1858* (London, Associated University Presses, 1995), pp. 54, 56–8.

23. Mary Ann Steggles, *Statues of the Raj* (London, British Association for Cemeteries in South Asia, 2000).

24. This has been suggested by Benedict Read in the preface to Mary Ann Steggles and Richard Barnes, *British Statuary in India: New View and Old Memories* (Kirstead, Norfolk, Frontier Publishing, 2011), p. 9.

25. James Douglas, *Glimpses of Old Bombay and Western India* (London, Sampson Low, 1900).
26. Mary Ann Steggles, 'Set in stone: Victoria's monuments in India', *History Today*, 51 (February 2001).
27. There were, for example, two in Cawnpore (Kanpur) alone, a particularly sensitive place because of the 1857 events there. One of these was in the unusual material of aluminium.
28. See: https://en.wikipedia.org/wiki/Embassy_of_the_United_Kingdom,_Bangkok (accessed 2 December 2019).
29. Cornwallis, who had surrendered to the Americans at Yorktown, continued his career in India and elsewhere.
30. A marble bust of Victoria was produced for the same museum.
31. Steggles and Barnes, *British Sculpture*, pp. 203, 230, 265 and 269. The sculptors were, respectively, Matthew Noble, James Forsyth, Alfred Gilbert and W. Hamo Thornycroft.
32. Martin Gilbert (ed.), *Servant of India: Sir James Dunlop Smith, Private Secretary to the Viceroy* (London Longmans, 1966), pp. 88–9.
33. One of these is the Scottish cemetery, recently the subject of survey and restoration. See, for example, https://scottishcemeterykolkata.wordpress.com/ (accessed 2 December 2019). The other is the more famous South Park Street cemetery, filled with grand tombs and memorials. There are a number of websites, the one containing the best illustrations is https://roadsandkingdoms.com/2015/city-of-forgotten-souls/ (accessed 2 December 2019).
34. The Catholic cemetery in Agra contains notable monuments, including an imitation of the Taj Mahal.
35. Vijaya Gupchup and T. Thomas (eds), *St. Thomas Cathedral, Bombay: Witness to History* (Bombay, Eminence Designs, 2005).
36. Steggles and Barnes, *British Statuary*, pp. 238–9.
37. Personal observation on a visit to Port Louis in 2004.
38. La Bourdonnais has an impressive statue at his birthplace, St Malo in Brittany.
39. See: https://en.wikipedia.org/wiki/List_of_public_art_in_the_City_of_Sydney (accessed 11 February 2022).
40. For the Australian examples, see Benjamin Wilkie, *The Scots in Australia, 1788–1938* (Woodbridge, Boydell Press, 2017), pp. 93–7.
41. See: https://en.wikipedia.org/wiki/Van_Wouw_Museum (accessed 31 March 2020). This was Anton van Wouw's last home and is now part of the University of Pretoria. Korhaan went to the USA and joined Barnum and Bailey's circus, staying with them for some thirty years. He thus became a twentieth-century equivalent of some of the African human spectacles of the nineteenth century.
42. A similar statue, by the same sculptor, Sir Thomas Brock, was erected in Sydney in the 1920s.
43. These have been charted in a major article by Paul McGarr, '"The viceroys are disappearing from the roundabouts in Delhi": British symbols of power in post-colonial India', *Modern Asian Studies*, 49, 3 (2015), pp. 787–831.
44. Personal observation.
45. The state of Uttar Pradesh removed all British statues, mainly because of sensitivities about the locations of the 1857 rising, while others such as Bihar and Tamil Nadu have been more relaxed.
46. See article by Nadir Sidiqqi and Shameen Khan in *Dawn*, 2 March 2014, https://widerimage.reuters.com/story/from-raj-to-architectural-riches (accessed 20 July 2018).
47. A.S. Bhalla, *Monuments, Power and Poverty in India: From Ashoka to the Raj* (London, I.B. Tauris, 2015). Bhalla wrote (p. 19) that it was 'to the credit of the Indian authorities' that this statue of Queen Victoria had survived.
48. McGarr suggests that this was moved into storage, but it is in fact in Coronation Park.
49. Bhalla, *Monuments*, p. 111. See also the, albeit incomplete, table of the 'Current status of the monuments of the Raj' on p. 126.

50. Seen in Chennai in January 2020.
51. See: www.alamy.com/stock-photo-a-statue-of-queen-empress-victoria-stands-in-the-gardens-of-madras-22527134.html (accessed 26 February 2020). In this image the statue is surrounded by an elaborate iron pavilion. This pavilion is absent in a photograph of c.1897, showing the statue outside the Victoria Memorial Hall, surrounded by a large number of local Indian citizens, www.alamy.com/stock-photo-statue-of-queen-victoria-madras-chennai-india-circa-1897-date-circa-105397017.html (accessed 26 February 2020).
52. See: www.newindianexpress.com/states/andhra-pradesh/2017/apr/08/iconic-queen-victoria-statue-loses-its-sheen-lies-in-utter-neglect-1591332.html (accessed 26 February 2020). The report dates from April 2017.
53. Francis G. Hutchins, *The Illusion of Permanence: British Imperialism in India* (Princeton, NJ, Princeton UP, 1967).
54. Churchill's celebrated 'If the British Empire and its Commonwealth should survive for a thousand years' seemed like an unfortunate echo of the Nazi 'thousand-year Reich'.
55. Christopher W. London, *Bombay Gothic* (Mumbai, India Book House, 2002), pp. 63–5; Julius Bryant and Susan Weber (eds), *John Lockwood Kipling: Arts and Crafts in the Punjab and London* (New Haven, CT, YUP, 2017), pp. 82–6.
56. Peter Donaldson, *Remembering the South African War: Britain and the Memory of the Anglo-Boer War, from 1899 to the Present* (Liverpool, Liverpool UP, 2013).
57. A Scottish example from the 1899–1902 Anglo-Boer War is the memorial in the Perthshire village of Alyth, which contains the names only of local landed gentry, officer casualties during the war. Casualties from 'other ranks' are not recorded. On the other hand, the memorial in the Angus village of Edzell unusually displays the names of all ranks from the local area.
58. Sir Donald Mackenzie Wallace, *The Web of Empire: A Diary of the Imperial Tour of their Royal Highnesses the Duke and Duchess of Cornwall and York in 1901* (London, Macmillan, 1902), p. 323.
59. See: https://nzhistory.govt.nz/media/photo/invercargill-memorial-south-african-war (accessed 10 February 2022).
60. Joy Damousi, 'War and commemoration: "The responsibility of empire"', in Deryck M. Schreuder and Stuart Ward (eds), *Australia's Empire* (Oxford, OUP, 2008), pp. 292–3.
61. Brian S. Osborne and Geraint B. Osborne, 'The cast[e]ing of heroic landscapes of power: constructing Canada's Pantheon on Parliament Hill', *Material History Review*, 60 (fall 2004), pp. 35–47.
62. Brian S. Osborne, 'Constructing landscapes of power: the George Etienne Cartier monument, Montreal', *Journal of Historical Geography*, 24, 4 (October 1998), pp. 431–58.
63. David A. Johnson, 'The Great War's impact on imperial Delhi', in Michael J.K. Walsh and Andrekos Varnava (eds), *The Great War and the British Empire: Culture and Society* (London, Routledge, 2016), pp. 249–63.
64. By 1968, after the death of Nehru and the rise of new generations of politicians, any residual respect for the British monarchy had declined. See Lucy Peck, *Delhi: A Thousand Years of Building* (New Delhi, Roli Books, 2005), p. 268. Funding for the museum was announced in *The Hindu*, 7 October 2015. See Gaurav Vivek Bhatnagar, 'National War Memorial takes shape six decades after being conceived', *The Wire*, 21 April 2018, https://thewire.in/urban/national-war-museum-delhi-india-gate (accessed 13 July 2018).
65. The other Burmese cemetery and memorial is Thanbyuzayat, south of Moulmein, and close to a new memorial museum to the Japanese Burma–Siam railway.
66. Nuala C. Johnson, 'Sculpting heroic histories: celebrating the centenary of the 1798 rebellion in Ireland', *Transactions of the Institution of British Geographers*, 19, 1 (1994), pp. 78–93.
67. Yvonne Whelan, 'Monuments, power and contested space – the iconography of Sackville Street (O'Connell Street) before independence (1922)', *Irish Geographer*, 34, 1 (2001), pp. 11–33.

68. Yvonne Whelan, 'The construction and destruction of a colonial landscape: monuments to British monarchs in Dublin before and after independence', *Journal of Historical Geography*, 28, 4 (2002), pp. 508–33; Yvonne Whelan, 'Symbolising the state – the iconography of O'Connell Street and environs after independence (1922)', *Irish Geographer*, 34, 2 (2001), pp. 135–56.

69. Kate O'Malley, *Ireland, India and Empire: Indo-Irish Radical Connections, 1919–64* (Manchester, MUP, 2008).

70. See: www.thejournal.ie/nelsons-pillar-destruction-myths-2647389-Dec2016/ (accessed 26 February 2020). See also Heather Stedman, 'Monuments to the Duke of Wellington in nineteenth-century Ireland: forging British and imperial identities', *Irish Geographer*, 46, 1–2 (2013).

71. Another statue which stands at the level of the viewer, a clear rejection of plinths, is an engaging one of the Scottish poet Robert Ferguson (1750–74) outside the Canongate Kirk Edinburgh, where the poet is buried. This statue is so humanly appealing that passers-by have been known to provide it with hats and gloves in winter and take 'selfies' arm in arm with it.

72. Charles Turley, *With the Prince Round the Empire* (London, Methuen, 1926), p. 70.

73. *The Times of India*, 22 November 1921.

74. See: www.dailymail.co.uk/indiahome/indianews/article-4064250/Statue-Shivaji-PM-Modi-lays-foundation-Shivaji-memorial-worth-Rs-3600-crore-Mumbai-irking-environmentalists-fishermen.html (accessed 30 July 2018). The cost converts into more than £400 million.

75. For these and others, www.atlasobscura.com/things-to-do/canada/statues (accessed 8 November 2019).

76. Such controversies have been featured in the British press, including *The Guardian*, 24 August 2017, www.theguardian.com/australia-news/postcolonial-blog/2017/aug/25/statues-are-not-history-here-are-six-in-australia-that-need-rethinking (accessed 8 November 2019).

77. See: www.cricketcountry.com/criclife/22-cricketers-who-are-immortalised-in-statue-at-a-cricket-ground-510729 (accessed 28 November 2019) and the more comprehensive site: C.B. Stride, F.E. Thomas and J.P. Wilson, 'The sporting statues project' (2012), www.sportingstatues.com (accessed 28 November 2019). W.G. Grace, the most celebrated English cricketer, lacked a statue until one was unveiled at Lord's (without much ceremony) in 2000. Graham Gooch also merited a statue. In Britain there are more statues of footballers and football managers.

78. Participating in an Oxford Union debate in May 2015, despite my sympathies, I was barracked by the Rhodes Must Fall movement. Earlier that day, I had noticed a bust of Rhodes in a side-street commemorating him having lodged in the building.

79. See: www.theguardian.com/uk-news/2016/mar/16/the-real-meaning-of-rhodes-must-fall (accessed 27 October 2019).

80. Richard Drayton, 'Rhodes must not fall?', *Third Text*, 33, 4–5 (2019), pp. 651–66.

81. See: www.change.org/p/glasgow-city-council-remove-the-racist-colonial-statue-of-frederick-roberts-in-the-kelvingrove-park. A more affectionate, though satirically disrespectful approach is reflected in the equestrian statue of the Duke of Wellington outside the city's Museum of Modern Art, which permanently sports a traffic cone on its head. Another Glasgow statue which has received some abuse is that of Donald Dewar, the original first minister of Scotland after devolution. He has been seen as a protagonist of the Union and has been plastered with independence stickers.

82. Attacks on statues spread to Canada in 2020, with statues as varied as 'Gassy Jack Deighton', a saloon keeper, and Captain George Vancouver, explorer of the West Coast, being attacked in Vancouver, British Columbia.

83. The Odessa authorities wished to revive the international character of the city, while the Cossacks objected to Catherine's destruction of the limited autonomy of Ukraine, as well as her efforts to suppress the Cossacks.

84. One of the first European travellers to see (in 1832) and enthuse about these statues, partly carved from the living stone, was Alexander Burnes, East India Company officer and explorer, killed in Kabul in 1841.
85. *The Guardian*, 14 December 2018, www.theguardian.com/world/2018/dec/14/racist-gandhi-statue-removed-from-university-of-ghana (accessed 8 November 2019).
86. *The Economic Times*, 21 December 2018, https://economictimes.indiatimes.com/news/international/world-news/ghana-to-reinstall-statue-of-mahatma-gandhi-at-prominent-location-in-accra/articleshow/67197361.cms (accessed 8 November 2019).

Chapter 6 Photography

1. For European art, see Dorothy Kosinski (ed.), *The Artist and the Camera* (New Haven, CT, YUP, 2000). In the case of India, see Brij Bhushan Sharma, 'Artists and photography: some Indian encounters', *History of Photography*, 12, 3 (1988), pp. 247-58.
2. Donald Simpson and Peter Lyon, *Commonwealth in Focus: 130 Years of Photographic History* (Melbourne, Clemenger Harvie, 1982), p. 117.
3. Examples included Dr Charles Eyles, Colonial Surgeon in the Gold Coast and British Honduras in the 1880s; Dr John Rowland in Lagos in the 1880s and 1890s, who produced an album of Lagos views in 1885; and Sir Benjamin Simpson, who became Surgeon General of the Indian Medical Service, joined missions to Bhutan and Burma, was particularly interested in ethnography, and exhibited a large number of Indian portraits at the 1862 London International Exhibition. Also Dr John Murray, who was in charge of the Agra Medical School after 1849 and published *Picturesque Views in the North-Western Province of India* (1859) and *Photographic Views of Agra and its Vicinity* (1858).
4. Examples included Thomas Alldridge, district commissioner in Sierra Leone; John Birch of the Ceylon and Straits Settlements civil services; Albert Hawes, who was a consul in East Africa and the Pacific islands; Charles Hose, a judge in Sarawak; John McNair in the Straits Settlements; Alfred Paul of the Indian Civil Service; Maurice Portman in the Andaman Islands; and W.S. Turton of the Public Works Department in Lagos.
5. There is a photograph of famine victims in the 1876-8 Madras famine in John Fabb, *The British Empire from Photographs: India* (London, Batsford, 1986), unpaginated, illustration 63.
6. The earliest picture postcards issued in Britain were probably products of Messrs George Stewart of Edinburgh. These were 'court'-sized cards, with small images in the top left-hand corner. By the end of the 1890s, Valentine's of Dundee had become significant postcard publishers. Tonie Holt and Valmai Holt, *Picture Postcards of the Golden Age* (London, Postcard Publishing Company, 1978), pp. 36-7.
7. Anandi Ramamurthy, *Imperial Persuaders: Images of Africa and Asia in British Advertising* (Manchester, MUP, 2003).
8. See: https://search.cam.ac.uk/web?query=Royal+tour+photographs&inst=CUL&offset=0&max=10. These are in the Royal Commonwealth photograph collection in Cambridge University Library.
9. The Brownie was first issued in 1900. Eaton S. Lothrop, 'The Brownie camera', *History of Photography*, 2, 1 (1978), pp. 1-10.
10. Republished by University of Toronto Press, 1994, with introduction by Marjory Harper. Other aristocratic travellers were Lord and Lady Brassey, who sailed extensively around the Empire after 1876 (until Lady Brassey's death in 1887) and took large numbers of photographs. Brassey was governor of Victoria, 1895-1900.
11. The former British Empire and Commonwealth Museum in Bristol collected no fewer than 500,000 photographs and 2,000 films, which are now in the archives of Bristol Museum, www.bristolmuseums.org.uk/bristol-museum-and-art-gallery/whats-on/empire-through-lens/ (accessed 29 March 2020). See also https://britishphotohistory.

ning.com/profiles/blogs/exhibition-empire-through-the-lens-pictures-from-the-british-empire (accessed 29 March 2020). London's Royal Geographical Society possesses an even larger collection of global significance, with many photos of imperial subjects, but only a small proportion currently digitised, https://images.rgs.org/ (accessed 30 March 2020).

12. Works include James R. Ryan, *Picturing Empire: Photography and the Visualisation of the British Empire* (London, Reaktion, 1997); James R. Ryan, *Photography and Exploration* (London, Reaktion, 2013); Joan M. Schwartz and James R. Ryan (eds), *Picturing Place: Photography and the Geographical Imagination* (London, I.B. Tauris, 2003); Eleanour M. Hight and Gary D. Sampson (eds), *Colonialist Photography: Imag(in)ing Race and Place* (London, Routledge, 2002); Jane Lydon, *Photography, Humanitarianism, Empire* (London, Bloomsbury 2016); also the essays in Paul S. Landau and Deborah D. Kaspin (eds), *Images and Empires* (Berkeley, University of California Press, 2002).

13. A special issue of the journal *History of Photography*, 'Anthropology and Colonial Endeavour', was guest edited by Elizabeth Edwards in 1997. The book series 'Photography, History; History, Photography', with a multi-disciplinary base, including sociology and anthropology, is published by Bloomsbury.

14. See Andrew Roberts, 'Photographs as sources for African history', papers presented at a conference in 1988' (SOAS, University of London, 1989); Roberts, 'Photographs and African history', review article, *Journal of African History* 29, 2 (1988), pp. 301–11; John Fabb, *The British Empire from Photographs: Africa* (London, Batsford, 1987); a work on photographs and the Boer War by Emanoel Lee, *To the Bitter End* (Harmondsworth, Penguin, 1987); Nicolas Monti (ed.), *Africa Then: Photographs 1840–1918* (London, Thames and Hudson, 1987). Other works on photography in Africa include M.W. Daly and H.E. Forbes, *The Sudan: Caught in Time* (Reading, Garnet, 1994), photographs from the Sudan Archive, Durham University Library; Colin Oman, *Egypt: Caught in Time* (Reading, Garnet, 1997) and 'Images of Africa', *African Research and Documentation, Journal of the SCOLMA*, 68 (1995); David Killingray and Andrew Roberts, 'An outline history of photography in Africa to c. 1940', *History in Africa*, 16 (1989), pp. 197–208. Also Heike Behrens, *Contesting Visibility: Photographic Practices on the East African Coast* (Bielefeld, Transcripts Verlag, 2013); Okwul Enwezor and Rory Bester (eds), *Rise and Fall of Apartheid Photography and the Bureaucracy of Everyday Life* (Munich, Prestel, 2013); John Peffer and Elisabeth L. Cameron (eds), *Portraiture and Photography in Africa* (Bloomington, IN, Indiana UP, 2013); Richard Vokes (ed.), *Photography in Africa: Ethnographic Perspectives* (Woodbridge, Suffolk, James Currey, 2012).

15. See Anne Maxwell, *Colonial Photography and Exhibitions: Representations of the 'Native' People and the Making of European Identities* (Leicester, Leicester University Press, 1999), which deals with photography and imperial exhibitions while also examining particular cases in the Pacific, Australasia and North America, with reciprocal effects on European identities.

16. Jane Lydon, *Imperial Emotions: The Politics of Empathy across the British Empire* (Cambridge, CUP, 2020).

17. A.D. Bensusan, *Silver Images: History of Photography in Africa* (Cape Town, Howard Timmins, 1966), p. 33.

18. Julian Cox and Colin Ford (eds), *Julia Margaret Cameron: The Complete Photographs* (Los Angeles, J. Paul Getty Trust Publications, 2003).

19. Joy Melville, *Julia Margaret Cameron: Pioneer Photographer* (Stroud, Sutton Publishing, 2003), p. 39. For the Herschel correspondence, see also Jeff Rosen, *Julia Margaret Cameron's 'Fancy Subjects': Photographic Allegories of Victorian Identity and Empire* (Manchester, MUP, 2016), chapters 2 and 3.

20. Sophie Gordon, 'Photography in India', *International Institute for Asian Studies Newsletter*, 44 (summer 2007), https://core.ac.uk/download/pdf/15600219.pdf (accessed 28 March 2020).

21. G. Thomas, 'Photography and the Elphinstone Institution of Bombay', *History of Photography*, 5, 3 (1981), pp. 245–7. The Company renewed its call in 1854.
22. The early photographer Roger Fenton, who went to the Crimea, travelled with a horse-drawn van, which served as a portable darkroom for his chemical processing. Richard Pare, 'Introduction', in *Roger Fenton* (New York, Aperture Foundation, 1987), p. 7.
23. Arthur Littlewood (ed.), *Indian Mutiny and Beyond: The Letters of Robert Shebbeare VC* (Barnsley, Pen and Sword, 2007), pp. 85, 88, 100, 102, 109, 116.
24. Though born in Venice, Beato was a British subject by virtue of living on Corfu from a young age, at a time when the Ionian Islands were part of the British Empire.
25. Images of the comprehensive destruction of the great city of Lucknow, taken by Beato, can be found in the Wellcome Collection: two are reproduced in John M. MacKenzie, *The British Empire through Buildings: Structure, Function and Meaning* (Manchester, MUP, 2020), pp. 37–8.
26. Sean Willcock, 'Aesthetic bodies: posing on sites of violence in India, 1857–1900', *History of Photography*, 39 (2015), pp. 142–59, considers the posing of live Indians in so many of the photographs indicative of colonial violence, and places this aesthetic convention into the tradition of the picturesque established by Hodges.
27. Other photographers who joined campaigns include Humphrey Lloyd Hime, of the photographic firm of Armstrong, Beere and Hime, on the Red River expedition in Canada in 1858, and John Burke, who was officially commissioned to join the second Afghan War campaign 1878–80. See *Commonwealth in Focus*, p. 117. Francis Gregson was appointed war correspondent to the 1898 Sudan campaign and may have taken photographs. A photograph of Mahdist prisoners owned by the Royal Collection Trust could be by him; see www.rct.uk/collection/2501845/the-first-batch-of-prisoners-leaving-the-battlefield-khartoum-1898 (accessed 27 March 2020).
28. Ryan, *Picturing Empire*, p. 73.
29. For the copy of views of Japan in the Getty Museum, California, see: www.getty.edu/art/collection/objects/32729/felice-beato-views-of-japan-english-about-1868/ (accessed 27 March 2020). In the V&A collection, *Views of Japan* is described as volume II: http://collections.vam.ac.uk/item/O1093644/views-of-japan-volume-ii-photograph-beato-felice/ (accessed 27 March, 2020). They are now exceptionally rare items, commanding enormous sums when sold.
30. See for example, Jim Masselos and Narayani Gupta, *Beato's Delhi, 1857 and Beyond* (Delhi, Rani Dayal, 2000) and Anne Lacoste, *Felice Beato: A Photographer on the Eastern Road* (Los Angeles, Getty Publications, 2010).
31. McCosh's calotypes are in the National Army Museum, London. Some of his photographs are illustrated in George Bruce, *The Burma Wars, 1824–86* (London, Hart Davis, 1973). See also Ray McKenzie, '"The laboratory of mankind": John McCosh and the beginnings of photography in British India', *History of Photography*, 11, 2 (1987), pp. 109–18. McCosh urged assistant surgeons to take up the camera for the professional rewards it would offer.
32. Andrew Jarvis, '"The myriad pencil of the photographer": seeing, mapping and situating Burma in 1855', *Modern Asian Studies*, 45, 5 (2001), pp. 791–823, emphasises the originality of Tripe's photographs in the context of the photographic cultural surveying of Empire. Between 1857 and 1860, Tripe was Photographer to the Government of Madras, charged with photographing architectural and other antiquities in South India before they were further damaged or destroyed. Some of his photographs are in the V&A Museum in London. G. Thomas, 'Linnaeus Tripe in Madras', *History of Photography*, 5, 4 (1981), pp. 329–37.
33. A large number of illustrated books have been published on photography in India, including Fabb, *The British Empire from Photographs: India*; Ray Desmond, *Victorian India in Focus: A Selection of Early Photographs from the Collection in the India Office Library and Records* (London, HMSO, 1982); John Falconer and Satish Sharma,

A Shifting Focus: Photography in India, 1850–1900 (London, British Council, 1997); John Falconer, *India: Pioneering Photographers 1850–1900* (London, British Library, 20001); Vidya Dehejia (ed.), *India through the Lens: Photography 1840–1911* (Washington, DC, Smithsonian Institution, 2000). They constitute a useful resource even when delivered with an unproblematic empiricism.

34. Omar Shah, *From Kashmir to Kabul: The Photographs of John Burke and William Baker, 1860–1900* (Ahmedabad, Mapin, 2002).
35. Hugh Rayner (ed.), *Photographic Journeys in the Himalayas, 1863–1866, Samuel Bourne* (Bath, Pagoda Tree Press, 2009).
36. Fred Bremner, *My Forty Years in India*, with an introduction by Hugh Rayner (Bath, Pagoda Tree Press, 2007). Also Brij Bhushan Sharma, 'Fred Bremner's Indian years', *History of Photography*, 13, 4 (1989), pp. 293–301; Sheila Asante, 'From Lucknow to Lahore: Fred Bremner's vision of India', *Asian Affairs*, 44, 1 (2013), pp. 89–96, which followed an exhibition of Bremner's photography in Edinburgh.
37. Bremner, *Forty Years*, p. 61.
38. L.H. Wilson was a Glasgow industrialist who took up photography and made a collection of photographs of India when a guest of the Maharaja of Alwar in 1926–7. Anne Buddle, 'India's associations in Scotland's national galleries', in Roger Jeffery, *India in Edinburgh* (New Delhi, Social Science Press, 2019), p. 86.
39. Ibid., p. 80.
40. Joanna Sassoon, 'Photography', *Historical Encyclopedia of Western Australia* (Crawley, University of Western Australia Press, 2009), pp. 686–8.
41. Bensusan, *Silver Images*, p. 33.
42. Julie Lawson, *James Robertson of Istanbul* (London, British Council, 1991). Lawson argued that Robertson brought the eye of an engraver to photography, turning it into an artistic medium with a considerable emphasis on detail, for example in architectural shots. Lawson suggested that in his Crimean photography Robertson contrasted order with chaos, neat lines of tents and the destruction and rubble of warfare.
43. Julie Brown and Margaret Maynard, 'Painter and photographer: Brisbane in the 1880s and 1890s', *History of Photography*, 2, 4 (1978), pp. 325–33.
44. See: https://collections.tepapa.govt.nz/topic/1059 (accessed 3 April 2020).
45. J. Russell Harper and Stanley Triggs (eds), *Portrait of a Period: A Collection of Notman Photographs* (Montreal, McGill UP, 1867, unpaginated). McGill University has 400,000 items relating to the Notman archives. The firm also had a Toronto branch. It is suggested in this book (which is unpaginated) that Notman took great delight in the Montreal winter, seeing it as a time of carnival and display, with ice palaces, rinks, etc.
46. Joan Schwartz, 'Frederick Dally', *The Canadian Encyclopedia*, www.thecanadianencyclopedia.ca/en/article/frederick-dally (accessed 27 April 2020).
47. Some photographs are in Peter Grant, *Victoria: A History in Photographs* (Vancouver, Altitude Publishing, 1995). Another work of photographs of the same region is Meredith Bain Woodward, *Land of Dreams: A History of Photography of the British Columbia Interior* (Vancouver, Altitude Publishing, 1993).
48. *Photographic Views of British Columbia, 1867–1870*, www.rct.uk/collection/2368804-a/photographic-views-of-british-columbia-1867-to-1870 (accessed 27 April 2020).
49. Colleen Skidmore, 'Women workers of Notman's Studio: young ladies of the printing room', *History of Photography*, 20, 2 (1996), pp. 122–8.
50. S. Muthiah, 'Three woman photographers', *The Hindu*, 17 July 2017, www.thehindu.com/society/history-and-culture/women-photographers-of-old-chennai/article19294060.ece (accessed 9 April 2020). Another of Muthiah's women photographers was the English wife of Ananda Coomeraswamy, who contributed photographs to her husband's publications.
51. By the 1880s, there were three professional photographers working in Apia, Samoa, issuing images of Samoa as an earthly paradise. Alison Devine Nordström, 'Early

photography in Samoa', *History of Photography*, 15 (1991), pp. 272–86. The anthropological and ideological significance of Thomas Andrew's photography in Samoa are considered by Nicholas Thomas, *Colonialism's Culture: Anthropology, Travel and Government* (Princeton, NJ, Princeton UP, 1994). The cover illustration is a classic colonial postcard, 'A study in black and white'.

52. Clark Worswick (ed.), *Princely India: Photographs by Raja Deen Dayal, Court Photographer (1884–1910) to the Premier Prince of India* (London, Hamish Hamilton, 1880).

53. Ibid., p. 20.

54. Gita Rajan, 'Evidence of another modernity: Lala Deen Dayal's 1904 Delhi Durbar photographs', in J.F. Codell (ed.), *Power and Resistance: The Delhi Coronation Durbars, 1877, 1903, 1911* (Ahmedabad, Mapin, 2012), pp. 160–73; Deepali Dewan, 'The limits of photography: the Dayal Studio's Coronation Album, 1903', ibid., pp. 142–59. For Bourne and Shepherd see Plate 25.

55. G. Thomas, 'Maharaja Sawai Ram Singh II of Jaipur, photographer-prince', *History of Photography*, 10, 3 (1986), pp. 181–91.

56. The illustration in *The Graphic*, 12 July 1879, of John Burke photographing the 'Ameer Yakoob Khan' indicates this clearly. This appears in Pratapaditya Pal and Vidya Dehejia, *From Merchants to Emperors: British Artists and India, 1757–1930* (Ithaca, NY, Cornell UP, 1986), p. 183.

57. Violet Jacob, *Diaries and Letters from India 1895–1900* (Edinburgh, Canongate 1990), p. 75.

58. Thomson had been apprenticed to an optical and scientific instrument maker in Edinburgh, a business with obvious connections to photography.

59. J. Thomson, *The Straits of Malacca, Indo-China and China or Ten Years' Travels, Adventures and Residence Abroad* (London, Sampson Low, 1875), pp. 188–9. This book, illustrated by sixty-eight engravings from Thomson photographs, is available on the web: https://archive.org/details/straitsmalacca00thomrich/page/n19/mode/2up (accessed 27 March 2020).

60. See: www.zanzibarhistory.org/Gomes_Gallery.htm (accessed 28 March 2020).

61. See: wwwe.lib.cam.ac.uk/CUL/rcs_photographers/entry.php?id=208. Some Gomes photographs in the collection of the Royal Commonwealth Society are in Cambridge University Library. There were other photographic studios in Zanzibar, all with Portuguese or Goan names, J.B. and Felix Coutinho and Pereira de Lord Brothers.

62. Julie Crooks, *Alphonso Lisk-Carew: Early Photography in Sierra Leone*, PhD thesis, SOAS, University of London, 2014, http://eprints.soas.ac.uk/18564. This considers the origins and development of the business, the social and intellectual role of its photography, as well as attitudes to colonialism, gender and so on.

63. Amy J. Staples, Flora Edouwayo Kaplan and Bryan M. Freyer, *Fragile Legacies: The Photographs of Solomon Osagie Alonge* (Washington, DC, Smithsonian Institution, 2016). Alonge's studio also issued postcards.

64. P.A. Klier represented striking internationalisation in British Burma. Arriving in Moulmein (Mawlamyine) in 1865 he joined Germans who were watchmakers, opticians and photographers. Moving to Rangoon in 1880, he became a noted photographer of street scenes, Burmese shows and individuals, www.chasingchinthes.com/ (accessed 6 April 2020). The Skeen family had studios in Colombo and Rangoon, with William Skeen having trained at the London School of Photography. Members were also government printers.

65. Clare Harris, *Photography and Tibet* (London, Reaktion 2016). It may be that the first photograph in Tibet was taken in 1863. On photography and the Younghusband expedition, see Simeon Koole, 'Photography as event: power, the Kodak camera and territoriality in early twentieth-century Tibet', *Comparative Studies in Society and History*, 59, 2 (2017), pp. 310–45.

66. G. Thomas, 'Rajendra Lall Mitra (1822–90)', *History of Photography*, 8, 3 (1984), pp. 223–6.

67. Noel F. Singer, *Burmah: A Photographic Journey, 1855–1925* (Gartmore, Stirlingshire, Kiscadale Publications, 1993), pp. 11–12.

68. Harper and Triggs (eds), *Portrait of a Period*. Notman was appointed official photographer to the visit of the Prince of Wales to Canada in 1860 and Lord Monck, Governor General of the Province of Canada (the combination of Upper and Lower Canada) ordered Notman stereoscopic views for the Prince.

69. The records of the Madras society survive. G. Thomas, 'The Madras Photographic Society, 1856–61', *History of Photography*, 16, 4 (1992), pp. 299–301.

70. An indication of the spread of photographic societies in India is revealed by the numbers joining the Federation of Indian Photography, formed in 1952, www.fip.org.in/fipweb/public/about-us (accessed 29 March 2020).

71. Bensusan, *Silver Images*, pp. 33–4.

72. Buddle, 'India associations', p. 80.

73. Ryan, *Photography and Exploration*; Leila Koivunen, *Visualizing Africa in Nineteenth-century British Travel Accounts* (Abingdon, Routledge, 2009). Also see works in note 12 of this chapter.

74. Koivunen, *Visualizing Africa*, p. 35.

75. Beau Riffenburgh and Liz Cruwys, *The Photographs of H.G. Ponting* (London, Discovery Gallery, 1998). Ponting was photographer with Scott's Antarctic expedition in 1910, but also travelled and photographed extensively in the empire.

76. Ryan, *Picturing Empire*, pp. 148–67.

77. Christopher Morton and Philip N. Grover (eds), *Wilfred Thesiger in Africa: A Unique Collection of Essays and Personal Photographs* (London, Harper Press, 2010).

78. Lydon, *Imperial Emotions*, p. 20 and chapter 6, pp. 143–63.

79. A set is in the National Portrait Gallery in London, www.npg.org.uk/collections/search/set/532/The+Life+and+Work+of+David+Livingstone (accessed 30 March 2020). Another different set is in the National Library of Scotland. www.nls.uk/exhibitions/david-livingstone/lantern-slides (accessed 30 March 2020).

80. T. Jack Thompson, *Light on Darkness? Missionary Photography of Africa in the Nineteenth and Early Twentieth Centuries* (Grand Rapids, MI, Eerdmans, 2012), pp. 196–9 and 207–38; Ryan, *Picturing Empire*, pp. 192–5. Donald Simpson published the pioneering 'Missions and the magic lantern', *IBMR*, 21, 2 (1997), pp. 13–15.

81. Ibid., p. 14.

82. The celebrated Scottish photographer George Washington Wilson branched out from Scotland to produce a lantern-slide lecture with the title 'Cannibal isles or rovings among the coral reefs and palms', with an accompanying booklet. These have been analysed by Michael Hayes in 'Photography and the emergence of the Pacific cruise: rethinking the representational crisis in colonial photography', in Hight and Sampson (eds), *Colonialist Photography*, pp. 172–87, particularly pp. 177–8. For Scott of Glasgow, see Thompson, *Light on Darkness*, p. 215.

83. See: www.africamuseum.be/en/discover/focus_collections/display_object?objectid=32815 (accessed 30 March 2020).

84. Lydon, *Imperial Emotions*, chapter 6.

85. Involuntary child migration continued until the 1960s and later became a significant aspect of child abuse enquiries in England and Scotland.

86. John M. MacKenzie, *Propaganda and Empire* (Manchester, MUP, 1984), pp. 162–6; Ryan, *Picturing Empire*, chapter 6. See also James R. Ryan, 'Visualizing imperial geography: Halford Mackinder and the Colonial Office Visual Instruction Committee, 1902–11', *Ecumene, a Journal of Environment, Culture, Meaning*, 1, 2 (1994), pp. 157–76.

87. Rather fancifully they have been described as 'the first art form of the unlettered person'. Christaud Geary and Virginia-Lee Webb, *Delivering Views: Distant Cultures in Early Postcards* (Washington, DC, Smithsonian Institution, 1998), p. 13.

88. There was a postcard exhibition at the Brunei Gallery, SOAS, London in 2018: 'From Madras to Bangalore: Picture Postcards and Urban History in Colonial India', www.thelookoutjournal.com/daily-art/2018/10/6/postcards-from-the-past (accessed 9 April 2020).

89. Malek Alloula, *The Colonial Harem* (Manchester, MUP, 1986).

90. Gilles Teulié, 'Southern (African) belles and the aesthetic forms of seduction: portraying Zulu women in early twentieth-century postcards', *L'Atelier*, 9, 2 (2017), pp. 62–96; and Teulié, 'Orientalism and the British picture postcard industry: popularising the empire in Victorian and Edwardian homes', *Cahiers Victoriens et Édouardiens* (Montpellier, Centre d'études et de recherches victoriennes et édouardiennes et contemporaines, 2019, 89), pp. 1–17. See also Rachel Ama Asaa Engmann, 'Under imperial eyes, black bodies, buttocks and breasts: British colonial photography and Asante fetish girls', *African Arts*, 45, 2 (2012), pp. 46–57.

91. Alan Beukers, *Exotic Postcards: The Lure of Distant Lands* (London, Thames and Hudson, 2007).

92. W.S. Johnston was another Creole from Sierra Leone. Geary and Webb, *Delivering Views*, p. 167.

93. Tuck was originally from Prussia and had been selling photographs in Britain from the 1860s.

94. Akande Akeyami, 'Early attempts at architectural photography in Lagos, Nigeria', *Lagos Journal of Architecture*, 2 (July 2016), pp. 19–33, https://ir.unilag.edu.ng/bitstream/handle/123456789/7178/Early%20Attempts%20Architectural%20Photography%20in%20Lagos.pdf?sequence=1&isAllowed=y (accessed 29 March 2020).

95. Many more postcard publishers in the British Empire can be found in Geary and Webb, *Delivering Views*.

96. Omar Khan, *Paper Jewels: Postcards from the Raj* (Ahmedabad, Mapin and Alkazi Collection of Photography, 2018). This contains no fewer than 519 illustrations.

97. John Falconer, '"A pure labor of love": a publishing history of *The People of India*', in Hight and Sampson (eds), *Colonialist Photography*, pp. 51–83.

98. See, among several examples, Peter Robb (ed.), *The Concept of Race in South Asia* (Delhi, OUP, 1995).

99. Tony Ballantyne, *Orientalism and Race: Aryanism in the British Empire* (Houndmills, Palgrave, 2002).

100. Photographs of Indian 'types' are almost legion and were published, for example, by Clifton of Bombay, Higginbotham of Madras, K.C. Mehra of Peshawar, Bremner of Lahore and Quetta, Herman Dass of Ambala and Dagshai, Mooli Dhur of Ambala, Del Tufo of Madras, D. Macropolo of Calcutta, the Society for the Propagation of the Gospel, and Scottish mission industries of Poona and Ajmer, and many others. They were also produced in Britain by A&C Black, Raphael Tuck and George Stewart of Edinburgh. The London Imperial Institute published cards of Indian products and their producers.

101. Many were issued by Ahuja of Rangoon.

102. Geary and Webb, *Delivering Views*, p. 3.

103. This is largely true of Thompson, *Light on Darkness?* and the articles in the *IBMR*, 26, 4 (2002), a journal associated with the US Overseas Ministries Study Centre. Articles include 'The beginnings of Moravian missionary photography in Labrador', by Hans Rollmann; 'Much more than illustrations of what we already know: experiences in the rediscovery of mission photography', by Paul Jenkins; and '"Fields of vision": photographs in the missionary collections at the School of Oriental and African Studies, London', by Samantha Johnson and Rosemary Seton.

104. Editorial in *IBMR*, 26, 4 (2002), p. 145.

105. Jeffrey Richards (ed.), *Imperialism and Juvenile Literature* (Manchester, MUP, 1989); MacKenzie, *Propaganda and Empire*, chapter 8; and Berny Sèbe, *Heroic Imperialists in Africa: The Promotion of British and French Colonial Heroes (1870–1939)* (Manchester, MUP, 2013).

106. Andrew Porter, 'Sir Roger Casement and the international humanitarian movement', *JICH*, 29, 2 (2001), pp. 59–74. Casement became genuinely anti-imperial as his role as an Irish nationalist became more pronounced, leading to his trial and execution as a traitor.

107. Thompson, *Light in Darkness?*, pp. 183–9. See also T. Jack Thompson, 'Light on the Dark Continent: the photography of Alice Seely Harris and the Congo atrocities of the early twentieth century', *IBMR*, 26, 4 (2002), p. 146.

108. Kevin Grant, 'Christian critics of empire: missionaries, lantern lectures and the Congo Reform Campaign in Britain', *JICH*, 29, 2 (2001), pp. 27–58. Grant includes useful lists of the number of lectures and meetings of the CRC in Britain in 1906 to 1908.

109. Catherina de Lorenzo, 'The imaging of Aborigines: commitment to land rights', *History of Photography*, 15, 3 (1991), pp. 228–35.

110. Lydon, *Photography, Humanitarianism, Empire*, particularly pp. 27–37.

111. MacKenzie, *British Empire through Buildings*, pp. 185–7.

112. Brenda Croft, 'Laying ghosts to rest', in Hight and Sampson (eds), *Colonialist Photography*, p. 28.

113. Kathleen Howe, 'Hooper, Colonel Willoughby Wallace (1837–1912)', entry in John Hannavy (ed.), *The Encyclopedia of Nineteenth-century Photography* (Abingdon, Routledge, 2008), pp. 713–14.

114. See also Christina Twomey, 'Framing photography and humanitarianism', *History of Photography*, 36 (2012), pp. 255–64.

115. See essays in Maria Antonella Pelizzari (ed.), *Traces of India: Photographing Architecture and the Politics of the Raj, 1850–1900* (New Haven, CT, Yale Center for British Art, 2003). One contributor, Tapati Guha-Thakurta, suggests that the nineteenth-century architectural commentator James Fergusson based many of his ideas on Indian architecture upon photographs. The work of Linnaeus Tripe in recording aspects of architecture is extolled by Janet Dewan in *Linnaeus Tripe, Documenting South Indian architecture* (London, Taylor and Francis, 1989).

116. During their conquest, the British army took over many monasteries, ejecting their monks, and inevitably causing damage.

117. Susie Protschky has charted these phenomena in considerable detail in respect of Indonesia and the Dutch royal family in *Photographic Subjects: Monarchy and Visual Culture in Colonial Indonesia* (Manchester, MUP, 2020).

118. See: https://blogs.bl.uk/endangeredarchives/2017/05/tamil-studio-photography.html (accessed 8 April 2020). For a wider study of photographic portraiture in India, see Christopher Pinney, *Camera Indica: The Social Life of Indian Photographs* (Chicago, University of Chicago Press, 1997).

119. Chris Gore, 'Neils Walwin Holm: radicalising the image in Lagos Colony, West Africa', *History of Photography*, 37, 3 (2013), pp. 283–300.

120. John McCracken, 'Mungo Murray Chisuse and the early history of photography in Malawi'. *Society of Malawi Journal*, 61, 2 (2008), pp. 1–18.

121. Bensusan, *Silver Images*, p. 69. See also the article on Sobukwe in SAHO (South African History Online), www.sahistory.org.za/people/robert-sobukwe (accessed 7 April 2020) and for some of his photographs, www.alamy.com/stock-photo/robert-sobukwe.html (accessed 7 April 2020).

122. This comes from an unpublished lecture, quoted by McCracken, 'Mungo Murray Chisuse', p. 12.

Chapter 7 The Press

1. The telegraph was significant for internal communications over vast distances in Canada, Australia and India. For India, see Deep Kanta Lahiri Choudhury, *Telegraphic Imperialism: Crisis and Panic in the Indian Empire, c. 1830* (Houndmills, Palgrave Macmillan, 2010).
2. In the Goethe tale, the sorcerer returns and breaks the spell, but European empires had no such saving figure.
3. When Walter Medhurst left for the London Missionary Society mission in Malacca in 1816, he 'stowed a new fount of English type'. Andrew Hillier, *Mediating Empire: An English Family in China, 1817–1927* (Folkestone, Renaissance Books, 2020), p. 6. He later adopted an advanced press, capable of printing in Chinese.
4. C.A. Bayly, *Empire and Information: Intelligence Gathering and Social Communication in India, 1780–1870* (Cambridge, CUP, 1997), p. 343.
5. Miles Ogborn, *Indian Ink: Script and Print in the Making of the English East India Company* (Chicago, University of Chicago Press, 2007), p. 269. Stories of ancient printing in India seem to be apocryphal.
6. Carrier pigeons were used from 1850 to 1857 to bring important news from ships at Pointe de Galle to Colombo.
7. The word 'gazette' may have come from Venice, where a *gazeta* or *gazzetta* was a Renaissance news sheet. Its origins may lie in the Italian for 'magpie'.
8. See: www.ggl.gi/gibraltar-chronicle/ (accessed 20 September 2021). The Gibraltar Garrison Library contains a full set of the paper.
9. See: www.thecanadianencyclopedia.ca/en/article/first-newspapers-in-canada (accessed 23 April 2020).
10. J. Don Vann and Rosemary T. Van Arsdel, *Periodicals of Queen Victoria's Empire: An Exploration* (Toronto, University of Toronto Press, 1996), p. 66.
11. See: https://novascotia.ca/archives/gazette/. This website has a complete facsimile of the two-page paper.
12. See: www.thecanadianencyclopedia.ca/en/article/first-newspapers-in-canada (accessed 27 April 2020).
13. A rare copy was held in the Royal Commonwealth Society Library, London, now in Cambridge University Library.
14. P.J. Marshall, 'The White Town of Calcutta under the rule of the East India Company', *Modern Asian Studies*, 34, 2 (2000), pp. 308–9.
15. Ogborn, *Indian Ink*, pp. 205–6.
16. A facsimile copy of these proposals can be found in https://en.wikipedia.org/wiki/Hicky%27s_Bengal_Gazette#/media/File:1780-00-Prospectus_of_Hicky's_Bengal_Gazette.png (accessed 27 April 2020).
17. *The Memoirs of William Hickey, 1775–1782* (London, Hurst and Blackett, 1918), p. 175.
18. Andrew Otis, *Hicky's Bengal Gazette: The Untold Story of India's First Newspaper* (New Delhi, Westland Publications, 2018). See also https://andrewotis.com/ (accessed 19 April 2020).
19. There are a number of different transliterated spellings of the word *Hurkaru* or *Harkara*. In Hindi it means 'messenger' or 'courier', a classic name for a newspaper.
20. For newspapers in Bengal see J. Natarajan, *History of Indian Journalism*. This book, constituting part II of the Report of the Press Commission, was published in 1955 by the Ministry of Information and Broadcasting of the Government of India. More recently, see G.N.S. Raghavan, *The Press in India* (New Delhi, Gyan Publishing House, 1994).
21. Sujit Sivasundaram, *Islanded* (Chicago, University of Chicago Press, 2013), pp. 306–9.
22. Frank Welsh, *A History of Hong Kong* (London, HarperCollins, 1993), p. 140.

23. Yizheng Zou, 'English newspapers in British colonial Hong Kong: the case of the *South China Morning Post*, 1903–1941', *Critical Arts: South–North Cultural and Media Studies*, 29, 1 (2015), pp. 26–40.

24. Michael Ng, 'When silence speaks: press censorship and rule of law in British Hong Kong, 1850s–1940s', *Law and Literature*, 29, 3 (2017), pp. 425–56.

25. Prasun Sonwalkar, 'Indian journalism in the colonial crucible: a nineteenth-century story of political protest', *Journalism Studies*, 16, 5 (2015), pp. 624–36.

26. C.A. Bayly, *Imperial Meridian: The British Empire and the World, 1780–1830* (Harlow, Pearson, 1989), chapter 7.

27. For Mackenzie's early career, see Chris Raible, *A Colonial Advocate: The Launching of his Newspaper and the Queenston Career of William Lyon Mackenzie* (Creemore, Curiosity House, 1999).

28. Chris Raible, *The Power of the Press: The Story of Early Canadian Printers and Publishers* (Toronto, James Lorimer, 2007).

29. Durham's report, prompted by the 1837 rebellion, proposed the introduction of responsible government and the uniting of Upper and Lower Canada.

30. John M. MacKenzie, '"To enlighten South Africa": the creation of a free press at the Cape in the early nineteenth century', in Chandrika Kaul (ed.), *Media and the British Empire* (Houndmills, Palgrave Macmillan, 2006), pp. 20–36.

31. Randolph Vigne, *Thomas Pringle: South African Pioneer, Poet and Abolitionist* (London, James Currey, 2012), part III 'The Stand Against Power', particularly chapter 9, 'An arrant dissenter', pp. 111–44. Although Pringle, like Mackenzie, was a Presbyterian secessionist, the absence of a secessionist church in the Cape ensured that he was often an adherent of the Church of Scotland. Denominational boundaries were very fluid at that time.

32. Sundaram, *Islanded*, p. 308.

33. Abiodun Salawu, 'Not Iwe Irohin, but Umshumayeli: a revisit of the historiography of the early African language press', *African Identities*, 13, 2 (2015), pp. 157–70.

34. Abiodun Salawu, 'The Yoruba and their language newspapers: origin, nature, problems and prospects', *Studies of Tribes and Tribals*, 2, 2 (2004), pp. 97–104.

35. See: www.thecanadianencyclopedia.ca/en/article/newspapers (accessed 27 April 2020).

36. Papers were also published to satisfy specific interest groups and diverse immigrant populations: Germans, Italians, East Europeans and Chinese soon had newspapers in their own languages.

37. For an analysis of the relationship of the South African press with Britain over a longer period, see John Lambert, '"The thinking is done in London": South Africa's English-language press and imperialism', in Kaul (ed.), *Media and the British Empire*, pp. 37–54.

38. It is intriguing that Scottish papers such as *The Scotsman* and *Inverness Courier* only appeared in the same year.

39. Frank Barton, *The Press of Africa: Persecution and Perseverance* (London, Macmillan, 1979), p. 17.

40. Andrew S. Thompson, *Imperial Britain: The Empire in British Politics c. 1880–1932* (Harlow, Essex, Pearson, 2000), particularly chapter 3; Simon J. Potter, *News and the British World: The Emergence of an Imperial Press System* (Oxford, OUP, 2003).

41. Donald Read, *The Power of News: The History of Reuters* (Oxford, OUP, 1999), chapter 1. Reuter's father was baptised as a Christian convert after arrival in England in 1845.

42. This hot metal machine, invented by a German immigrant to the USA, enabled its operator to set up an entire line of type on a keyboard through the creation of moulds for the letters, replacing the older technique of setting up each individual character. It was in use, remarkably, from the 1890s to the 1970s and 1980s, when it was replaced by phototypesetting and computer systems.

43. Uniquely among these examples, the *Montreal Gazette* had news on the first page, perhaps influenced by American papers available in the city.

44. Culture and entertainment includes church affairs.
45. Includes all Australian news even though pre-Confederation at this date.
46. Eight-page, 8 col. paper, plus four-page 7 col. entertainment supplement.
47. Local news for these three newspapers includes China.
48. Local news for these three newspapers includes the Malay Peninsula and Borneo.
49. Local news for these three newspapers includes all of modern-day Canada.
50. Andrew Griffiths, *The New Journalism, the New Imperialism and the Fiction of Empire, 1870–1900* (Houndmills, Palgrave Macmillan, 2015).
51. For chapters on the British press and the Anglo-Boer War, see Simon Potter (ed.), *Newspapers and Empire in Ireland and Britain; Reporting the British Empire c. 1857–1921* (Dublin, Four Courts Press, 2004).
52. *The Daily News*, 19 May 1900, p. 5 and 21 May, p. 4, J.S. Battye History Library, State Library of Western Australia.
53. *Otago Daily News*, 18, 19 and 21 May, the Hocken Library, Dunedin. There were torch-light processions, general rejoicings and mass meetings.
54. *Halifax Morning Chronicle*, 19 and 21 May 1900; *Halifax Herald*, 19 and 21 May 1900, also the *Acadian Recorder*: Halifax Archives.
55. Boer War material can be found in the Halifax, Nova Scotia Archives.
56. John Griffiths, *Imperial Culture in Antipodean Cities, 1880–1939* (Houndmills, Basingstoke, Palgrave Macmillan, 2014), pp. 41–3. In the case of Britain, the activities of working-class clubs tend to refute the lower middle class and youths analysis, see John M. MacKenzie, *Propaganda and Empire* (Manchester, MUP, 1984), pp. 61–3.
57. From a considerable literature, see Andrea Bosco, *The Round Table Movement and the Fall of the 'Second' British Empire (1909–1919)* (Newcastle, Cambridge Scholars, 2017).
58. Tom Clarke, *Northcliffe in History: An Intimate Study of Press Power* (London, Hutchinson, 1950), p. 155.
59. Griffiths, *Imperial Culture*, pp. 111–12.
60. Stephanie Newell, 'Paradoxes of press freedom in British West Africa', *Media History*, 22, 1 (2016), pp. 101–22.
61. John D. Chick, 'The Ashanti Times: a footnote to Ghanaian press history', *African Affairs*, 76, 302 (1977), pp. 80–94.
62. For the earlier period see Barton's *Press of Africa*.

Chapter 8 Theatre

1. Music hall became the most popular form of light musical and other entertainment in Britain during the nineteenth century. Later, it transformed into variety, consisting of a string of unrelated items by different types of performer, including singers, comedians, magicians, acrobats, jugglers, dancers, some even involving animals. In music hall/variety a master of ceremonies often introduces the acts. Vaudeville was the American version.
2. Noel F. Singer, *Burmah: A Photographic Journey 1855–1925* (Gartmore, Kiscadale, 1993), pp. 23–4. A nineteenth-century photograph of a Burmese orchestra and actors is reproduced on p. 22.
3. See: World Encyclopedia of Puppetry Arts, https://wepa.unima.org/en/asia/ (accessed 10 June 2020). See also Inge C. Orr, 'Puppet theatre in Asia', *Asian Folklore Studies*, 33, 1 (1974), pp. 69–84.
4. See: www.thecanadianencyclopedia.ca/en/article/asian-canadian-theatre (accessed 11 June 2020). Korean and Filipino immigrants later performed their own theatrical traditions.
5. Ousmane Diakhaté and Hansel Ndumbe Eyoh, 'The roots of African theatre ritual and orality in the pre-colonial period', *International Association of Theatre Critics Journal (IATC journal/Revue de l'AICT)*, 15 (2017), www.critical-stages.org/15/the-roots-of-

african-theatre-ritual-and-orality-in-the-pre-colonial-period/ (accessed 10 June 2020). Accounts of African pre-colonial theatre can be found in Martin Banham (ed.), *A History of Theatre in Africa* (Cambridge, CUP, 2002).

6. Malyaban Chattopadhyay, 'A historical study of ancient Indian theatre-communication in the light of *Natyasastra*', www.caluniv.ac.in/global-mdia-journal/ARTICLE-DEC2013/Article_12_Malyaban_Chattopadhyay.pdf (accessed 22 June 2020).

7. Durgodas Mukhopadhyay, 'Ancient Indian stage and its conventions', *Annals of the Bhandarkar Oriental Research Institute*, 69, 1/4 (1988), pp. 243–8, www.jstor.org/stable/41693771?seq=1 (accessed 22 June, 2020).

8. Rashna Darius Nicholson, 'Troubling Englishness: the eastward success and westward failure of the Parsi theatre', *Nineteenth-Century Theatre and Film*, 44, 1 (2017), pp. 75–91.

9. See: www.thecanadianencyclopedia.ca/en/article/french-language-theatre (article by Michel Tremblay, accessed 9 June 2020).

10. Brian Kennedy, *The Baron Bold and the Beauteous Maid: A Compact History of Canadian Theatre* (Toronto, Playwrights Canada Press, 2004), Prologue.

11. *Weekly Chronicle*, 22 January 1819, p. 3, column 2. Nova Scotia Archives, Halifax.

12. J. Linden Best, 'Box, pit and gallery: the Theatre Royal, Spring Gardens [Halifax]' *Dalhousie Review*, 53, 3 (1923), pp. 520–8. The Nova Scotian archives are rich in material on theatrical performances in Halifax.

13. *The Acadian Recorder*, 1 May 1858, p. 2, column 6. Nova Scotia Archives, Halifax.

14. *British Colonist*, 27 July 1858, p. 2, column 6. Nova Scotia Archives, Halifax.

15. Lawrence D. Smith, 'Spectacular remedies to colonial conflicts: tableaux vivants, proto-cinema and global performance in Dion Boucicault's *Jessie Brown*', *Nineteenth-Century Theatre and Film*, 41, 2 (2014), pp. 29–49, quotation on p. 46.

16. Description of amateur theatricals, Halifax Archives, AK F28 C66. *Furlough* was a travel play, involving scenes in the United States, Upper and Lower Canada and the Maritimes.

17. Kennedy, *Baron Bold*, pp. 31–41.

18. Marty Gould, *Nineteenth Century Theatre and the Imperial Encounter* (London, Routledge 2011).

19. The Toronto journal, *The Week*, reviewed the performances in the Opera House, particularly of *The Merchant of Venice* on 28 February, p. 204, https://archive.org/stream/weekcanadianjour01toro#page/n102/mode/1up (accessed 10 June 2020).

20. Keith Garebian and Ralph Berry, updated by Eli Yarhi, 'The Stratford Festival', *The Canadian Encyclopedia*, www.thecanadianencyclopedia.ca/en/article/stratford-shakespeare-festival (accessed 10 June 2020).

21. See: www.canadiantheatre.com/dict.pl?term=Canadian%20Theatre%20History (accessed 11 June 2020).

22. James B. Hartman, 'On stage, theatre and theatres in early Winnipeg', *Manitoba History*, 43 (2002), www.mhs.mb.ca/docs/mb_history/43/theatrehistory.shtml (accessed 11 June 2020).

23. Sushil K. Mukherjee, *The Story of the Calcutta theatres, 1753–1980* (Calcutta, Bagchi, 1982).

24. Geoffrey Moorhouse, *Calcutta: The City Revealed* (Harmondsworth, Penguin, 1974), p. 61.

25. Ian Talbot and Tahir Kamran, *Colonial Lahore: A History of the City and Beyond* (London, Hurst, 2016), pp. 15, 53–4.

26. See: http://olioweb.me.uk/plays/ (accessed 19 June 2020).

27. John Golder and Richard Madelaine (eds), *O Brave New World: Two Centuries of Shakespeare on the Australian Stage* (Sydney, Century Press, 2001); also review by Ann Blake in *Theatre Research International*, 27, 2 (2002), pp. 214–15.

28. Neville Beckwith, 'Drama in Western Australia, 1829–1900', typescript in J.S. Battye History Library, State Library of Western Australia, Perth. Also Jenny Gregory and Jan Gothard (eds), *Historical Encyclopedia of Western Australia* (Perth, University of Western Australia Press, 2009).

29. S.L. Goldberg and F.B. Smith (eds), *Australian Cultural History* (Cambridge, CUP, 1981), p. 181.

30. Lindis Taylor, 'Story: Opera and musical theatre' in A.H. McLintock (ed.), *Te Ara, the Encyclopedia of New Zealand*. Revised and republished from 2004: *Te Ara – The Encyclopedia of New Zealand* online (Wellington, Manatū Taonga Ministry for Culture and Heritage, Government of New Zealand).

31. Brooke performed for a week in the Garrison Theatre in Cape Town. The Cape was a convenient stopping-off point for actors voyaging to Australia or India, often securing star performers.

32. Jonathan Mane-Wheoki, 'The high arts in a regional culture – from Englishness to self-reliance', in John Cookson and Graeme Dunstall (eds), *Southern Capital: Christchurch, Towards a City Biography 1850–2000* (Christchurch, Canterbury University Press, 2000), pp. 310–11.

33. Ann Blake, '"Our Shakespeare": the Melbourne Shakespeare Society, 1884–1930', *Nineteenth-Century Theatre and Film*, 36, 1 (2009), pp. 73–86.

34. Law Kar and Frank Bren, *Hong Kong Cinema: A Cross-cultural View* (Lanham, MD, Scarecrow Press, 2004), pp. 4–5.

35. Marlis Schweitzer, '"Too much tragedy in real life": theatre in post-emancipation Jamaica', *Nineteenth-Century Theatre and Film*, 44, 1 (2017), pp. 8–27.

36. E.M. Forster, *A Passage to India* (Harmondsworth, Penguin, 1976, first published 1924), p. 25.

37. The Kendal acting company was particularly popular in Bangalore, which Felicity described as the most anglicised city in India. Felicity Kendal, *White Cargo* (London, Michael Joseph, 1998), p. 119.

38. Gillian Tindall, *City of Gold: The Biography of Bombay* (Hounslow, Temple Smith, 1982), pp. 164–5.

39. J.P. Losty (ed.), *Sita Ram's Painted Views of India: Lord Hastings's Journey from Calcutta to the Punjab, 1814–1815* (London, Thames and Hudson, 2015), p. 238.

40. Rimli Bhattacharya, 'Promiscuous spaces and economies of entertainment: soldiers, actresses and hybrid genres in colonial India', *Nineteenth-Century Theatre and Film*, 41, 2 (2014), pp. 50–75, particularly pp. 56–65. See also P. Trivedi, 'Garrison theatre in colonial India', in C. Cochrane and J. Robinson (eds), *Theatre History and Historiography* (London, Palgrave Macmillan, 2016), pp. 103–20.

41. Ibid., p. 73.

42. Laurence Wright, 'Shakespeare in South Africa; alpha and omega', keynote address at a Shakespeare conference in Launceston, Tasmania, February 2002, www.researchgate. net/publication/29807055_Shakespeare_in_South_Africa_Alpha_and_'Omega' (accessed 22 February 2022). It is possible that some troops performed *Hamlet* in Fort Frederick above Algoa Bay (now Port Elizabeth) about the same time.

43. Yvette Hutchison, 'South African theatre', in Banham (ed.), *History of Theatre in Africa*, pp. 312–79. See also Temple Hauptfleisch, 'The shaping of South African theatre', in Susan Arndt and Katrin Brendt (eds), *Words and Worlds: African Writing, Literature and Society* (Trenton, NJ, Africa Press, 2007).

44. Damian Shaw, 'Two "Hottentots", some Scots and a West Indian slave: the origins of Kaatje Kekkelbek', *English Studies in Africa*, 52, 2 (2009), pp. 4–17.

45. Ciarunji Chesaina and Even Mwangi, 'Kenya', in Banham (ed.), *History of Theatre*, p. 217.

46. David Kerr with Stephen Chifunyise, 'Southern Africa', Banham (ed.), *History of heatre*, p. 278; Amandina Lihamba, 'Tanzania', in Banham (ed.), *History of Theatre*, p. 237.

47. Frances Pollon, 'Parramatta, the Cradle City of Australia' (City of Parramatta, 1983).
48. See: https://teara.govt.nz/en/theatres-cinemas-and-halls (accessed 23 June 2020).
49. Raja Bhasin, *Simla: The Summer Capital of British India* (New Delhi, Viking, 1992), p. 141. Doz's book was called *Simla in Ragtime* and was published at the Station Press in Simla in 1913.
50. However, the Kendal family touring company performed there after independence when Geoffrey Kendal tacked an Indian flag over the viceroy's insignia. Kendal, *White Cargo*, p. 42.
51. Emily Eden, *Up the Country* (London, Curzon, 1978), pp. 139–40.
52. Ibid., p. 287.
53. Bhasin, *Simla*, p. 138.
54. Pamela Kanwar, *Imperial Simla: The Political Culture of the Raj* (New Delhi, OUP 1990), pp. 78–9.
55. Fred Bremner, *My Forty Years in India* (Bath, Pagoda Tree Press, 2007), p. 61. Bremner took the photographs of many of the casts.
56. Personal observation, February 2020.
57. Mollie Panter-Downes, *Ooty Preserved: A Victorian Hill Station in India* (London, Century, 1967), pp. 68 and 70.
58. Robin C. Whittaker, '"Entirely free of any amateurishness": private training, public taste and the Women's Dramatic Club of University College, Toronto (1905–21)', *Nineteenth-Century Theatre and Film*, 38, 2 (2011), pp. 51–66. See also the account of pageants for juvenile and women performers, as well as other theatrical events in Ontario in Eva-Marie Kröller, *Writing the Empire: The McIlwraiths, 1853–1948* (Toronto, University of Toronto Press, 2021), pp. 174–7.
59. For examples of such transnational lives, see Desley Deacon, Penny Russell and Angela Woollacott (eds), *Transnational Lives: Biographies of Global Modernity, 1700–present* (London, Palgrave Macmillan, 2010).
60. As suggested in the *Bulletin of the National Operatic and Dramatic Association* in 1937, quoted in Tobias Becker, 'Entertaining the empire: theatrical touring companies and amateur dramatics in colonial India', *Historical Journal*, 57, 3 (2014), pp. 699–725, particularly p. 702.
61. Ibid., p. 705.
62. *The Examiner*, Monday 6 May 1901, p. 6, https://trove.nla.gov.au/newspaper/article/35398700 (accessed 15 June, 2020). This article quoted a review of an earlier performance of *Boy Jim* from the *Bendigo Daily Advertiser*.
63. *San Francisco Call*, 98, 13, 13 June 1905, p. 4. California Digital Newspaper Collection. https://cdnc.ucr.edu/cgi-bin/cdnc?a=d&d=SFC19050613.2.40&e=-------en--20--1--txt-txIN--------1 (accessed 15 June 2020).
64. Members of the troupe were prosecuted for indecency. *Ashburton Guardian*, 30 October, 1879, https://paperspast.natlib.govt.nz/newspapers/AG18791030.2.16?query=burlesque (accessed 21 June 2020).
65. Bhattacharya, 'Promiscuous spaces', pp. 61–2.
66. For minstrelsy, see Michael Pickering, 'Mock blacks and racial mockery: the "nigger" minstrel and British imperialism', in J.S. Bratton et al., *Acts of Supremacy: The British Empire and the Stage, 1790–1930* (Manchester, MUP, 1991), pp. 179–236.
67. David Holloway, *Playing the Empire: The Acts of the Holloway Touring Company* (London, Harrap, 1979).
68. Diana Morgan, revised by K.D. Reynolds, 'Dame (Florence) Lilian Braithwaite (1873–1948)', *Oxford Dictionary of National Biography*. For other female transnational performers, such as Margaret Anglin and Katherine Dunham, see essays in D. Deacon et al. (eds), *Transnational Lives: Biographies of Global Modernity*.
69. *The Times of India*, 23 November 1911, p. 8. ProQuest Historical Newspapers.

70. In an interview in 1911, Bandmann commented on the immense popularity of Shakespeare among Indians, that they invariably brought their copies with them and then complained about the cuts. Christopher B. Balme, *The Globalization of the Theatre, 1870–1930: The Theatrical Networks of Maurice E. Bandmann* (Cambridge, CUP, 2020), pp. 148–9. This book and the research project lying behind it have unveiled the complexity of Bandmann's operations in the British World and beyond. While the Lang-Holloway company was in Bombay, another company, that of Allan Wilkie, was performing at the Empire Theatre, with plays including Irving's favourite, *The Bells*, as well as *Cramond Brig, Julius Caesar* and *The Cardinal. The Times of India*, 30 November 1911, p. 9. ProQuest Historical Newspapers.
71. Holloway, *Playing the Empire*, p. 146.
72. Balme, *Globalization of the Theatre*, p. 2.
73. *Straits Times*, 5 August 1911, p. 3 reported the details of an interview Bandmann had given to *The Referee*, https://eresources.nlb.gov.sg/newspapers/Digitised/Article/strait-stimes19110805-1.2.6 (accessed 21 June 2020).
74. *The Times of India*, 20 May 1907, p. 5, reported the negotiations with Bombay City Council for the building of this temporary theatre. ProQuest Historical Newspapers.
75. Ibid., pp. 74–80.
76. It was said that when the Bandmann Company arrived in Shanghai, the numbers of the chorus girls had been depleted by marriage and concubinage after tours of India and other territories. On the other hand, extras were supplied by the local Amateur Dramatic Society who had already learned the words and music for their own production. Ibid., p. 176.
77. Kendal, *White Cargo*, p. 14.
78. Trivedi, 'Garrison theatre', p. 103.
79. Gauri Viswanathan, *Masks of Conquest: Literary Study and British Rule in India* (New York, Columbia UP, 1989) and Jyotsna Singh, 'Different Shakespeare: the Bard in colonial/postcolonial India', *Theatre Journal*, 41 (1989), pp. 445–58.
80. Leah S. Marcus, *How Shakespeare Became Colonial: Editorial Tradition and the British Empire* (London, Routledge, 2017).
81. Kendal, *White Cargo*.

Chapter 9 Film and Radio

1. See: https://thecanadianencyclopedia.ca/en/article/the-history-of-film-in-canada (accessed 17 May 2020); Peter Morris, *Embattled Shadows: A History of Canadian Cinema 1895–1939* (Montreal, McGill-Queen's UP, 1979).
2. Andrew D. Roberts, 'Africa on film to 1940', *History in Africa*, 14 (1987), p. 191.
3. Annette Kuhn and Guy Westwell (eds), *A Dictionary of Film Studies* (Oxford, OUP, 2012), entry for 'South Africa, Film'.
4. The first date is given in Karina Aveyard, 'Cinema history trends', www.screenaustralia. gov.au/fact-finders/cinema/industry-trends/historical-admissions/before-1900 (accessed 14 April 2020), the second in https://en.wikipedia.org/wiki/Cinema_of_Australia (accessed 14 April 2020).
5. Jenny Gregory and Jan Gothard (eds), *Historical Encyclopedia of Western Australia* (Perth, University of Western Australia Press, 2009), p. 198.
6. See: https://teara.govt.nz/en/screen-industry/page-2 and www.ngataonga.org.nz/blog/film/moving-pictures-arrive-in-new-zealand/ (both accessed 17 May 2020).
7. *Otago Daily Times*, 18 April 1898.
8. See: http://eresources.nlb.gov.sg/history/events/1c727764-2ade-4ece-819d-76d4b0d36318 (accessed 17 May 2020).
9. Law Kar and Frank Bren, *Hong Kong Cinema: A Cross-cultural View* (Lanham, MD, Scarecrow Press, 2004), pp. 5-6. The Edison system reached the Far East from the western USA.

10. James Chapman and Nicholas J. Cull, *Projecting Empire: Imperialism and Popular Cinema* (London, I.B. Tauris, 2009) and Lee Grieveson and Colin MacCabe (eds), *Empire and Film* (London, Palgrave Macmillan, 2011).

11. James Burns, *Cinema and Society in the British Empire 1895–1940* (Houndmills, Palgrave Macmillan, 2013). Burns concentrates on India, Africa and the Caribbean. See also Burns, 'Excessive Americanisms: Hollywood in the British Empire, 1918–1930', *Britain and the World*, 7, 2 (2014), pp. 196–211.

12. John Grierson is credited with coining the term 'documentary' for factual film in 1926. In the 1960s, he presented television programmes about documentaries, in a series titled *This Wonderful World*.

13. John M. MacKenzie, *The British Empire through Buildings: Structure, Function and Meaning* (Manchester, MUP, 2020), pp. 156–7; Navin Ramani and Laura Cerwinske, *Bombay Art Deco Architecture* (Delhi, Roli Books, 2007) identifies five major Art Deco cinemas in Bombay.

14. Ting-yan Cheung and Pablo Sze-pang Tsoi, 'From an imported novelty to an indigenous practice: Hong Kong Cinema in the 1920s', in Emilie Yeuh-yu Yeh (ed.), *Early Film Culture in Hong Kong, Taiwan and Republican China* (Ann Arbor, MI, University of Michigan Press, 2018), pp. 71–100.

15. This growth can be charted in Josef Gugler (ed.), *The Urbanization of the Third World* (Oxford, OUP, 1988).

16. Burns, *Cinema and Society*, p. 11.

17. Ibid., p. 60.

18. Lord Hailey, *An African Survey: A Study of Problems Arising in Africa South of the Sahara* (London, OUP, 1938), p. 1302.

19. Hailey, *African Survey Revised 1956* (published in 1957), p. 1253.

20. James Burns, *Flickering Shadows: Cinema and Identity in Colonial Zimbabwe* (Athens, OH, Ohio UP 2002), p. 29.

21. Burns, *Cinema and Society*, pp. 49–52.

22. James Burns, 'Excessive Americanisms'. See also Joy Damousi, '"The filthy American twang": elocution, the advent of American "talkies" and Australian cultural identity', *American Historical Review*, 112, 2 (2007), pp. 394–416.

23. Burns, *Cinema and Society*, p. 14.

24. For propaganda, Greg Kennedy and Christopher Tuck (eds), *British Propaganda and Wars of Empire* (Farnham, Ashgate, 2014).

25. I am grateful to James Burns for this information.

26. For showings in Scotland, John M. MacKenzie, 'Exhibiting empire at the Delhi Durbar of 1911: imperial and cultural contexts', in John McAleer and John M. MacKenzie, *Exhibiting the Empire* (Manchester, MUP, 2015), pp. 194–219. For showings overseas, see Stephen Bottomore, 'Have you seen the Gaekwar Bob? Filming the 1911 Delhi Durbar', *Historical Journal of Film, Radio and Television*, 17, 3 (1997), pp. 309–45 and www.colonialfilm.org.uk/node/1455 (accessed 19 May 2020).

27. This can be seen at: www.youtube.com/watch?v=4VCpkplKUf8&feature=emb_rel_end (accessed 19 May 2020) or https://benbeck.co.uk/firsts/1_Technology/movie3t.htm (accessed 19 May 2020).

28. See: www.youtube.com/watch?v=6qlB8UVocY8 (accessed 6 July 2020).

29. See: www.colonialfilm.org.uk/genre/newsreels (accessed 19 May 2020). British Movietone and Associated Press newsreels relating to India can be found at: www.livemint.com/Consumer/9VIAMhObcPXD2gl7MuSX9O/What-the-newsreels-tell-us-about-India-of-the-1900s.html (accessed 19 May 2020).

30. See: www.colonialfilm.org.uk/production-company/missionary-societies (accessed 18 May 2020). This is the website of the 'Colonial Film: Moving Images of the British Empire' Arts and Humanities Research Council project, 2007–10, conducted in association with the British Film Institute and the then British Empire and Commonwealth Museum in Bristol.

31. J. Merle Davis, *Modern Industry and the African* (first published 1933, 2nd edn, London, Frank Cass, 1967).

32. See: www.colonialfilm.org.uk/node/1844 (accessed 19 May 2020). See also Dean Rapp and Charles W. Weber, 'British film, empire and society in the twenties: the Livingstone film, 1923-25', *Historical Journal of Film, Radio and Television*, 9, 1 (1989), pp. 3-17.

33. Jeffrey Richards, *Films and British National Identity* (Manchester, MUP, 1997), pp. 46-7.

34. Tom Rice, 'Exhibiting Africa: British Instructional Films and the Empire Series (1925-28)', in Grieveson and MacCabe (eds), *Empire and Film*, pp. 115-33.

35. Rosaleen Smyth, 'The development of British colonial film policy, 1927-1939, with special reference to East and Central Africa', *Journal of African History*, 20, 3 (1979), pp. 437-50. See also Roberts, 'Africa on film' and Burns, *Cinema and Society*, pp. 93-132.

36. Smyth, 'The development of British colonial film policy', p. 438.

37. Davis, *Modern Industry*.

38. Ibid., pp. 307 and 324-5. Davis focused on the copper mines of Northern Rhodesia (Zambia).

39. Scott Anthony, 'Imperialism and internationalism: the British documentary movement and the legacy of the Empire Marketing Board', in Grieveson and MacCabe (eds), *Empire and Film*, pp. 135-48. The GPO made some imperial films.

40. Aaron Windel, 'The Bantu Educational Kinema Experiment and the political economy of community development', in Grieveson and MacCabe (eds), *Empire and Film*, pp. 207-25. See also the chapter in that volume by Aboubakar Sanogo.

41. Smyth, 'The development of British colonial film policy', pp. 442-7.

42. Hailey, *African Survey*, pp. 1292, pp. 1301-3. In the revised 1956 edition of the *Survey*, p. 1253, Hailey detailed the number of cinemas in West Africa in the 1950s, including 40 in Nigeria and 26 in the Gold Coast. In Anglophone Africa, he claimed that 70 per cent of the films shown were American.

43. See: www.bfi.org.uk/films-tv-people/4ce2b9439f5e7 (accessed 23 May 2020).

44. The most detailed study of such films is Tom Rice, *Films for the Colonies: Cinema and the Preservation of the British Empire* (Oakland, CA, University of California Press, 2019), which carries the story through to the 1950s and the establishment of local units. Also chapters by James Burns, Tom Rice, David Trotter and Priya Jaikumar in Grieveson and MacCabe (eds), *Empire and Film*. John Grierson apparently saw the objectives of 'simple' films as being the outcome he was most proud of. Rosaleen Smyth, 'Grierson, the British Documentary Film Movement and colonial cinema in British colonial Africa', *Film History*, 25, 4 (2013), pp. 82-113.

45. Terri Francis, 'Sounding the nation: Martin Rennells and the Jamaican Film Unit, 1951-1961', *Film History*, 23 (2011), pp. 110-28.

46. Ikechukwu Obiaya, 'A break with the past: the Nigerian video film industry in the context of colonial filmmaking', *Film History*, 23 (2011), pp. 129-46.

47. Burns, *Flickering Shadows*, p. xix.

48. Ibid., chapter 3 and p. 129.

49. Educated Africans often decried such films as well. Ibid., pp. 164-5.

50. John M. MacKenzie, 'David Livingstone, the construction of the myth', in Graham Walker and Tom Gallagher (eds), *Sermons and Battle Hymns* (Edinburgh, EUP, 1990), pp. 24-42 and Joanna Lewis, *Empire of Sentiment: The Death of Livingstone and the Myth of Victorian Imperialism* (Cambridge, CUP, 2018), chapters 4-7.

51. Jeffrey Richards, 'Boy's Own empire: feature films and imperialism in the 1930s', in John M. MacKenzie (ed.), *Imperialism and Popular Culture* (Manchester, MUP, 1986), pp. 140-64.

52. Chapman and Cull, *Projecting Empire*.

53. Prem Chowdhry, *Colonial India and the Making of Empire Cinema: Image, Ideology and Identity* (Manchester, MUP, 2000), p. 240.
54. Ibid., p. 39.
55. John M. MacKenzie, *Propaganda and Empire* (Manchester, MUP, 1984), pp. 68–95, in which pp. 91–3 are devoted to the radio.
56. Lee Grieveson, 'The cinema and the (Common) Wealth of Nations . . .', in Grieveson and MacCabe (eds), *Empire and Film*, p. 100.
57. Chowdhry, *Colonial India*, p. 38.
58. The Cinematograph Film Act of 1927 decreed that 7.5 per cent of all films distributed in Britain had to be British according to a sequence of definitions. The quota was raised to 20 per cent in 1935.
59. See: www.thecanadianencyclopedia.ca/en/article/the-history-of-film-in-canada (accessed 24 May 2020) and https://encyclopediecanadienne.com/en/article/canadian-film-history-1939-to-1973 (accessed 24 May 2020).
60. Scott Mackenzie, 'A screen of one's own: early cinema in Quebec and the public sphere, 1906–28', *Screen*, 41, 2 (2000), pp. 183–202.
61. See: www.researchgate.net/publication/332751636_History_and_Evolution_of_Indian_Film_Industry (accessed 24 May 2020).
62. Their activities have been celebrated by Robin's daughter, Vilasnee Tampoe-Hautin. See https://en.wikipedia.org/wiki/Robin_Tampoe. This study has been much extended in Ian Conrich and Vilasnee Tampoe-Hautin, *The Cinema of Sri Lanka: South Asian Film in Texts and Contexts* (London, I.B. Tauris, 2019).
63. Aitor Anduaga, *Wireless and Empire: Geopolitics, Radio Industry and Ionosphere in the British Empire, 1918–1939* (Oxford, OUP, 2009).
64. John M. MacKenzie, '"In touch with the infinite": the BBC and the Empire, 1923–53', in John M. MacKenzie (ed.), *Imperialism and Popular Culture* (Manchester, MUP, 1986), pp. 165–91. See also Thomas Hajkowski, *The BBC and National Identity in Britain, 1922–53* (Manchester, MUP, 2010), which examines the role of radio in national events, in creating British imperial culture, in royal tours and also in the development of separate identities in Scotland and Wales.
65. Simon J. Potter, *Broadcasting and Empire: The BBC and the British World, 1922–1970* (Oxford, OUP, 2012).
66. Vincent Kuitenbrouwer, '"The brightness you bring into our otherwise very dull existence": responses to Dutch Global Radio broadcasts from the British Empire in the 1920s and 1930s', in Stephanie Barczewski and Martin Farr (eds), *The MacKenzie Moment and Imperial History* (Houndmills, Palgrave Macmillan, 2020), pp. 361–82.
67. Ruth Teer-Tomaselli, 'Language, programming and propaganda during the SABC's first decade', *African Media Studies*, 35. 2 (2015), pp. 59–76.
68. Sethunya Tsepho Mosime, 'Media control, colonialism and the making of an authoritarian postcolonial African state: the case of Botswana', *African Journalism Studies*, 36, 2 (2015), pp. 45–58. See also Everette Ndlovu, 'Three waves of media repression in Zimbabwe', in the same issue of the journal, pp. 25–44. These three waves were Southern Rhodesia in the Federal period, Rhodesia after 1963 and Zimbabwe after 1980.
69. Potter, *Broadcasting Empire*, p. 172.

Conclusion

1. David Cannadine argued (not entirely convincingly) that this reputation was a relatively recent phenomenon: 'The context, performance and meaning of ritual: the British monarchy and the "invention of tradition", c. 1820–1977', in Eric Hobsbawm and Terence Ranger (eds), *The Invention of Tradition* (Cambridge, CUP 1983), pp. 101–64.

2. A major conduit for translating these events into Britain was through the imperial exhibitions of the late nineteenth and early twentieth centuries.

3. Any member of a film audience in Africa can identify elements of cultural difference, as when Africans laugh at moments of poignancy in white action (what have they got to be sad about?), the opposite reaction to that intended, while white people react to supposedly strange (yet normal) practices in ethnic films with equal hilarity.

BIBLIOGRAPHY

PRIMARY SOURCES

Beckwith, Neville, 'Drama in Western Australia, 1829–1900', typescript in J.S. Battye History Library, State Library of Western Australia, Perth.

Fraser, Lovat, *At Delhi* (Bombay, *Times of India*, 1903).

Government of India, *Official Directory with Maps, Coronation Durbar 1911* (Delhi, Government Printing, 1911).

Hailey, Lord, *An African Survey: A Study of Problems Arising in Africa South of the Sahara* (London, OUP, 1938).

Yule, Henry, and Burnell, A.C., *Hobson-Jobson: An Anglo-Indian Dictionary* (Ware, Herts, Wordsworth Editions, 1986, first published 1886).

Many newspapers, cited in the footnotes, were consulted on the web and in archives and libraries in Adelaide, Hobart, Melbourne, Perth and Sydney in Australia; Wellington, New Zealand; Halifax NS and Vancouver BC, in Canada; Singapore; in South Africa, Cape Town and Pietermaritzburg.

DIARIES, LETTERS AND MEMOIRS

Adcock, St John, *The Prince of Wales' African Book: A Pictorial Record of the Journey to West Africa, South Africa and South America* (London, Hodder and Stoughton, 1925).

Bremner, Fred, *My Forty Years in India*, with an introduction by Hugh Rayner (Bath, Pagoda Tree Press, 2007).

Butler, Sir W.F., *Sir William Butler: An Autobiography* (London, Constable, 1911).

Churchill, Winston S., *My Early Life* (London, Odhams, 1947).

Clutterbuck, George W., *In India or Bombay the Beautiful* (London, Ideal Publishing Union, 1899).

Earle, Augustus, *A Narrative of Nine Months' Residence in New Zealand in 1827* (Christchurch NZ, Whitecombe and Tombs 1909, first published 1832).

Eden, Emily, *Portraits of the Princes and People of India with 28 hand-coloured lithograph plates* (London, Dickinson, 1844).

—— *Up the Country: Letters written to her sister from the Upper Provinces of India*, introduction and notes by Edward Thompson (London, Curzon Press, 1978, 1st edn 1930).

Frew, A.A., *Prince George's African Tour* (London, Blackie, 1934).

Gilbert, Martin (ed.), *Servant of India: A Study of Imperial Rule 1905–1910 as told through the correspondence and diaries of Sir James Dunlop Smith, Private Secretary to the Viceroy* (London, Longmans, 1966).

Headlam, Cecil, *Ten Thousand Miles through India and Burma: An Account of the Oxford University Authentics' Cricket Tour . . . in the year of the Durbar* (London, Dent, 1903).

Hickey, William, and Spencer, Alfred (ed.), *Memoirs of William Hickey*, vol. II, *1775–82* (London, Hurst and Blackett, 1918).

Hobbes, John Oliver (Mrs Pearl Craigie), *Imperial India: Letters from the East* (London, Fisher Unwin, 1903).

Hodges, William, *Select Views in India, drawn on the spot, in the years 1780, 1781, 1782, and 1783, and executed in aqua tinta, by William Hodges, R.A.* (London, printed for the author and sold by J. Edwards, 1785).

—— *Travels in India, during the Years 1780, 1781, 1782, & 1783. By William Hodges, R.A.* (London, printed for the author and sold by J. Edwards, 1793).

Ingall, Francis, *The Last of the Bengal Lancers* (London, Leo Cooper, 1988).

Jacob, Violet, *Diaries and Letters from India 1895–1900* (Edinburgh, Canongate, 1990).

James, B.A. 'Jimmy' (ed.), *High Noon of Empire: The Diary of Lt. Col. Henry Tyndall 1895–1915* (Barnsley, Pen and Sword, 2007).

King George's Jubilee Trust, *Their Majesties' Visit to Canada, the United States and Newfoundland, 1939* (London, Macmillan, 1939).

Littlewood, Arthur (ed.), *Indian Mutiny and Beyond: The Letters of Robert Shebbeare VC* (Barnsley, Pen and Sword, 2007).

Menpes, Mortimer, *The Durbar* (London, Adam and Charles Black, 1903).

Mountbatten, Pamela, *India Remembered: A Personal Account of the Mountbattens during the Transfer of Power* (London, Pavilion Books, 2007).

Mundy, General Godfrey Charles, *Journal of a Tour in India* (London, John Murray, 1858, 3rd edn).

Murray, Dr John, *Photographic Views in Agra and its Vicinity*, accompanying captions by J. Middleton (London, J. Hogarth, 1858).

—— *Picturesque Views in the North-Western Provinces of India* (London, J. Hogarth, 1859).

O'Connor, V.C. Scott, *The Empire Cruise* (London, printed privately for the author, 1925).

Phillips, Sir Percival, *The Prince of Wales' Eastern Book: A Pictorial Record of the Voyages of HMS Renown, 1921–1922* (London, Hodder and Stoughton, 1923).

Price, G. Ward, *Through South Africa with the Prince* (London, Gill, 1926).

Rayner, Hugh (ed.), *Photographic Journeys in the Himalayas, 1863–1866, Samuel Bourne* (Bath, Pagoda Tree Press, 2009).

Roberts, Field Marshal Lord, of Kandahar, *Forty-one Years in India: From Subaltern to Commander-in-Chief*, 2 vols (London, Richard Bentley, 1897).

Steer, Valentia, *The Delhi Durbar of 1902–3: A Concise Illustrated History* (London, Marshall, 1903).

Syiemlieh, David R. (ed.), *Robert Lindsay (1754–1836), Anecdotes of an Indian Life* (Shillong, North-Eastern Hill University Publications, 1997).

Thomson, J., *The Straits of Malacca, Indo-China and China or Ten years' Travels, Adventures and Residence Abroad* (London, Sampson Low, 1875).

Turley, Charles, *With the Prince Round the Empire* (London, Methuen, 1926).

Wallace, Donald Mackenzie, *The Web of Empire: A Diary of the Imperial Tour of their Royal Highnesses the Duke and Duchess of Cornwall and York in 1901* (London, Macmillan, 1902).

Wallis, J.P.R. (ed.), *The Northern Goldfields Diaries of Thomas Baines*, 3 vols (London, Chatto and Windus, 1946).

Wheeler, H. Talboys, *The History of the Imperial Assemblage at Delhi, held on 1ˢᵗ January 1877 to celebrate the Assumption of the Title of Empress of India by H.M. the Queen, including historical sketches of the Indian Princes, Past and Present* (London, Longmans Green, 1877).

Wheeler, Stephen, *A History of the Delhi Coronation Durbar held on 1ˢᵗ January 1903 to Celebrate the Coronation of His Majesty King Edward VII, Emperor of India, Compiled from Official Papers* (London, John Murray, 1904).

ARTICLES AND THESES

Akeyami, Akande, 'Early attempts at architectural photography in Lagos, Nigeria', *Lagos Journal of Architecture*, 2 (July 2016), pp. 19–33.

Aldrich, Robert, 'Commemorating colonialism in a post-colonial world', *e-Rea* (online journal), 10, 1 (2012), http://journals.openedition.org/erea/2803 (accessed 7 December 2021; doi: https://doi.org/10.4000/erea.2803

Asante, Sheila, 'From Lucknow to Lahore: Fred Bremner's vision of India', *Asian Affairs*, 44, 1 (2013), pp. 89–96.

Auerbach, Jeffrey, 'The picturesque and the homogenization of empire', *British Art Journal*, 5, 1 (spring/summer 2004), pp. 47–54.

August, Tom, 'Art and empire – Wembley, 1924', *History Today*, 43 (October 1993), pp. 38–44.

Becker, Tobias, 'Entertaining the empire: theatrical touring companies and amateur dramatics in colonial India', *Historical Journal*, 57, 3 (2014), pp. 699–725.

Best, J. Linden, 'Box, pit and gallery: the Theatre Royal, Spring Gardens [Halifax]', *Dalhousie Review*, 53, 3 (1923), pp. 520–8.

Bhattacharya, Rimli, 'Promiscuous spaces and economies of entertainment: soldiers, actresses and hybrid genres in colonial India', *Nineteenth-Century Theatre and Film*, 41, 2 (2014), pp. 50–75.

Blake, Ann, '"Our Shakespeare": the Melbourne Shakespeare Society, 1884–1930', *Nineteenth-Century Theatre and Film*, 36, 1 (2009), pp. 73–86.

Bottomore, Stephen, 'Have you seen the Gaekwar Bob? Filming the 1911 Delhi Durbar', *Historical Journal of Film, Radio and Television*, 17, 3 (1997), pp. 309–45.

Bradlow, Frank R., 'The colourful Thomas Baines', *South African Library Bulletin*, 29 (1975), pp. 138–43.

Bridge, Carl and Fedorowich, Kent (eds), 'The British world: diaspora, culture, identity', special issue of the *JICH*, 31, 2 (May 2003).

Brown, Julie and Maynard, Margaret, 'Painter and photographer: Brisbane in the 1880s and 1890s', *History of Photography*, 2, 4 (1978), pp. 325–33.

Brownfoot, Janice N., '"Healthy bodies, healthy minds": sport and society in colonial Malaya', *IJHS*, 19, 2–3 (2002), pp. 129–56.

Burns, James, 'Excessive Americanisms: Hollywood in the British Empire, 1918–1930', *Britain and the World*, 7, 2 (2014), pp. 196–211.

Campbell, J.D., '"Training for sport is training for war": sport and the transformation of the British army, 1860–1914', *IJHS*, 17, 4 (2000), pp. 21–58.

Chattopadhyay, Malyaban, 'A historical study of ancient Indian theatre-communication in the light of *Natyasastra*', *Global Media Journal – Indian Edition*, online, sponsored by the University of Calcutta, Article 12, 4, 2 (December 2013), unpaginated.

Chick, John D., 'The *Ashanti Times*: a footnote to Ghanaian press history', *African Affairs*, 76, 302 (1977), pp. 80–94.

Colvin, Ian D., 'South African aquatints: Samuel Daniell and his work', *The State*, 6, 6 (December 1911), pp. 557–65.

Crooks, Julie, *Alphonso Lisk-Carew, Early Photography in Sierra Leone*, PhD thesis, SOAS, University of London, 2014.

Curzon, Marquess, of Kedleston, 'The cradle of polo', in *Leaves from a Viceroy's Notebook and Other Papers* (London, Macmillan, 1926), pp. 79–90.

Damousi, Joy, '"The filthy American twang": elocution, the advent of American "talkies" and Australian cultural identity', *American Historical Review*, 112, 2 (2007), pp. 394–416.

Dasgupta, Shamya, 'An inheritance from the British: the Indian boxing story', *IJHS*, 21, 3–4 (2004), pp. 31–51.

Davis, Ann, 'The Wembley controversy in Canadian art', *Canadian Historical Review*, 54, 1 (March 1993), pp. 48–74.

De Lorenzo, Catherina, 'The imaging of Aborigines: commitment to land rights', *History of Photography*, 15, 3 (1991), pp. 228–35.

Deschamps, Simon, 'Freemasonry and the Indian Parsi community: a late meeting on the level', *Journal of Freemasonry and Fraternalism*, 3, 1 (2012), pp. 61–72.

Diakhaté, Ousmane and Eyoh, Hansel Ndumbe, 'The roots of African theatre ritual and orality in the pre-colonial period', *International Association of Theatre Critics Journal* (*IATC journal/Revue de l'AICT*) online, 15 (2017).

Drayton, Richard, 'Rhodes must not fall?', *Third Text*, 33, 4–5 (2019), pp. 651–66.

Dubow, Saul, 'How British was the British World? The case of South Africa', *JICH*, 37, 1 (2009), pp. 1–27.

Edwards, Elizabeth (ed.), 'Anthropology and colonial endeavour', special issue, *History of Photography*, 21, 1 (1997).

Elsaesser, Luise, '"Dashing about with the greatest gallantry": polo in India and the British metropole, 1862–1914', *Sport in History*, 40, 1 (May 2019), pp. 1–27.

Engmann, Rachel Ama Asaa, 'Under imperial eyes, black bodies, buttocks and breasts: British colonial photography and Asante fetish girls', *African Arts*, 45, 2 (2012), pp. 46–57.

Etherington, Norman, 'Barbarians ancient and modern', *American Historical Review*, 116, 1 (February 2011), pp. 31–57.

Foster, Sir William, 'British artists in India', *Journal of the Royal Society of Arts*, 98, 4820 (May 1950), pp. 518–25.

Francis, Terri, 'Sounding the nation: Martin Rennells and the Jamaican Film Unit, 1951–1961', *Film History*, 23 (2011), pp. 110–28.

Gordon, Sophie, 'Photography in India', *International Institute for Asian Studies Newsletter*, 44 (summer 2007), pp. 10–11.

Gore, Chris, 'Neils Walwin Holm: radicalising the image in Lagos Colony, West Africa', *History of Photography*, 37, 3 (2013), pp. 283–300.

Grant, Kevin, 'Christian critics of empire: missionaries, lantern lectures and the Congo Reform Campaign in Britain', *JICH*, 29, 2 (2001), pp. 27–58.

Guha, Ramachandra, 'Cricket and politics in colonial India', *Past and Present*, 161 (November 1998), pp. 155–90.

Hartman, James B., 'On stage, theatre and theatres in early Winnipeg', *Manitoba History*, 43 (2002), pp. 15–24.

Hay, Iain, Hughes, Andrew and Tutton, Mark, 'Monuments, memorials and marginalisation in Adelaide's Prince Henry Gardens', *Geografiska Annales*, Series B, Human Geography, 86, 3 (September 2004), pp. 200–16.

Hercock, Marion, 'A history of hunting with hounds in Western Australia', *Early Days, the Journal of the Royal Western Australia Historical Society*, 11, part 6 (2000), pp. 695–712.

Hichberger, J.W.M., 'Democratising glory? The Victoria Cross paintings of Louis Desanges', *Oxford Art Journal*, 7, 2 (1984), pp. 42–51.

Hoorn, Jeanette, 'Joseph Lycett: the pastoral landscape in early colonial Australia', *Art Bulletin of Victoria*, 26 (1986), pp. 4–14. Now digitised by the National Gallery of Victoria and available online in *Art Journal*, 26 (24 June 2014), unpaginated.

Hopkins, A.G., 'Back to the future: from national history to imperial history', *Past and Present*, 164 (August 1999), pp. 198–243.

Horton, Peter A., 'Rugby Union football and its role in the socio-cultural development of Queensland, 1882–91', *IJHS*, 9, 1 (1992), pp. 119–31.

—— '"Padang or paddock": a comparative view of sport in two imperial territories', *IJHS*, 14, 1 (1997), pp. 1–20.

—— 'The "green" and the "gold": the Irish-Australians and their role in the emergence of the Australian sports culture', *IJHS*, 17, 2–3 (2000), pp. 65–92.

—— 'Pacific Islanders in global rugby: the changing currents of sports migration', *IJHS*, 29, 27 (2012), pp. 1288–2404.

Hyam, Ronald, 'Empire and sexual opportunity', *JICH*, 14, 2 (1986), pp. 34–90.

—— 'Concubinage and the Colonial Service: the Crewe Circular', *JICH*, 14, 3 (1986) pp. 170–86.

Jarvis, Andrew, '"The myriad pencil of the photographer": seeing, mapping and situating Burma in 1855', *Modern Asian Studies*, 45, 5 (2001), pp. 791–823.

Jenkins, Paul, 'Much more than illustrations of what we already know: experiences in the rediscovery of mission photography', *IBMR*, 26, 4, (2002), pp. 157–62.

Johnson, Nuala C., 'Sculpting heroic histories: celebrating the centenary of the 1798 Rebellion in Ireland', *Transactions of the Institution of British Geographers*, 19, 1 (1994), pp. 78–93.

Johnson, Samantha and Seton, Rosemary, '"Fields of vision": photographs in the missionary collections at the School of Oriental and African Studies, London', 26, 4 (Oct. 2002), pp. 164–8.

Killingray, David and Roberts, Andrew, 'An outline history of photography in Africa to c. 1940', *History in Africa*, 16 (1989), pp. 197–208.

Kirk-Greene, A.H.M., 'The thin white line: the size of the civil service in Africa', *African Affairs*, 79, 314 (1980), pp. 25–44.

Koole, Simeon, 'Photography as event: power, the Kodak camera and territoriality in early twentieth-century Tibet', *Comparative Studies in Society and History*, 59, 2 (2017), pp. 310–45.

Kubicek, R.V., 'The role of shallow-draft steamboats in the expansion of the British Empire, 1820–1914', *International Journal of Maritime Research*, 6, 1 (June 1994), pp. 85–106.

Lothrop, Eaton S., 'The Brownie camera', *History of Photography*, 2, 1 (1978), pp. 1–10.

McCracken, John, 'Mungo Murray Chisuse and the early history of photography in Malawi', *The Society of Malawi Journal*, 61, 2 (2008), 1–18.

McDevitt, Patrick, 'The king of sports: polo in late Victorian and Edwardian India', *IJHS*, 20, 1 (2003), pp. 1–27.

McDowell, Matthew L., 'Sport and social relations in the Falkland Islands up to 1982', *JICH*, 48, 6 (2020), pp. 1078–1108.

McGarr, Paul, '"The viceroys are disappearing from the roundabouts in Delhi": British symbols of power in post-colonial India', *Modern Asian Studies*, 49, 3 (2015), pp. 787–831.

MacKenzie, John M., 'Irish, Scottish, Welsh and English worlds? A four-nation approach to the history of the British Empire', *History Compass* (online journal), 6, 5 (Sept. 2008), pp. 1244–63.

—— 'The British Empire: ramshackle or rampaging? A historiographical reflection' in the *JICH*, 43, 1 (March 2015), pp. 99–124.

McKenzie, Ray, '"The laboratory of mankind": John McCosh and the beginnings of photography in British India', *History of Photography*, 11, 2 (1987), pp. 109–18.

Mackenzie, Scott, 'A screen of one's own: early cinema in Quebec and the public sphere, 1906–28', *Screen*, 41, 2 (2000), pp. 183–202.

Majumdar, Boria, 'Cricket in colonial India: the Bombay Pentangular, 1892–1946', *IJHS*, 19, 2–3 (2002), pp. 157–88.

—— 'Imperial tool for nationalist resistance: the games ethic in Indian history', *IJHS*, 21, 3–4 (2004), pp. 384–401.

—— 'Maharajahs and cricket: self, state, province and nation', *IJHS*, 22, 4 (2005), pp. 639–48.

—— 'The golden years of Indian Hockey: "We climb the victory stand"', *IJHS*, 25, 12 (2008), pp. 1592–611.

Mangan, J.A. and McKenzie, Callum, '"Blooding" the martial male: the imperial officer, field sports and big-game hunter', *IJHS*, 25, 9 (August 2008), pp.1057–79.

Marshall, P.J., 'The White Town of Calcutta under the rule of the East India Company', *Modern Asian Studies*, 34, 2 (2000), pp. 307–31.

Mosime, Sethunya Tsepho, 'Media control, colonialism and the making of an authoritarian postcolonial African state: the case of Botswana', *African Journalism Studies*, 36, 2 (2015), pp. 45–58.

Mukhopadhyay, Durgodas, 'Ancient Indian stage and its conventions', *Annals of the Bhandarkar Oriental Research Institute*, 69, 1/4 (1988), pp. 243–8.

Ndlovu, Everette, 'Three waves of media repression in Zimbabwe', *African Journalism Studies*, 36, 2 (2015), pp. 25–44.

Nead, Lynda, 'The secret of England's greatness', *Journal of Victorian Culture*, 19, 2 (2014), pp. 161–82.

Newell, Stephanie, 'Paradoxes of press freedom in British West Africa', *Media History*, 22, 1 (2016), pp. 101–22.

Ng, Michael, 'When silence speaks: press censorship and rule of law in British Hong Kong, 1850s–1940s', *Law and Literature*, 29, 3 (2017), pp. 425–56.

Nicholson, Rashna Darius, 'Troubling Englishness: the eastward success and westward failure of the Parsi theatre', *Nineteenth-Century Theatre and Film*, 44, 1 (2017), pp. 75–91.

Nielsen, Erik, '"Indian hockey (and football) tricks": race, magic, wonder and empire in Australian–Indian sporting relations, 1926–38', *Sport in Society*, 15, 4 (2012), pp. 551–64.

Nordström, Alison Devine, 'Early photography in Samoa', *History of Photography*, 15 (1991), pp. 272–86.

Obiaya, Ikechukwu, 'A break with the past: the Nigerian video film industry in the context of colonial filmmaking', *Film History*, 23 (2011), pp. 129–46.

Orr, Inge C., 'Puppet theatre in Asia', *Asian Folklore Studies*, 33, 1 (1974), pp. 69–84.

Osborne, Brian S., 'Constructing landscapes of power: the George Etienne Cartier monument, Montreal', *Journal of Historical Geography*, 24, 4 (October 1998), pp. 431–58.

—— and Osborne, Geraint B., 'The Cast[e]ing of heroic landscapes of power: constructing Canada's Pantheon on Parliament Hill', *Material History Review*, 60 (fall 2004), pp. 35–47.

Perkin, Harold J., 'Teaching the nations how to play: sport in the British Empire and Commonwealth', *IJHS*, 6, 2 (1980), pp. 145–55.

Porter, Andrew, 'Sir Roger Casement and the international humanitarian movement', *JICH*, 29, 2 (2001), pp. 59–74.

Ranger, Terence, 'Making Northern Rhodesia imperial: variations on a royal theme, 1924–1938', *African Affairs*, 79, 316 (1980), pp. 362–5.

Rapp, Dean and Weber, Charles W., 'British film, empire and society in the twenties: the Livingstone film, 1923–25', *Historical Journal of Film, Radio and Television*, 9, 1 (1989), pp. 3–17.

Roberts, Andrew, 'Photographs and African history', Review article, *Journal of African History*, 29, 2 (1988), pp. 301–11.

—— 'Africa on film to 1940', *History in Africa*, 14 (1987), pp. 189–227.

Rollman, Hans, 'The beginnings of Moravian missionary photography in Labrador', *IBMR*, 26, 4 (2002), pp. 150–6.

Ruskin, Pamela, 'George French Angas, pioneer artist', *Walkabout*, 33 (1967), pp. 32–5.

Ryan, James R., 'Visualizing imperial geography: Halford Mackinder and the Colonial Office Visual Instruction Committee, 1902–11', *Ecumene, a Journal of Environment, Culture, Meaning*, 1, 2 (1994), pp. 157–76.

Sacks, Benjamin, 'A footnote to sport history: twenty years of cricket, conflict and contestation in Samoa, 1880–1900', *IJHS*, 34, 14 (2017), pp. 1483–500.

Salawu, Abiodun, 'The Yoruba and their language newspapers: origin, nature, problems and prospects', *Studies of Tribes and Tribals*, 2, 2 (2004), pp. 97–104.

—— 'Not Iwe Irohin, but Umshumayeli, a revisit of the history of the early African language press', *African Identities*, 13, 2 (2015), pp. 157–70.

Schweitzer, Marlis, '"Too much tragedy in real life": theatre in post-emancipation Jamaica', *Nineteenth-Century Theatre and Film*, 44, 1 (2017), pp. 8–27.

Sharma, Brij Bhushan, 'Artists and photography: some Indian encounters', *History of Photography*, 12, 3 (1988), pp. 247–58.

—— 'Fred Bremner's Indian Years', *History of Photography*, 13, 4 (1989), pp. 293–301.

Shaw, Damian, 'Two "Hottentots", some Scots and a West Indian slave: the origins of Kaatje Kekkelbek', *English Studies in Africa*, 52, 2 (2009), pp. 4–17.

Simpson, Donald, 'Missions and the magic lantern', *IBMR*, 21, 2 (1997), pp. 13–15.

Singh, Jyotsna, 'Different Shakespeare: the bard in colonial/postcolonial India', *Theatre Journal*, 41 (1989), pp. 445–58.

Skidmore, Colleen, 'Women workers of Notman's Studio: young ladies of the printing room', *History of Photography*, 20, 2 (1996), pp. 122–8.

Smith, Lawrence D., 'Spectacular remedies to colonial conflicts: tableaux vivants, proto-cinema and global performance in Dion Boucicault's *Jessie Brown*', *Nineteenth-Century Theatre and Film*, 41, 2 (2014), pp. 29–49.

Smyth, Rosaleen, 'The development of British colonial film policy, 1927–1939, with special reference to East and Central Africa', *Journal of African History*, 20, 3 (1979), pp. 437–50.

—— 'Grierson, the British Documentary Film Movement and colonial cinema in British colonial Africa', *Film History*, 25, 4 (2013), pp. 82–113.

Sonwalkar, Prasun, 'Indian journalism in the colonial crucible: a nineteenth-century story of political protest', *Journalism Studies*, 16, 5 (2015), pp. 624–36.

Stedman, Heather, 'Monuments to the Duke of Wellington in nineteenth-century Ireland, forging British and imperial identities', *Irish Geographer*, 46, 1–2 (2013), pp. 129–59.

Steggles, Mary Anne, 'Set in stone: Victoria's monuments in India', *History Today*, 51 (February 2001), pp. 44–9.

Stoddart, Brian, 'Sport, cultural imperialism and colonial response', *Comparative Studies in Society and History*, 30, 4 (1988), pp. 649–73.

Swart, Sandra, 'Horses, power and settler society, the Cape c. 1654–1840', *Kronos: Southern African Histories* (University of the Western Cape), 29 (November 2003), pp. 47–63.

Tam, Wing Sze, 'Public space and British colonial power, the transformation of Hong Kong Statues Square, 1890s–1920s', MPhil thesis, Lingnan University, 2014.

Teer-Tomaselli, Ruth, 'Language, programming and propaganda during the SABC's first decade', *African Media Studies*, 35, 2 (2015), pp. 59–76.

Teulié, Gilles, 'World War Two iconoclasm: the destruction and reconstruction of memorials to Queen Victoria and Edward VII on the French Riviera', *e-Rea* (online journal), 14, 2 (2017), http://journals.openedition.org/erea/5809 (accessed 8 December 2021); doi: https://doi.org/10.4000/erea.5809

—— 'Southern (African) belles and the aesthetic forms of seduction: portraying Zulu women in early twentieth-century postcards', *L'Atelier*, 9, 2 (2017), pp. 62–96.

—— 'Orientalism and the British picture postcard industry: popularising the empire in Victorian and Edwardian homes', *Cahiers Victoriens et Edouardiens* (Montpellier, Centre d'études et de recherches victoriennes et édouardiennes et contemporains, 2019), pp. 1–17.

Thomas, G., 'Photography and the Elphinstone Institution of Bombay', *History of Photography*, 5, 3 (1981), pp. 245–7.

—— 'Linnaeus Tripe in Madras', *History of Photography*, 5, 4 (1981), pp. 329–37.

—— 'Rajendra Lall Mitra (1822–90)', *History of Photography*, 8, 3 (1984), pp. 223–6.

—— 'Maharaja Sawai Ram Singh II of Jaipur, photographer-prince', *History of Photography*, 10, 3 (1986), pp. 181–91.

—— 'The Madras Photographic Society, 1856–61', *History of Photography*, 16, 4 (1992), pp. 229–301.

Thompson, T. Jack, 'Light on the Dark Continent: The photography of Alice Seely Harris and the Congo atrocities of the early twentieth century', *IBMR*, 26, 4 (2002), pp. 146–9.

Tillotson, G.H.R., 'The Indian travels of William Hodges', *Journal of the Royal Asiatic Society*, third series, 2, 3 (1992), pp. 377–98.

Tola, Mulualem Daba, 'The historiography and values of statue construction: focus on global perspectives', *Humanities and Social Sciences*, 5, 2 (2017), pp. 53–9.

Tucker, Abigail, 'Sketching the earliest views of the New World', *The Smithsonian Magazine* online (December 2008), unpaginated.

Twomey, Christina, 'Framing atrocity: photography and humanitarianism', *History of Photography*, 36, 3 (2012), pp. 255–64.

Vasili, Phillip, '"The right kind of fellows": Nigerian football tourists as agents of Europeanisation', *IJHS*, 11, 2 (1994), pp. 191–211.

West, J. Thomas, 'Thoroughbred racing', in *The Canadian Encyclopedia*, 15 December 2013, Historica Canada, www.thecanadianencyclopedia.ca/en/article/thoroughbred-racing.

Whelan, Yvonne, 'Monuments, power and contested space – the iconography of Sackville Street (O'Connell Street) before independence (1922)', *Irish Geographer*, 34, 1 (2001), pp. 11–33.

—— 'Symbolising the state – the iconography of O'Connell Street and environs after independence (1922)', *Irish Geographer*, 34, 2 (2001), pp. 135–56.

—— 'The construction and destruction of a colonial landscape: monuments to British monarchs in Dublin before and after independence', *Journal of Historical Geography*, 28, 4 (2002), pp. 508–33.

Whittaker, Robin C., '"Entirely free of any amateurishness": private training, public taste and the Women's Dramatic Club of University College, Toronto (1905–21)', *Nineteenth-Century Theatre and Film*, 38, 2 (2011), pp. 51–66.

Willcock, Sean, 'Aesthetic bodies: posing on sites of violence in India, 1857–1900', *History of Photography*, 39, 2 (2015), pp. 142–59.

Woolford, J.V., 'Africa through the eyes of a painter-explorer', *Geographical Magazine*, 55, 3 (March 1983), pp. 148–53.

Zou, Yizheng, 'English newspapers in British colonial Hong Kong: the case of the *South China Morning Post*, 1903–1941', *Critical Arts: South-North Cultural and Media Studies*, 29, 1 (2015), pp. 26–40.

BOOKS

Aberdeen and Temair, Ishbel Gordon, Marchioness of, and Harper, Marjory (ed.), *Through Canada with a Kodak* (Toronto and London, University of Toronto Press, 1994, originally published Edinburgh, E.H. White, 1893).

Adas, Michael, *Machines as the Measure of Men: Science, Technology and Ideologies of Western Dominance* (Ithaca, NY, Cornell UP, 1989).

Aldrich, Robert, *Vestiges of the Colonial Empire in France: Monuments, Museums and Colonial Memories* (Basingstoke, Palgrave Macmillan, 2005).

—— *Banished Potentates: Dethroning and Exiling Indigenous Monarchs under British and French colonial rule, 1815–1955* (Manchester, MUP, 2018).

—— and McCreery, Cindy (eds), *Royals on Tour: Politics, Pageantry and Colonialism* (Manchester, MUP, 2018).

Ali, Abdullah Yusuf, *A Cultural History of India during the British Period* (New York, AMS Press, 1976, first published 1945).

Alloula, Malek, *The Colonial Harem* (Manchester, MUP, 1986).

Ames, Eric, Klotz, Marcia and Wildenthal, Lora (eds), *Germany's Colonial Pasts* (Lincoln, NE, University of Nebraska Press, 2005).

Anduaga, Aitor, *Wireless and Empire: Geopolitics, Radio Industry and Ionosphere in the British Empire, 1918–1939* (Oxford, OUP, 2009).

Anon., *Rock Paintings in Africa* (Claremont, Cape Town, South African Archaeological Society, 1960).

Appleyard, Ron, *S. T. Gill: The South Australian Years, 1839–1852* (Adelaide, Art Gallery of South Australia, 1986).

Archer, Mildred, *India and British Portraiture 1770–1825* (London, Sotheby's Publications, 1979).

—— *Early Views of India: Picturesque Journeys of Thomas and William Daniell, 1786–1794* (London, Thames and Hudson, 1980).

—— *Visions of India: The Sketchbooks of William Simpson, 1859–1862* (London, Phaidon, 1986).

—— *Company Paintings, Indian Paintings of the British Period* (London, V&A Museum, 1992).

—— and Falk, Toby, *India Revealed: The Art and Adventures of James and William Fraser, 1801–1835* (London, Cassell, 1989).

—— and Lightbown, Ronald, *India Observed: India as Viewed by British Artists, 1760–1860* (London, V&A Museum, 1982).

Arndt, Susan and Brendt, Katrin (eds), *Words and Worlds: African Writing, Theatre and Society* (Trenton, NJ, Africa World Press, 2007).

Auerbach, Jeffrey A., *Imperial Boredom: Monotony and the British Empire* (Oxford, OUP, 2018).

Auhl, Ian and Marfleet, Denis, *Australia's Earliest Mining Era, 1841–1851: Paintings by S. T. Gill* (Adelaide, Rigby, 1975).

Baden-Powell, Robert, *Scouting for Boys* (London, Cox, 1908).

Baker, William J. and Mangan, James A. (eds), *Sport in Africa: Essays in Social History* (New York, Africana Publishing, 1987).

Ballantyne, Tony, *Orientalism and Race: Aryanism in the British Empire* (Basingstoke, Palgrave, 2002).

Balme, Christopher B., *The Globalization of the Theatre, 1870–1930: The Theatrical Networks of Maurice E. Bandmann* (Cambridge, CUP, 2020).

Banham, Martin (ed.), *A History of Theatre in Africa* (Cambridge, CUP, 2002).

Barczewski, Stephanie, *Country Houses and the British Empire, 1700–1930* (Manchester, MUP, 2014).

—— and Farr, Martin (eds), *The MacKenzie Moment and Imperial History* (Basingstoke, Palgrave Macmillan, 2020).

Barringer, Tim, Quilley, Geoff and Fordham, Douglas (eds), *Art and the British Empire* (Manchester, MUP, 2007).

Barton, Frank, *The Press of Africa: Persecution and Perseverance* (London, Macmillan, 1979).

Battiss, Walter, *The Artists of the Rocks* (Pretoria, Red Fawn Press, 1948).

Bayly, C.A., *Imperial Meridian: The British Empire and the World, 1780–1830* (Harlow, Pearson, 1989).

—— (ed.), *The Raj: India and the British 1600–1947* (London, National Portrait Gallery, 1990).

—— *Empire and Information: Intelligence Gathering and Social Communication in India, 1780–1870* (Cambridge, CUP, 1997).

—— *The Birth of the Modern World, 1780–1914* (Malden, MA, Blackwell, 2004).

Beckles, Hilary McD. and Stoddart, Brian (eds), *Liberation Cricket: West Indies Cricket Culture* (Manchester, MUP, 1995).

Behrens, Heike, *Contesting Visibility: Photographic Practices on the East African Coast* (Bielefeld, Transcripts Verlag, 2013).

Beinart, William and Hughes, Lotte, *Environment and Empire* (Oxford, OUP, 2007).

Belich, James, *Making Peoples, a History of the New Zealanders: From Polynesian Settlement to the End of the Nineteenth Century* (London, Allen Lane, 1996).

—— *Paradise Reforged: A History of the New Zealanders from the 1880s to the year 2000* (London, Allen Lane, 2001).

—— *Replenishing the Earth: The Settler Revolution and the Rise of the Anglo-World, 1783–1939* (Oxford, OUP, 2009).

Bell, Duncan, *Reordering the World: Essays on Liberalism and Empire* (Princeton, NJ, Princeton UP, 2016).

—— *The Idea of Greater Britain: Empire and the Future of World Order, 1860–1900* (Princeton, NJ, Princeton UP, 2007).

Bensusan, A.D., *Silver Images: History of Photography in Africa* (Cape Town, Howard Timmins, 1966).

Berger, Carl, *The Sense of Power: Studies in the Ideas of Canadian Imperialism, 1867–1914* (Toronto, Toronto UP, 1970).

Berman, Esmé, *Art and Artists in South Africa: An Illustrated Biographical Dictionary and Survey of Painters and Graphic Artists since 1875* (Cape Town, A.A. Balkema, 1974).

Berton, Pierre, *Canada from Sea to Sea* (Ottawa, Department of External Affairs, Government of Canada, 1958).

Beukers, Alan, *Exotic Postcards: The Lure of Distant Lands* (London, Thames and Hudson, 2007).

Beveridge, Lord, *India Called Them* (London, Allen and Unwin, 1947).

Bhalla, A.S., *Monuments, Power and Poverty in India: From Ashoka to the Raj* (London, I.B. Tauris, 2015).

Bhasin, Raja, *Simla: The Summer Capital of British India* (New Delhi, Viking, 1992).

Bickers, Robert, *Empire Made Me: an Englishman Adrift in Shanghai* (London, Allen Lane, 2003).

—— (ed.), *Settlers and Expatriates* (Oxford, OUP, 2010).

Bindman, David, Gates, Henry Louis et al. (eds), *The Image of the Black in Western Art*, vols 2 and 3 (Cambridge, MA, Belknap Press, Harvard UP, 2010 and 2011).

Black, David R. and Nauright, John, *Rugby and the South African Nation* (Manchester, MUP, 1998).

Blanchard, Pascal, Lemaire, Sandrine, Boncel, Nicolas and Thomas, Dominic, *Colonial Culture in France since the Revolution*, trans. Alexis Pernsteiner (Bloomington, IN, University of Indiana Press, 2014).

—— Boncel, Nicolas, Boetson, Gilles, Deroo, Eric, Lemaire, Sandrine and Forsdick, Charles (eds), *Human Zoos: Science and Spectacle in the Age of Colonial Empires* (Liverpool, Liverpool UP, 2008).

Bosco, Andrea, *The Round Table Movement and the Fall of the 'Second' British Empire (1909–1919)* (Newcastle, Cambridge Scholars, 2017).

Bradley, Mark (ed.), *Classics and Imperialism in the British Empire* (Oxford, OUP, 2010).

Bradlow, Frank R., *Thomas Baines: His Art in Rhodesia from the Original Paintings in the Central African Archives* (Salisbury, Central African Archives, Southern Rhodesia, 1956).

Bragg, Melvyn, *The Adventure of English: 500 AD to 2000: The Biography of a Language* (London, Hodder and Stoughton, 2003).

Bratton, J.S. et al., *Acts of Supremacy: The British Empire and the Stage, 1790–1930* (Manchester, MUP, 1991).

Brown, Stewart J. (ed.), *William Robertson and the Expansion of Empire* (Cambridge, CUP, 2008).

Bruce, George, *The Burma Wars, 1824–86* (London, Hart Davis, 1973).

Bryant, Julius and Weber, Susan (eds), *John Lockwood Kipling: Arts and Crafts in the Punjab and in London* (New Haven, CT, YUP, 2017).

Bueltmann, Tanja, *Clubbing Together: Ethnicity, Civility and Formal Sociability in the Scottish Diaspora to 1930* (Liverpool, Liverpool UP, 2014).

Buettner, Elizabeth, *Europe after Empire: Decolonization, Society and Culture* (Cambridge, CUP, 2016).

Burbank, Jane and Cooper, Frederick, *Empires in World History* (Princeton, NJ, Princeton UP, 2010).

Burke, Peter, *What is Cultural History?* (Cambridge, Polity, 2004).

Burns, James, *Flickering Shadows: Cinema and Identity in Colonial Zimbabwe* (Athens, OH, Ohio UP 2002).

—— *Cinema and Society in the British Empire 1895–1940* (Basingstoke, Palgrave Macmillan, 2013).

Burton, Antoinette (ed.), *After the Imperial Turn: Thinking with and through the Nation* (Durham, NC, Duke UP, 2003).

—— *The Trouble with Empire* (Oxford, OUP, 2015).

Bush, Barbara, *Imperialism and Postcolonialism* (London, Routledge, 2006).

Butler, Sarah J., *Britain and its Empire in the Shadow of Rome: The Reception of Rome in Socio-political Debate from the 1850s to the 1920s* (London, Bloomsbury, 2012).

Calloway, Colin G., *White People, Indians and Highlanders: Tribal Peoples and Colonial Encounters in Scotland and America* (Oxford, OUP, 2008).

Cannadine, David, *Ornamentalism: How the British Saw Their Empire* (London, Allen Lane, 2001).

Chapman, James and Cull, Nicholas J., *Projecting Empire: Imperialism and Popular Cinema* (London, I.B. Tauris, 2009).

Chisholm, Alec H., *The Australian Encyclopaedia*, vol. 4 (Sydney, Angus and Robertson, 1958).

Choudhury, Deep Kanta Lahiri, *Telegraphic Imperialism: Crisis and Panic in the Indian Empire, c. 1830* (Basingstoke, Palgrave Macmillan, 2010).

Chowdhry, Prem, *Colonial India and the Making of Empire Cinema: Image, Ideology and Identity* (Manchester, MUP, 2000).

Churchill, Winston S., *The Story of the Malakand Field Force* (London, Leo Cooper, 1989, first published 1898).

Clarke, Tom, *Northcliffe in History: An Intimate Study of Press Power* (London, Hutchinson, 1950).

Cochrane, C. and Robinson, J. (eds), *Theatre History and Historiography* (London, Palgrave Macmillan, 2016).

Codell, Julie F. (ed.), *Power and Resistance: The Delhi Coronation Durbars 1877, 1903, 1911* (Ahmedabad, Mapin Publishing, 2012).

Cohn, Bernard S., *Colonialism and its Forms of Knowledge: The British in India* (Princeton, NJ, Princeton UP, 1996).

Colley, Linda, *Britons: Forging the Nation 1707–1837* (New Haven, CT, YUP, 1992).

Comaroff, Jean and Comaroff, John, *Of Revelation and Revolution: Christianity, Colonialism and Consciousness in South Africa*, 2 vols (Chicago, University of Chicago Press, 1991 and 1997).

Conrich, Ian and Tampoe-Hautin, Vilasnee, *The Cinema of Sri Lanka: South Asian Film in Texts and Contexts* (London, I.B. Tauris, 2019).

Constantine, Stephen, *Buy and Build: The Advertising Posters of the Empire Marketing Board* (London, HMSO, 1986).

Cookson, John and Dunstall, Graeme (eds), *Southern Capital: Christchurch, towards a City Biography 1850–2000* (Christchurch, Canterbury UP, 2000).

Coombes, Annie E., *Reinventing Africa: Museums, Culture and the Popular Imagination in Late Victorian and Edwardian England* (New Haven, CT, YUP, 1994).

—— *History after Apartheid: Visual Culture and Public Memory in a Democratic South Africa* (Durham, NC, Duke UP, 2003).

Cooper, Frederick and Stoler, Ann Laura (eds), *Tensions of Empire: Colonial Cultures in a Bourgeois World* (Berkeley, University of California Press, 1997).

Cotton, Evan, *East Indiamen: The East India Company's Maritime Service* (London, Batchworth Press, 1999).

Coutu, Joan, *Persuasion and Propaganda: Monuments and the Eighteenth-century British Empire* (Montreal and Kingston, McGill-Queen's UP, 2006).

Cox, Julian and Ford, Colin (eds), *Julia Margaret Cameron: The Complete Photographs* (Los Angeles, J. Paul Getty Trust Publications, 2003).

Craft, Aimée, *Breathing Life into the Stone Fort Treaty* (Vancouver, UBC Press, 2013).

Craggs, Ruth and Wintle, Claire, *Cultures of Decolonisation: Transnational Productions and Practices* (Manchester, MUP, 2016).

Cromer, Earl of, *Modern Egypt* (London, Macmillan, 1908).

Crosbie, Barry and Hampton, Mark (eds), *The Cultural Construction of the British World* (Manchester, MUP, 2016).

Crosby, Alfred W., *Ecological Imperialism: The Biological Expansion of Europe, 900–1900* (Cambridge, CUP, 1996).

Crowley, John E., *Imperial Landscapes: Britain's Global Visual Culture, 1745–1820* (New Haven, YUP, 2011).

Dabydeen, David, *Hogarth's Blacks: Images of Blacks in Eighteenth-century English Art* (Manchester, MUP, 1987).

Dalrymple, William, *The Anarchy: The East India Company, Corporate Violence and the Pillage of an Empire* (London, Bloomsbury, 2019).

—— (ed.), *Forgotten Masters: Indian Painting for the East India Company* (London, Philip Wilson for the Wallace Collection, 2019).

Daly, M.W. and Forbes, H.E., *The Sudan: Caught in Time* (Reading, Garnet, 1994).

Darian-Smith, Kate, Grimshaw, Patricia and McIntyre, Stuart (eds), *Britishness Abroad: Transnational Movements and Imperial Cultures* (Melbourne, Melbourne UP, 2006).

Darwin, John, *After Tamerlane: The Global History of Empire* (London, Allen Lane, 2007).

Davis, J. Merle, *Modern Industry and the African* (London, Frank Cass, 1967, first published 1933).

De Courcy, Anne, *The Fishing Fleet: Husband-hunting in the Raj* (London, Weidenfeld and Nicolson, 2012).

De Guise, Lucien, *Beyond Orientalism: How the West was Won over by Islamic Art* (Islamic Arts Museum, Malaysia, 2008).

Deacon, Desley, Russell, Penny and Woollacott, Angela (eds), *Transnational Lives: Biographies of Global Modernity, 1700–present* (London, Palgrave Macmillan, 2010).

Dehejia, Vidya, *Impossible Picturesqueness: Lear's Indian Watercolours, 1973–75* (New York, Columbia UP, 1990).

—— (ed.), *India through the Lens: Photography 1840–1911* (Washington, Smithsonian Institution, 2000).

Desmond, Ray, *Victorian India in Focus: A Selection of Early Photographs from the Collection in the India Office Library and Records* (London, HMSO, 1982).

Devine, T.M., *To the Ends of the Earth: Scotland's Global Diaspora 1750–2010* (London, Allen Lane, 2011).

—— *The Scottish Clearances: A History of the Dispossessed* (London, Allen Lane, 2018).

Dimeo, Paul and Mills, James (eds), *Soccer in South Asia: Empire, Nation, Diaspora* (London, Frank Cass, 2001).

Dirks, Nicholas B. (ed.), *Colonialism and Culture* (Ann Arbor, MI, Michigan UP, 1992).

—— Eley, Geoff and Ortner, Sherry B. (eds), *Culture/Power/History: A Reader in Contemporary Social Theory* (Princeton, NJ, Princeton UP, 1994).

—— *The Scandal of Empire: India and the Creation of Imperial Britain* (Cambridge, MA, Harvard UP, 2006).

Docking, Gil, *Two Hundred Years of New Zealand Painting* (Melbourne, Lansdowne, 1971).

Donaldson, Peter, *Remembering the South African War: Britain and the Memory of the Anglo-Boer War, from 1899 to the Present* (Liverpool, Liverpool UP, 2013).

Doornbos, Martin R., *Regalia Galore: The Decline and Collapse of Ankole Kingship* (Nairobi, East African Literature Bureau, 1975).

Douglas, James, *Glimpses of Old Bombay and Western India* (London, Sampson Low, 1900).

Droth, Martina, Edwards, Jason and Hatt, Michael (eds), *Sculpture Victorious: Art in an Age of Invention, 1837–1901* (New Haven, CT, YUP, 2014).

Dubin, Steven C., *Transforming Museums: Mounting Queen Victoria in a Democratic South Africa* (New York, Palgrave, 2006).

Dunn, Michael, *New Zealand Painting: A Concise History* (Auckland, Auckland UP, 2003).

Dutta, Krishna, *Calcutta: A Cultural and Literary History* (Oxford, Signal, 2008).

Enwezor, Okwul and Bester, Rory (eds), *Rise and Fall of Apartheid Photography and the Bureaucracy of Everyday Life* (Munich, Prestel, 2013).

Evans, Martin (ed.), *Empire and Culture: The French Experience, 1830–1940* (Basingstoke, Palgrave Macmillan, 2004).

Fabb, John, *The British Empire from Photographs: India* (London, Batsford, 1986).

—— *The British Empire from Photographs: Africa* (London, Batsford, 1987).

Falconer, John, *India: Pioneering Photographers 1850–1900* (London, British Library, 2001).

—— and Sharma, Satish, *A Shifting Focus: Photography in India, 1850–1900* (London, British Council, 1997).

Farr, Martin and Guégan, Xavier (eds), *The British Abroad since the Eighteenth Century*, vol. 2 (Basingstoke, Palgrave Macmillan, 2013).

Fawaz, Leila Tarazi and Bayly, C.A. (eds), *Modernity and Culture* (New York, Columbia UP, 1998).

Fedorowich, Kent and Thompson, Andrew S., *Mapping the Contours of the British World* (Manchester, MUP, 2013).

Ferguson, Niall, *Empire: How Britain Made the Modern World* (London, Allen Lane, 2003).

Gailey, Andrew, *The Lost Imperialist: Lord Dufferin and Mythmaking in An Age of Celebrity* (London, John Murray, 2013).

Garlake, Peter, *The Painted Caves: An Introduction to the Prehistoric Art of Zimbabwe* (Harare, Zimbabwe, Modus, 1987).

Geary, Christaud and Webb, Virginia-Lee, *Delivering Views: Distant Cultures in Early Postcards* (Washington and London, Smithsonian Institution, 1998).

Geertz, Clifford, *The Interpretation of Cultures: Selected Essays* (New York, Basic Books, 1973).

Giblin, John and Spring, Chris, *South Africa: The Art of a Nation* (London, Thames and Hudson, 2016).

Goldberg, S.L. and Smith, F.B. (eds), *Australian Cultural History* (Cambridge, CUP, 1981).

Golder, John and Madelaine, Richard (eds), *O Brave New World: Two Centuries of Shakespeare on the Australian Stage* (Sydney, Century Press, 2001).

Goody, Jack, *The Culture of Flowers* (Cambridge, CUP, 1993).

—— *Food and Love: A Cultural History of East and West* (London, Verso, 1998).

Goswamy, B.N., *Daniells' India: Views from the Eighteenth Century* (New Delhi, Nyogi Books, 2013).

Gott, Richard, *Britain's Empire: Resistance, Repression, Revolt* (London, Verso, 2011).

Gould, Marty, *Nineteenth Century Theatre and the Imperial Encounter* (London, Routledge 2011).

Grant, Peter, *Victoria: A History in Photographs* (Vancouver, Altitude Publishing, 1995).

Greenwood, Adrian, *Victoria's Scottish Lion: The Life of Colin Campbell Lord Clyde* (Stroud, History Press, 2015).

Greenwood, William and de Guise, Lucien, *Inspired by the East: How the Islamic World Influenced Western Art* (London, British Museum, 2019).

Gregory, Jenny and Gothard, Jan (eds), *Historical Encyclopaedia of Western Australia* (Crawley, WA, University of Western Australia Press, 2009).

Grieveson, Lee and MacCabe, Colin (eds), *Empire and Film* (London, Palgrave Macmillan, 2011).

Griffiths, Andrew, *The New Journalism, the New Imperialism and the Fiction of Empire, 1870–1900* (Basingstoke, Palgrave Macmillan, 2015).

Griffiths, John, *Imperial Culture in Antipodean Cities, 1880–1939* (Basingstoke, Palgrave Macmillan, 2014).

Groseclose, Barbara, *British Sculpture and the Company Raj: Church Monuments and Public Statuary in Madras, Calcutta and Bombay to 1858* (London, Associated University Presses, 1995).

Grossman, Loyd, *Benjamin West and the Struggle to be Modern* (London, Merrell, 2015).

Gugler, Josef (ed.), *The Urbanization of the Third World* (Oxford, OUP, 1988).

Guha, Ramachandra, *Wickets in the East: An Anecdotal History* (Delhi, OUP, 1992).

—— *A Corner of a Foreign Field: The Indian History of a British Sport* (London, Picador, 2002).

Guha-Thakurta, Tapati, *The Making of a New 'Indian' Art: Artists, Aesthetics and Nationalism in Bengal, c. 1850–1920* (Cambridge, CUP, 1992).

Gupchup, Vijaya and Thomas, T. (eds), *St. Thomas Cathedral, Bombay: Witness to History* (Bombay, Eminence Designs, 2005).

Hagerman, C., *Britain's Imperial Muse* (Basingstoke, Palgrave Macmillan, 2013).

Hajkowski, Thomas, *The BBC and National Identity in Britain, 1922–53* (Manchester, MUP, 2010).

Hall, Catherine (ed.), *Cultures of Empire: A Reader* (Manchester, MUP, 2000).

—— and Rose, Sonya O., *At Home with the Empire: Metropolitan Culture and the Imperial World* (Cambridge, CUP, 2006).

—— and McClelland, Keith (eds), *Race, Nation and Empire: Making Histories, 1750 to the Present* (Manchester, MUP, 2010).

Hannavy, John (ed.), *The Encyclopedia of Nineteenth-century Photography* (New York and London, Taylor and Francis, 2008).

Harper, J. Russell, *Painting in Canada: A History* (Toronto, University of Toronto Press, 1977).

—— and Triggs, Stanley (eds), *Portrait of a Period: A Collection of Notman Photographs* (Montreal, McGill UP, 1867).

Harper, Tobias, *From Servants of the Empire to Everyday Heroes: The British Honours System in the Twentieth Century* (Oxford, OUP, 2020).

Hauptman, William (ed.), *John Webber 1751–1793: Pacific Voyager and Landscape Artist* (Bern, Kunstmuseum, and Manchester, Whitworth Art Gallery, 1996).

Hay, Roy, *Aboriginal People and Australian Football in the Nineteenth Century* (Newcastle, Cambridge Publishing, 2019).

—— and Murray, Bill, *A History of Football in Australia: A Game of Two Halves* (Melbourne, Hardie Grant, 2014).

Harris, Clare, *Photography and Tibet* (London, Reaktion, 2016).

Headrick, Daniel R., *The Tools of Empire: Technology and European Imperialism in the Nineteenth Century* (New York, OUP, 1981).

—— *The Invisible Weapon: Telecommunications and International Politics 1851–1945* (New York, OUP, 1991).

Hercock, Marion with Harrison, Zoe, *A History of Dressage in Western Australia* (Carlisle, Western Australia, Hesperian Press, 2019).

Hevia, James L., *Animal Labor and Colonial Warfare* (Chicago, University of Chicago Press, 2018).

Hichberger, J.W.M, *Images of the Army: The Military in British Art 1815–1914* (Manchester, MUP, 1988).

Hight, Eleanour M. and Sampson, Gary D. (eds), *Colonialist Photography: Imag(in)ing Race and Place* (London, Routledge, 2002).

Hillier, Andrew, *Mediating Empire: An English Family in China, 1817–1927* (Folkestone, Renaissance Books, 2020).

Hobsbawm, Eric and Ranger, Terence (eds), *The Invention of Tradition* (Cambridge, CUP, 1983).

Holland, Robert, Williams, Susan and Barringer, Terry A. (eds), *The Iconography of Independence: 'Freedoms at Midnight'* (Abingdon, Routledge, 2010).

Holloway, David, *Playing the Empire: The Acts of the Holloway Touring Company* (London, Harrap, 1979).

Holt, Tonie and Holt, Valmai, *Picture Postcards of the Golden Age* (London, Postcard Publishing Company, 1978).

Hoock, Holger, *Empires of the Imagination: Politics, War and the Arts in the British World 1750–1850* (London, Profile, 2010).

Horton, Melanie, *Empire Marketing Board Posters* (London, Scala, 2010).

Hoselitz, Virginia, *Imagining Roman Britain: Victorian Responses to a Roman Past* (Woodbridge, Suffolk, Boydell Press, 2007).

Hubbard, R.H., *Antoine Plamondon (1802–1895), Théophile Hamel (1817–1670). Two Painters of Quebec / Deux Peintres de Québec* (Ottawa, National Gallery of Canada, 1970).

Huggins, Mike, *Flat Racing and British Society, 1790–1914* (London, Frank Cass, 2000).

—— *Horse Racing and the British* (Manchester, MUP, 2004).

—— *Horse Racing and British Society in the Long Eighteenth Century* (Martlesham, Suffolk, Boydell, 2018).

Hughes, Robert, *Art of Australia* (Harmondsworth, Penguin, 1984).

Hunt, Tristram, *Ten Cities that made an Empire* (London, Allen Lane, 2014).

Hutchins, Francis G., *The Illusion of Permanence: British Imperialism in India* (Princeton, NJ, Princeton UP, 1967).

Hyam, Ronald, *Britain's Imperial Century 1815–1914: A Study of Empire and Expansion* (London, Batsford, 1976).

—— *Sexuality and Empire* (Manchester, MUP, 1990).

Hyde, Ralph, *Panoramania! The Art and Entertainment of the All-embracing View* (London, Trefoil and Barbican Art Gallery, 1988).

Jackson, Ashley, *Mad Dogs and Englishmen: A Grand Tour of the British Empire at its Height 1850–1945* (London, Quercus, 2009).

—— and Tomkins, David, *Illustrating Empire: A Visual History of British Imperialism* (Oxford, Bodleian Library, 2011).

—— *Buildings of Empire* (Oxford, OUP, 2013).

Jackson, S., *Constructing National Identities in Canadian and Australian Classrooms* (Basingstoke, Palgrave Macmillan, 2018).

James, C.L.R., *Beyond a Boundary* (London, Stanley James, 1993).

Jeffery, Roger (ed.), *India in Edinburgh* (New Delhi, Social Science Press, 2019).

Jasanoff, Maya, *Edge of Empire: Conquest and Collecting in the East, 1750–1850* (London, Fourth Estate, 2005).

Johnston, Basil, *Ojibway Ceremonies* (Lincoln, NE, University of Nebraska Press, 1990).

—— *Manitous, the Spiritual World of the Ojibway* (St Paul, MN, Minnesota Historical Society Press, 1995).

Johnston, David A., *New Delhi: The Last Imperial City* (Basingstoke, Palgrave Macmillan, 2015).

Johnstone, Christopher, *Landscape Paintings of New Zealand: A Journey from North to South* (Auckland, Random House, 2006).

Kamensky, Jane, *A Revolution in Color: The World of John Singleton Copley* (New York, Norton, 2016).

Kanwar, Pamela, *Imperial Simla: The Political Culture of the Raj* (New Delhi, OUP, 1990).

Kar, Law and Bren, Frank, *Hong Kong Cinema: A Cross-cultural View* (Lanham, MD, Scarecrow Press, 2004).

Kaul, Chandrika, *Reporting the Raj: The British Press and India, c. 1880–1922* (Manchester, MUP, 2003).

—— (ed.), *Media and the British Empire* (London, Palgrave Macmillan, 2006).

Kendal, Felicity, *White Cargo* (London, Michael Joseph, 1998).

Keneally, Thomas et al, *Australia* (London, Royal Academy of Arts, 2013).

Kennedy, Brian, *The Baron Bold and the Beauteous Maid: A Compact History of Canadian Theatre* (Toronto, Playwrights Canada Press, 2004).

Kennedy, Dane, *The Magic Mountains: Hill Stations and the British Raj* (Berkeley, University of California Press, 1996).

Kennedy, Greg and Tuck, Christopher (eds), *British Propaganda and Wars of Empire* (Farnham, Ashgate, 2014).

Khan, Omar, *Paper Jewels: Postcards from the Raj* (Ahmedabad, Mapin and Alkazi Collection of Photography, 2018).

Killingray, David, Lincoln, Margarette and Rigby, Nigel (eds), *Maritime Empires: British Imperial Maritime Trade in the Nineteenth Century* (Woodbridge, Suffolk, Boydell Press, 2004).

Kincaid, Dennis, *British Social Life in India 1608–1937* (London, Routledge, 1938).

Koivunen, Leila, *Visualizing Africa in Nineteenth-century British Travel Accounts* (Abingdon, Routledge, 2009).

Korr, Chuck and Close, Marvin, *More than Just a Game: Football v Apartheid* (London, Collins, 2008).

Kosinski, Dorothy (ed.), *The Artist and the Camera* (New Haven, CT, YUP, 2000).

Kröller, Eva-Marie, *Writing the Empire: The McIlwraiths, 1853–1948* (Toronto, University of Toronto Press, 2021).

Kuhn, Annette and Westwell, Guy (eds), *A Dictionary of Film Studies* (Oxford, OUP, 2012).

Kumari, Mamta, *The Life and Times of Gopal Krishna Gokhale* (New Delhi, Ocean Books, 2018).

Lacoste, Anne, *Felice Beato: A Photographer on the Eastern Road* (Los Angeles, Getty Publications, 2010).

Laffaye, Horace A., *The Evolution of Polo* (Jefferson, NC, McFarland, 2009).

Laird, Dorothy, *Paddy Henderson: The Story of P. Henderson and Company, 1834–1961* (Glasgow, Outram, 1961).

Landau, Paul S. and Kaspin, Deborah D. (eds), *Images and Empires* (Berkeley, University of California Press, 2002).

Lawson, Julie, *James Robertson of Istanbul* (London, British Council, 1991).

Lee, Emanoel, *To the Bitter End* (Harmondsworth, Penguin, 1987).

Levine, Philippa (ed.), *Gender and Empire* (Oxford, OUP, 2004).

—— and Grayzel, Susan R. (eds), *Gender, Labour, War and Empire: Essays on Modern Britain* (Basingstoke, Palgrave Macmillan, 2009).

Lewis, Joanna, *Empire of Sentiment: The Death of Livingstone and the Myth of Victorian Imperialism* (Cambridge, CUP, 2018).

Lieven, Dominic, *Empire* (London, Pimlico, 2003).

London, Christopher W., *Bombay Gothic* (Mumbai, India Book House, 2002).

Longair, Sarah and McAleer, John (eds), *Curating Empire: Museums and the British Imperial Experience* (Manchester, MUP, 2012).

Lorcin, Patricia (ed.), *A Cultural History of Western Empires in the Modern Age, 1920–2000*, vol. 6 (London, Bloomsbury, 2019).

Lorimer, Douglas J., *Colour, Class and the Victorians* (Leicester, Leicester UP, 1978).
—— *Race, Race Relations and Resistance: A Study of the Discourse of Race in Late Victorian and Edwardian Britain, 1870–1914* (Manchester, MUP, 2013).
Losty, J.P., *Delhi 360 Degrees: Mazhar Ali Khan's View from the Lahore Gate* (New Delhi, Roli Books, 2012).
—— (ed.), *Sita Ram's Painted Views of India: Lord Hastings's Journey from Calcutta to the Punjab, 1814–1815* (London, Thames and Hudson, 2015).
Lutyens, Mary, *The Lyttons in India: Lord Lytton's Viceroyalty* (London, John Murray, 1979).
Lydon, Jane, *Photography, Humanitarianism, Empire* (London, Bloomsbury 2016).
—— *Imperial Emotions: The Politics of Empathy across the British Empire* (Cambridge, CUP, 2020).
McAleer, John, *Representing Africa: Landscape, Exploration and Empire in Southern Africa 1780–1870* (Manchester, MUP, 2010).
—— *Picturing India: People, Places and the World of the East India Company* (London, British Library, 2017).
—— and MacKenzie, John M. (eds), *Exhibiting the Empire: Cultures of Display and the British Empire* (Manchester, MUP, 2015).
McCarthy, Angela and MacKenzie, John M. (eds), *Global Migrations: The Scottish Diaspora since 1600* (Edinburgh, EUP, 2016).
McCrae, Alister, *Scots in Burma* (Edinburgh, Kiscadale, 1990).
—— and Prentice, Alan, *Irrawaddy Flotilla* (Paisley, James Paton, 1978).
MacKenzie, John M. (ed.), *Propaganda and Empire: The Manipulation of British Public Opinion, 1880–1960* (Manchester, MUP, 1984).
—— (ed.), *Imperialism and Popular Culture* (Manchester, MUP, 1986).
—— *The Empire of Nature: Hunting, Conservation and British Imperialism* (Manchester, MUP, 1988).
—— (ed.), *Popular Imperialism and the Military* (Manchester, MUP, 1991).
—— *Orientalism: History, Theory and the Arts* (Manchester, MUP, 1995).
—— (ed.), *David Livingstone and the Victorian Encounter with Africa* (London, National Portrait Gallery, 1996).
—— with Dalziel, Nigel R., *The Scots in South Africa* (Manchester, MUP, 2007).
—— *Museums and Empire: Natural History, Human Cultures and Colonial Identities* (Manchester, MUP, 2009).
—— and Devine, T.M. (eds), *Scotland and the British Empire* (Oxford, OUP, 2011).
—— (ed.), *Wiley-Blackwell Encyclopedia of Empire* (Malden, MA, Wiley-Blackwell, 2016).
—— *The British Empire through Buildings: Structure, Function and Meaning* (Manchester, MUP, 2020).
McKenzie, Kirsten (ed.), *A Cultural History of Western Empires in the Age of Empire 1800–1920*, vol. 5 (London, Bloomsbury, 2019).
McKenzie, R., *Sculpture in Glasgow: An Illustrated Handbook* (Glasgow, Foulis Archive, 1999).
Mackintosh, C.W., *Coillard of the Zambezi* (London, Fisher Unwin, 1907).
McLintock, A.H. (ed.), *An Encyclopaedia of New Zealand,* 3 vols (Wellington, Government of New Zealand, R.E. Owen, Government Printer, 1966). Revised and republished from 2004 as *Te Ara – The Encyclopedia of New Zealand* online (Wellington, Manatū Taonga Ministry for Culture and Heritage, Government of New Zealand).
Magee, Gary B. and Thompson, Andrew S., *Empire and Globalisation: Networks of People, Goods and Capital in the British World, c.1850–1914* (Cambridge, CUP, 2010).
Mandala, Vijaya Ramadas, *Shooting a Tiger: Big-game Hunting and Conservation in Colonial India* (New Delhi, OUP, 2019).
Mangan, J.A., *Athleticism in the Victorian and Edwardian Public School: The Emergence and Consolidation of an Educational Ideology* (Cambridge, CUP, 1981).

396

—— *The Games Ethic and Imperialism: Aspects of the Diffusion of an Ideal* (London, Frank Cass, 1988).

—— (ed.), *The Cultural Bond: Sport, Empire, Society* (London, Frank Cass, 1992).

Marcus, Leah S., *How Shakespeare Became Colonial: Editorial Tradition and the British Empire* (London, Routledge, 2017).

Marshall, Andrew, *The Trouser People: The Quest for the Victorian Footballer who Made Burma Play the Empire's Game* (London, Viking, 2002).

Marshall, P.J. (ed.), *The Cambridge Illustrated History of the British Empire* (Cambridge, CUP, 1996).

Mason, Tony and Riedi, Eliza, *Sport and the Military: The British Armed Forces 1880–1960* (Cambridge, CUP, 2010).

Masselos, Jim and Gupta, Narayani, *Beato's Delhi, 1857 and Beyond* (Delhi, Rani Dayal, 2000).

Mathur, Saloni, *An Indian Encounter: Portraits for Queen Victoria by Rudolf Swoboda* (London, National Gallery, 2002).

Maxwell, Anne, *Colonial Photography and Exhibitions: Representations of the 'Native' People and the Making of European Identities* (Leicester, Leicester UP, 1999).

Mayer, Marc, *Art in Canada* (Ottawa, National Gallery of Canada, 2017).

Mazrui, Ali A., 'Africa's triple heritage of play: reflections on the gender gap', in Baker and Mangan (eds), *Sport in Africa: Essays in Social History* (New York, Africana Publishing, 1987), pp. 217–28.

Mbikusita, Godwin, *Yeta III's Visit to England* (Lusaka, Northern Rhodesia, Government Printer, 1940).

Meghani, Kajal, *Splendours of the Subcontinent: A Prince's Tour of India 1875–6* (London, Royal Collection Trust, 2017).

Melville, Joy, *Julia Margaret Cameron, Pioneer Photographer* (Stroud, Sutton Publishing, 2003).

Metcalf, Thomas R., *Ideologies of the Raj* (Cambridge, CUP, 1995).

Milroy, Sarah and Dejardin, Ian, *From the Forest to the Sea: Emily Carr in British Columbia* (Fredericton, New Brunswick, Goose Lane Editions, 2015).

Mitchem, John C., *Race and Imperial Defence in the British World, 1870–1914* (Cambridge, CUP, 2016).

Mitter, Partha, *Much-maligned Monsters: A History of European Reactions to Indian Art* (Oxford, OUP, 1977).

—— *Art and Nationalism in Colonial India 1850–1922* (Cambridge, CUP, 1994).

Monti, Nicolas (ed.), *Africa Then: Photographs 1840–1918* (London, Thames and Hudson, 1987).

Moorhouse, Geoffrey, *Calcutta: The City Revealed* (Harmondsworth, Penguin, 1974).

Morris, Jan, *Pax Britannica, The Climax of an Empire* (London, Faber, 1968).

—— *Heaven's Command: An Imperial Progress* (London, Faber, 1973).

—— *Farewell the Trumpets: An Imperial Retreat* (London, Faber, 1978).

—— *The Spectacle of Empire* (London, Faber, 1982).

—— with Winchester, Simon, *Stones of Empire: Buildings of the Raj* (Oxford, OUP, 1983).

Morris, Peter, *Embattled Shadows: A History of Canadian Cinema 1895–1939* (Montreal, McGill-Queen's UP, 1979).

Morton, Christopher and Grover, Philip N. (eds), *Wilfred Thesiger in Africa: A Unique Collection of Essays and Personal Photographs* (London, Harper Press, 2010).

Mount, Ferdinand, *Tears of the Rajahs: Mutiny, Money and Marriage in India 1805–1905* (London, Simon and Schuster, 2015).

Mukasa, Ham, *Uganda's Katikiro in England* (Manchester, MUP, 1998).

Mukherjee, Sushil K., *The Story of the Calcutta Theatres, 1753–1980* (Calcutta, Bagchi, 1982).

Murray, Craig, *Sikunder Burnes, Master of the Great Game* (Edinburgh, Birlinn, 2016).

Murray, Joan, *The Best of the Group of Seven* (Toronto, McClelland and Stewart, 1984).

Nanda, B.R., *Gokhale: The Indian Moderates and the British Raj* (Princeton, NJ, Princeton UP, 1977).

Natarajan, J., *History of Indian Journalism, Part II of the Report of the Press Commission* (New Delhi, Ministry of Information and Broadcasting, Government of India, Publications Division, 1955).

Nauright, John and Chandler, Timothy J.L. (eds), *Making Men: Rugby and Masculine Identity* (London, Frank Cass, 1999).

Netton, Ian Richard (ed.), *Orientalism Revisited: Art, Land and Voyage* (Abingdon, Routledge, 2013).

Nicholls, C.S., *Red Strangers: The White Tribe of Kenya* (London, Timewell Press, 2005).

Noltie, H.J., *Indian Botanical Drawings 1793–1868* (Edinburgh, Royal Botanic Garden, 1999).

—— *The Dapuri Drawings: Alexander Gibson & the Bombay Botanic Gardens* (Edinburgh, the Antique Collectors' Club in association with the Royal Botanic Garden, 2002).

—— *The Cleghorn Collection: South Indian Botanical Drawings 1845–1860* (Edinburgh, Royal Botanic Garden, 2016).

O'Malley, Kate, *Ireland India and Empire: Indo-Irish Radical Connections, 1919–64* (Manchester, MUP, 2008).

Ogborn, Miles, *Indian Ink: Script and Print in the Making of the English East India Company* (Chicago, University of Chicago Press, 2007).

Oleksijczuk, Denise Blake, *The First Panoramas: Visions of British Imperialism* (Minneapolis, MN, University of Minnesota Press, 2011).

Oman, Colin, *Egypt: Caught in Time* (Reading, Garnet, 1997).

Otis, Andrew, *Hicky's Bengal Gazette: The Untold Story of India's First Newspaper* (New Delhi, Westland Publications, 2018).

Pal, Pratapaditya and Dehejia, Vidya, *From Merchants to Emperors: British Artists and India, 1757–1930* (Ithaca, NY, Cornell UP, 1986).

Panter-Downes, Mollie, *Ooty Preserved: A Victorian Hill Station in India* (London, Century Publishing, 1985).

Pare, Richard, *Roger Fenton*. Aperture Masters of Photography (New York, Aperture Foundation, 1987).

Parsons, Neil, *King Khama, Emperor Joe and the Great White Queen: Victorian Britain through African Eyes* (Chicago, University of Chicago Press, 1998).

Parsons, Timothy H., *The Rule of Empires* (Oxford, OUP, 2010).

Patterson, Brad, Brooking, Tom and McAloon, Jim, *Unpacking the Kists: The Scots in New Zealand* (Montreal, McGill-Queen's UP, 2013).

Peck, Lucy, *Delhi: A Thousand Years of Building* (New Delhi, Roli Books, 2005).

Peffer, John and Cameron, Elisabeth L. (eds), *Portraiture and Photography in Africa* (Bloomington, IN, Indiana UP, 2013).

Pelizzari, Maria Antonella (ed.), *Traces of India: Photographing Architecture and the Politics of the Raj, 1850–1900* (New Haven, CT, Yale Center for British Art, 2003).

Pinney, Christopher, *Camera Indica: The Social Life of Indian Photographs* (Chicago, University of Chicago Press, 1997).

Pocock, J.G.A., *Barbarism and Religion*, vol. 4: *Barbarians, Savages and Empires* (Cambridge, CUP, 2005).

Pollon, Frances, *Parramatta, Cradle City of Australia* (City of Parramatta NSW, 1983).

Porter, Andrew, *Religion versus Empire? British Protestant Missionaries and Overseas Expansion, 1700–1914* (Manchester, MUP, 2004).

Porter, Bernard, *The Absent-minded Imperialists: Empire, Society and Culture in Britain* (Oxford, OUP, 2004).

Potter, Simon J., *News and the British World: The Emergence of an Imperial Press System* (Oxford, OUP, 2003).

—— (ed.), *Newspapers and Empire in Ireland and Britain: Reporting the British Empire c. 1857–1921* (Dublin, Four Courts Press, 2004).

—— *Broadcasting and Empire: the BBC and the British World, 1922–1970* (Oxford, OUP, 2012).

Prain, Michelle (ed.), *The British Legacy in Valparaiso* (Santiago, Ril Editores, 2011).

Prakash, Om, *A Cultural History of India* (New Delhi, New Age International Publishers, 2004).

Prior, Mary Ann, *An Indian Portfolio, the Life and Work of Emily Eden* (London, Quartet Books, 2012).

Protschky, Susie, *Photographic Subjects: Monarchy and Visual Culture in Colonial Indonesia* (Manchester, MUP, 2020).

Quilley, Geoff and Bonehill, John (eds), *William Hodges 1744–1897: The Art of Exploration* (New Haven, CT, YUP, 2004).

Raghavan, G.N.S., *The Press in India* (New Delhi, Gyan Publishing House, 1994).

Raible, Chris, *A Colonial Advocate: The Launching of his Newspaper and the Queenston Career of William Lyon Mackenzie* (Creemore, Curiosity House, 1999).

—— *The Power of the Press: The Story of Early Canadian Printers and Publishers* (Toronto, James Lorimer, 2007).

Ramamurthy, Anandi, *Imperial Persuaders: Images of Africa and Asia in British Advertising* (Manchester, MUP, 2003).

Ramani, Navin and Cerwinske, Laura, *Bombay Art Deco Architecture* (New Delhi, Lustre Press, Roli Books, 2007).

Ranger, Terence O., *Dance and Society in Eastern Africa, 1890–1970: The Beni Ngoma* (London, Heinemann, 1975).

Read, Donald, *The Power of News: The History of Reuters* (Oxford, OUP, 1999).

Reed, Charles V., *Royal Tourists, Colonial Subjects and the Making of a British World, 1860–1911* (Manchester, MUP, 2016).

Reid, Dennis, *A Concise History of Canadian Painting* (Don Mills, Ontario, OUP, 1988).

Rice, Tom, *Films for the Colonies: Cinema and the Preservation of the British Empire* (Oakland, CA, University of California Press, 2019).

Richards, Eric, *Destination Australia: Migration to Australia since 1901* (Sydney, University of NSW Press, 2008).

Richards, Jeffrey (ed.), *Imperialism and Juvenile Literature* (Manchester, MUP, 1989).

—— *Films and British National Identity* (Manchester, MUP, 1997).

Riffenburgh, Beau and Cruwys, Liz, *The Photographs of H.G. Ponting* (London, Discovery Gallery, 1998).

Robb, Peter (ed.), *The Concept of Race in South Asia* (Delhi, OUP, 1995).

Roberts, Andrew D. (ed.), *Photographs as Sources for African History: Papers Presented at a Workshop Held at the SOAS, London, May 12–13, 1988* (SOAS, University of London, 1989).

Robertson, Helen, *Constantia and its Neighbours* (Wynberg, Houghton House, 2014).

Rock, D., *The British in Argentina* (Basingstoke, Palgrave Macmillan, 2019).

Rosen, Jeff, *Julia Margaret Cameron's 'Fancy Subjects': Photographic Allegories of Victorian Identity and Empire* (Manchester, MUP, 2016).

Ross, Robert, *Clothing: A Global History or, The Imperialists' New Clothes* (Cambridge, Polity Press, 2008).

Ryan, James R., *Picturing Empire: Photography and the Visualisation of the British Empire* (London, Reaktion, 1997).

—— *Photography and Exploration* (London, Reaktion, 2013).

Said, Edward W., *Culture and Imperialism* (London, Chatto and Windus, 1993).

Salmon, Edward and Longden, Major A.A., *The Literature of the Empire and the Art of the Empire* (London, Collins, 1924).

Salmond, Anne, *Hui: A Study of Maori Ceremonial Gatherings* (Wellington, Reed, 1977).

—— *Tears of Rangi: Experiments across Worlds* (Auckland, Auckland UP, 2017).

Sanghera, Sathnam, *Empireland: How Imperialism Has Shaped Modern Britain* (London, Penguin, 2021).

Schildkrout, Enid and Keim, Curtis A. (eds), *The Scramble for Art in Central Africa* (Cambridge, CUP, 1998).

Schreuder, Deryck M. and Ward, Stuart (eds), *Australia's Empire* (Oxford, OUP, 2008).

Schwartz, Joan M. and Ryan, James R. (eds), *Picturing Place: Photography and the Geographical Imagination* (London, I.B. Tauris, 2003).

Sèbe, Berny, *Heroic Imperialists in Africa: The Promotion of British and French Colonial Heroes, 1870–1939* (Manchester, MUP, 2013).

Seeley, J.R., *The Expansion of England* (London, Macmillan, 1883).

Sen, Satadru, *Migrant Races, Empire, Identity and K.S. Ranjitsinhji* (Manchester, MUP, 2004).

Shah, Omar, *From Kashmir to Kabul: The Photographs of John Burke and William Baker, 1860–1900* (Ahmedabad, Mapin, 2002).

Sidney, Richard J.H., *In British Malaya Today* (London, Hutchinson, c.1927).

Silcox, David, *The Group of Seven and Tom Thomson* (Toronto, Firefly Books, 2001).

Simpson, Donald and Lyon, Peter, *Commonwealth in Focus: 130 Years of Photographic History* (Melbourne, Clemenger Harvie, 1982).

Singer, Noel F., *Burmah: A Photographic Journey, 1855–1925* (Gartmore, Stirlingshire, Kiscadale Publications, 1993).

Singh, Jaisal, *Polo in India* (New Delhi, Lustre Press, Roli Books, 2007).

Sivasundaram, Sujit, *Islanded: Britain, Sri Lanka and the Bounds of an Indian Ocean Colony* (Chicago, University of Chicago Press, 2013).

Smith, Alison, Brown, David Blayney and Jacobi, Carol (eds), *Artist and Empire: Facing Britain's Imperial Past* (London, Tate Publishing, 2015).

Smith, Bernard, *Place, Taste and Tradition: A Study of Australian Art since 1788* (Melbourne, OUP, 1979, originally published 1945).

—— *European Vision and the South Pacific* (New Haven, CT, YUP, 1985, originally published by Oxford, Clarendon Press, 1960).

—— with Joppien, Rüdiger, *The Art of Captain Cook's Voyages*, 3 vols (Oxford, OUP, 1985–7).

Spence, Daniel Owen, *Colonial Naval Culture and British Imperialism, 1922–67* (Manchester, MUP, 2015).

Springhall, John O., *Youth, Empire and Society: A Social History of British Youth Movements* (Brighton, Croom Helm, 1977).

—— (ed.), *Sure and Stedfast: A History of the Boys' Brigade, 1883–1983* (London, Collins, 1983).

Stanard, Matthew G., *The Leopard, the Lion and the Cock: Colonial Memories and Monuments in Belgium* (Leuven, Leuven UP, 2019).

Staples, Amy J., Kaplan, Flora Edouwayo and Freyer, Bryan M., *Fragile Legacies: The Photographs of Solomon Osagie Alonge* (Washington, DC, Smithsonian Institution, 2016).

Steggles, Mary Anne, *Statues of the Raj* (London, British Association for Cemeteries in South Asia, 2000).

—— and Barnes, Richard, *British Statuary in India: New View and Old Memories* (Kirstead, Norfolk, Frontier Publishing, 2011).

Stern, Philip J., *The Company State: Corporate Sovereignty and the Early Modern Foundations of the British Empire in India* (Oxford, OUP, 2011).

Stockwell, Sarah (ed.), *The British Empire: Themes and Perspectives* (Oxford, Blackwell, 2008).

Stoddart, Brian and Sandiford, Keith (eds), *The Imperial Game* (Manchester, MUP, 1998).

Stonechild, Blair, *The Knowledge Seeker: Embracing Indigenous Spirituality* (Regina, University of Regina Press, 2016).

Summers, Roger (ed.), *Prehistoric Rock Art of the Federation of Rhodesia and Nyasaland* (Salisbury, National Publications Trust, 1959).

Sykes, Sir Percy, *Sir Mortimer Durand: A Biography* (London, Cassells, 1926).

Talbot, Ian and Kamran, Tahir, *Colonial Lahore: A History of the City and Beyond* (London, Hurst, 2016).

Teo, Hsu-Ming and White, Richard (eds), *Cultural History in Australia* (Sydney, New South Wales UP, 2003).

Thomas, Nicholas, *Entangled Objects: Exchange, Material Culture and Colonialism in the Pacific* (Cambridge, MA, Harvard UP, 1991).

—— *Colonialism's Culture: Anthropology, Travel and Government* (Princeton, NJ, Princeton UP, 1994).

Thompsell, Angela, *Hunting Africa: British Sport, African Knowledge and the Nature of Empire* (Basingstoke, Palgrave Macmillan, 2015).

Thompson, Andrew S., *Imperial Britain: The Empire in British Politics c. 1880–1932* (Harlow, Essex, Pearson, 2000).

Thompson, T. Jack, *Light on Darkness? Missionary Photography of Africa in the Nineteenth and Early Twentieth Centuries* (Grand Rapids, MI, Eerdmans, 2012).

Tindall, Gillian, *City of Gold: The Biography of Bombay* (London, Temple Smith, 1982).

Tobin, Beth Fowkes, *Picturing Imperial Power: Colonial Subjects in Eighteenth-century British Painting* (Durham, NC, Duke UP, 1999).

Tromans, Nicholas (ed.), *The Lure of the East: British Orientalist Painting* (London, Tate Publishing, 2008).

Turner, Frank, *Contesting Cultural Authority: Essays in Victorian Intellectual Life* (Cambridge, CUP, 1993).

Turner, John, *Joseph Lycett: Governor Macquarie's Convict Artist* (Newcastle, NSW, Hunter History Publications, 1997).

Van Duinan, Jared, *The British World and an Australian National Identity: Anglo-Australian Cricket, 1860–1901* (London, Palgrave Macmillan, 2018).

Vance, Jonathan F., *A History of Canadian Culture: From Petroglyphs to Product, Circuses to the CBC* (Don Mills, Ont., OUP, 2009).

Vann, J. Don and Van Arsdel, Rosemary T., *Periodicals of Queen Victoria's Empire: An Exploration* (Toronto, University of Toronto Press, 1996).

Vigne, Randolph, *Thomas Pringle: South African Pioneer, Poet and Abolitionist* (London, James Currey, 2012).

Viswanathan, Gauri, *Masks of Conquest: Literary Study and British Rule in India* (New York, Columbia UP, 1989).

Vokes, Richard (ed.), *Photography in Africa: Ethnographic Perspectives* (Suffolk, James Currey, 2012).

Walker, Graham and Gallagher, Tom (eds), *Sermons and Battle Hymns* (Edinburgh, EUP, 1990).

Walsh, Michael J.K. and Varnava, Andrekos (eds), *The Great War and the British Empire: Culture and Society* (London, Routledge, 2016).

Walton, John K. (ed.), *Histories of Tourism: Representation, Identity and Conflict* (Clevedon, Channel View Publications 2005).

Webster, Wendy, *Englishness and Empire 1939–1965* (Oxford, OUP, 2005).

Welsh, Frank, *A History of Hong Kong* (London, HarperCollins, 1993).

Wiener, Martin J., *English Culture and the Decline of the Industrial Spirit, 1850–1980* (Cambridge, CUP, 1981, 2nd edn, 2004).

Wilcox, Scott, *Edward Lear and the Art of Travel* (New Haven, CT, Yale Center for British Art, 2000).

Wilkie, Benjamin, *The Scots in Australia, 1788–1938* (Woodbridge, Boydell Press, 2017).

Williams, Glyn, *The Death of Captain Cook: A Hero Made and Unmade* (London, Profile, 2008).

Wilson, Kathleen (ed.), *The Sense of the People: Politics, Culture and Imperialism in England, 1715–1785* (Cambridge, CUP, 1995).

—— (ed.), *A New Imperial History: Culture, Identity and Modernity in Britain and the Empire, 1660–1940* (Cambridge, CUP, 2004).

Woodward, Meredith Bain, *Land of Dreams: A History of Photography of the British Columbia Interior* (Vancouver, Altitude Publishing, 1993).

Woollacott, Angela, *Gender and Empire* (Basingstoke, Palgrave Macmillan, 2006).

Worster, Donald, *Nature's Economy: A History of Ecological Ideas* (Cambridge, CUP, 1977).

Worswick, Clark (ed.), *Princely India: Photographs by Raja Deen Dayal, Court Photographer (1884–1910) to the Premier Prince of India* (London, Hamish Hamilton, 1880).

Yeh, Emilie Yeuh-yu (ed.), *Early Film Culture in Hong Kong, Taiwan and Republican China* (Ann Arbor, MI, University of Michigan Press, 2018).

Young, James E., *The Texture of Memory: Holocaust Memorials and Meaning* (New Haven, CT, YUP, 1993).

INDEX

Note: Italicised numbers refer to illustrations